Global Patient Safety

This book explores patient safety themes in developed, developing and transitioning countries. A foundation premise is the concept of 'reverse innovation' as mutual learning from the chapters challenges traditional assumptions about the construction and location of knowledge. This edited collection can be seen to facilitate global learning. This book will, hopefully, form a bridge for those countries seeking to enhance their patient safety policies. Contributors to this book challenge many supposed generalisations about human societies, including consideration of how medical care is mediated within those societies and how patient safety is assured or compromised. By introducing major theories from the developing world in the book, readers are encouraged to reflect on their impact on the patient safety and health quality debate. The development of practical patient safety policies for wider use is also encouraged. The volume presents a ground-breaking perspective by exploring fundamental issues relating to patient safety through different academic disciplines. It develops the possibility of a new patient safety and health quality synthesis and discourse relevant to all concerned with patient safety and health quality in a global context.

John Tingle is a Barrister and Associate Professor in Law at Nottingham Law School, Nottingham Trent University, UK.

Clayton Ó Néill is a Lecturer in Law at Nottingham Law School, Nottingham Trent University, UK.

Morgan Shimwell is a Lecturer in Law at Nottingham Law School, Nottingham Trent University, UK.

Global Patient Safety

Law, Policy and Practice

Edited by John Tingle, Clayton Ó Néill and Morgan Shimwell

Routledge
Taylor & Francis Group
LONDON AND NEW YORK

First published 2019
by Routledge
2 Park Square, Milton Park, Abingdon, Oxon, OX14 4RN

and by Routledge
52 Vanderbilt Avenue, New York, NY 10017, USA

First issued in paperback 2020

Routledge is an imprint of the Taylor & Francis Group, an informa business

British Library Cataloguing in Publication Data
A catalogue record for this book is available from the British Library

Library of Congress Cataloging-in-Publication Data
Names: Tingle, John, editor. | Ó Néill, Clayton, editor. | Shimwell, Morgan, editor.
Title: Global patient safety : law, policy and practice / Edited by John Tingle, Clayton Ó Néill, and Morgan Shimwell.
Description: New York, NY : Routledge, 2019. | Includes bibliographical references and index.
Identifiers: LCCN 2018015640| ISBN 9781138052789 (hbk) | ISBN 9781351683456 (web pdf) | ISBN 9781351683449 (epub) | ISBN 9781351683432 (mobipocket)
Subjects: LCSH: Patients—Legal status, laws, etc. | Medical care—Law and legislation. | Patients—Safety measures. | Medical errors—Prevention—Law and legislation.
Classification: LCC K3601 .G56 2019 | DDC 344.04/1—dc23
LC record available at https://lccn.loc.gov/2018015640

ISBN 13: 978-0-367-58718-5 (pbk)
ISBN 13: 978-1-138-05278-9 (hbk)

Typeset in Galliard
by Swales & Willis Ltd, Exeter, Devon, UK

This edited collection is dedicated to patients, healthcare professionals and all those who strive to improve patient safety.

Contents

Contributors

Agnese Bankava is a practising Lawyer and Researcher at the University of Latvia.

John Blenkinsopp is Professor of Management at Newcastle Business School, Northumbria University, UK.

Huw Davies is Professor of Health Care Policy and Management at the School of Management, University of St Andrews, UK.

Charles Foster is a Barrister and Fellow of Green Templeton College, University of Oxford, UK.

Tim Freeman is an Associate Professor in Leadership at the Department of Management, Leadership and Organisations, Middlesex University, UK.

Jonathan Herring is DM Wolfe-Clarendon Fellow in Law at Exeter College, Vice Dean and Professor of Law at the Faculty of Law, University of Oxford, UK.

Rachel Jokela is Adverse Health Events Program Director at the Division of Health Policy, Minnesota Department of Health, USA.

Regina Kamoga is the Executive Director for Community Health and Information Network (CHAIN) in Uganda. She was also a Member of the Expert Review Committee for the Access to Medicine Index 2016. She is a Patient Safety Champion under the WHO Patients for Patient Safety programme.

Piyawan Limpanyalert is Deputy Director of the Healthcare Accreditation Institute, Thailand.

Jean V. McHale is Professor of Healthcare Law and Director of the Centre for Health Law, Science and Policy at Birmingham Law School, University of Birmingham, UK.

Ahmed Al-Mandhari is the Director of the WHO Eastern Mediterranean Regional Office. He is a Senior Consultant family physician in the Department of Family Medicine and Public Health at the Sultan Qaboos University Hospital in Oman.

Russell Mannion is Professor of Health Systems at the Health Services Management Centre, University of Birmingham, UK.

Aisha Rashid Al Maqbali is Director of Primary Health Care in the Directorate General of Health Services, North Batinah Governorate in Oman, and is also a Senior Specialist in Family Medicine and Public Health.

Ross Millar is a Senior Lecturer and Director of Learning and Teaching at the Health Services Management Centre, University of Birmingham, UK.

Barbara A. Noah is Professor of Law at Western New England University School of Law, Western New England University, USA.

Azhin Omer is a Doctoral Researcher and Lecturer in Law at Nottingham Law School, Nottingham Trent University, UK.

Clayton Ó Néill is a Lecturer in Law at Nottingham Law School, Nottingham Trent University, UK.

Cheluchi Onyemelukwe is Associate Professor in Health Law and Policy at the Babcock School of Law and Security Studies, Babcock University, Nigeria and Partner at Health Ethics and Law Consulting, Nigeria.

Evija Palceja is a Paediatrician and Patient Safety Manager at the Children's University Hospital, Latvia. She is also a Lecturer and Researcher at the University of Latvia.

Martin Powell is Professor of Health and Social policy at the Health Services Management Centre, University of Birmingham, UK.

Kay Seden is an MRC Population health science Fellow based at the Infectious Diseases Institute, Makerere University, Uganda and the University of Liverpool, UK.

Morgan Shimwell is a Lecturer in Law at Nottingham Law School, Nottingham Trent University, UK.

Roy Smith is Course Leader in the MA in International Development at Nottingham Trent University, UK.

Nick Snowden is the Academic Director of the Hull MBA, in the Faculty of Business, Law and Politics at the University of Hull, UK.

John Tingle is a Barrister and Associate Professor in Law at Nottingham Law School, Nottingham Trent University, UK.

Shin Ushiro is Professor and Director of the Patient Safety Division of Kyushu University Hospital and Executive Board Member of the Japan Council for Quality Health Care.

Preface

John Tingle, Clayton Ó Néill and Morgan Shimwell

Since the publication of *Patient Safety, Law, Policy and Practice* in 2011,[1] the patient safety debate has, in at least one important way, moved on. There has been an increasing focus on patient safety as a *global issue*, challenging nations at all stages of economic, social and political development. The World Health Assembly substantively launched its programme for global health quality and safety reform in 2002, closely followed by the establishment of the World Alliance for Patient Safety in 2004 and the patient-led Patients for Patient Safety framework. Three Global Patient Safety Challenges have been successively initiated in 2004 ('*Clean Care is Safer Care*'), 2008 ('*Safe Surgery Saves Lives*') and most recently in 2017 ('*Medication Without Harm*'). However, until 2015, the involvement of high-level policy-makers and Ministers of Health in the process of organised global patient safety change has been limited. Since then, there have been two Global Ministerial Summits. Fifteen years since the launch of an international patient safety agenda, it has taken until 2017 for governments from forty-five countries to pledge a commitment to a global patient safety movement and to make patient safety a global health priority.

This book aims to present a snapshot of how these commitments to patient safety are being carried out in practice around the world. The various chapters address health governance, regulation, legal and professional accountability, open disclosure, the litigation system and the concept of health regulation. A diverse range of patient safety tools are profiled, including adverse patient safety incident systems, reporting, and closed claims analysis.

The chapters provide a practical illustration of national experiences of patient safety in England, the Kurdistan Region of Iraq, Uganda, Nigeria, the United States of America, Japan, Oman, Latvia and Thailand. These countries are all in various stages of patient safety policy development. This diversity of experience provides opportunities for comparative discussion of issues such as access to litigation, redress mechanisms and how these can have an impact on care delivery through concepts such as defensive medicine, the 'safe investigative space' and the duty of candour.

New emerging areas, not always traditionally associated with patient safety, law, policy and practice are explored. Social policy, business management,

1 J. Tingle and P. Bark, *Patient Safety: Law, Policy and Practice*, Routledge, 2011.

international development, ethics as well as law all find a voice in the chapters of this book. The book reflects on how these perspectives relate to each other and identifies key themes and trends in healthcare systems across the globe.

A key conceptual theme in the book is that patient safety policy, particularly in England, has developed in an ad hoc manner, with little conceptual foundation. Patient safety in the National Health Service (NHS) is still a major concern twenty years after the issue became mainstream. The Care Quality Commission (CQC), the health and social care regulator of England, still regards patient safety as its major concern. We offer NHS patient safety experience as a model of a developed system with a long history of quality and safety interventions. There is much to admire about the UK's commitment to patient welfare within the healthcare system. However, our authors have not shied from criticism of their national patient safety frameworks. Rather, this book casts the enduring problems and failures into the light, as much as the success stories. These systemic problems are a vital learning opportunity, to recognise the shared difficulties of striving to improve the healthcare experience. This book aims to help spread the message of both the good and bad in patient safety policy development, to share success and failure and to help inform international patient safety policy development throughout the world.

Of course, patient safety is a heightened challenge for developing and transitioning countries. These carry a disproportionate burden of the human costs of patient safety failures. Definitive data on health quality is difficult to obtain in these countries and patient safety agendas have had limited success. Efforts can be seen to be marked by a lack of sustainability, hampered by poor health infrastructures. The chapters on patient safety in Nigeria and Uganda provide a perspective of the challenges faced in poor resource environments. However, as the reader will see from the chapters dealing with developed countries, such as the USA and England, the availability of resources does not necessarily correlate with more successful safety interventions. There is a startling degree of global commonality in the challenges of patient safety.

A central premise of the book is the concept of 'reverse innovation': a process of mutual learning between countries; a meaningful exchange of ideas, concepts, initiatives and practices across the development divide. Some chapters will challenge traditional assumptions about patient safety knowledge production, where and how it resides. By introducing major theories from a multitude of areas, such as social policy, business management, international development, ethics and the law, readers will be encouraged to reflect on their impact on the patient safety and health quality debate. This book will explore the possibility of a new patient safety and health quality synthesis and discourse, relevant to all those concerned with improving our healthcare systems and experiences.

We would like to thank those who supported us throughout this project: our supportive families, the authors of the chapters, Barbara Legg, Alison Kirk, Chloe James and our colleagues at Nottingham Law School, Nottingham Trent University.

John Tingle, Clayton Ó Néill and Morgan Shimwell
Nottingham
March 2018

1 Patient safety policy development in the NHS in England

John Tingle

The year 2000 was a watershed moment in the history of patient safety policy development in the NHS in England. The year saw the publication of the seminal patient safety policy document, *An Organisation with a Memory* with its underpinning concept of, 'Clinical Governance'.[1] Around the same time in the USA the Institute of Medicine published *To Err is Human*[2] which did the same job and focused patient safety policy development not only in the USA, but also elsewhere. In the light of these two patient safety policy development publications, it seems appropriate to take the year 2000 as a common starting year for contemporary patient safety policy development and to reflect on how much progress there has been on policy development and initiatives since.

In reading *Organisation with a Memory*, it is useful to reflect on whether the National Health Service (NHS) has moved significantly forward since 2000 in the intervening years in developing an ingrained patient safety culture. Unfortunately, however, only incremental progress in developing an ingrained patient safety culture in the NHS has occurred: we still have a long way to go! The problems outlined in *Organisation with a Memory* are still largely very much with us today:

> The Way Forward, the time is right for a fundamental re-thinking of the way that the NHS approaches the challenge of learning from adverse health care events. The NHS often fails to learn the lessons when things go wrong, and has an old-fashioned approach in this area compared to some other sectors.[3]

The issues and the conceptual tools, such as clinical governance, remain very pertinent today. The concept of clinical governance was, at the time, an excellent and simple quality organising concept and tool. In terms of definition, it could mean anything you wanted it to mean. Essentially, it was about doing your job well and providing good quality care. Today, we talk about *Intelligent Transparency*

1 Chief Medical Officer, *An organisation with a memory: report of an expert group on learning from adverse events in the NHS*, London: TSO, 2000. http://webarchive.nationalarchives.gov.uk/20130105144251/http://www.dh.gov.uk/prod_consum_dh/groups/dh_digitalassets/@dh/@en/documents/digitalasset/dh_4065086.pdf

2 Institute of Medicine, *To err is human: building a safer health system*, Washington DC: The National Academies Press, 2000. https://doi.org/10.17226/9728 (accessed 16 March 2018).

3 Chief Medical Officer, *Organisation with a memory*, p. ix.

'as a guiding patient safety policy principle'.[4] In re-reading *Organisation with a Memory*, it was interesting to note that the 1955 guidance on dealing with serious incidents was still in use in 2000.[5,6]

Following *Organisation with a Memory* new guidance was issued in 2001 in the form of *Building a safer NHS: Implementing Organisation with a Memory.*[7] This report set out the role of a new National Patient Safety Agency (NPSA) and determined what was to be the National Reporting and Learning System (NRLS). This included a plan to introduce new, mandatory schemes for 'near misses' and 'adverse care events'. It was hoped that that this would enhance patient safety by 'harnessing learning throughout the NHS when something goes wrong'.[8]

In 2006, *Safety First a report for patients, clinicians and healthcare managers*,[9] was published. Problems with the NPSA and the NRLS were discussed and recommendation 4 stated:

> The objectives, functions and accountabilities of the NPSA need to be recast as part of a renewed national strategy for patient safety. This is particularly marked in relation to reporting and learning. Despite the high volume of incident reports collected by the NPSA to date, there is little evidence that these have resulted in actionable learning for local NHS organisations. The NRLS is not yet delivering high-quality, routinely available information on patterns, trends and underlying causes of harm to patients.[10]

Despite a rocky start, the NPSA did function as a good champion of patient safety in the NHS. It focused attention on the issue and developed some excellent tools and publications, such as RCA – Root Cause Analysis – and the 'Seven Steps to Patient Safety', which are still in use today.[11]

On Friday 1 June 2012, the key functions and expertise for patient safety developed by the NPSA transferred to the NHS Commissioning Board Special

4 Jeremy Hunt, 'Learning from post-accident investigations to ensure patient safety', 28 September 2017. www.gov.uk/government/speeches/learning-from-post-accident-investigations-to-ensure-patient-safety (accessed 16 March 2018) (accessed 16 March 2018).

5 The report stated: '[f]ormal Department of Health guidance on untoward incident reporting was first issued in 1955. Somewhat surprisingly, this guidance is still current'.

6 Chief Medical Officer, *Organisation with a Memory*, p. 50.

7 Department of Health, Building a safer NHS for patients: implementing an organisation with a memory, London: TSO, 2001.

8 Ibid., p. 2.

9 Sir Ian Carruthers OBE and Pauline Philip, *Safety first, a report for patients, clinicians and healthcare managers*, London: Department of Health, 2006. http://webarchive.nationalarchives.gov.uk/20130105032616/http://www.dh.gov.uk/prod_consum_dh/groups/dh_digitalassets/@dh/@en/documents/digitalasset/dh_064159.pdf (accessed 16 March 2018).

10 Ibid., p. 5.

11 'Seven steps to patient safety', London: NPSA. http://www.nrls.npsa.nhs.uk/resources/collections/seven-steps-to-patient-safety/ (accessed 16 March 2018).

The NPSA established 'Seven steps to patient safety', as follows:

Step 1 – Build a safety culture.

Step 2 – Lead and support your staff.

Step 3 – Integrate your risk management activity.

Health Authority and the NPSA was abolished as part of the review of NHS arm's length bodies.[12] The NHS, arguably, lost an important patient safety focus point that left a vacuum in policy development, education, training and capacity. The Government shot itself in the foot when it abolished the NPSA.[13]

What has happened since? The intervening years

Regulatory organisations have come and gone and have been morphed into others. The structure of the NHS has also changed: Strategic Health Authorities, Primary Care Trusts have all been consigned to the history books, along with the NPSA. In many senses of the word, the NHS is seemingly a bit of a political football and change is a constant feature. Patient safety policy documents from 2000 until the present day all sound alarmingly familiar in terms of the progress being made: slow and incremental through the years, and the same in the present day. In 2005, the National Audit Office (NAO)[14] looked at patient safety in the NHS and made several findings. They recognised that improvements in safety culture has taken place as a result of the development of risk management systems. However, they reported that 'trusts are still predominantly reactive in their response to patient safety issues and parts of some organisations still operate a blame culture'.[15] They stressed that under-reporting remained a significant problem.[16] All was not doom and gloom in the report: it was stated that the culture within NHS trusts was more open and fair and the clinical governance concept had helped drive improvements.

In 2006, the Healthcare Commission,[17] which later changed into the Care Quality Commission (CQC) that we have today, also looked at patient safety

Step 4 – Promote reporting.

Step 5 – Involve and communicate with patients and the public.

Step 6 – Learn and share safety lessons.

Step 7 – Implement solutions to prevent harm.

12 Department of Health, *Liberating the NHS: review: report of the arm's length bodies review*, London: Department of Health, 2010. www.gov.uk/government/uploads/system/uploads/attachment_data/file/216278/dh_118053.pdf (accessed 16 March 2018).

13 Ibid. The report stated that: 'Following the last review of arm's-length bodies, a number of other discrete functions related to patient safety were brought together within the National Patient Safety Agency. The functions of the organisation, whilst necessary within a system supporting wider quality and safety improvement, do not of themselves need to be performed at arm's-length of the Department and could be delivered elsewhere in the system. We propose to abolish the National Patient Safety Agency. Some National Patient Safety Agency functions will become part of the remit of the NHS Board, while others will be supported to continue in other ways'. Pp. 26–27.

14 National Audit Office, 'A Safer place for patients: learning to improve patient safety', HC 456 Session 2005–2006, 3, Department of health, London: TSO, 2005. www.nao.org.uk/wp-content/uploads/2005/11/0506456.pdf (accessed 16 March 2018).

15 Ibid., p. 2.

16 Ibid.

17 Healthcare Commission, *State of healthcare 2006*, London: Commission for Healthcare Audit and Inspection, 2006. http://www.wales.nhs.uk/documents/State_of_Healthcare_2006.pdf (accessed 16 March 2018).

and found that NHS trusts need to take patient safety more seriously. In 2006, they said that one in ten healthcare organisations could not guarantee that they met the required standards regarding safety.[18] The themes, *inter alia*, expressed in these reports are still relevant today and a comparison with modern reports echoes many of the themes found twelve years ago and before.

In 2006 the Department of Health published *Safety First* and that report stated that the pace of change in patient safety in the NHS was too slow and its profile needed to be higher on trust agendas. Again, it had to be taken more seriously as an issue.[19] This report stated that more effective learning from error is needed. A key point made was that those who manage trusts seemed more focused on balancing the financial budget than on the safety of patients. Some trusts were, in the future, to seriously take their eye off the patient safety ball to balance the books: the Mid Staffordshire crisis is a case in point. The only constant feature in the patient safety landscape has been the National Health Service Litigation Authority (NHSLA), formed in November 1995 as a special health authority. It is now known under its new operating name, NHS Resolution, to better reflect its work in handling and resolving negligence claims.

NHS Resolution (NHSLA)

This organisation survived the arm's length review which saw the demise of the NPSA and has been a consistent and stable feature of the NHS patient safety and clinical negligence management landscape since its formation. It has contributed positively through its litigation management role for trusts and independent sector providers of NHS care in England who are members of their indemnity schemes. It has set patient safety standards through trust membership of its main indemnity risk pooling scheme for clinical claims, the Clinical Negligence Scheme for Trusts. Member Trusts of the CNST were inspected against CNST patient standards. In its 2004 report, *A Review of the NHSLA Incident Reporting and Management and Learning from Experience Standards, Assessment Outcomes*, the NAO observes:

> It is probably true that the CNST standards were the first set of clinical risk management standards that included the assessment of how well NHS organisations were reporting clinical incidents. Back in 1995, only a minority of trusts were reporting and recording clinical incidents. This was due to a variety of reasons including the culture and acceptance that clinical incidents were to some degree 'expected' side effects or complications to treatment. Such an approach was coupled with a general acceptance by the public that 'doctor knows best'. Today, of course, a more knowledgeable and probing public demand a great deal more from the NHS.[20]

18 Ibid., pp 8–9.

19 Carruthers and Philip, *Safety First*, p. 19.

20 National Audit Office, *A review of the NHSLA incident reporting and management and learning from experience standards assessment outcomes April 2003–March 2004*, London: NAO, 2004.

This inspection process ceased from April 2014 onwards and the NHSLA standards, as they became known, were no longer updated. The NHSLA reflected on the value of the CNST inspection process and moved to a more facilitative, supportive educational approach by creating a Safety and Learning Service. This service includes targeted workshops for special groups such as claims managers, clinicians and trust board members; a safety and learning library, local network events and information and analysis in relation to a member's organisation's claims data on a secure extranet.

The NHSLA can rightly be regarded as one of the NHS patient safety success stories. It has been a constant stabilising influence in managing clinical negligence litigation and in properly managing cases with the help of case managers and specialist law firms. It has helped develop a real sense of professionalism in managing cases and has also helped share good patient safety practices through its indemnity schemes and safety and learning service. There is now a much more informed view of the reasons for clinical negligence litigation and the NHSLA is spending more time on focusing on patient safety and helping to stop errors occurring. It also contributes to policy development through its long experience of claims and litigation management in the NHS. Its claims database has provided some useful data which has informed the development of safer practices in areas such as maternity care.[21]

A sense of history

Having given a sense of history to patient safety policy development in England and the associated institutions, a move can now be made to look at contemporary issues and how far progress has been made since 2000. To discuss this, the terrible events that unfolded in the Mid Staffordshire crisis must be discussed. That crisis represented the NHS's darkest moment and exposed the real underbelly of patient safety in the NHS. It revealed a fractured regulatory system where duplication and confusion of function was rife. Patient safety horrors flew under the regulatory radar and people died as a result. These events, however, were not isolated and several other hospital trusts were very closely looked at and improvement called for. The scale of the horrific events found at Mid Staffordshire were unique, but other trusts were also found to have major patient safety failings. The Government response to Mid Staffordshire and the subsequent policies, reforms and actions taken now define our current patient safety system. To understand this system, we need to know more about what went on and analyse the report of the chair of the inquiry, Sir Robert Francis QC. A fundamental question is to ask whether such events could ever happen again in the NHS. Sadly, it might possible if we look at the current NHS funding tensions and CQC reports about patient safety compliance but, hopefully,

21 NHSLA, *Ten years of maternity claims: an analysis of NHS Litigation Authority data – key findings*, London: NHSLA, 2012. http://www.nhsla.com/Safety/Documents/Ten%20Years%20of%20Maternity%20Claims%20-%20An%20Analysis%20of%20the%20NHS%20LA%20Data%20-%20October%202012.pdf (accessed 16 March 2018).

not on the same scale. Disquiet about the pace of progress was articulated in 2009, when the House of Commons Health Committee stated:

> We are, however, concerned that Lord Darzi's emphasis on quality and safety is an indication that, for all the policy innovations of the past decade, insufficient progress has been made in making NHS services safer.[22]

The Mid Staffordshire crisis

A disputed estimate suggested that between 400 and 1,200 patients died because of poor care over the 50 months between January 2005 and March 2009 at Stafford hospital, Staffordshire.[23] The final inquiry report was published on 6 February 2013. Conditions of appalling care were found. Harrowing personal stories chronicling major neglect were told to the inquiry. These included cases where patients were left in excrement in soiled bed clothes for lengthy periods of time. Water was left out of reach, assistance was not provided with feeding for patients who could not eat without help, toilets and wards were in an unacceptable state, no assistance was given to patients who requested help in their toileting, and '[s]taff treated patients and those close to them with what appeared to be callous indifference'.[24]

Two hundred and ninety recommendations were made in the report designed to change the NHS culture, making sure that patients come first. Patient safety fell through the cracks at Mid Staffordshire, as the Trust was more focused on financial matters and targets. Financial concerns and a need to balance the budget, which formed part of the root causes of the problems found, should not be prioritised. What happened in this crisis appeared also to fly under the radar of regulatory bodies and provides evidence of a degree of ineffectiveness in the structure and operation of these bodies. The Trust culture was certainly a negative one. For example, they failed to understand the seriousness of what was occurring, reacted extremely slowly and downplayed matters significantly. Their over-focus on targets and finances highlighted 'an engrained culture of tolerance of poor standards'.[25]

The Francis Report talks about secrecy, self-promotion, an acceptance of poor standards and a failure to put the patient first, looking inwards not outwards.[26] Recommendations included formalising in the NHS principles of openness, transparency and candour:

22 House of Commons Health Committee Session 2008–09, *Health Committee – sixth report patient safety*, HC. https://publications.parliament.uk/pa/cm200809/cmselect/cmhealth/151/15102.htm para 32 (accessed 16 March 2018).

23 Denis Campbell, 'Mid Staffs hospital scandal: the essential guide', *The Guardian*, 06 February 2013. www.theguardian.com/society/2013/feb/06/mid-staffs-hospital-scandal-guide (accessed 16 March 2018).

24 Robert Francis QC, *Report of the Mid Staffordshire NHS Foundation Trust public inquiry executive summary*, London: TSO, 2013, p, 13. www.gov.uk/government/publications/report-of-the-mid-staffordshire-nhs-foundation-trust-public-inquiry (accessed 16 March 2018).

25 Ibid., pp. 43–44.

26 Ibid.

> A common culture made real throughout the system – an integrated hierarchy of standards of service. No provider should provide, and there must be zero tolerance of, any service that does not comply with fundamental standards of service. Standards need to be formulated to promote the likelihood of the service being delivered safely and effectively, to be clear about what has to be done to comply, to be informed by an evidence base and to be effectively measurable.[27]

The Government of the time could not be accused of being slow in responding to the report and responded in six weeks. The Government accepted most of the recommendations made either in principle or absolutely.[28] The Francis report set up an urgent patient safety reform agenda and, in 2018, at the time of writing the report is five years of age. Things did change after Francis, and the CQC system of inspection was reformed and made more effective and thorough. Trusts had to say how they were responding to the Francis Report. More reports followed, and these included the Berwick Report.[29] This report echoed others and talked about culture development and also penalties, which was an interesting focus. Offences of ill-treatment or wilful neglect now form Sections 20 to 25 of the Criminal Justice and Courts Act 2015:

> We support responsive regulation of organisations, with a hierarchy of responses. Recourse to criminal sanctions should be extremely rare, and should function primarily as a deterrent to wilful or reckless neglect or mistreatment.[30]

The initial response to the Francis Report was well articulated and strong on direction. The Government was clearly very determined to instigate effective positive changes in the NHS and to bring about a caring culture which puts the patient first. This Government's drive and determination has been consistent and continuous. The Nuffield Trust produced a report on the Francis report,[31] one year on, and found that the report had been well received by staff interviewed in the study. Leaders of trusts said, however, that culture change does take time, it's not an instant thing.[32] The Francis report has certainly made a

27 Ibid., p. 87.
28 Department of Health, *Hard truths, the journey to putting patients first*, London: Department of Health, 2014.
29 National Advisory Group on the Safety of Patients in England, *A promise to learn – a commitment to act: improving the safety of patients in England*, London: Williams Lea, 2013.
30 Ibid., p. 33.
31 Ruth Thorlby, Judith Smith, Sally Williams and Mark Dayan, *February, The Francis Report: one year on. The response of acute trusts in England*, London: Nuffield Trust, 2014.
32 Ibid., p. 6. The report stated that: 'Many senior leaders of the acute trusts said that the publication of the Francis Report had prompted them to reflect in greater depth on the quality of care being delivered in their organisations. It had also added legitimacy to their efforts to give greater weight to improve and assure the quality of care, alongside meeting financial and performance targets. Although the Francis Report was cited by senior leaders as reinforcing their efforts to prioritise quality of care as equal to, or more important than, financial performance, there remains a profound tension between the two goals.'

difference! Moving on to today, where are we with developing an ingrained, reflective patient safety culture in the NHS which always puts the patient first? We can get a true sense of this from the annual reports of the CQC on the state of care in the NHS in England and from certain political speeches on patient safety policy.[33]

What next? Rising clinical negligence costs and patient safety

What happens next in England about patient safety is a difficult question to answer. The patient safety debate now can be seen to be very closely related to the rising costs of clinical negligence issue.

In England, we currently face what some regard as unsustainably high costs of clinical negligence litigation. This, some argue, is eating into front line care services and they, understandably, want it controlled. At the same time, patients, injured by those who were meant to care for them, have a right to reasonable access to legal services to seek compensation for the harm caused. We have an adversarial civil compensation system which makes establishing a case in a very real sense a contest between opposing parties. Clinical negligence litigation is also expensive: it depends on expert evidence from doctors and others and causation can be a difficult issue. This area of legal practice requires expert legal help because it can be a very complex area, even for low-value claims. *Organisation with a Memory* reported the costs then (2000):

> The NHS paid out around £400 million in clinical litigation settlements in the financial year 1998/99 and has a potential liability of around £2.4 billion from existing and expected claims; when analysed many cases of litigation show potentially avoidable causes.[34]

The NAO gives current figures and state that the cost of clinical negligence claims is rising at a faster rate year-on-year than NHS funding. As a result, trusts are spending a higher proportion of their income on clinical negligence.[35] In terms of one year, the figures are causing acute levels of concern at many different policy levels.

33 Jeremy Hunt, 'Learning from post-accident investigations'.

34 Chief Medical Officer, *Organisation with a memory*, p. 5.

35 NAO, Department of Health, Managing the costs of clinical negligence in trusts, HC 305 Session 2017–2019 7, London: NAO, 2017, www.nao.org.uk/wp-content/uploads/2017/09/Managing-the-costs-of-clinical-negligence-in-trusts.pdf (accessed 16 March 2018). p 22: 'NHS Resolution estimated that liabilities for existing claims through the Clinical Negligence Scheme for Trusts, that involve future payments or are not yet settled, and potential clinical negligence claims for incidents that have already occurred but not yet made, were £60 billion in 2016–17, up from £51 billion in 2015–16. The total provision across all NHS Resolution's schemes was £65 billion in 2016–17, up from £56 billion in 2015–16.'

> In 2016–17, NHS Resolution spent £1.6 billion on the Clinical Negligence Scheme for Trusts, comprising £974 million on damages, £602 million on legal costs (£480 million on claimants' legal costs and £122 million on defence costs) and £10 million on claims operations. There are two ways of measuring the annual cost of clinical negligence claims. Costs are growing according to either measure.[36]

The UK has the highest costs of litigation in Europe.[37] The NAO feel that the current Government measures to try and control the escalation of costs are not going to solve the problem, which will only get worse.[38] The statistics provided by the NAO provide stark testimony to spiralling costs:

> The provision for existing or potential clinical negligence claims through this scheme was £60 billion in 2016–17. The implication of the rising costs of clinical negligence claims is that in an already constrained financial environment, this reduces the proportion of the health budget available to deliver healthcare to patients. It also creates an increasing cost on public finances for future years.[39]

Policy development in this area has been too narrow and has not engaged sufficiently with stake holders across the full spectrum of interests. The causes of clinical negligence can reside in patient safety failures, but that is not the whole story. Patients' motivations for suing and complaining need further research. Doctors, nurses and patients may hold different views of what competence is.

The Medical Protection Society (MPS) argue:

> What constitutes an adverse outcome or patient safety incident also appears to be evolving, and may be viewed from different perspectives by the patient and the doctor. The patient's view may include disappointment in outcomes, poor doctor–patient interactional experience, service and quality, while doctors can tend to focus on whether medical error occurred.
>
> Existing evidence tells us that there is not a strong correlation between clinical error and claims or complaints.[40]

36 Ibid.

37 See NHS National Institute for Health Research, 'Commissioning brief – supporting information', Health Service and Delivery Research Programme, 2018.

38 Ibid., p. 7. It is stated in the report that '[t]he government lacks a coherent cross-government strategy, underpinned by policy, to support measures to tackle the rising cost of clinical negligence. The Department and NHS Resolution, working with others including the Ministry of Justice, have identified many of the factors contributing to the rising costs of clinical negligence. But some of the biggest factors influencing costs fall within the remit of more than one government department or are largely outside of the health system's control.'

39 NAO, *Department of Health, Managing the costs of clinical negligence in trusts*, HC 305 Session 2017–2019 7, London: NAO, 2017, p. 5.

40 Medical Protection Society, *The rising cost of clinical negligence: who pays the price?*, London: MPS, 2017, www.medicalprotection.org/docs/default-source/sab-docs/5892-striking-a-balance-policy-paper-web.pdf (accessed 16 March 2018), p, 13.

At the same time, the NHS has been very slow to learn the patient safety lessons of the past. This is a consistent theme in many reports from 2000 to today. The NRLS which came into being in late 2003 has provided a useful tool to learn about patient safety failures. That system is, however, being reviewed and a new one is on the horizon.

The NRLS

The NRLS is being reformed to make it much more fit for purpose as several failings have been identified. A DPSIMS (Development of the Patient Safety Incident Management System) project is currently underway in the NHS which will succeed the NRLS.[41] The NRLS currently receives over two million incident reports each year.[42]

NHS Improvement discusses some failings of the NRLS which identify complexity as one issue. The new DPSIMS system will, hopefully, be easier to use for both staff and patients.[43] It is envisaged that there will also be a better central sharing of information across organisations that require it. The new system needs to work across the whole of healthcare. NHS Improvement states:

> Currently, only larger organisations that have purchased a local risk management system, mostly hospitals and large community and mental health services, can batch-upload their incidents. Others have to submit them individually on e-forms. This discourages them from sharing their information and has resulted in very low participation from primary care, for example.[44]

Other purported benefits of the new system will be that it will allow for better use of safety data, provide improved feedback to the people who record patient safety incidents and result in the NHS learning from incidents in order to prevent harm.[45] The NRLS clearly has its failings and NHS Improvement provides a road map on some of the new system thinking which, hopefully, will work to greatly improve matters.[46]

Conclusion

In terms of effort in developing a patient safety culture in the NHS, successive Governments can be seen to have worked hard to develop a patient safety

41 NHS Improvement, ***Development of the Patient Safety Incident Management System (DPSIMS) project***, Alpha phase update, December, London: NHS Improvement, 2017. https://improvement.nhs.uk/documents/2194/20171221_Development_of_the_Patient_Safety_Incident_Management_System_-_Alpha__WL9a8gA.pdf (accessed 16 March 2018).

42 NHS Improvement, Patient safety review and response report, October 2016 to March 2017: A summary of how we reviewed and responded to the patient safety issues you reported, London: NHS Improvement, 2018. https://improvement.nhs.uk/resources/patient-safety-review-and-response-October-march-2017/

43 Medical Protection Society, *The rising cost of clinical negligence*.

44 Ibid., pp. 3–4.

45 Ibid., p. 4.

46 Ibid.

infrastructure. The NRLS, Healthcare Commission, CQC, NPSA, NHSLA, CNST, and the NRLS have all been success stories. The reformed CQC methods of inspection are fit for purpose and have brought positive changes which can be seen in the regular reports of the CQC. The problem is, however, that only incremental progress has been made in developing what can be best termed an ingrained patient safety culture in the NHS. The NHS is still patently bad at learning from the errors of the past and patient safety is still the major concern of the CQC eighteen years after *Organisation with a memory* was published. In many senses of the term, the NHS can be seen to running to stand still in patient safety. At the time of writing in 2018, the NHS is facing lots of cost pressures and it seems all too easy to distract the attention of those who manage hospitals to balance the budgets. Another Mid Staffordshire crisis may appear remote, but it's not totally improbable.

References

Campbell, Denis, 'Mid Staffs hospital scandal: the essential guide', *The Guardian*, 6 February 2013. www.theguardian.com/society/2013/feb/06/mid-staffs-hospital-scandal-guide (accessed 16 March 2018).

Care Quality Commission, *The state of care in NHS acute hospitals: 2014 to 2016 findings from the end of CQC's programme of NHS acute comprehensive inspections*, London: CQC, 2016. www.cqc.org.uk/sites/default/files/20170302b_stateofhospitals_web.pdf (accessed 16 March 2018).

Care Quality Commission, *The state of health care and adult social care in England 2016/17*, London: CQC, 2017. www.cqc.org.uk/sites/default/files/20171123_stateofcare1617_report.pdf (accessed 16 March 2018).

Carruthers, Sir Ian, OBE and Philip, Pauline, *Safety First, a report for patients, clinicians and healthcare managers*, London: Department of Health, 2006. http://webarchive.nationalarchives.gov.uk/20130105032616/http://www.dh.gov.uk/prod_consum_dh/groups/dh_digitalassets/@dh/@en/documents/digitalasset/dh_064159.pdf (accessed 16 March 2018).

Chief Medical Officer, *An organisation with a memory: report of an expert group on learning from adverse events in the NHS*, London: TSO, 2000. http://webarchive.nationalarchives.gov.uk/20130105144251/; www.dh.gov.uk/prod_consum_dh/groups/dh_digitalassets/@dh/@en/documents/digitalasset/dh_4065086.pdf (accessed 16 March 2018).

Department of Health, *Building a safer NHS for patients implementing organisation with a memory*, London: TSO, 2001. http://webarchive.nationalarchives.gov.uk/20120106001900/http://www.dh.gov.uk/prod_consum_dh/groups/dh_digitalassets/@dh/@en/documents/digitalasset/dh_4058094.pdf (accessed 16 March 2018).

Department of Health, *Hard truths, the journey to putting patients first*, London: Department of Health, 2014.

Department of Health, *Liberating the NHS: review: report of the arm's length bodies review*, London: Department of Health, 2010. www.gov.uk/government/uploads/system/uploads/attachment_data/file/216278/dh_118053.pdf (accessed 16 March 2018).

Francis, Robert, QC, *Report of the Mid Staffordshire NHS Foundation Trust Public Inquiry Executive summary*, London: TSO, 2013. www.gov.uk/government/publications/report-of-the-mid-staffordshire-nhs-foundation-trust-public-inquiry (accessed 16 March 2018).

Healthcare Commission, *State of healthcare 2006*, London: Commission for Healthcare Audit and Inspection, 2006. www.wales.nhs.uk/documents/State_of_Healthcare_2006.pdf (accessed 16 March 2018).

House of Commons Health Committee Session 2008-09, *Health Committee – sixth report patient safety*, HC. https://publications.parliament.uk/pa/cm200809/cmselect/cmhealth/151/15102.htm (accessed 16 March 2018).

Hunt, Jeremy, 'Learning from post-accident investigations to ensure patient safety', 28 September 2017. www.gov.uk/government/speeches/learning-from-post-accident-investigations-to-ensure-patient-safety (accessed 11 February 2018).

Institute of Medicine, *To err is human: building a safer health system*, Washington, DC: The National Academies Press, 2000. https://doi.org/10.17226/9728 (accessed 16 March 2018).

Medical Protection Society, *The rising cost of clinical negligence. Who pays the price?*, London: MPS, 2017. www.medicalprotection.org/docs/default-source/sab-docs/5892-striking-a-balance-policy-paper-web.pdf (accessed 16 March 2018).

National Advisory Group on the Safety of Patients in England, *A promise to learn – a commitment to act, improving the safety of patients in England*, London: Williams Lea, August 2013. www.gov.uk/government/uploads/system/uploads/attachment_data/file/226703/Berwick_Report.pdf.

National Audit Office, *Department of Health, managing the costs of clinical negligence in trusts*, HC 305 Session 2017–2019 7, London: NAO, 2017. www.nao.org.uk/wp-content/uploads/2017/09/Managing-the-costs-of-clinical-negligence-in-trusts.pdf (accessed 16 March 2018).

National Audit Office, *Managing the costs of clinical negligence in trusts*, London: NAO, 7 September 2017. www.nao.org.uk/wp-content/uploads/2017/09/Managing-the-costs-of-clinical-negligence-in-trusts.pdf (accessed 16 March 2018).

National Audit Office, *A review of the NHSLA incident reporting and management and learning from experience standards assessment outcomes April 2003–March 2004*, London: NAO, 2004. www.nao.org.uk/wp-content/uploads/2005/11/NHSLA_review.pdf (accessed 16 March 2018).

National Audit Office, *A safer place for patients: learning to improve patient safety*, London: Department of Health, November 2005. www.nao.org.uk/wp-content/uploads/2005/11/0506456.pdf (accessed 16 March 2018).

NHS Improvement, *Development of the patient safety incident management system (DPSIMS) project, Alpha phase update*, London: NHS Improvement, 2017. https://improvement.nhs.uk/documents/2194/20171221_Development_of_the_Patient_Safety_Incident_Management_System_-_Alpha__WL9a8gA.pdf (accessed 16 March 2018).

NHS Improvement, *Patient safety review and response report, October 2016 to March 2017: A summary of how we reviewed and responded to the patient safety issues you reported 17 January*, London: NHS Improvement, 2018. https://improvement.nhs.uk/resources/patient-safety-review-and-response-October-march-2017/ (accessed 16 March 2018).

NHSLA Web site, 'Patient Safety'. www.nhsla.com/Safety/Pages/Home.aspx (accessed 16 March 2018).

NHSLA, *Ten Years of maternity claims: an analysis of NHS Litigation Authority data – key findings*, London: NHSLA, 2012. www.nhsla.com/Safety/Documents/Ten%20Years%20of%20Maternity%20Claims%20-%20An%20Analysis%20of%20the%20NHS%20LA%20Data%20-%20October%202012.pdf (accessed 16 March 2018).

NHS National Institute for Health Research, 'Commissioning brief – supporting information', Health Service and Delivery Research Programme, 2018.

Seven steps to patient safety, London: NPSA, 2018. www.nrls.npsa.nhs.uk/resources/collections/seven-steps-to-patient-safety/ (accessed 16 March 2018).

Thorlby, Ruth, Smith, Judith, Williams, Sally, and Dayan Mark, *The Francis Report: one year on. The response of acute trusts in England*, London: Nuffield Trust, 2014. www.nuffieldtrust.org.uk/files/2017-01/francis-report-one-year-on-web-final.pdf (accessed 16 March 2018).

Vernon, Helen, 'Improving safety – reducing costs'. https://nhsproviders.org/media/1428/2-helen-vernon_patients-and-quality-first.pdf (accessed 16 March 2018).

2 The health law, ethics and patient safety interface

Jonathan Herring

Introduction

Hospitals are dangerous places. Each year more people die from medical errors than motor vehicle accidents, breast cancer or AIDS.[1] It has been estimated that even across Europe one in every ten hospital patients experience a preventable harm or adverse event.[2] These not only cause harm to patients and their families, but add to the financial and resource pressures on health care systems. Increasing risks in hospitals reflect, in part, the current sophistication of technological treatments and medicines. These mean that health care settings are often dealing with patients who are in a precarious state of health and exhibit a complex combination of conditions. Further, economic constraints have required health care systems to deal with ever larger numbers of patients with pressurised resources.

The interest in health safety has been growing in recent years and it is now a major theme in health care management and academic study.[3] Arguably the issue first became widely acknowledged with the American report in 1999, *To Err is Human*, which claimed that between 44,000 and 98,000 patient deaths per year were due to medical errors.[4] Not long afterwards, the NHS acknowledged the issue in *An Organisation with a Memory*.[5] In recent years it was the Francis Reports which have put patients' safety at the centre of public attention.

Francis Reports

The Francis Reports[6] were produced as a result of a public inquiry into events at the Mid Staffordshire NHS Foundation Trust between January 2005 and March

1 O. Quick, 'Outing medical errors: questions of trust and responsibility', *Medical Law Review* 2006, 14:30.

2 World Health Organisation, *Patient safety*, Geneva: WHO, 2017.

3 National Patient Safety Foundation, *Free from harm: accelerating patient safety improvement fifteen years after To err is human*, Washington: NPSF, 2015.

4 US Institute of Medicine, *To err is human*, Washington: US Institute of Medicine, 1999.

5 NHS, *An organisation with a memory*, London: NHS, 2000.

6 R. Francis, *The Report of the Mid Staffordshire NHS Foundation Trust public inquiry*, London: The Stationery Office, 2013; HC 898 I–III. R. Francis, *Independent inquiry into care provided by Mid Staffordshire NHS Foundation Trust January 2005–March 2009*, London: The Stationery Office, 2010.

2009. They disclosed a lack of basic care in many wards and departments of the hospital. During the four years some 400–1,200 patients may have died from mistreatment and neglect. The personal stories uncovered were distressing and included patients being left in excrement; being abandoned on a commode for hours; lying in soiled bed clothes for long periods of time; calling out for help and not receiving it; needing assistance to eat but not being given it; being left naked on their beds in full view of others; and being treated with a lack of basic kindness. Patients were left feeling ashamed, afraid and undignified.

These failings were seen as primarily not about the fault of individual nursing staff, but rather reflected deeper problems within the Trust. These included that the Trust's Board had 'an insidious negative culture involving a tolerance of poor standards and a disengagement from managerial and leadership responsibilities'.[7] The Inquiry summarised the issues as including the following:

> a corporate focus on process at the expense of outcomes; a failure to listen to those who have received care through proper consideration of their complaints; staff disengaged from the process of management; insufficient attention to the maintenance of professional standards; lack of support for staff through appraisal, supervision and professional development; a weak professional voice in management decisions; a failure to meet the challenge of the care of the elderly through provision of an adequate professional resource . . .[8]

Chillingly they concluded that the issues facing the Trust were 'not . . . of such rarity or improbability that it would be safe to assume that it has not been and will not be repeated.'[9]

What was needed across the NHS were:

> common values, shared by all putting patients and their safety first; we need a commitment by all to serve and protect patients and to support each other in that endeavour, and to make sure that the many committed and caring professionals in the NHS are empowered to root out any poor practice around them.

Work is required in five key areas to achieve these goals:

1. Clear standards

Standards are seen to be at the heart of patient safety. These standards must be clearly set out; there must be inspections to check for compliance; and enforcement where non-compliance is identified.[10] The Francis Report expounded on these:

7 Francis Report 2013, p. 3.
8 Ibid.
9 Ibid., para 76.
10 R. Brownsword, 'Regulating patient safety: is it time for a technological response?', *Law, Innovation and Technology* 2014, 6:1.

> [A] structure of clearly understood fundamental standards and measures of compliance, accepted and embraced by the public and healthcare professionals, with rigorous and clear means of enforcement: we need a list of standards, about patient safety, the effectiveness of treatment, and basic care – the requirements we will all agree should be in place to permit any hospital service to continue. These standards should be defined by what patients and the public want and are entitled to, and what healthcare professionals agree can be delivered. Non-compliance with these fundamental standards cannot be tolerated. Any organisation unable consistently to comply should be prevented from continuing a service which exposes patients to risk. To cause death or serious harm to a patient by non-compliance with fundamental standards should be a criminal offence . . .
>
> Fundamental standards must be policed by the Care Quality Commission. It is this inquiry's firm conclusion that physical inspection by well qualified, trained and experienced hospital inspectors is the most effective means of monitoring compliance with standards in hospitals.[11]

2. Openness, transparency and candour

Promoting safety requires organisations to learn lessons from errors. If that is to happen it means that where adverse events occur people should be open about what has happened. There two key reasons why this is important. First, this is better for the patient because it means a proper assessment can be made about their current condition and what treatment they need to recover from the incident. It also means that the patient can better come to terms with the incident if they are being treated with honesty and respect. Second, it means the hospital can then learn from what has happened and put in place procedures to ensure it is not repeated.

The Francis Report emphasises the need for openness, transparency and candour:

- Openness means enabling concerns and complaints to be raised freely and fearlessly, and questions to be answered fully and truthfully.
- Transparency means making accurate and useful information about performance and outcomes available to staff, patients, the public and regulators.
- Candour means informing any patient who has or may have been avoidably harmed by a healthcare service of that fact and a remedy offered where appropriate regardless of whether a complaint has been made or a question asked about it . . .[12]

With candour and openness it is possible to adopt the attitude that 'every error is a treasure' and a resource to improve safety.[13]

11 Francis, *Report of the Mid Staffordshire NHS Foundation Trust public inquiry*, Chairman's statement, p. 5.

12 Ibid, p. 6.

13 C. Vincent, *Patient safety*, London: Elsevier, 2006, p. 12.

3. Improvements in support and training

The Francis Report also emphasises the importance of training:

> improved support for compassionate caring and committed nursing: proper standards of nursing care lie at the heart of what is required to protect patients when in hospital. The majority of nurses are compassionate, caring and committed. They should be given effective support and recognition, and be empowered to use these qualities to maintain standards. Entrants to the profession should be assessed for their aptitude to deliver and lead proper care, and their ability to commit themselves to the welfare of their patients. Training standards need to be created to ensure that qualified nurses are competent to deliver compassionate care to a consistent standard and their training must incorporate the need to experience hands-on patient care. Named clinicians should be responsible for the welfare and care of each patient in hospital.[14]

Of course training and support is only part of the picture. Resources are key too. The number of patients nurses have to look after and the hours they have to care are hugely important. No amount of training can ensure an exhausted overstretched health care professional can deal appropriately with an unreasonable number of patients.

4. Patient-centered leadership

The Francis Report noted that safety culture had to be reinforced by leadership within the health care service so it becomes part of every aspect of health care. There needs to be a common code of ethics and conduct for all leaders and senior managers. That needs to be reinforced by managers who are held to account when they have not applied the core values. There also needs to be a registration system so that only fit and proper persons are eligible to be directors of NHS organisations.[15]

5. Accurate useful and relevant information

The Francis Report sets out the importance of recording and using information:

> accurate, useful and relevant information: information is the lifeblood of an open transparent and candid culture. All professionals, individually and collectively, should be obliged to take part in the development, use and publication of more sophisticated measurements of the effectiveness of what they do, and of their compliance with fundamental standards. Patients, the public, employers, commissioners and regulators need access to accurate,

14 Francis, *Report of the Mid Staffordshire NHS Foundation Trust public inquiry*, 2013, Chairman's statement, pp. 6–7.

15 Ibid., p. 7.

> comparable and timely information. Improvements are needed in the core information systems for the collection of data about patients, to support both their individual treatment and the accurate collation of information for statistical purposes. Difficulties in achieving this are no excuse for inaction . . . It should be a criminal offence to be a party to a wilful or reckless false statement as to compliance with safety or fundamental standards.[16]

To implement all five of these goals the Francis Report produced around 290 proposals including the following:

- The introduction of a new statutory duty of candour.
- The establishment of a single regulator to deal with care quality and financial matters, looking at patient safety across the trust.
- Powers to prosecute or suspect boards or individuals for low standards of care.
- A registration system to ensure only registered people could provide care for patients.
- A common set of core values and standards throughout the NHS and particularly recognising and applying the value of transparency, honesty and candour.

Definition of safety

Clearly, improving patient safety was at the heart of the Francis Report and extensive work has been undertaken to put it into effect. But what, exactly, does patient safety mean? The World Health Organisation proposes the following definition:

> The simplest definition of patient safety is the prevention of errors and adverse effects to patients associated with health care.[17]

A fuller definition is proposed by Oliver Quick:

> It involves planning the design of systems, products, processes and influencing the behaviour of individuals and institutions in order to prevent harm, and is demonstrated by reference to evidence, for example surgical complication rates.[18]

As these definitions indicate, tackling safety involves an appreciation of why adverse events occur and efforts being put in place to avoid them. Nowadays there is widespread agreement that it is rarely possible to identify a single cause for an error. Rather, typically, errors result from a combination of events and cultures. That was precisely the explanation found in the Francis Reports. Even

16 Francis, *Report of the Mid Staffordshire NHS Foundation Trust public inquiry*, p. 3.

17 World Health Organisation, *Patient safety*.

18 O. Quick, 'Patient safety and the problem and potential of law', *Professional Negligence* 2012. 28:68.

the ideal health care professional will make mistakes. The job of the health care services is to put in place structures to avoid these mistakes leading to bad outcomes. Punishing or retraining of the practitioner would do little if the error lay at the system level and so the underlying problem was not resolved. A good example is errors that result from fatigue.[19] If an error occurred due to the fatigue of a surgeon one could rework the surgeon's schedule or retrain the surgeon to be alert to the signs of fatigue, but if nothing was done for the schedule of surgeons generally or steps were not put in place to detect fatigue it would be highly likely a fatigue-related event would occur again.[20]

There is, however, a danger here. The systems approach to patient safety is not a reason for denying all personal responsibility. Ulrich Beck[21] is concerned that under a systems approach:

> causes dribble away into a general amalgam of agents and conditions, reactions and counter-reactions, which brings social certainty and popularity to the concept of system. This reveals in exemplary fashion the ethical significance of the system concept: *one can do something and continue doing it without having to take personal responsibility for it.*

I would suggest that the response to these concerns is to be accepting of the fact that everyone will make mistakes. It is the responsibility of the system to put in place checks and balances to ensure these mistakes are caught and do not result in harm to patients. However, there are limits to the kind of mistakes a system can catch. Deliberate attempts to harm a patient or to undermine the protections a system put in place are very hard to prevent and blame for them lies primarily with the individual. A health care professional who relies on the system to protect a patient, rather than their own skills, deserves to be held to account.

Techniques of improving safety

The best way to tackle safety issues is to seek to put in place procedures at different layers. James Reason's[22] Swiss Cheese Model captures this well. It imagines a pile of slices of cheese with holes in. Something may fall through a hole in the first layer, and even through a similarly placed hole in the second layer, but by the third or fourth it should meet a piece of solid cheese. Similarly we need layers of safety procedures, realising that each individual procedure will not capture every error, but if there are an adequate number in place one of them will. At a broad level we might identify at least six layers.[23]

19 Royal College of General Practitioners, *Patient safety implications of general practice workload*, London: RCGP, 2015.

20 C. Vincent, *Patient safety*, p. 16.

21 U. Beck, *Risk society: towards a new modernity*, London: Sage, 1992, p. 33.

22 J. Reason, 'Human error: models and management', *British Medical Journal* 2000, 320:768.

23 For a wider discussion see C. Newdick, 'From Hippocrates to commodities: three models of NHS governance', *Medical Law Review* 2014, 22:162.

1. Personal professional responsibility.

Health care professionals have a responsibility to take care of their patients. Their skill is, of course, a key component of patient safety. Central to improving patient safety is finding ways of ensuring that health care professionals have the skills, training and work place frameworks to be able to keep patients safe. Further, that they are held to account if they fail to live up to the standards expected. However, as is now clear, relying on personal responsibility is insufficient on its own. As Professor Sir Ian Kennedy, in 2001, at the Bristol Heart Inquiry acknowledged:

> healthcare professionals often monitored their own work at local level, reviewing for example, deaths and complications. But . . . there were no systems, either within the hospital or elsewhere, to identify poor clinical outcomes or take action, unless or until some scandal broke, or a pattern of performance was so poor as to attract public attention . . .[24]

The primary means of enforcement of care standards will be clinical negligence and professional regulation. The difficulty with these is that they tend to discourage openness and focus on individual misconduct. As the *Bristol* report said of medical negligence:

> the culture and the practice of clinical negligence litigation work against the interests of patients' safety. The system is positively counter-productive, in that it provides a clear incentive not to report, or to cover up, an error or incident. And once covered up, no one can learn from it and the next patient is exposed to the same or similar risk.[25]

A further problem is that efficacy of medical negligence depends on the wealth and determination of patients to peruse their claim. This means that the issues that come to court or before the professional bodies are not necessarily those that reflect the greatest need for a response.

2. Teamwork

A second key theme in the promotion of safety is to encourage health care professionals to work in teams. The obvious point is that if health care professionals work in teams, then if one person makes an error, the hope is that another will spot it. This can be reinforced by requiring second opinions or double checks before potentially dangerous interventions. This, however, is not a foolproof system. It works if members of the team feel free to criticise each other, but not if power structures within the group prevent that. There is also a danger that the 'double checking' becomes routinised if staff members come to trust their colleagues to such an extent they cannot imagine a colleague making an error.

24 Bristol Royal Infirmary Inquiry, *Learning from Bristol*, Cm5207, 2001.
25 Ibid.

3. Regulation and inspection

While regulation has an important part to play in ensuring the provision of safety mechanisms it is clear that regulation alone cannot ensure safety. Indeed, it is worth noting that the Mid-Staffordshire events occurred even though the hospital was subject to a regulatory regime. Francis Fukuyama[26] notes that:

> [N]o regulatory regime is ever fully leak-proof . . . But this misses the point of social regulation: no law is ever fully enforced. Every country makes murder a crime and attaches severe penalties to homicide, and yet murders nonetheless occur. The fact that they do has never been a reason for giving up on the law or on attempts to enforce it.

Nevertheless, regulation has a bad reputation in health contexts, for good reasons.

First, there is a concern that regulations produced in the name of patient safety are in fact designed to promote factors other than patients' safety, particularly financial ones. The Healthcare Commission recognised that had happened and commented:

> . . . it is not acceptable – nor is it necessary – for the safety of patients to be compromised by any other objectives, no matter how compelling these may seem, at the time, to be.[27]

Second, there is a danger that in following the letter of a regulation sight can be lost of the greater goal of patient safety. Christopher Newdick claims that that occurred in Mid Staffordshire where concerns about breaching waiting-time targets meant that less urgent cases were dealt with before more urgent ones.[28]

Thirdly, it is possible for regulation to fail. Roger Brownsword identifies some of the reasons why this might happen:[29]

> Broadly speaking, where there is a lack of regulatory effectiveness, the locus of the problem will be (i) with the regulators themselves, or (ii) with the response (including the resistance) of regulatees, or (iii) with some disruptive factors external to the regulators and regulatees – and, quite possibly, the problem will be found to lie in more than one of these loci.

From these concerns it is possible to draw out a number of key points about successful regulation. First, its success depends on the co-operation of those being regulated.[30] Working with the strong ethical code of most health professionals is more effective than imposing an alien set of targets. Regulation works best when

26 F. Fukuyama, *Our posthuman future*, London: Profile Books, 2002, p. 192.

27 Healthcare Commission, *Learning from investigations*, London: Healthcare Commission, 1998.

28 Newdick, 'From Hippocrates to commodities'.

29 Brownsword, 'Regulating patient safety'.

30 J. Healy, *Improving health care safety and quality: reluctant regulators*, Aldershot: Ashgate, 2011.

those being regulated own the process and want to have their processes checked so they can be improved if they are failing. It works best when it is seen as a collaborative effort involving medical professionals, patients and the regulators.[31]

Second, the regulation must have a coherent message. Sets of arbitrary rules are unlikely to demand respect or promote safety. As Judith Healy identifies the problems with bad regulation:

> The proliferation of externally set priorities and the number of different agencies and actors created what we termed 'priority thickets' – dense patches of overlapping or disjointed goals that commanded very substantial attention and resources, but did not necessarily provide clear direction or facilitate the development of clear goals, internally coherent visions or strategies linked to local priorities.[32]

Third, effective regulation is positive and acknowledges the things the organisation is doing well and seeks to build on those.[33]

Fourth, a sophisticated range of enforcement mechanisms are needed. These can range from 'soft' enforcement where organisations are encouraged to continue and develop good practices and to extend them to other areas of their work. Moving up to 'harder' enforcement through formal warnings and ultimately criminal or civil penalties as a last resort.

Fifth, and more controversially, there may need to be a range of regulators. Judith Healy recommends a range of regulators arguing that 'one single regulatory actor alone cannot expect to have all the knowledge and to have full command over all the influence and actions necessary to implement change in a complex health care system.'[34] Indeed a well-functioning organisation will want to use self-regulation alongside the external regulation to ensure the most effective response. However, having a range of disparate regulations can be problematic. Quick argues:

> There appears to be little method in the madness of multiple agencies performing similar tasks yet leaving organisations and individuals confused and often conflicted in how to respond. Constant change to the remit and legal responsibilities of regulators, as well as regular name changes, cannot help them in their task of making an impact with the regulated.[35]

This, however, is an argument against disorganised regulation, rather than a coherent set of regulators who have different areas of specialisation and techniques

31 O. Quick, *Regulating patient safety: the end of professional dominance?* Cambridge University Press, 2016.

32 M. Dixon-Woods et al., 'Culture and behaviour in the English National Health Service: overview of lessons from a large multimethod study', *BMJ Quality and Safety Journal* 2014, 23:106.

33 J. Healy, *Improving patient safety through responsive regulation*, London: The Health Foundation, 2013.

34 Ibid.

35 O. Quick, 'Regulating and legislating safety: the case for candour', *BMJ Quality and Safety* 2014, 23:614.

of regulation. It is suggested the 'Swiss cheese' analogy can apply to regulators as it can to safety systems.

4. Patients

Patients (including the families and friends of patients) can be best placed to know if there are shortfalls in the basic care of patients. Empowering patients is an important way of promoting safety.[36] Of course, it would not appropriate to see patients as being responsible for their own safety, but part of the problem in Mid Staffs was the failure to take seriously the complaints by families of patients and to listen to the comments of patients themselves.

5. Technology

Roger Brownsword[37] advocates the use of technologies to promote safety. These can include the use of constraints or 'forcing functions' that makes an error impossible. For example, arranging apparatus which makes it impossible to insert the wrong tube. The use of computing technology can alert practitioners when unusual data had been entered or a surprising amount of medicine prescribed.

Such proposals are relatively uncontroversial. More so would be the use of surveillance technologies, for example video monitoring of patients. This could be targeted at patients who are perceived to be particularly vulnerable, such as those at risk of falling or on suicide watch. Supporters of such surveillance will argue they offer a deterrent from abuse and a record that can be used to investigate abuse. In some settings it might be argued that surveillance offers greater freedom, if, for example, it allows patients greater freedom of movement.

Of course, there are concerns. Inevitably the use of cameras in wards raises privacy and dignity concerns, particularly if the cameras cover areas where intimate examinations or activities might take place, such as bathrooms or toilets. There are also concerns (relying on evidence from the use of CCTV in cities) that bad behaviour is displaced to areas where there are no cameras, although in most health settings it may be possible to provide comprehensive coverage. Further there is a concern that the cameras may not prioritise patient safety as an internal value. As Brownsword puts it:

> 'in moral communities, and in all walks of life, the aspiration is to do the right thing; respecting persons, and respecting patients and their safety, is doing the right thing; and it matters to moral communities that such respect is shown for the right reason – not because we know that we are being observed.'[38]

36 World Health Organisation, *Exploring patient participation in reducing health-care-related safety risks*, Geneva: WHO, 2013.

37 Brownsword, 'Regulating Patient Safety'.

38 Ibid., p. 13.

6. Candour

At the heart of patient safety must be idea that we learn from mistakes. Only if we know what mistakes have happened can we discover why they have happened and what processes can be put in place to ensure they do not happen again. However, fear of blame or litigation and loss of reputation are strong incentives not to disclose a mistake has been made. These have been seen as a significant barrier to promoting safety and hence a legal duty of candour was created in Regulation 20 of the Health and Social Care Act 2008 (Regulated Activities) Regulations 2014.

Regulation 20 requires 'registered persons' to act 'in an open and transparent way' with patients. In particular if there is a 'notifiable safety incident' they must notify the patient and inform them of 'all the facts the registered person knows about the incident as at the date of the notification' and 'include an apology'. The patient must be informed as soon as possible after a notifiable safety incident has occurred. The NHS Standard Contract requires that to be within 20 working days. That notification must be given in person and explained to the best of the health service body's knowledge of all the facts. It must advise what further enquiries are appropriate; issue an apology; and keep a written record. Regulation 20 defines a notifiable safety incident as including incidents that in the reasonable opinion of a health care professional could result in death, moderate harm, severe harm or prolonged psychological harm. To be clear, this means the regulations do not apply to a 'near miss' if that has not resulted in harm, or only a lower level of harm. As the primary purpose of disclosure is to prevent future harms it is surprising that the duty does not apply to the potential for harm, rather than the actual harm suffered. Further, it may raise difficult questions of interpretation in the case of a very sick patient when it is not clear if their injury has occurred as a result of their underlying condition or harm.[39]

Law

What is the role of the law in all of patient safety? It is perhaps natural following investigations such as the Francis Reports that Governments and others turn to legal regulation as the solution to promote patient safety. However, there are some good reasons to doubt the ability of the law to do more than play a relatively small role in promoting safety.

Limitations on the effectiveness of law in patient safety

The primary direct legal interventions in the area of patient safety are through criminal law sanctions and order for payments under tort law. The criminal law may become involved in cases of deliberate abuse, when the normal law on assaults will apply. Where a patient dies a charge of gross negligence

39 Care Quality Commission, *Learning, candour and accountability*, London: CQC, 2016.

manslaughter can be brought. In relation to tort law the most likely to be used is negligence, which can lead to compensation payments being made. However, these legal interventions are primarily retrospective rather than forward looking. They are designed to allocate responsibility and ensure compensation is paid, rather than preventing a repeat of the harms.[40] Direct legal actions also come with costs. They encourage secrecy and can cause emotional and financial costs for those pursuing claims or defending them. Indeed Oliver Quick is adamant: 'There is no clear evidence connecting the threat of civil action with safer healthcare.'[41]

Further, the law's enforcement mechanisms are typically aimed at preventing harmful behaviour, rather than promoting good behaviour. Generally the criminal law will not punish you for being rude; insensitive; or for failing to help someone in need, and will only intervene if you have actually caused someone harm. The law of tort punishes those who fall below the standard of the reasonable person, but does not require them to live up to the highest standards. While, therefore, it may be designed to prevent the most egregious harms to patients, it sets the bar relatively low.

Another limitation on the effectiveness of law as a method of promoting patient safety is that one of the foundational legal principles is the 'rule of law'. That requires the law to be sufficiently certain so that citizens can know in advance what the law requires of them. This, in part, creates the 'tick box' mentality for which the law is sometimes criticised. The law sets down in precise rules what is required so that an individual can know what the law requires.

For all these reasons, although direct legal action can have some role to play in improving safety it is a rather limited one. However, it would be too quick to dismiss the usefulness of legal intervention.

Effective use of the law to promote patient safety

Although, therefore, there are reasons to be wary about legal intervention it would be wrong to dismiss its role entirely. Direct legal intervention through the law of tort and criminal law is only rarely used, but this does not mean it lacks value. It is important to have the threat of criminal punishment of the most serious of cases. After all if something would be a criminal offence outside a hospital setting there is no reason it should not be inside. There are also some helpful offences designed to protect patients. Most notable is the offence of ill treatment or neglect, found in s. 20 Criminal Justice and Courts Act 2015:

> It is an offence for an individual who has the care of another individual by virtue of being a care worker to ill-treat or wilfully to neglect that individual.

40 Quick, 'Outing medical errors'.
41 Quick, 'Patient safety and the problem and potential of law'.

Section 21 allows a care provider to be convicted if:

(a) an individual who has the care of another individual by virtue of being part of the care provider's arrangements ill-treats or wilfully neglects that individual,
(b) the care provider's activities are managed or organised in a way which amounts to a gross breach of a relevant duty of care owed by the care provider to the individual who is ill-treated or neglected, and
(c) in the absence of the breach, the ill-treatment or wilful neglect would not have occurred or would have been less likely to occur.

More importantly the law is not just about legal actions brought in court rooms. Contract law is primarily designed to deter people from breaching a contract or guide parties as to how to (extra-judicially) resolve disputes if a breach has taken place. Very few contract cases reach court, and yet the legal framework has a significant impact on many daily transactions. Further, the law can promote general attitudes and values. The intense debate over same-sex marriage, for example, was largely about the positive message sent about same-sex relationships through marriage. The Mental Capacity Act 2005 encourages those who care for people who lack capacity to act in the best interests of the person lacking capacity. So too it might be said the law can have a role in promoting an ethos or culture of promotion of patient safety, even if it will be rare for a case to come before the courts. Just as contract law creates an environment in which contracts are complied with and respected, so too the law might have a role in creating an environment in which patient safety is a key value.

The law can also become involved by setting up systems of regulation and inspection. The regulators are empowered by the law to have rights of access to buildings and require measures to remedy problems identified. Here the work is done not directly by the courts, but by the regulators, empowered and backed up by the law.

The National Health Service

The NHS Constitution has become a key document for the NHS. Under section 2 of the Health Act 1989 a wide range of NHS bodies are required to have regard to it. It has plenty to say about patient safety. Principle 3 states 'the NHS aspires to the highest standards of excellence and professionalism'. Similarly a key NHS Value is a commitment to quality of care. When it comes to the rights of patients, they are given the 'right to be cared for in a clean, safe, secure and suitable environment.' It also states:

> You have the right to expect NHS bodies to monitor, and make efforts to improve continuously, the quality of healthcare they commission or provide. This includes improvements to the safety, effectiveness and experience of services.

In relation to staff the Constitution lists some important legal duties, including:

> You have a duty to take reasonable care of health and safety at work for you, your team and others, and to co-operate with employers to ensure compliance with health and safety requirements.

There are also various expectations, which are not per se legal duties. These include the need to:

- provide all patients with safe care, and to do all you can to protect patients from avoidable harm
- follow all guidance, standards and codes relevant to your role, subject to any more specific requirements of your employers
- maintain the highest standards of care and service, treating every individual with compassion, dignity and respect, taking responsibility not only for the care you personally provide, but also for your wider contribution to the aims of your team and the NHS as a whole
- find alternative sources of care or assistance for patients, when you are unable to provide this (including for those patients who are not receiving basic care to meet their needs)
- take up training and development opportunities provided over and above those legally required of your post
- play your part in sustainably improving services by working in partnership with patients, the public and communities
- raise any genuine concern you may have about a risk, malpractice or wrongdoing at work (such as a risk to patient safety, fraud or breaches of patient confidentiality), which may affect patients, the public, other staff or the organisation itself, at the earliest reasonable opportunity
- involve patients, their families, carers or representatives fully in decisions about prevention, diagnosis, and their individual care and treatment
- be open with patients, their families, carers or representatives, including if anything goes wrong; welcoming and listening to feedback and addressing concerns promptly and in a spirit of co-operation
- contribute to a climate where the truth can be heard, the reporting of, and learning from, errors is encouraged and colleagues are supported where errors are made . . .

Within the NHS patient safety is the responsibility of a body named NHS Improvement. The NHS Outcomes Framework sets out the response to particular issues facing the NHS and these will include for those issues particular needs for a safe environment. The 'never event' list has been created which sets out incidents that can cause death or severe harm where the NHS has clear guidance and tools to ensure they do not happen. They tackle issues such as leaving objects in a patient's body. Between 1 April 2015 and 31 March 2016 there were 447 serious incidents that fell within the definition of a 'never event';[42] 351 were reported between 1 April 2016 and 31 January 2017.[43] This demonstrates how even with targeted responses at the most serious incidents it is difficult to ensure they never occur.

42 NHS, *Never events reported as occurring between 1 April 2015 and 31 March 2016 – final update 2017*, London: NHS, 2017.

43 Ibid.

A recent creation is the Healthcare Safety Investigation Branch. This has operated since April 2016 and will offer support and guidance to NHS organisations on investigations, and carry out certain investigations itself.[44] The expert advisory group states: 'The purpose of this new safety investigation body is to act as an enabler, exemplar and catalyst for learning-oriented safety investigation.'

The General Medical Council

The GMC provides guidance which promotes patient safety. It requires that:

> You must protect patients from risk of harm posed by another colleague's conduct, performance or health . . . If you have concerns that a colleague may not be fit to practise, you must take appropriate steps without delay, so that the concerns are investigated and patients protected where necessary.[45]

The GMC also requires: 'effective systems . . . to give early warning of any failure, or potential failure, in clinical performance, and that such failures are addressed quickly and effectively'.[46] It explains that 'If a patient under your care has suffered harm or distress, you must act immediately to put matters right, if that is possible. You should offer an apology and explain fully and promptly to the patient what has happened . . . '[47]

Nursing and Midwifery Council

The NMC Code also addresses patient safety. It requires nurses to 'be open and candid with all service users about all aspects of care and treatment, including when any mistakes or harm have taken place.'[48] If someone has suffered actual harm then a nurse must put the situation right and 'explain fully and promptly what has happened, including the likely effects, and apologise to the person affected and, where appropriate, their advocate, family or carers.'[49]

More generally the Code creates a duty to raise concerns about patient safety. This requires nurses to 'raise and, if necessary, escalate any concerns you may have about patient or public safety, or the level of care people are receiving in your workplace or any other healthcare setting and use the channels available to you in line with our guidance and your local working practices'.[50]

44 P. Walsh, 'Will the independent patient safety investigation service make a difference?', *Clinical Risk* 2015, 21:75.
45 GMC, *Good management practice*, London: GMC, 2013, Annex C, para 1.
46 Ibid.
47 GMC, *Raising and acting on concerns about patient safety*, London: GMC, 2016, p. 2.
48 NMC, *The code for nurses and midwives*, London: NMC, 2016.
49 Ibid.
50 Ibid.

Conclusion

Patient safety is now a major concern for health care professionals and organisations. It would be foolhardy to suggest that there is a 'magic bullet' that can ensure patients will always be safe in hospitals. An ideal system of patient safety involves using a range of regulations, inspections, technologies and systems that can begin to tackle the issue. The NHS is beginning to utilise these, particularly following the Francis Reports. However, as this chapter has emphasised there was extensive regulation even at the time of the events in Mid Staffs. As patients' safety mechanisms are improved two points particularly should be emphasised. The first is that patients themselves are an invaluable source of information and have an important role to play in safety promotion. Second, regulatory regimes must reward and acknowledge good practice, as well as identifying where improvements need to be made.

References

Beck, U., *Risk society: towards a new modernity*, London: Sage, 1992.

Bristol Royal Infirmary Inquiry, *Learning from Bristol*, Cm5207, 2001.

Brownsword, R., 'Regulating patient safety: is it time for a technological response?', *Law, Innovation and Technology* 2014, 6:1.

Care Quality Commission, *Learning, candour and accountability*, London: CQC, 2016.

Dixon-Woods, M., et al. 'Culture and behaviour in the English National Health Service: overview of lessons from a large multimethod study', *BMJ Quality and Safety Journal* 2014, 23:106.

Francis, R., *Independent inquiry into care provided by Mid Staffordshire NHS Foundation Trust January 2005–March 2009*, London: The Stationery Office, 2010.

Francis, R., *The Report of the Mid Staffordshire NHS Foundation Trust Public Inquiry*, London: The Stationery Office, 2013; HC 898 I–III.

Fukuyama, F., *Our posthuman future*, London, Profile Books, 2002.

GMC, *Good management practice*, London: GMC, 2013.

GMC, *Raising and acting on concerns about patient safety*, London: GMC, 2016.

Healy, J., *Improving health care safety and quality: reluctant regulators*, Aldershot: Ashgate, 2011.

Healy, J., *Improving patient safety through responsive regulation*, London: The Health Foundation, 2013.

Healthcare Commission, *Learning from investigations*, London: Healthcare Commission, 1998.

National Patient Safety Foundation, *Free from harm: accelerating patient safety improvement fifteen years after To err is human*, Washington: NPSF, 2015.

Newdick, C., 'From Hippocrates to commodities: three models of NHS governance', *Medical Law Review* 2014, 22:162.

NHS, *An organisation with a memory*, London: NHS, 2000.

NHS, *Never events reported as occurring between 1 April 2015 and 31 March 2016 – final update 2017*, London: NHS, 2017.

NMC, *The code for nurses and midwives*, London: NMC, 2016.

Quick, O., 'Outing medical errors: questions of trust and responsibility', *Medical Law Review* 2006, 14:22.

Quick, O., 'Patient safety and the problem and potential of law', *Professional Negligence* 2012, 28:68.

Quick, O., 'Regulating and legislating safety: the case for candour', *BMJ Quality and Safety* 2014, 23:614.

Quick, O., *Regulating patient safety: the end of professional dominance?* Cambridge University Press, 2016.

Reason, J., 'Human error: models and management', *British Medical Journal* 2000, 320:768.

Royal College of General Practitioners, *Patient safety implications of general practice workload*, London: RCGP, 2015.

US Institute of Medicine, *To err is human*, Washington: US Institute of Medicine, 1999.

Vincent, C., *Patient safety*, London, Elsevier; 2006.

Walsh, P., 'Will the independent patient safety investigation service make a difference?', *Clinical Risk* 2015, 21:75.

World Health Organisation, *Exploring patient participation in reducing health-care-related safety risks*, Geneva: WHO, 2013.

World Health Organisation, *Patient safety*, Geneva: WHO, 2017.

3 Patient safety and substantive English medical law

Charles Foster

Introduction

Fear of civil litigation is likely to be a significant factor in determining clinical practice, and thus in ensuring patient safety.

Litigation itself, whatever the outcome, is always stressful. Clinicians wish to avoid that stress and the alleged errors that resulted in litigation. A finding of breach of duty may be devastating for personal and professional morale, and may affect a clinician's professional career. Clinicians are bombarded by frightening case studies from their defence organisations.[1] The organisations naturally want to avoid their members making similar (expensive) mistakes in the future. NHS Resolution seeks to teach clinicians the lessons learned from litigation. The authors and promulgators of local and national clinical guidelines no doubt have regard to the errors exposed by litigation. The courts pay close regard to clinical guidelines in determining the standard of care expected, and in deciding whether or not a clinical duty has been breached, and thus clinical guidelines themselves can come to determine the legal acceptability of particular practices. In this way the results of litigation involving clinical guidelines (although not usually determining formally, by reference to the doctrine of precedent, the acceptability of a practice) can come, indirectly, to determine future practice.

This chapter examines the role of English law in patient safety. It focuses on the changes in the substantive law, and assumes that those changes affect the behaviour of clinicians in the ways outlined above.

The existence and extent of a duty

We have a duty to take reasonable care to avoid acts or omissions which it is reasonably foreseeable would be likely to injure our neighbours, says the famous case of *Donoghue v Stevenson*.[2] But who is my neighbour? Lord Atkin said that:

1 E.g. the MDU's 'Journal', the MPS's 'Casebook', and the MDDUS's 'Summons'.
2 [1932] AC 562.

> The answer seems to be – persons who are so closely and directly affected by my act that I ought reasonably to have them in contemplation as being so affected when I am directing my mind to the acts or omissions which are called in question.[3]

The neighbours of clinicians, for the purposes of the law of clinical negligence, are (with some important caveats) patients. A doctor, generally, can choose whether or not to create a doctor–patient relationship. Where there is no choice about it, it is the law of contract, not of tort, that has forced the creation of the relationship, although, once created, the law of negligence (sometimes, in the case of private patients, supplemented by contract) that determines the obligations that that relationship entails.

It is usually obvious when a patient is a patient. The law has been reluctant to extend doctors' obligations beyond obvious patients. Thus a claimant who had declared on a questionnaire that she had sickle cell anaemia, could not sue a doctor, employed by the a potential employer to which the claimant had applied, for alleged negligence in concluding from the questionnaire that the claimant would be likely to have an increased rate of absence from work.[4] A doctor does not owe a duty to all potential sexual partners of a patient to whom she gives contraceptive advice (though she may owe a duty to the patient's spouse).[5] The liability to third parties for injury caused by violent patients who should have been contained is currently unclear: the law continues to evolve. But it is very unlikely that a court would find that a clinician owes a duty to the entire world in such circumstances.[6]

These exceptions to the general principle that a doctor owes a duty to her patient can be regarded as legal exotica. Cases of doctors' liability to third parties are insufficiently numerous or financially significant to dilute the rhetorical power of legal and quasi-legal statements about liability to patients. The liability of doctors to patients is the bread and butter of clinical negligence litigators and indemnifiers. Insofar as safety is affected by litigation, it is patient safety, not non-patient safety, that is the main beneficiary.

While non-patient safety may be ethically important, the principles that determine liability for non-patient safety are so uncertain, and so hedged round with policy considerations, that the law of negligence cannot be said to be a major contributor to non-patient safety.

The standard of care

The cornerstone case in the law of clinical negligence is *Bolam v Friern Hospital Management Committee*.[7] The important part is McNair J's direction to the jury,

3 P. 580.

4 *Kapfunde v Abbey National plc* [1999] Lloyd's Rep Med 48; [1998] EWCA Civ 535.

5 *Goodwill v British Pregnancy Advisory Services* [1996] 2 All ER 161.

6 *Palmer v Tees Health Authority* [1999] Lloyd's Rep Med 351; see too *Dorset Yacht Co. Ltd v Home Office*; *Caparo Industries v Dickman* [1990] 2 AC 605.

7 [1957] 1 W.L.R. 583.

which has become the canonical statement of the standard expected of medical professionals. It has metastasised well beyond medical law, and is fairly ubiquitous in professional law generally. A doctor is not negligent, he said, 'if he has acted in accordance with a practice accepted as proper by a responsible body of medical men skilled in that particular art . . . Putting it the other way round, a man is not negligent, if he is acting in accordance with such a practice, merely because there is a body of opinion who would take a contrary view, if he has acted in accordance with a practice accepted as proper by a responsible body of medical men skilled in that particular art.'[8]

This test has been repeatedly endorsed by the courts. Thus, for instance, in *Maynard v West Midlands Regional Health Authority*,[9] Lord Scarman said:

> . . . I have to say that a judge's 'preference' for one body of distinguished professional opinion to another also professionally distinguished is not sufficient to establish negligence in a practitioner whose actions have received the seal of approval of those whose opinions, truthfully expressed, honestly held, were not preferred. If this was the real reason for the judge's finding, he erred in law even though elsewhere in his judgment he stated the law correctly. For in the realm of diagnosis and treatment negligence is not established by preferring one *respectable* body of professional opinion to another. Failure to exercise the ordinary skill of a doctor (in the appropriate speciality, if he be a specialist) is necessary.[10]

Note that *Bolam* prescribes both a rule of substantive law and a rule of evidence. The law requires clinicians to act in a way that would be endorsed by a responsible body of clinicians in the relevant specialty. And the way that the courts decide whether or not the claimant has discharged the burden of proving that the defendant has not acted in such a way is by hearing evidence from experts in the specialty. The claimant has to clear a high bar: she has to show that there are no responsible people in that specialty who would have acted as the defendant did. 'Responsible' does not entail being in the majority. In *De Freitas v O'Brien*[11] only four or five clinicians in the world could be identified who would have acted as the defendant did. The fact that the defendant was in a tiny minority did not mean that he was not 'responsible': he was, the court held, and the claimant failed.

De Freitas indicated an entirely appropriate judicial protection of medical innovation. To criticise the use of new technologies or medical approaches on the ground that 'responsible' has to be judged by reference to the number of people who do things in a particular way would stop medical progress – to the ultimate detriment of patients.

8 At 587.
9 [1984] 1 W.L.R. 634.
10 At 639.
11 [1995] 6 Med LR 108.

Yet there is no doubt that the *Bolam* test was abused by patients. It is not hard to fashion some sort of a defence for many distinctly sub-optimal medical practices, and where those defences were delivered authoritatively by well remunerated expert consultants, judges were often inappropriately deferential.

This deference came to an abrupt halt after the House of Lords decision in *Bolitho v City and Hackney Health Authority.*[12]

Lord Browne-Wilkinson (who gave the only substantive judgment) said there:

> . . . in my view, the court is not bound to hold that a defendant doctor escapes liability for negligent treatment or diagnosis just because he leads evidence from a number of medical experts who are genuinely of opinion that the defendant's treatment or diagnosis accorded with sound medical practice. In the *Bolam* case itself, McNair J. stated [1957] 1 W.L.R. 583, 587, that the defendant had to have acted in accordance with the practice accepted as proper by a '*responsible* body of medical men'. Later, at p. 588, he referred to 'a standard of practice recognised as proper by a competent *reasonable* body of opinion'. Again, in the passage which I have cited from *Maynard's* case, Lord Scarman refers to a 'respectable' body of professional opinion. The use of these adjectives – responsible, reasonable and respectable – all show that the court has to be satisfied that the exponents of the body of opinion relied upon can demonstrate that such opinion has a logical basis. In particular in cases involving, as they so often do, the weighing of risks against benefits, the judge, before accepting a body of opinion as being responsible, reasonable or respectable, will need to be satisfied that, in forming their views, the experts have directed their minds to the question of comparative risks and benefits and have reached a defensible conclusion on the matter . . .
>
> . . . in cases of diagnosis and treatment there are cases where, despite a body of professional opinion sanctioning the defendant's conduct, the defendant can properly be held liable for negligence (I am not here considering questions of disclosure of risk). In my judgment that is because, in some cases, it cannot be demonstrated to the judge's satisfaction that the body of opinion relied upon is reasonable or responsible. In the vast majority of cases the fact that distinguished experts in the field are of a particular opinion will demonstrate the reasonableness of that opinion. In particular, where there are questions of assessment of the relative risks and benefits of adopting a particular medical practice, a reasonable view necessarily presupposes that the relative risks and benefits have been weighed by the experts in forming their opinions. But if, in a rare case, it can be demonstrated that the professional opinion is not capable of withstanding logical analysis, the judge is entitled to hold that the body of opinion is not reasonable or responsible.
>
> . . . I emphasise that in my view it will very seldom be right for a judge to reach the conclusion that views genuinely held by a competent medical

12 [1998] AC 232.

> expert are unreasonable. The assessment of medical risks and benefits is a matter of clinical judgment which a judge would not normally be able to make without expert evidence. As the quotation from Lord Scarman makes clear, it would be wrong to allow such assessment to deteriorate into seeking to persuade the judge to prefer one of two views both of which are capable of being logically supported. It is only where a judge can be satisfied that the body of expert opinion cannot be logically supported at all that such opinion will not provide the bench mark by reference to which the defendant's conduct falls to be assessed.'[13]

Despite Lord Browne-Wilkinson's caution, expressed in the last paragraph quoted, this produced convulsions in the legal and medical worlds. Clinicians were worried that it would give non-medically qualified judges carte blanche to second-guess their judgments and the judgments of the experts called on their behalf. Yet *Bolitho* contained no new statement of substantive law. It merely called attention to the word 'responsible' that had always been the central plank of the *Bolam* test, and reiterated the uncontroversial principle that the courts, not the doctors, should decide what standard the law expected doctors to reach, and whether, in a particular case, that standard had been reached.

Although it was not legally revolutionary, *Bolitho* undoubtedly produced a profound change of culture. It swept away, almost overnight, the old culture of deference to experts. It gave judges renewed confidence: they could, and sometimes did, reject the evidence of qualified experts. Judges and counsel interrogated experts not just about their expertise or the factual basis of their conclusions, but about their reasoning.

Experts had previously been seen by the courts as medical practitioners generally had been seen by laymen: as uncontradictable gods. *Bolitho* dealt a death blow to medical paternalism in the courts, and in doing so, since what happens in the courts gradually filters out into the wider world, dealt a severe (but not yet mortal) blow to medical paternalism generally.

Has this improved patient safety? It is difficult to know, but the intuitive answer would seem to be yes. Questionable practices, hallowed by mere convention, can now be questioned. The requirement that a practice, to be defensible, has to be capable of standing up to scrutiny, has had the effect of enhancing the status of evidence-based medicine.[14] The process of drafting an authoritative clinical guideline necessarily involves an examination of the literature and a canvassing of opinions from a variety of experts. There is much less room, in the world of evidence-based medicine endorsed by *Bolitho*, for dangerous mavericks.

The decay of paternalism, however, was seen much more dramatically (but with much less effect on patient safety), in the law relating to consent.

13 241–3.

14 Ash Samanta, et al., 'The role of clinical guidelines in medical negligence litigation: a shift from the *Bolam* standard'. *Medical Law Review* (2006) 14(1); 321–66.

Medical consent

Ever since Auschwitz the law, in most western jurisdictions, has paid at least lip service to patient autonomy. This respect for autonomy found a legal home in Article 8 of the European Convention on Human Rights – that most elastic of all the provisions of the Convention – and inter alia, in the common law relating to confidentiality and consent.

To do something to a patient without her consent can be, if the patient does not know the nature and quality of the act, an assault (actionable both as a criminal and a civil assault), but the courts have actively discouraged the invocation of assault in most medical consent cases[15] and in the overwhelming majority of such cases the claimant contends that it is negligent to do the act without the requisite consent.

The leading case on the law relating to negligent failings in the consent process used to be *Sidaway v Board of Governors of the Bethlem Royal Hospital and the Maudsley Hospital*.[16] The ratio of *Sidaway* has always been contentious (there were four speeches in the House of Lords, each advocating a rather different view) but for many years there was an uneasy consensus, at least amongst legal and medical practitioners, that Lord Diplock won the day. He had said:

> The merit of the Bolam test is that the criterion of the duty of care owed by a doctor to his patient is whether he has acted in accordance with a practice accepted as proper by a body of responsible and skilled medical opinion . . . To decide what risks the existence of which a patient should be voluntarily warned and the terms in which such warning, if any, should be given, having regard to the effect that the warning may have, is as much an exercise of professional skill and judgment as any other part of the doctor's comprehensive duty of care to the individual patient, and expert medical evidence on this matter should be treated in just the same way. The *Bolam* test should be applied.[17]

At the other end of the spectrum was the prescient Lord Scarman. His time would come, but he had to wait thirty years. He had said that if a 'failure to warn a patient of the risks inherent in the operation which is recommended does constitute a failure to respect the patient's right to make his own decision, I can see no reason in principle why, if the risk materialises and injury or damage is caused, the law should not recognise and enforce a right in the patient to compensation by way of damages'.[18] The decision about whether or not to consent to treatment did not involve merely medical criteria:

> The doctor's concern is with health and the relief of pain. These are the medical objectives. But a patient may well have in mind circumstances, objectives, and values which he may reasonably not make known to the doctor but

15 *Chatterton v Gerson* [1981] QB 432
16 [1985] AC 871
17 893, 895
18 884–5

> which may lead him to a different decision from that suggested by a purely medical opinion.[19]

It followed, he said, that:

> . . . English law must recognise a duty of the doctor to warn his patient of risk inherent in the treatment which he is proposing: and especially so, if the treatment be surgery. The critical limitation is that the duty is confined to material risk. The test of materiality is whether in the circumstances of the particular case the court is satisfied that a reasonable person in the patient's position would be likely to attach significance to the risk. Even if the risk be material, the doctor will not be liable if upon a reasonable assessment of his patient's condition he takes the view that a warning would be detrimental to his patient's health.[20]

The temporary triumph of Diplock and the temporary eclipse of Scarman were curious. They were illustrations of lawyers' and doctors' appetites for an easy answer. The easy answer here was that one principle – *Bolam* – ruled all negligence claims, whether they related to consent or to anything else. Academics railed against the oversimplification of *Sidaway,* and, as we have seen, Lord Browne-Wilkinson in *Bolitho* had restricted his highly influential comments about the *Bolam* test to '. . . cases of diagnosis and treatment . . .' In expounding *Bolam* he was not, he explicitly said, 'considering questions of disclosure of risk . . .'[21]

This more nuanced understanding of *Sidaway* gradually crept back into the courts, and in *Pearce v United Bristol Healthcare NHS Trust*[22] Lord Woolf MR, in a distinct but cautious retreat from Lord Diplock in *Sidaway*, articulated the 'reasonable patient' test:

> In a case where it is being alleged that a plaintiff has been deprived of the opportunity to make a proper decision as to what course he or she should take in relation to treatment, it seems to me to be the law, as indicated in the cases to which I have just referred, that if there is a significant risk which would affect the judgment of a reasonable patient, then in the normal course it is the responsibility of a doctor to inform the patient of that significant risk, if the information is needed so that the patient can determine for him or herself as to what course he or she should adopt.[23]

This 'reasonable patient' test became canonical, despite the difficulty of reconciling it with *Sidaway*, but *Pearce*, though a clear step away from *Sidaway*, hardly revolutionised legal or medical practice.

19 885–6.
20 889–90.
21 243.
22 [1999] PIQR P 53.
23 Para 21.

In *Chester v Afshar*[24] there was an opportunity for the law to repent emphatically of its historic refusal to read three out of the four speeches in *Bolitho*. Here, the claimant was not properly warned about the risk of cauda equina syndrome resulting from a planned laminectomy. The evidence was that if she had been warned she would still have undergone the operation, but would have undergone it on a different day. The claimant had the operation: cauda equina syndrome eventuated – as a non-negligent consequence of the procedure. She claimed damages for the cauda equina syndrome.

The majority of the House of Lords decided that the breach to the claimant's right to sovereignty over her own body required a remedy (which is uncontroversial), and that the appropriate remedy was damages for the full value of the cauda equina syndrome (which is, it is respectfully contended, perverse).

There was a blistering dissent from Lord Hoffmann, who said that the operation was analogous to a game of roulette. The chances of winning or losing did not depend on which day the game was played: they were always identical. The argument that persuaded the majority was:

> . . . about as logical as saying that if one had been told, on entering a casino, that the odds on No 7 coming up at roulette were only 1 in 37, one would have gone away and come back next week or gone to a different casino. The question is whether one would have taken the opportunity to avoid or reduce the risk, not whether one would have changed the scenario in some irrelevant detail. The judge found as a fact that the risk would have been precisely the same whether it was done then or later or by that competent surgeon or by another.[25]

The House of Lords could have decided, with perfect coherence, to find that the claimant did have compensable loss: her autonomy right under Article 8 of the European Convention on Human Rights had been violated. It could and should have granted her the modest damages usually awarded for such violations. Instead, *Chester* threw the long-established law of causation into convulsions. It did declare the importance of respect for patient autonomy, but did so in such an intellectually disreputable way that the message was not broadcast as loudly as it should have been. *Chester* is generally thought to have been wrongly decided, and has not been widely followed.

The Supreme Court revisited the question of tortious liability for failure to provide proper information to patients in *Montgomery v Lanarkshire Health Board*.[26] The case was a classic illustration of medical paternalism. An obstetrician had chosen not to warn a pregnant woman about the risk of shoulder dystocia associated with vaginal delivery. Had she been told, it was found, she would have opted for a caesarean section, which would have avoided the shoulder dystocia.

24 [2005] 1 AC 134.
25 At para 31.
26 [2015] AC 1430.

Sidaway, the Supreme Court concluded, was incorrectly decided:

> An adult person of sound mind is entitled to decide which, if any, of the available forms of treatment to undergo, and her consent must be obtained before treatment interfering with her bodily integrity is undertaken. The doctor is therefore under a duty to take reasonable care to ensure that the patient is aware of any material risks involved in any recommended treatment, and of any reasonable alternative or variant treatments. The test of materiality is whether, in the circumstances of the particular case, a reasonable person in the patient's position would be likely to attach significance to the risk, or the doctor is or should reasonably be aware that the particular patient would be likely to attach significance to it.
>
> The doctor is, however, entitled to withhold from the patient information as to a risk if he reasonably considers that its disclosure would be seriously detrimental to the patient's health. The doctor is also excused from conferring with the patient in circumstances of necessity, as for example where the patient requires treatment urgently but is unconscious or otherwise unable to make a decision.[27]

Lady Hale said that it was now well recognised 'that the interest which the law of negligence protects is a person's interest in their own physical and psychiatric integrity, an important feature of which is their autonomy, their freedom to decide what shall and shall not be done with their body . . .'[28]

What has all this to do with patient safety?

On one hand it might be argued that a crucial aspect of patient safety is the protection of patient autonomy, and that a violation of autonomy is as egregious as physical injury. Indeed a medically induced wound (such as is created by a surgeon's scalpel) is not defined as an injury at all if it has been created with the patient's consent. An identical wound, absent that consent, is an injury. Breaches of autonomy and actionable physical injuries are thus intimately related.[29]

Undoubtedly the law now protects patient autonomy much better than it did. But it is not obvious that this is necessarily a good thing. The requirement to inform patients thoroughly is onerous and open-ended. It is impossible to notify the patient about all the risks associated with a procedure or a medication that have been recorded in the literature, and even if it were possible, to mention remote possibilities would simply generate angst, discourage patients

27 Paras 87–88, per the joint judgment of Lords Kerr and Reed, with which Lords Neuberger, Clarke, Wilson and Hodge agreed.

28 Para 108.

29 Though it is important to observe that there is a real dissonance between the law's insistence, in the realm of medical law, on the centrality of autonomy and on the individual's sovereignty over her own body, and the law's insistence, in the realm of criminal law, that there are some acts (such as mutually consensual sado-masochism causing serious bodily injury) which are unlawful notwithstanding fully informed consent on the part of the person suffering the injury: see *R v Brown* [1994] 1 AC 212.

from treatment that was likely to be beneficial, and take up a huge amount of time that would be better spent treating patients. The 'reasonable patient' caveat deals pragmatically with some of these objections, but even so, the consenting process has become time-consuming and (in the eyes of many clinicians) an unwarranted diversion from the real business of medicine – to the detriment of patient safety. The right *not* to know is almost unprotected by the law: the option of relaxing, happily secure in the (usually justified) belief that 'doctor knows best' has been removed.[30]

Confidentiality

The right to have ones medical (and other) confidences respected is protected both by the common law and by Article 8 of the European Convention on Human Rights.

The position in the common law can be briefly stated: the disclosure of information that is prima facie confidential will not be an *actionable* breach of confidence if the public interest in disclosure outweighs the public interest in non-disclosure.[31] The Article 8 analysis looks at first blush similar: Article 8(1) confers a personal right to have confidences kept confidential. But this is a qualified right: it is subject to the broader, societal considerations articulated in Article 8(2).[32]

The common law analysis is more stoutly protective of personal confidences than Article 8. Once a piece of information is identified as confidential, it will be unlawful to disclose it unless the public interest defence applies. There is, so far, only one case in which the common law has imposed on clinicians a positive duty of disclosure. That was in a case of allegedly negligent non-disclosure of information about a claimant's genetic constitution, and the court indicated there that there were reasons for seeing the disclosure of genetic information as an exception to the general rule.[33] The general rule would not force disclosure, even if non-disclosure would result in serious personal injury. There are various statutory obligations of disclosure (for instance in cases of suspected terrorism). But if a doctor (for instance) knows that one of his HIV positive patients intends to go home after the clinic and have unprotected sex with a known partner, the law will not compel the doctor to notify the partner: it will merely excuse her if she does breach the confidence. This is a dramatic lacuna in English patient safety law.

The 'genetic information' exception identified in *ABC* surely cannot survive. There are compelling analogies between genetic and other diseases, and

30 Jonathan Herring and Charles Foster, 'Please don't tell me: the right not to know', *Cambridge Quarterly of Healthcare Ethics* (2012) 21(1): 20–9.

31 *W v Egdell* [1990] Ch 400; X v Y [1998] 2 All ER 648.

32 Article 8 provides: '1. Everyone has the right to respect for his private and family life, his home and his correspondence. 2. There shall be no interference by a public authority with the exercise of this right except such as is in accordance with the law and is necessary in a democratic society in the interests of national security, public safety or the economic well-being of the country, for the prevention of disorder or crime, for the protection of health or morals, or for the protection of the rights and freedoms of others.'

33 *ABC v St. George's Healthcare NHS Foundation Trust* [2017] EWCA Civ 336.

compelling public policy reasons for imposing a positive obligation to disclose – at least where failure to do so might result in death or serious injury.

Article 8(2), however, has the potential to impose a positive duty. The English court in *ABC* thought that Article 8 had nothing to add to the domestic law. It was wrong: if the common law proves insufficiently flexible to extend to non-genetic cases, Article 8(2) might have to do the job.

Best interests and patient identity

The law assumes that there is never any difficulty about identifying the patient whose safety is in issue, or to whom a duty is owed. The person in the dementia ward is, for all purposes, the same as the person who, ninety years before, was born. The fact that her name was the same in the register of births as it will be in the register of deaths tells a story which the law thinks is satisfactory.

This does not reflect the complexity of human life and pathology.[34] Dementia may strip away all memory, all preferences, and all distinguishing characteristics. Person 1 may cease to exist: Person 2 may be birthed, and inhabit a body composed of some of the cells that served Person 1 while she was alive. The fact that Person 1 and Person 2 were sequential tenants is hardly justification for treating them as identical.

In such circumstances Person 2 will be incapacitous. The law, in deciding how Person 2 should be treated, applies the Mental Capacity Act 2005. The governing principles are set out in section 1:

> 1. (2) A person must be assumed to have capacity unless it is established that he lacks capacity.
>
> (3) A person is not to be treated as unable to make a decision unless all practicable steps to help him to do so have been taken without success.
>
> (4) A person is not to be treated as unable to make a decision merely because he makes an unwise decision.
>
> (5) An act done, or decision made, under this Act for or on behalf of a person who lacks capacity must be done, or made, in his best interests.
>
> (6) Before the act is done, or the decision is made, regard must be had to whether the purpose for which it is needed can be as effectively achieved in a way that is less restrictive of the person's rights and freedom of action.
>
> Note the underlying assumption: that (even in the case of permanent incapacity) the pre-morbid patient is the same as the post-morbid patient.
>
> Section 4 contains a list of criteria which must be considered in ascertaining the best interests of the patient. Section 4(6) provides that the decision-maker

34 Charles Foster and Jonathan Herring, *Identity, Personhood and the Law*, Springer, 2017.

> (6) . . . must consider, so far as is reasonably ascertainable –
>
> (a) the person's past and present wishes and feelings (and, in particular, any relevant written statement made by him when he had capacity),
>
> (b) the beliefs and values that would be likely to influence his decision if he had capacity, and
>
> (c) the other factors that he would be likely to consider if he were able to do so.

If there is anything in the observation that Person 1 may have given way to Person 2, these provisions, from the point of view of patient safety, are terrifying. Person 2 is tyrannised by the dead Person 1. Autonomy is the watchword of the Mental Capacity Act, and yet the only autonomy protected is that of a corpse. The real interests of the existing patient are ignored.

This case of personality transformation is of course rather unusual. In most cases there will be an obvious continuity, of real ethical, metaphysical and legal significance, between the patient at time x and the patient at time x + y years, and the Mental Capacity Act will do a workmanlike, if rather philosophically rough and unexamined, job. But it should not be impossible for the law to look beyond the names on the statutory registers, and identity the real patient whose safety is in issue.

Conclusion

The English common law has been and continues to be a powerful device for protecting patients. Since the articulation of the *Bolam* test in 1957, which entrenched medical paternalism, medical law has moved the patient dramatically to centre stage. Patient autonomy is now the principal draftsman of the English common law, and although (and particularly in relation to the law relating to civil liability for the consenting process) it might be argued that this has compromised patient safety, it cannot seriously be questioned that, overall, this focus on autonomy has made patients safer – or at least the authors of their own dangers.

There is still work for the common law to do – notably in grappling (as the philosophers have done for millennia) with the issue of personal identity in a way that recognises that personhood (or at least the attributes which should determine the law's attitude to non-capacitous patients) might change over time, and in imposing positive duties for breaches of confidentiality that affect patient safety.

References

Foster, Charles and Herring, Jonathan, *Identity, personhood and the law*, Springer, 2017.

Herring, Jonathan and Foster, Charles, 'Please don't tell me: the right not to know', *Cambridge Quarterly of Healthcare Ethics* (2012) 21(1):20–29.

Samanta, Ash, Mello, Michelle M., Foster, Charles, Tingle, John and Samanta, Jo, 'The role of clinical guidelines in medical negligence litigation: a shift from the *Bolam* standard', *Medical Law Review* (2006) 14(1):321–366.

4 Board governance for better, safer healthcare

Russell Mannion, Huw Davies, Ross Millar and Tim Freeman

Governing patient safety

Health care scandals, such as the most recent at Mid Staffordshire in the English NHS, have demonstrated that uncaring and ineffective practices can flourish in hospitals when the organisational context goes wrong.[1] When this happens, patients not only have unpleasant experiences during care but they can be hurt or even die as a consequence. Addressing quality and safety failings has emerged over the past few decades as one of the key challenges in modern hospital management, and it is clear that these challenges are not confined to a few 'failing' organisations but that they are (a) endemic and (b) embedded in system arrangements and organisational practices.[2]

Hospital Boards, usually comprised of a mix of executive and non-executive directors, take ultimate responsibility for steering the hospital organisation where much of care is delivered. Their primary concerns are with financial and clinical performance alongside regulatory compliance. Central to these tasks is assuring and improving quality and securing better, safer care. While health care financing and delivery systems vary markedly across the globe, in almost all jurisdictions large health care facilities secure governance and managerial oversight through some kind of executive board.

In the English NHS, hospitals are largely organised as free-standing NHS 'Trusts'. These Trusts have Boards with statutory responsibility for upholding the quality and safety of care delivered by their organisation. However, as in many other jurisdictions, recent high-profile reports into failings in the quality of hospital care in the NHS raise concerns over the ability of hospital Trust Boards to discharge these legal duties effectively.

1 R. Francis, The Mid Staffordshire NHS Foundation Trust public inquiry, London: The Stationery Office; 2013.

2 R. Millar, R. Mannion, T. Freeman and HTO Davies, 'Hospital Board oversight of patient safety: a narrative review and synthesis of relevant empirical research', *Milbank Quarterly* 2013, 91:738–70; R Francis, *Freedom to speak up: an independent review into creating an open and honest reporting culture in the NHS*, London: The Stationery Office, 2015; J. Braithwaite, Y. Matsuyama, R. Mannion and J. Johnson, *healthcare reform, quality and safety: perspectives, participants, partnerships and prospects in 30 countries*, Abingdon: Ashgate Publishers, 2015.

Hospital Boards in the English NHS have traditionally operated along the lines of the Anglo-Saxon private sector unitary board model[3] which typically comprises a chair, chief executive, executive directors and non-executive directors who are, with the chair, in the majority. All Board members share corporate responsibility for formulating strategy, ensuring accountability and shaping culture. However, there are also distinctive roles for members of the Board: the Chair leads the Board, taking overall responsibility for the effectiveness of Board processes (and for Foundation Trusts, the Chair also chairs the Council of Governors). Alongside the Chair, the Chief Executive leads the executive functions within the organisation, taking overall responsibility for service delivery. Other key Board roles include Finance Director, Medical Director and Director of Nursing; non-executive directors (NEDs) may also take on distinct roles, leading for example on quality or patient engagement. Within this structure all members of the Board bear the same responsibility, individually and collectively, for the performance of services provided by their organisation. In addition, free-standing Foundation Trusts (FTs) have a Board of Governors drawn from the local community to provide additional governance mechanisms attuned to local needs.[4]

In this chapter, then, we explore some of the theoretical framings that can link hospital Boards to the organisation and delivery of front-line care, and we summarise some of the empirical work that has examined the impact of Boards on important staff perceptions and patient outcomes. Drawing on a large multi-method project funded by the UK National Institute for Health Research (NIHR), we can begin to see the potential importance of Boards for better, safer care, but there is much that yet remains to be unravelled by further careful study.[5]

Theoretical framings of Board governance

Several theoretical frameworks of Board governance have been developed and we can make the distinction between whether Boards are conceptualised in either *instrumental* or *symbolic* terms. Guidance on the role and conduct of NHS Boards is most usually informed by instrumentalist assumptions of the role of Boards,

3 B. Garratt, *The fish rots from the head – the crisis in our boardrooms: developing the crucial skills of the competent director*, 2nd edition, London: Harper Collins Publishers 2010; N. Chambers, G. Harvey, R. Mannion, J. Bond, J. Marshall, 'Towards a framework for enhancing the performance of NHS boards: a synthesis of the evidence about board governance, board effectiveness and board development', 2013, *Health Services and Delivery Research*, 1 (6).

4 R. Millar, R. Mannion, T. Freeman and H. T. O. Davies (2018). '"Of course, we will look into that for you": a deliberative analysis of hospital governance in England', *Journal of Social Policy* (under review).

5 R. Mannion, T. Freeman, R. Millar, H. Davies, 'Effective board governance of safe care: a (theoretically underpinned) cross-sectioned examination of the breadth and depth of relationships through national quantitative surveys and in-depth qualitative case studies', *Health Services and Delivery Research* 2016, 4 (4).

where they are seen as *fora* for deliberation, conciliation and decision-making. On these terms, a 'successful' Board is one that is able to take decisions on corporate strategy in an efficient and effective manner, and can monitor its implementation through to organisational success.[6] In contrast, *symbolic* framings of governance suggest that formal governance processes are but an elaborate 'front' or charade that obscure the ways in which decisions are really taken elsewhere. Both conceptual groupings may be important for understanding the dynamics of governance in healthcare, and we take them here in turn.[7]

Understandings of governance that have seen by far the most attention are those framings that posit governance as having instrumental (not just symbolic) value. Four key instrumentalist frameworks can be discerned in the literature: *Agency Theory*; *Stewardship Theory*; *Stakeholder Theory* and *Resource Dependency Theory*.

> *Agency theory* is based on the assumption that, unless scrutinised, staff will seek to pursue their own interests rather than wider organisational objectives (opportunism). Here the Board is conceptualised as a monitoring device set up to ensure compliance by developing systems of checking, monitoring and control to hold staff accountable for their actions. This approach has previously been used to understand and classify clinical governance strategies in UK hospitals.[8]
>
> *Stewardship theory* works on the assumption that staff are motivated by more than their own narrow self-interests, and that managers want to do a good job and serve as effective stewards of an organisation's resources.[9] The theory assumes a high degree of trust, with the focus of the Board being on creating a framework for shared values and enabling staff, rather than monitoring and coercing performance.
>
> *Stakeholder theory* assumes a multiplicity of competing and cooperative interests within organisations, and focuses on how various stakeholder interests can be addressed, integrated and balanced.[10] The role of Board members within this framework is to understand and represent the views of all those with a stake in the organisation, and it is recognised that the Board may need to manage complex trade-offs between stakeholders, including staff, patients and the public.

6 N. Chambers and C. Cornforth, 'The role of corporate governance and Boards in organisational performance', in K. Walshe and G. Harvey (eds) *From knowing to doing: connecting knowledge and performance in public services*, Cambridge: Cambridge University Press, 2010.

7 Mannion et al., 'Effective board governance of safe care'.

8 R. Mannion, H. T. O. Davies, 'A principal-agent perspective on clinical governance' in D. Kernick (ed), *Getting Health Economics into Practice*, Oxford: Radcliffe Medical Press, 2002, pp. 67–78.

9 C. Cornforth, The governance of public and non-profit organisations: what do boards do? London: Routledge, 2003.

10 S-Y. D. Lee, J. A. Alexander, V. Wang, F. S. Margolin and J. R. Combes, 'An empirical taxonomy of hospital governing board roles', *Health Services Research* 2008, 43:12–43.

Resource dependency theory derives from the strategic management literature and was originally developed particularly by Zahra and Pearce.[11] From this perspective, the organisation is seen as an amalgam of tangible and intangible assets and dynamic capabilities. The main function of the Board is to successfully manage internal and external relationships to leverage influence and resources. Board members are selected for their background, contacts and skills in mediation and 'boundary spanning'.

In spite of their differences, all four of these instrumentalist theories assume that Board members are able to exercise influence over staff and, via this influence, that they lever beneficial change and enhance organisational performance. Garratt[12] has integrated the insights from both agency and stewardship theories and posits two main areas of Board foci, which he terms 'conformance' and 'performance' (see Table 4.1). *Conformance* has both external and internal dimensions: *external accountability* includes compliance with regulatory and legal requirements, as well as accountability to external stakeholders. In contrast, the *internal dimension* is associated with management control. The *conformance dimension* therefore shares many similarities with the agency theory perspective on governance. The *performance dimension*, according to Garratt, involves governing the organisation to enhance its achievement of goals and objectives. This again consists of two main functions: *policy formulation* and *strategic thinking*. The performance dimension thus links closely to the stewardship theory of corporate governance.

Table 4.1 The main functions of hospital Boards.[13]

	Short term focus on 'conformance'	*Long term focus on 'performance'*
External Focus	*Accountability* • Ensuring external accountabilities are met, e.g. to stakeholders, funders, regulators. • Meeting audit, inspection and reporting requirements	*Policy formulation* • Setting and safeguarding the organisation's mission and values • Deciding long-term goals • Ensuring appropriate policies and systems in place
Internal Focus	*Supervision* • Appointing and rewarding senior management • Overseeing management performance • Monitoring key performance indicators • Monitoring key financial and budgetary controls • Managing risks	*Strategic thinking* • Agreeing strategic direction • Shaping and agreeing long-term plans • Reviewing and deciding major resource decisions and investments

11 S Zahra, J Pearce, 'Boards of directors and corporate financial performance: a review and integrative model', *Journal of Management* 1989, 15:291–334.

12 Garratt, The fish rots from the head.

13 Adapted from Garratt, *The fish rots from the head*; Chambers and Cornforth, 'The role of corporate governance'.

This framework (illustrated in Table 4. 1) suggests that Boards need to focus on both their conformance and performance aspects of corporate governance, and that blended perspectives on agency/stewardship may be necessary.

While popular management literature and government documents tend to idealise Board members' activities through the use of 'heroic' narratives[14] there is considerable debate over the extent to which Boards undertake the classic instrumentalist functions of establishing objectives and core strategies. Within the empirical and critical theory literature, Boards have been characterised as performing largely non-instrumental roles by acting primarily as legitimating institutions that formally declare decisions negotiated elsewhere. These perspectives indicate the potential importance of the symbolic and ceremonial value of Boards and the need to explore efficacy of Board performances in a more dramaturgical sense. In this regard, Hajer[15] has outlined a framework for the analysis of the performative dimension of governance. The approach opens up the day-to-day interactions of Board members for analysis through consideration of the setting in which deliberation takes place; the scripting in terms of the actors involved in the decision-making forum; the staging in terms of deliberate attempts to organise the interaction between participants by drawing on existing symbols; and the performance in terms of the way in which the interaction constructs new knowledge, understandings and power relationships that project forward to shape future interactions and provide opportunities for challenge and change over time.[16]

These diverse theories provide multiple and complementary perspectives on Board governance. Instrumentalist theories allow for the formulation and testing of specific hypotheses linking Board attitudes, competencies and behaviours to managerial action and healthcare organisational performance. The more dramaturgical perspectives on Board 'performance' provide a counter-balancing caution against too rational and instrumentalist perspectives, drawing attention to the importance of power, status, conflict and subterfuge when interpreting Board activities and impacts. It is not that any particular perspective is necessarily more 'right' or 'wrong' than another: the multiplicity of views in parallel (since integration across may not be possible) broadens and diversifies understandings and opens up new ways of seeing (and hence influencing) these important governance processes.

Empirical work relating governance and performance

Careful review of previously published empirical research linking hospital governance to hospital performance (including aspects of quality and safety)

14 M. Learmonth, 'NHS Trust Chief Executives as Heroes?', *Health Care Analysis* 2010, 9:417–33.

15 M. Hajer, *Setting the stage: a dramaturgy of policy implementation*, Amsterdam School for Social Science Research Working Paper 04/06 Amsterdam: University of Amsterdam, 2004); M Hajer, 'Setting the stage: a dramaturgy of policy deliberation', *Administration and Society* 2005, 36:624–47; M. Hajer, W. Versteeg, 'Performing governance through networks', *European Political Science* 2005, 4:340–7.

16 T Freeman, R Millar, R Mannion and H Davies, 'Enacting corporate governance of healthcare safety and quality: a dramaturgy of hospital boards in England', *Sociology of Health & Illness*, 38:233–51.

has revealed four key organisational governance issues requiring significant attention:[17] leading for safer care; measuring safe care; internal Board oversight; and external regulation and accountability. Much of this empirical work has been carried out in the US, with less frequent (and usually smaller) studies in the UK.[18] Nonetheless, there are lessons to be learnt from across this international literature that are worthy of drawing out, so each of these themes is examined in turn. More recently, our own national survey of NHS Boards in acute hospitals[19] has offered some tantalising glimpses of possible empirical relationships between Boards and wards.

Leading for safer care

The recent policy emphasis on Board oversight of patient safety tends to reflect a key message from the quality improvement literature as a whole: that strong and committed leadership from the top is vital to the success of quality improvement programmes. Clear leadership is associated with recognising that lapses in patient safety arise most often as a problem of the system rather than with individual employees' competencies or motivations, and with words and actions that promote a culture that encourages the identification of mistakes, and emphasises system improvements that reduce variability and make safety a priority.

Empirical evidence from cross-sectional surveys in the US suggests that boards that demonstrate such a leadership focus have a positive impact on the safety performance of their organisations: boards that place a high priority on quality and safety are associated with higher performance,[20] as are boards that set strategic goals for quality improvement and demand reports on the progress of action in response to adverse events. Yet securing board attention to these matters can be difficult. Survey data from the US suggested that fewer than half of CEOs regarded their governing boards as 'very effective' in overseeing quality, and while most boards had strategic goals for quality many did not have specific objectives with clearly defined targets.[21] Research in the UK backs up this finding, with many chief nursing officers perceiving that their Board

17 Millar et al., '"Of course, we will look into that for you"'.

18 Ibid.

19 Mannion, R., Davies, H., Millar, R., Freeman, T., Jacobs, R. and Kasteridis, P., 'Overseeing oversight: governance of quality and safety by hospital boards in the English NHS', *Journal of Health Services Research and Policy* 2015, 20 (15):9–16; Mannion, R., Freeman, T., Millar, R., Davies, H., 'Effective board governance of safe care'; R. Mannion, H. T. O. Davies, R. Jacobs, P. Kasteridis, R. Millar, and T. Freeman, T., 'Do hospital boards matter for better, safer, patient care?', *Social Science & Medicine* 2017, 177:278–87.

20 H. J. Jiang, C. Lockee, K. Bass and I. Fraser, 'Board oversight of quality: any differences in process of care and mortality?', *Journal of Healthcare Management* 2009, 54:15–30; L. D. Prybil, D. R. Bardach and D. W. Fardo, 'Board oversight of patient care quality in large nonprofit health systems', *American Journal of Medical Quality* 2013, 28(6):536–8.

21 G. R. Baker, J. L. Denis, M. P. Pomey, A. M. Murray, Effective governance for quality and patient safety in Canadian healthcare organizations: a report to the Canadian Health Services Research Foundation and the Canadian Patient Safety Institute. Ottawa: CHSRF/CPSI, 2010.

members were only moderately engaged with quality improvement initiatives.[22] Recent qualitative research in the English NHS concluded that Boards of healthcare organisations with high 'quality improvement maturity': prioritised quality improvement; combined a focus on short-term (external) priorities with long-term (internal) investment in quality improvement; used data for quality *improvement*, not just assurance; engaged staff and patients and had a culture of *continuous* improvement.[23]

Perceptions remain then that – despite the obvious need for clear Board leadership on quality – Boards are primarily focused on financial issues, with assumptions that care quality issues are adequately dealt with by clinical leadership.

Measuring and assessing safe care

Board oversight of quality and patient safety rests on Board directors' ability to obtain, process and interpret information, assess current performance, and then to set strategic direction using a range of metrics that are tailored to local circumstances. A variety of expert advice has been produced to encourage Boards to understand the big picture on quality and safety performance through the use of checklists and dashboards.[24] Empirical evidence from hospital surveys suggests that Boards that engage in reviewing and tracking their organisation's performance through the collection and analysis of internally generated data (quality dashboards or scorecards) and national benchmarks are likely to have better outcomes in relation to quality.[25]

This (largely US) survey research is backed up by case study work in the UK NHS that found that scorecard data in a hospital offered a view of the organisation as a whole and facilitated ward-specific analysis and feedback on the governance of safety challenges such as healthcare-associated infections.[26] Alongside the use of formal performance metrics, research also emphasises the role of 'soft intelligence' in capturing the qualitative experience of patients and staff, which often defies simple coding and quantification.[27] Leadership walk-arounds, front-line

22 S. Machell, P. Gough, D. Naylor, V. Nath and K. Steward, (2010) *Putting quality first in the boardroom: improving business of caring*, London: King's Fund, 2010.

23 J. Jones, L. Pomeroy, G. Robert, S. Burnett, J. E. Anderson and N. J. Fulop, 'How do hospital boards govern for quality improvement? A mixed methods study of 15 organisations in England' *BMJ quality & safety* 2017, doi:10.1136/bmjqs-2016-006433.

24 E. Kroch, T. Vaughn, M. Koepke, S. Roman, D. Foster, S. Sinha et al., 'Hospital boards and quality dashboards', *Journal of Patient Safety* 2006, 2:10-19; M. Pugh and J. Reinertsen, 'Reducing harm to patients: using patient safety', *Healthc Exec* 2007, 22(6):62, 64–5.

25 Jiang, Lockee, Bass and Fraser, 'Board oversight of quality'.

26 A. Ramsay, C. Magnusson, and N. Fulop, 'The relationship between external and local governance systems: the case of health care associated infections and medication errors in one NHS trust', *Quality & Safety in Health Care* 2010, 19:1–8.

27 A. Frankel, E. G. Baker, C. Neppl, T. Simmonds, M. Gustafson, T. K. Gandhi, 'Patient safety leadership walkrounds', *Joint Committee Journal Quality & Safety* 2003, 26:16–26; K. McDonagh and R. Limbdenstock, 'Hospital governing boards: a study of their effectiveness in relation to organisational performance', *Journal of Healthcare Management* 200651(6):377–89.

storytelling and paying careful attention to patient and carer voices can all provide contextual and balancing information alongside formal metrics.[28]

Patient safety metrics are clearly important then in any strategy that is designed to improve care, but the evidence to-date suggests a need for considerable effort: to improve the credibility, validity and reliability of formal data; to increase Board members' proficiency in the use and interpretation of these metrics; and to balance a focus on measured trends with soft intelligence.

Internal Board oversight

The increasing interest in Board oversight of patient safety has focused attention on the formal organisational structures and processes for safeguarding care, as well as on the informal relationships and dynamics between Boards and professional groups. The formal structure of Boards has been found to be related to the effective oversight of patient safety and survey data from the US shows that boards with a separate quality committee are more likely than those without to be high performing.[29] High-performing organisations are also more likely to use quality dashboards or scorecards, issue written policy throughout the organisation and establish strategic goals for quality improvement

Effective Board oversight of safety also requires attention to be paid to dynamics and tensions within and between Boards, medical staff and senior leaders.[30] In particular, having a physician leader on a Board quality committee has been suggested as a means to enhance performance by facilitating communication and building trust and confidence.[31] Indeed, hospitals in which representatives with clinical expertise served on the Board quality committee were seen to have performed significantly better on process and outcomes of care than did hospitals that had no such expertise on their Boards.[32] Collaborative retreats with multidisciplinary staff groups and internal collaboratives, built around safety initiatives, have also been found to enhance safeguarding processes

Collaborative, multi-professional dynamics are needed at the heart of Boards, but research highlights the need for development in this area.[33] Nursing leadership, for example, remains conspicuously absent from many Board deliberations.[34]

28 McDonagh and Limbdenstock, Hospital governing boards'.
29 Jiang, Lockee, Bass and Fraser, 'Board oversight of quality'.
30 Millar, et al., '"Of course, we will look into that for you"'.
31 A. K. Jha and A. M. Epstein, 'Hospital governance and the quality of care', *Health Affairs* 2010, 29:182–7.
32 G. Veronesi, I. Kirkpatrick and F. Vallascas, 'Clinicians on the board: what difference does it make?' *Social Science Med* 2013, 77:147–55; F. Sarto, and G. Veronesi, 2016, 'Clinical leadership and hospital performance: assessing the evidence base', *BMC Health Services Research* 2016, 16.
33 Peter J. Pronovost, C. M. Armstrong, R. Demski, R. R. Peterson, P. B. Rothman, 'Next level of board accountability in health care quality', *Journal of Health Organization and Management* 2018, https://doi.org/10.1108/JHOM-09-2017-0238
34 L. MacLeod, 'Nursing leadership: ten compelling reasons for having a nurse leader on the hospital board', *Nurse Leader* 2010, 8:44–47; M. F. Mastal, M. Joshi and K. Schulke, 'Nursing leadership: championing quality and patient safety in the boardroom', *Nursing Economics* 2007, 25:323–30.

And combining professional and managerial roles is far from easy: there are serious ethical conflicts and ambiguities that can arise when Board members combine professional and clinical interests with corporate roles and duties.[35] Boards' relationships with wider patient and carer communities also need further consideration and strengthening, issues so far somewhat neglected in the empirical literature.

External regulation and accountability

The primary focus so far has been on internal processes for Board oversight of patient safety, but we have also uncovered research into the external accountability of Boards. For example, hospital organisations often struggle to reconcile the information needed for external accountability with that required to inform local improvements,[36] and a recurring dilemma is about whether and how to make local performance data publicly available.[37]

Qualitative research by the Healthcare Commission in England found that, despite the onus on commissioners or purchasers of services to drive up quality and safety through contracting and payment systems, there were local variations in the extent to which commissioners had robust information systems in place for holding hospitals to account for the quality of care that they provided.[38] Commissioning practice in holding provider organisations to account varied across health economies from ad hoc requests to providers for reports of serious untoward incidents to the systematic benchmarking of providers against indicators of quality and safety. The research found that the most effective accountability arrangements between commissioners and providers were those that were supported through 'relational contracting' and which built on strong personal relationships and collaborative, rather than competitive, partnerships between organisations.

Thus, there is a relationship – as yet not fully articulated or untangled – between the external reporting and regulatory requirements and the role of Boards in driving internal change. The extent to which external contextual factors encourage or impede local Board actions remains a fertile area for further study.

Recent large-scale study in the NHS

Much of the important literature discussed above has been created in the US context, albeit with some complementary and broadly consistent findings from

35 B. H. Gray, L. Weiss, 'The role of trustees and the ethics of trusteeship: findings from an empirical study', in B. Jennings, B. H. Gray, V. A Sharpe and A. R Fleischman (eds), *The Ethics of Hospital Trustees*, Washington, DC: Georgetown University Press, 2004, pp. 90–133.

36 Baker et al., Effective governance for quality.

37 R. Mannion and H. Davies, 'Reporting health care performance: learning from the past, prospects for the future, *Journal of Evaluation in Clinical Practice* 2002, 8(2)215–28.

38 Healthcare Commission, Safe in the Knowledge: How Do NHS Trust Boards Ensure Safe Care for Their Patients? London: Healthcare Commission, 2009.

smaller-scale studies in the NHS. However, we believe that there is considerable read-across between different healthcare jurisdictions. While recognising the significant inter-country differences in healthcare policy, finance and regulation, there are also important commonalities of structure, challenge and professional dynamics. So, it makes sense to look as widely as possible when seeking insights into Board governance, its design, operation and impacts. Nonetheless, country-specific analyses do have a direct appeal. In this final section, we highlight the largest and most recent exploration of the relationship between hospital Boards and overall organisational performance in the context of the UK NHS.

As part of the larger portfolio of work noted above[39] we conducted the first ever national-scale study that sought to examine quantitative relationships between the competencies of hospital Boards and the achievement of overall standards of quality and safety.[40] The study used a previously validated scale of Board competencies, which was further validated for use in the UK context[41] (Mannion et al, 2017). The Board Self-Assessment Questionnaire (BSAQ) assesses Board competencies across six domains (see Box 1, Fig. 4.1) and runs to 65 items for self-completion.

In gathering data on Boards, 334 individual Board members from across 95 acute hospitals provided self-reported data that assessed their competencies across all six domains. Aggregate competency scores at Board level were then linked to a raft of outcome measures of whole-hospital performance (such as mortality, readmissions, healthcare associated infections and patient safety incidents). In addition, we also explored relationships between Board competencies and process measures of staff attitudes (taken from the NHS National Staff Survey,[42] such as likelihood to report near misses, and confidence that the organisation responds appropriately to clinical errors. Multivariate analysis of these linked data sets, adjusting for mediating variable such as hospital size, type and financial performance, produced some inconclusive but nonetheless intriguing findings.[43]

We did not find any statistically significant relationship between Board competencies (as measured by BSAQ) and any whole-hospital mortality and patient safety measures. Although the overall patterning was consistent with positive Board effects, the effect sizes were small and they did not reach statistical significance. However, we *did* find a significant relationship between two dimensions of the BSAQ and two specific-and-related National Staff Survey organisational 'process' measures: staff 'feeling safe' to raise concerns about errors, near misses, and incidents; and staff 'feeling confident' that their organisation would address their concerns if raised. In particular, the correlational results are positive and significant for staff 'feeling safe' in the contextual, analytical, political and strategic domains of BSAQ, although the effect is strongest in the contextual dimension. This context dimension of Board competencies explores how the Board takes cognisance of the organisation's values

39 Mannion, et al., 'Effective board governance of safe care'.
40 Mannion, et al., 'Overseeing oversight'; Mannion et al., 'Effective board governance of safe care'.
41 Mannion, et al., 'Do hospital boards matter for better, safer, patient care?'
42 *National Staff Survey 2015*, NSS, Department of Health, London, 2015.
43 Mannion et al., 'Effective board governance of safe care'.

1. **Contextual dimension**. The board understands and takes into account the culture, values and norms of the organisation it governs.
2. **Educational dimension**. The board takes the necessary steps to ensure that all board members are well-informed about the organisation and the professions working there as well as the board's own roles, responsibilities and performance.
3. **Interpersonal dimension**. The board nurtures the development of board members as a group, attends to the board's collective welfare, and fosters a sense of cohesiveness.
4. **Analytical dimension**. The board recognises complexities and subtleties in the issues it faces and draws upon multiple perspectives to dissect complex problems and to synthesise appropriate responses.
5. **Political dimension**. The board accepts as one of its primary responsibilities the need to develop and maintain healthy relationships among key stakeholders.
6. **Strategic dimension.** The board helps envision and shape institutional direction and helps ensure a strategic approach to the organisation's future.

Figure 4.1 The Six BSAQ Dimensions of Board Competencies.

and norms, and positive orientations here may support a more open and transparent culture around speaking up, thus enabling staff to feel safe to raise quality concerns. Results were also positive and significant for staff 'feeling confident' for the contextual and strategic BSAQ dimensions, suggesting that a focus on the organisational values and institutional direction gives staff a sense of security and assurance that patient safety concerns will be dealt with. These findings from the NHS, then, do suggest some important associations between Board governance and staff ability to address issues around patient safety.

Discussion

Hospital Boards as corporate entities have a fundamental strategic role in developing the strategy, systems and cultures for their organisations. These approaches can be 'hard', for example the setting and monitoring of policies, standards and procedures, or 'soft', for example nurturing appropriate values and beliefs. In understanding governance, we can envisage a range of Board practices that address both instrumental and symbolic/dramaturgical aims. The diversity of theoretical framings available (e.g. agency theory; stewardship theory; stakeholder theory and resource dependency theory) and attempts at integration across these (e.g. Garratt's conformance/performance framing[44] offer a rich set of theoretical tools from which empirical insights can be hypothesised and tested.

From the extant empirical literature – rather dominated by quantitative US studies – a number of key structural, attitudinal and behavioural aspects of Boards are highlighted for effective governance. These include: strong and committed leadership that maintains a clear focus on quality and safety; time given over in

44 Garratt, The fish rots from the head.

Boards to detailed discussion of quality and safety backed up by comprehensive and trustworthy metrics; effective sub-structures from Boards such as quality and safety committees; and full use being made of integrated clinical leadership. Alongside these 'within Board' activities, the literature also draws attention to the important work that takes place outside of Boards, such as informal engagements with front-line staff, patients and carers, and institutional responses to external regulatory regimes.

Taken together, the instrumentalist empirical literature suggest that empirical studies of patient safety governance are informed by the broad assumption that failures in safety (adverse events) are not brought about solely by individual human error but are conditioned, precipitated and exacerbated by wider systemic and latent factors in the work environment and organisational context, and are therefore amenable to control and prevention. This assumption functions as a latent programme theory in the field of enquiry, and its influence is clearly seen in the nature of the dependent and independent variables selected in the more recent large-scale quantitative studies considered above.

Perhaps most intriguing from this set of literature is the suggestion (from recent wide-scale NHS study) that Board competencies may be related to important 'staff attitude' variables such as feeling 'safe' to report quality and safety issues, and 'confidence' that any matters reported would be addressed. Such a finding draws attention to some of the putative mechanisms by which Board activities may impact on quality and safety: through the collective mindsets (or cultures) of front-line and mid-tier staff, both clinical and managerial. Moreover, the Board competencies approach explicitly draws on diverse underlying theories. For example: the *contextual* dimension of BSAQ reflects the monitoring and accountability aspects of Board operations as proposed by *agency theory*; the *political* dimension emphasises the Board's wider connections as highlighted in *resource dependency theory*; and the *analytical* and *educational* dimensions of competence are central to *group decision process theories.*

Moreover, the many insights from the instrumentalist literature that dominates study of Board governance can be put into fresh and revealing light by considering the more symbolic and dramaturgical aspects of Board 'performance'.[45] In-depth qualitative and ethnographic study not only draws attention to important subjectivities, contingencies and contextuality, but also highlights how 'performances' in Boards may have as much to do with power, position, status and professional identity projects as they do with 'getting things done'. We ignore such insights at our peril, although much of the policy prescriptions and Board 'guidance literature' seem reluctant to engage with these rather occulted issues.

Funding acknowledgement

The research was funded by the National Institute for Health Research (NIHR) Health Services and Delivery (HSDR) programme (grant number. 10/1007/02;

45 Freeman et al., 'Enacting corporate governance of healthcare safety'.

project title 'Effective Board Governance of safe Care'; co-applicants Russell Mannion, Tim Freeman and Huw Davies). The views and opinion expressed therein are those of the authors and do not necessarily reflect those of the HSDR programme.

References

Baker, G. R., Denis, J. L., Pomey, M. P. and Murray, A. M., *Effective governance for quality and patient safety in Canadian healthcare organizations: a report to the Canadian Health Services Research Foundation and the Canadian Patient Safety Institute*, Ottawa: CHSRF/CPSI, 2010.

Braithwaite, J., Matsuyama, Y., Mannion, R. and Johnson, J., *Healthcare reform, quality and safety: perspectives, participants, partnerships and prospects in 30 countries.* Abingdon: Ashgate, 2015.

Chambers, N. and Cornforth, C., 'The role of corporate governance and Boards in organisational performance', in Walshe, K. and Harvey, G. (eds), *From knowing to doing: connecting knowledge and performance in public services*, Cambridge: Cambridge University Press, 2010.

Chambers, N., Harvey, G., Mannion, R., Bond, J. and Marshall, J., 'Towards a framework for enhancing the performance of NHS boards: a synthesis of the evidence about board governance, board effectiveness and board development', *Health Services and Delivery Research* 2013, 1:6.

Cornforth, C., *The governance of public and non-profit organisations: what do boards do?* London: Routledge, 2003.

Francis, R., *The Mid Staffordshire NHS Foundation Trust public inquiry.* London: The Stationery Office, 2013.

Francis, R., *Freedom to speak up: an independent review into creating an open and honest reporting culture in the NHS*, London: The Stationery Office, 2015.

Frankel, A., Baker, E. G., Neppl, C., Simmonds, T., Gustafson, M. and Gandhi, T. K., 'Patient safety leadership walkrounds', *Joint Commission Journal on Quality and Safety* 2003, 29:16–26.

Freeman, T., Millar, R., Mannion, R. and Davies, H., 'Enacting corporate governance of healthcare safety and quality: a dramaturgy of hospital boards in England', *Sociology of Health & Illness 2016, 38:233–51.*

Garratt, B., *The fish rots from the head – the crisis in our boardrooms: developing the crucial skills of the competent director*, 2nd edition, London: Harper Collins Publishers, 2010.

Gray, B. H. and Weiss, L., 'The role of trustees and the ethics of trusteeship: findings from an empirical study', in Jennings, B., Gray, B. H., Sharpe, V. A., Fleischman, A. R. (eds), *The ethics of hospital trustees.* Washington, DC: Georgetown University Press, 2004.

Hajer, M., *Setting the stage: a dramaturgy of policy implementation.* Amsterdam School for Social Science Research Working Paper 04/06. Amsterdam: University of Amsterdam.

Hajer, M., 'Setting the stage: a dramaturgy of policy deliberation', *Administration and Society* 2005, 36:624–47.

Hajer, M. and Versteeg, W., 'Performing governance through networks', *European Political Science* 2005, 4:340–7.

Healthcare Commission, *Safe in the knowledge: how do NHS Trust boards ensure safe care for their patients?*, London: Healthcare Commission, 2009.

Jha, A. K. and Epstein, A. M., 'Hospital governance and the quality of care', *Health Affairs* 2010, 29:182–7.

Jiang, H. J., Lockee, C., Bass, K. and Fraser, I., 'Board oversight of quality: any differences in process of care and mortality?' *Journal of Healthcare Management* 2009, 54:15–30.

Jones, L., Pomeroy, L., Robert, G., Burnett, S., Anderson, J. E. and Fulop, N. J., 'How do hospital boards govern for quality improvement? A mixed methods study of 15 organisations in England', *BMJ Quality & Safety* 2017, doi:10.1136/bmjqs-2016-006433.

Kroch, E., Vaughn, T., Koepke, M., Roman, S., Foster, D., Sinha, S., et al., 'Hospital boards and quality dashboards', *Journal of Patient Safety* 2006, 2:10–19.

Learmonth, M., 'NHS Trust chief executives as heroes?', *Health Care Analysis* 2010, 9:417–33.

Lee, S-Y. D., Alexander, J. A., Wang, V., Margolin, F. S. and Combes, J. R., 'An empirical taxonomy of hospital governing board roles', *Health Services Research* 2008, 43:12–43.

Machell, S., Gough, P., Naylor, D., Nath, V. and Steward K., *Putting quality first in the boardroom: improving business of caring*. London: King's Fund, 2010.

MacLeod, L., 'Nursing leadership: ten compelling reasons for having a nurse leader on the hospital board', *Nurse Leader* 2010, 8:44–7.

Mannion, R. and Davies, H. T. O., 'A principal-agent perspective on clinical governance', in Kernick, D. (ed), *Getting health economics into practice*. Oxford: Radcliffe Medical Press, 2002.

Mannion, R. and Davies, H., 'Reporting health care performance: learning from the past, prospects for the future', *Journal of Evaluation in Clinical Practice* 2002, 8(2):215–28.

Mannion, R., Davies, H., Millar, R., Freeman, T., Jacobs, R. and Kasteridis, P., 'Overseeing oversight: governance of quality and safety by hospital boards in the English NHS', *Journal of Health Services Research and Policy* 2015, 20 (15):9–16.

Mannion, R., Davies, H .T. O., Jacobs, R., Kasteridis, P., Millar, R. and Freeman, T., 'Do hospital boards matter for better, safer, patient care?', *Social Science & Medicine* 2017, 177:278–87.

Mannion, R., Freeman, T., Millar, R. and Davies, H., 'Effective board governance of safe care: A (theoretically underpinned) cross-sectioned examination of the breadth and depth of relationships through national quantitative surveys and in-depth qualitative case studies', *Health Services and Delivery Research* 2016, 4(4).

Mastal, M. F., Joshi, M. and Schulke. K., 'Nursing leadership: championing quality and patient safety in the boardroom', *Nursing Economics* 2007, 25:323–30.

McDonagh, K. and Limbdenstock, R., 'Hospital governing boards: a study of their effectiveness in relation to organisational performance', *Journal of Healthcare Management* 2006, 51(6):377–89.

Millar, R., Mannion, R., Freeman, T. and Davies, H. T. O., 'Hospital Board oversight of patient safety: a narrative review and synthesis of relevant empirical research', *Milbank Quarterly* 2013, 91:738–70.

Millar, R., Mannion, R., Freeman, T. and Davies, H. T. O., '"Of course, we will look into that for you": A deliberative analysis of hospital governance in England', *Journal of Social Policy* 2018 (under review).

National Staff Survey 2015 (NSS 2015). London: Department of Health.

Pronovost, Peter J., Armstrong, C. M., Demski, R., Peterson, R. R. and Rothman, P. B., 'Next level of board accountability in health care quality', *Journal of Health Organization and Management* 2018, https://doi.org/10.1108/JHOM-09-2017-0238.

Prybil, L. D., Bardach, D. R. and Fardo, D.W., 'Board oversight of patient care quality in large nonprofit health systems', *American Journal of Medical Quality* 2013, 28(6):536–8.

Pugh, M. and Reinertsen, J., 'Reducing harm to patients: using patient safety', *Healthc Exec* 2007, 22(6):62, 64–5.

Ramsay, A., Magnusson, C. and Fulop, N., 'The relationship between external and local governance systems: the case of health care associated infections and medication errors in one NHS trust', *Quality & Safety in Health Care* 2010, 19:1–8.

Sarto, F. and Veronesi, G., 'Clinical leadership and hospital performance: assessing the evidence base', *BMC Health Services Research*, vol 16, 2016.

Veronesi, G., Kirkpatrick, I. and Vallascas, F., 'Clinicians on the board: what difference does it make?' *Social Science Med*, 2013, vol 77, pp. 147–55.

Zahra, S. and Pearce, J., 'Boards of directors and corporate financial performance: a review and integrative model', *Journal of Management* 1989, 15:291–334.

5 Speaking up or blowing the whistle for better, safer care

Russell Mannion, Huw Davies, John Blenkinsopp, Jean V. McHale, Ross Millar, Martin Powell and Nick Snowden

Seeking better, safer care

In modern healthcare systems, not all care is as good or as safe as it could be and (although estimates vary) there is growing evidence to suggest about one in ten patients admitted to hospital may be harmed as a result of their admission.[1] Sub-optimal care and significant patient harm were first brought to prominence by the US Institute of Medicine with its ground-breaking report *To Err is Human*[2] and in the UK by the equally pivotal *An Organisation with a Memory*,[3] but these risks are seen across all health systems worldwide.[4] Moreover, patient harm is not limited to minor events but is often serious, including delayed diagnosis (with concomitant poorer prognoses), misapplications of treatments (including under-, over- and contraindicated use), major iatrogenic harm, hospital-acquired infections, falls and avoidable deaths. As well as human suffering, financial costs are significant, with prolonged hospital stays alone adding significant extra costs. In response to this evidence of widespread harm there have been concerted efforts to make healthcare safer and of higher overall quality.

Most harm to patients in hospital settings is not deliberate, negligent or the result of serious incompetence, but an emergent outcome of a complex system where typically competent (but variably able) clinicians, professionals and managers interact in inadequate systems, with limited resources, embedded in unsafe organisational environments. The focus of organisational improvement in healthcare has therefore shifted towards better understanding how organisations and systems can be improved, and the role and protection of front-line voices in driving that improvement. This chapter draws on some recent work funded by the UK National Institute for Health Research[5] to explore the ways in which

1 World Health Organization (WHO) *Patient safety: making health care safer*. Geneva: World Health Organization, 2017.

2 L. T. Kohn, J. Corrigan, M. S. Donaldson, *To err is human: building a safer health system*, Washington, DC: National Academy Press, 2000.

3 Department of Health, *An organisation with a memory*, London: The Stationery Office, 2000.

4 WHO, *Patient safety*.

5 Mannion et al., 'Understanding the knowledge gaps in whistleblowing and speaking up in healthcare: narrative reviews of the research literature and formal Inquiries, a legal analysis and stakeholder interviews' (2017) HSDR (forthcoming).

front-line voices are heard or silenced in the English NHS. Central to this is an understanding of the nature and role of whistleblowing.

In this chapter, we explore various aspects of whistleblowing and the organisational actions (and, in many cases, inactions) seen in response. We sketch out the policy background and the legal protections afforded to whistleblowers and conclude that there is much more yet to be done if front-line staff are to be given an effective (and protected) voice.

Whistleblowing: the canary in the mine?

Employee whistleblowing – loosely, the raising of concerns or 'speaking up' about unsafe, unethical or poor-quality care by employees to persons able to effect action – has emerged as a central issue in debates over quality and safety in many health systems.[6] In the English NHS, recent inquiries and reports into poor standards of care have highlighted the vital contribution that whistleblowing can play in the detection and prevention of harm to patients.[7] Yet for all its importance the act of whistleblowing is no simple issue:[8] it is fraught with ambiguity and contestation. Not all practices raised as concerns by whistleblowers – whether professional or managerial – can neatly be categorised as either conducive or inimical to safe and high-quality care; and the motives of those making such judgements may be questioned or impugned. Individual whistleblowers may be perceived as heroes by some (for championing patients' interests, for promoting better care and for challenging management) but as villains by others (for denigrating services, fracturing organisational relationships and damaging professional and organisational reputations). This ambiguity is reflected in media portrayals of them either as 'courageous employees' who act at great personal cost or 'disloyal malcontents' who pursue their own interests regardless of the dysfunctional consequences for individuals and organisations.

Moreover, it would be naïve to assume that all whistleblowers are necessarily motivated entirely by genuine concerns about patient care: some may be motivated in addition by work grievances or personality clashes; in the extreme, concerns may even be of a malicious nature. In fact, clear delineation between such labels is problematic. Whistleblowing may arise out of complex and contested circumstances since what is 'safe' and what is 'acceptable' (in terms of quality) are disputable and subject to shaping by local discursive practices. Therefore, binary distinctions (such as hero/villain; loyal/disloyal; warranted/unwarranted) are often unhelpful and disguise the complexity and ambiguity of whistleblowers and whistleblowing.

6 Braithwaite et al., *Healthcare reform, quality and safety: perspectives, participants, partnerships and prospects in 30 countries*, Abingdon: Ashgate Publishers, 2015.

7 R Francis, *Freedom to speak up: an independent review into creating an open and honest reporting culture in the NHS*, London: The Stationery Office, 2015.

8 R. Mannion and H. T. Davies, 'Cultures of silence and cultures of voice: the role of whistleblowing in healthcare organisations', *International Journal of Health Policy and Management*, 2015.

Speaking up – and being heard

When concerns are raised it is important organisations respond positively, learning from any mistakes and putting effective policies in place to prevent them from happening again. Unfortunately, in the NHS there have been all-too-many high-profile examples where serious concerns raised by front-line staff have not been adequately dealt with by the organisation. Patients have suffered as a result, and staff too may have been harmed from the direct and indirect consequences of their raising concerns. As Sir Robert Francis's independent review – *Freedom to speak up* – concluded, 'there is a culture within many parts of the NHS which deters staff from raising serious and sensitive concerns and which not infrequently has negative consequences for those brave enough to raise them'.[9]

The challenge then, in understanding speaking up and whistleblowing, lies as much in the organisational responses to new messages from the front line as it does in the encouragement of those messages in the first place. Speaking up may be necessary, but it is insufficient: *being heard*, with effective action to follow, is required if care quality and safety are to improve. More darkly, *protection* of those who do speak up from deleterious reactions is paramount.

Reluctant 'voice'

Numerous surveys across different professional groups confirm significant shortcomings (or, at least, *perceptions* of significant shortcomings) in the protection and support offered to whistleblowers raising concerns about poor or unsafe patient care in the NHS. A possible reason for this is the widespread perception among health professionals that they will be victimised, ostracised or bullied if they raise concerns about colleagues or poor standards of care.[10] This is not a new development. Almost two decades ago, the Bristol Royal Infirmary Inquiry noted many staff, particularly junior staff, remained silent in the face of poor care or wrongdoing as they were fearful of raising concerns and/or challenging superiors because of the possible repercussions: 'There is a real fear among staff (particularly among junior doctors and nurses) that to comment on colleagues, particularly consultants, is to endanger their future work prospects. The junior needs a reference and a recommendation; nurses want to keep their jobs. This is a powerful motive for keeping quiet'.[11]

These concerns remain current. The 2015 NHS staff survey found that, when asked whether their organisation treated staff involved in near misses, errors and incidents *fairly*, less than half (43%) reported this was the case. In addition, only half of staff (50%) reported feedback was given by their organisation about any

9 Francis, *Freedom to speak up*, p. 1.

10 Medical Protection Society (MPS), *Whistleblowing doctors afraid to speak out*, London: MPS, 2012.

11 I Kennedy, The report of the public inquiry into children's heart surgery at the Bristol Royal Infirmary 1984–1995. Learning from Bristol. Report no. CM 5207(I), 2001.

changes that had been made in response to the reported error or incident.[12] A 2013 Royal College of Nursing poll of its members found almost a quarter (24%) had been warned off or discouraged from whistleblowing and 45% said their employer took no action even when they had spoken out. Similarly, a survey of doctors undertaken in 2012 by the Medical Protection Society (MPS) reported only 11% of respondents would be confident of the process if they blew the whistle, and 49% of doctors reported that 'fear of consequences' is why the whistleblowing process is ineffective.[13]

That there should be so much uncertainty and disquiet about speaking out should not come as a surprise. Local discursive practices (e.g. on the nature of success, failure, risk and performance) and local operational contingencies (such as resource constraints, service rivalries and stakeholder pressure) will have a powerful influence on the willingness of employees to raise concerns and the ability and willingness of employers to respond appropriately. Of course, whatever the local contingencies and discourses, these play out within a larger political, policy and legal context, and it is to these we now turn.

Political and legal context

Various legal frameworks provide a backdrop against which whistleblower activity plays out. These include: employment law; human rights legislation and various regulatory frameworks. Current protection for whistleblowers in England is enshrined entirely within an employment context and is contained in the Employment Rights Act 1996 (ERA) as amended by the 1998 Public Interest Disclosure Act (PIDA). PIDA was passed to protect whistleblowers in the wake of the Bristol paediatric cardiac surgery scandal and provides legal protection against detriment for workers who raise concerns in the public interest (also known as making a 'protected disclosure') about a danger, risk, malpractice or wrongdoing in the workplace that affects others. To be protected, the disclosure must be in the public interest, the worker must have a reasonable belief that the information shows that one of the categories of wrongdoing listed in the legislation has occurred or is likely to occur, and the concern must be raised in the correct way. It should be noted therefore that even actions widely understood as whistleblowing (such as those made by the anaesthetist Dr Bolsin that sparked the inquiries into Bristol) may not actually fall under this legal definition, as Kennedy duly noted in his Inquiry report.[14]

Such legal protections are now enshrined in the NHS Constitution, which mandates that:

12 *NHS Staff Survey 2015*, London: NHS England, 2016.

13 MPS, Whistleblowing doctors afraid to speak out.

14 Kennedy, The Report of the Public Inquiry into children's heart surgery at the Bristol Royal Infirmary.

- staff should raise concerns at the earliest opportunity;
- NHS organisations should support staff by ensuring their concerns are fully investigated and that there is someone independent, outside of their team, who can provide support;
- there is a legal right for staff to raise concerns about safety, malpractice or other wrongdoing without suffering any detriment.

Whistleblowing policies have also been mandated and promoted for many years outside of any strict legal framework – for example, by healthcare employers, regulators and professional associations – aimed particularly at securing safe and effective services. Professional bodies, including the Royal College of General Practitioners and the UK Nursing and Midwifery Council, have professional codes that place obligations on registrants to report untoward incidents to their employers and have produced guidance for doctors and nurses, midwives and students raising concerns about quality of care. In 2012 NHS Employers launched the *Speaking Up Charter*, which encouraged NHS organisations to pledge publically a commitment to creating cultures and policies that support staff in raising concerns and a continuous review and evaluation of such policies to ensure they remain effective. The Department of Health has also commissioned a *Whistleblowing Helpline* which provides free advice and support to staff on whether and how to raise concerns at work. Since 2015 a statutory duty of candour has operated which requires NHS bodies and all CQC-registered providers (rather than individuals) to be open and honest when an unintended or unexpected incident has resulted in, or could result in, death, severe or moderate physical harm, or prolonged psychological harm. In such instances, providers must notify the patient involved, offer an apology and follow up the incident in writing.

The report of the independent *Freedom to Speak Up* review (FTSU) chaired by Sir Robert Francis[15] identified 20 Principles and associated Actions that should underpin whistleblowing polices in the NHS, and recommended the Secretary of State for Health should review at least annually the progress made in their implementation. These Principles and Actions include:

- A common policy and procedure for raising concerns including better investigations and promoting a model of good practice in the handling of concerns;
- training for managers and all staff in the raising and handling of concerns;
- cultural change towards creating more open, transparent and learning cultures which value communication and staff engagement;
- Freedom to Speak Up Guardians to be appointed to each NHS organisation, supported by an Independent National Officer (INO);
- legal changes to anti-discrimination laws to protect whistleblowers from discrimination in recruitment;
- additions to the list of prescribed persons to whom protected disclosures can be made.

15 Francis, *Freedom to speak up*.

In July 2015, the Secretary of State confirmed the steps to be taken to develop a culture of safety, including the appointment of a National Guardian alongside a local guardian in every NHS trust, with the goal of promoting the raising of concerns across the NHS. Although all NHS organisations are now required to have policies and procedures in place that urge staff to 'speak up' when necessary, there is no requirement for uniformity. More recent arrangements, such as the formation of the Healthcare Safety Investigation Branch (HSIB) and its proposals to create 'safe spaces' prohibiting the disclosure of certain information beyond the investigatory body, add further levels of complexity. As noted by Francis,[16] different sources of guidance express themselves differently and there is therefore a risk that such a plethora of information, advice and guidance may be confusing for staff working in the NHS. For example, staff may not know where to go for the best advice or whether having spoken to a particular organisation they still need to report their concerns elsewhere; they may also be confused as to what disclosures are, or (more worryingly) are *not*, 'protected'. Many of these issues are explored in more depth elsewhere in this volume.[17]

As the foregoing account demonstrates: raising concerns, speaking out and blowing the whistle are complex social acts, embedded in rich organisational settings, and shaped by a multifaceted backdrop of political, legal and policy-related considerations. In what follows, then, we seek first to explore the varied ways in which whistleblowing has been conceptualised and locate these in the organisational dynamics of response or inertia. We then set out and examine some of the legal underpinnings that support (or, indeed, inhibit) front-line workers giving voice. Finally, we conclude with some observations about the mismatch between the needs of a health service for free flows of information for improvement, and the cumbersome legal and policy architecture that only rarely supports these needs.

Unpacking whistleblowing

Metaphorical origins of whistleblowing

There are three competing explanations for the origins of the term 'whistleblowing', and each provides useful insights into the tensions and ambiguities that still surround the practice. The most frequently encountered explanation of whistleblowing is that it comes from an analogy with police officers blowing a whistle, to attract the attention of an individual to whom the officer wished to speak, or to bring other officers in the vicinity to the scene (in the days before mobile communications). Such an analogy draws attention to notions of wrongdoing, culpability and the alerting of relevant authorities to 'bring to book' miscreants.

16 R Francis, *Report of the Mid Staffordshire NHS Foundation Trust public inquiry*, The Mid Staffordshire NHS Foundation Trust, 2013.

17 See Chapter 6.

Another suggestion – along similar lines – is that the analogy is with the use of a whistle by referees in sport to call a halt to a game after a foul has been committed. This again highlights adjudication over wrongdoing, the calling to account of offenders and the rectification of any wrongs through the administration of sanctions or the allocation of advantage.

A third, perhaps less likely but nonetheless intriguing explanation, is that the term derives from 19th century US legislation that required train drivers to sound a whistle when they approached crossings (to warn of risk). Failure to do so could lead to fines, and moreover, citizens calling attention to these failures could receive payment for doing so. Indeed, in the US legal system it remains the case today that whistleblowers over financial irregularities can sometimes stand to gain personally from the reporting of such wrongdoing. This articulation of whistleblowing speaks to the still-current concern that whistleblowers might be motivated by personal gain.

Taken together then, these putative etymologies describe whistleblowing with varying emphases as calling for help, crying foul or informing the authorities (perhaps) for personal gain. It is worth noting then that lay understandings of whistleblowing, perhaps derived from these metaphors, may convey unhelpful concepts that impede effective voice in organisations, suggesting the terminology used may matter a great deal if we are to develop more effective self-correcting organisations.

Categorisations and continua of whistleblowing action

Over 30 years ago Near and Miceli defined whistleblowing as 'the disclosure by organisation members (former or current) of illegal, immoral, or illegitimate practices under the control of their employers, to persons or organisations that may be able to effect action'.[18] This definition quickly gained almost universal acceptance and application, and remains the standard definition to this day. However, within the healthcare field, many researchers prefer to cite McDonald and Ahern, who define a whistleblower as someone 'who identifies an incompetent, unethical or illegal situation in the workplace and reports it to someone who may have the power to stop the wrongdoing'.[19] Although this is effectively a paraphrasing of the earlier standard definition, it is not often presented as such, and as a result the healthcare literature on whistleblowing is sometimes less connected to the mainstream literature than would be desirable.

The 'standard' definition of whistleblowing draws attention to a continuum of activity from raising concerns (informally and internally), through speaking out (formally, but internal to the organisation) to out-and-out whistleblowing to external authorities (the more usual lay understanding). All of these have their place in any organisation aiming to be sensitive to messages from the front line, and concerned with the rapid remedying of identified defects in quality and safety.

18 J. P Near and M. P. Miceli, 'Organizational dissidence: the case of whistle-blowing', *Journal of Business Ethics* 1985, 4:1–16.

19 S. McDonald and K. Ahern, 4 (8), *Journal of Professional Nursing Management* 2000, 4(8):503–5.

Understanding the diversity of ways of raising concerns allows us to develop categorisations of such actions. Park et al. developed a typology of whistleblowing, suggesting that individuals who have decided to raise concerns face three key choices: (i) to raise issues informally or formally, (ii) to do so anonymously or on the record, and (iii) to choose channels that are either internal or external to their organisation.[20] Interestingly, this latter point is a key legal issue for the NHS, as it is not clear whether the National Guardian is a prescribed person for the purposes of making a protected disclosure under the Public Interest Disclosure Act (see later discussion).

The typology outlined above suggests eight different types of actions, only some of which would fit with what most people would understand as whistleblowing. For example, before deciding to blow the whistle employees usually find themselves trying to work out exactly what is happening, often through engaging in dialogue with colleagues.[21] Such behaviour could be consistent with the informal/identified/internal whistleblowing pathway,[22] but it seems unlikely that staff would perceive such conversations as a form of whistleblowing. Table 5.1 details how the Park et al. typology might translate into a healthcare context.

The academic literature has traditionally focused on a dichotomous choice between giving voice to concerns and remaining silent – that is, when faced with wrongdoing, an employee makes a conscious choice either to remain silent or to act by raising concerns.[23] Yet this simplistic dichotomy obscures a range of alternative strategies to whistleblowing that may be just as effective in identifying

Table 5.1 Types of whistleblowing (adapted from Park et al., 2008)

		Examples
Informal	Anonymous, Internal	Unsigned note sent to a manager in the internal mail; phone call to HR (or similar) giving no name
	Anonymous, External	Tip off to a journalist; anonymous web postings
	Identified, Internal	Discussing one's concerns with a colleague
	Identified, External	Posts on social media criticising one's employer
Formal	Anonymous, Internal	Leaving a message on a drug error hotline.
	Anonymous, External	Medication error reporting programmes
	Identified, Internal	Raising concerns with a speaking up guardian
	Identified, External	Raising concerns with a regulator; approaching an MP; speaking to a journalist

20 Park et al., 'Cultural orientation and attitudes towards types of whistle-blowing: a comparison of Turkey, South Korea and the UK', *Journal of Business Ethics* 2008, 82(4):929–39.

21 L. Blenkinsopp and M. S. Edwards, 'On not blowing the whistle: quiescent silence as an emotion episode', in Zerbe et al. (eds), *Emotions, ethics and decision-making (research on emotion in organizations*, vol. 4, Emerald Group Publishing Limited, 2008, pp. 181–206.

22 Park et al., 'Cultural orientation and attitudes'.

23 H. Teo and D. Caspersz, 'Dissenting discourse: exploring alternatives to the whistleblowing/silence dichotomy', 104 (2), *Journal of Business Ethics* 2011, 104(2):237–49.

and preventing wrongdoing.[24] Such strategies might include interpersonal approaches such as the use of humour or sarcasm to signal discontent, or informal and off-the-record discussions with managers and employees. For example, recent detailed ethnographic research in English hospital trusts found that staff often used 'pre-emptions' (informal actions used to intervene directly when patients were at immediate risk) and included strategies such as gentle reminders, use of humour or sharp words to sensitise staff to the need to alter their behaviour. When a breach of safety had already occurred the study found that informal 'sanctions' were applied, including 'a quiet word, bantering, public exposure or humiliation, scoldings and brutal reprimands'. These 'informal and circumlocutory'[25] channels of communication and low-level forms of social control may be valuable organisational mechanisms for addressing poor standards of care; indeed, they can often prove more effective than formal reporting systems, as they may be more likely to circumvent the 'deaf effect' (see below).

From an employee perspective then, the act of 'raising concerns' may sometimes be a relatively 'low-risk' act, something which might be done routinely, perhaps even just in passing (e.g. 'I think the new Healthcare Assistant is a little brusque with the older patients'). In contrast, 'speaking up' is potentially more serious: the very phrasing implies raising one's voice or breaking a silence. The perceived level of risk may not always be very great: in some cases the employee may only risk feeling foolish if s/he is mistaken, though their concern over this may in itself be enough to ensure they remain silent.[26] Whistleblowing is a more significant act, to which the organisation may respond negatively. Alford has argued that whistleblowers are defined *post hoc*, by the organisation's response to their action.[27] Using the NHS terminology, someone who thought they were just raising concerns or speaking up can discover they are a whistleblower if the organisation responds negatively. The general perception among NHS staff and the wider public is that NHS whistleblowers tend to fare badly,[28] so staff thinking about speaking up may, from the outset, be concerned they will get a very negative response. This may therefore lead to individuals with relatively low-level concerns to refrain from raising them.

Identifying the focus of concern

In a healthcare context, another important distinction between raising concerns and whistleblowing may be the focus of the concern. Whistleblowing is often seen as being about 'wrongdoing', yet many issues that could affect care quality

24 A. Jones and D. Kelly, 'Whistle-blowing and workplace culture in older peoples' care: qualitative insights from the healthcare and social care workforce', *Sociology of Health and Illness* 2014, 36(7):986–1002.

25 Ibid.

26 Blenkinsopp and Edwards, 'On not blowing the whistle'.

27 C. F. Alford, *Whistleblowers: broken lives and organizational power*, Ithaca: Cornell University Press, 2001.

28 Jones and Kelly, 'Whistle-blowing and workplace culture'.

and patient safety, and about which we would hope staff would raise concerns, are complex and ambiguous. Staffing levels, poor judgement or poor performance (whether innate or episodic, for example, from a colleague dealing with difficult personal problems) are all issues that could have a detrimental effect upon patient care, but would probably not be viewed by most staff as wrongdoing *per se*. Moreover, healthcare work often requires judgement based on hard-to-codify knowledge, alongside skills and expertise that may be imperfectly expressed, in situations of risk and uncertainty. Unsurprisingly then, identifying concerns that need to be raised is difficult and fraught with ambiguity, requiring not just judgements about the actions and inactions of others, but also assessments of their motives.

More subtly, a decision to speak out formally or to more senior staff about unaddressed issues is implicitly speaking up about earlier failures to address the problem. Typically, such action is more consistent with lay understandings of whistleblowing, and highlights an important point that is often missed: whistleblowers are often described as blowing the whistle about a specific issue (e.g. poor practice), but they are often effectively blowing the whistle on management's *failure to act* once made aware of the original issue.

Being heard, and clear sight of problems

Recent discussion of speaking up[29] tends to frame the problem in terms of creating environments in which staff feel more able to voice their concerns; recent policy responses too (such as the creation of 'safe spaces') collude with this framing. Yet, as Francis[30] and Kelly and Jones[31] observe, in many scandals staff had indeed voiced their concerns; the problem was getting someone to listen. This is consistent with the 'deaf effect', a term originally coined by Keil and Robey[32] to describe the reluctance of senior managers to hear, accept *and act on* challenging observations from lower down the organisation. Whilst it is widely recognised that it takes a degree of courage for someone to blow the whistle, it is less immediately obvious that it may also take courage for a manager to take on board the issues and act on them. Just as the whistleblower knows the line manager may not want to hear bad news, so the line manager knows senior management may be similarly reluctant to be informed of breaches or the requirements for remediation. Whistleblowing recipients in management roles may know that their actions in raising concerns may get a negative response from further up the management

29 E.g. Okuyama et al., 'Speaking up for patient safety by hospital-based health care professionals: a literature review', *BMC Health Sericesv Reearch* 2014, 14:61; Milligan et al., 'Supporting nursing, midwifery and allied health professional students to raise concerns with the quality of care: a systematic literature review', Council of Deans of Health (Commissioned Report) 2016; Francis, *Freedom to speak up*.

30 Francis, Report of the Mid Staffordshire NHS Foundation Trust Public Inquiry.

31 Jones and Kelly, Whistle-blowing and workplace culture'.

32 M. Keil and D. Robey, 'Blowing the whistle on troubled software projects', *Communications of the Academy of Management* 2001, 44(4):87–93.

hierarchy, and may even lead to the sort of retaliation and victimisation that can sometimes be experienced by whistleblowers themselves.

For this reason, there is a need to understand how managers 'have the courage to hear'.[33] In addition, senior management may also suffer from 'collective myopia',[34] a shared inability to see a problem. This is potentially even more problematic than the deaf effect, as it leaves those in management positions genuinely unable to see what the whistleblower is trying to bring to their attention. An example of this might be that what staff in a unit describe as bullying may be perceived by senior management as firm and effective performance management; another example might be divergent perspectives on the appropriate allocation of resources. Such situations may lead to escalation from raising concerns to speaking up to whistleblowing, not in search of 'someone willing to listen' but in search of 'someone able to see'.

As we have seen, then, in healthcare the events and circumstances worthy of speaking up about are complex and contested, and the organisational dynamics in which they must be spoken about are similarly complex and challenging. Taken together these complexities are likely to inhibit both initiating voice and responsive action to the detriment of patient care. Moreover, when voices are raised, and inaction ensues, escalation to formal whistleblowing brings organisational action under the purview of legal frameworks, and it is to these we now turn. (For a fuller discussion of this legal backdrop, see Chapter 6).

The legal underpinnings

Recent legal developments concerning whistleblowing in the NHS can be seen as deriving from the case of Grahame Pink, a nurse at Stockport General Infirmary who blew the whistle about poor patient care at the hospital in the late 1980s.[35] Meanwhile, there were also wider concerns surrounding standards in public life, as well as safety in transport and in the workplace, as exemplified by the Nolan Report, the Clapham Junction Rail Crash Report and the Piper Alpha disaster.[36] Against this background, legislation providing some protection for whistleblowers was finally enacted in 1998 in the form of the Public Interest Disclosure Act (PIDA), which amended earlier employment rights legislation.

The Public Interest Disclosure Act (PIDA)

The Public Interest Disclosure Act (PIDA) was enacted some three years before the publication of the Bristol Royal Infirmary Inquiry Report, that great

33 Vandekerckhove et al., 'Managerial responsiveness to whistleblowing: expanding the research horizon', in Brown et al. (eds), *International handbook of whistleblowing research* Cheltenham, UK: Edward Elgar Publishing, 2014, pp. 298–327.

34 N. Chikudate, 'Collective myopia and disciplinary power behind the scenes of unethical practices: a diagnostic theory on Japanese organization', *Journal of Management Studies* 2002, 39(3):289–307.

35 J. V. McHale, 'Whistle Blowing in the NHS', *Journal of Social Welfare and Family Law* 1992, 5:363.

36 J Bowers, *Whistleblowing Law and Practice* 2nd edition, Oxford: Oxford University Press, 2012: paras 1, and 03-1.1.2.

way-marker in NHS self-examination, and was subsequently reformed by the Enterprise and Regulatory Reform Act (ERRA) 2013. It is based on an understanding that the employer–employee relationship is one of trust and confidence, where the emphasis is more usually on *non-disclosure* rather than freedom of expression. However, the law does sanction departure from this understanding in certain situations where this is in the public interest (*Initial Services v Putterill* [1968] 1 QB 396).

In examining the scope of the PIDA legislation we will now focus on several distinct areas: the employees who come under the scope of the Act; the types of disclosures that are protected; and the actors to whom disclosures can lawfully be made. We will then consider the role of contractual confidentiality clauses (so-called 'gagging clauses'), before looking at the remedies available when detriment has been suffered, and the impact of the legislation in relation to whistleblowing in healthcare.

Employees under PIDA

The ERA safeguards disclosures made by a range of employees. 'Employees' refers to those in a contractual relationship and also would include, for example, nurses employed via an agency working for the NHS.[37] The Public Concern at Work Whistleblowing Commission (henceforth PCAW) has suggested the legislation should be extended to incorporate others, such as applicants for jobs, student health professionals, volunteers and interns, and non-executive directors (PCAW 2013). The scope of the legislation was subsequently extended to include primary care healthcare professionals such as GPs and nurses by amendments made to the ERA by the ERRA 2013 (section 20), and nursing students have now been included via regulations amending the primary legislation in 2015.[38]

Protected disclosures

It should be noted from the outset that the courts have taken a purposive approach, seeing the aim of the Act as being to facilitate responsible whistleblowing.[39] However, encouragement is not universal, and the words 'is made in the public interest' were included in section 43B in the amendments made to the 1996 Act by the ERRA 2013.

The ERA safeguards what are known as 'protected disclosures'. Statute identifies the kinds of disclosure that qualify, including (*inter alia*) notification of criminal offences, failure to comply with legal obligations, and health and safety breaches. A qualifying (or protected) disclosure refers to information where in the 'reasonable belief' of the worker making it, it tends to show a relevant failure.

37 *McTigue v University Hospital Bristol NHS Foundation Trust*, UKEAT /0354/15/JOJ; Peter Breakey, 'Whistleblowing protection', *New Law*, 7715, 23 September 2016.

38 2015 Regulations.

39 *BP Plc v Elstone and Petrotechnics Limited* [2010] IRLR 558; *Babula v Waltham Forest College* [2007] ICR 1026).

A disclosure may fall within this provision even in a situation in which it is shown later to be an incorrect belief.[40]

Actors to whom disclosures can lawfully be made

The Act operates to safeguard and privilege what are classed as 'three tiers' of disclosure. First, protected disclosures include disclosure to an employer.[41] This is unsurprising as it retains disclosure within the relationship of trust and of confidence. Disclosure to a legal advisor is also included.[42] This is in line with the special position accorded to lawyer–client disclosures more generally in English law through the doctrine of legal professional privilege. This provision does not include disclosure to persons who may be performing related advice functions, e.g. trade union representatives.[43] Disclosures to Ministers of the Crown are also safeguarded in this way,[44] as are disclosures to what are known as 'prescribed persons' (as set out in Regulations).[45] Included in this category are the CQC, NHS Commissioning Board, NHS Trust Development Authority and Health and Safety Executive,[46] and Monitor and Healthwatch.[47] In addition, other healthcare regulators such as the General Chiropractor Council, General Dental Council, General Pharmaceutical Council, and Health and Care Professions Council are also included.

The Act thus operates to facilitate *internal* organisational disclosure as well as *external* alarm-raising. But if this were all, the legislation would be of limited use: the Act goes beyond this and sanctions external disclosures too. Specifically, section 43H provides that in cases of disclosure of exceptionally serious failure then there is no need to go through internal procedures before disclosing. The worker must reasonably believe that information disclosed or allegations made are substantially true, the failure here is exceptionally serious, and it is reasonable to make the disclosure in these circumstances, taking into account to whom disclosure is made. It must not be made for personal gain.

Suffering detriment

The Act provides that the employee has a right not to be subject to detriment from his or her specific disclosure.[48] What constitutes detriment is not defined in the legislation, but the FTSU report gives as examples 'bullying, harassment or victimisation'.[49] While threats of detriment are not explicitly included in the

40 *Darnton v University of Surrey* [2003] IRLR 133 EAT .
41 Section 43C.
42 Section 43D.
43 PCAW 2013, page 23.
44 Section 43E.
45 Section 43F.
46 Public Interest Disclosure (Prescribed Persons) Order 2014: SI No 2418.
47 Public Interest Disclosure (Prescribed Persons) (Amendment) (No 2) Order 2015.
48 Section 47B; ERA 1996.
49 Francis, *Freedom to speak up*, para, 2.2.7.

legislation it is envisaged that they would be implicitly included.[50] Moreover, the Act imposes vicarious liability on employers and also personal liability on workers. Where an employee has made a protected disclosure, but is dismissed, then section 103A provides that this is an unfair dismissal. The causation tests for detriment and dismissal are different, however: in detriment, the test being more favourable for whistleblowing claimants.

Contractual confidentiality clauses

One point of controversy for some time has been the use of contractual confidentiality clauses inserted with the aim of stopping further disclosure by an employee (at times referred to as 'gagging clauses'.[51] The first Francis Report[52] commented that use of such clauses was widespread and that 'any clause restricting an individual's liberty to make a disclosure or imposing a duty of confidentiality should be limited to the minimum necessary to protect the public interest and not the reputation of any organisation or individual'.[53] Going further, Francis recommended that gagging clauses should be prohibited in relation to healthcare organisation, regulators and commissioners to the extent to which these inhibit what are *bona fide* disclosures of public interest questions of safety of care. In 2013 the Secretary of State for Health, Jeremy Hunt, told the press that gagging orders in the NHS would be banned.[54] However, use of gagging clauses still continued.

Remedies

Actions under the ERA may be brought against the employer or an employee who is claimed to be responsible for the detriment suffered. Where a worker has not been dismissed then a declaration can be sought to establish that the complaint was justified, along with compensation. Dismissal due to a protected disclosure will constitute an unfair dismissal. If the worker is found to be unfairly dismissed then they can be awarded compensation, and an order may be made for reinstatement (historically, reinstatement is rare however). The FTSU report commented that it was often not practicable to force individuals to be reinstated but that the NHS had 'a moral obligation to support those staff whose performance is sound but who have suffered as a result of speaking up'.[55] The extent to which this can be effectively achieved, however, remains an issue

Impact of the legislation in relation to whistleblowing in healthcare

Now the PIDA legislation has been in existence for around two decades, we can ask: how effective has it been? In relation to the impact of the Act in general,

50 Bowers, Whistleblowing law and practice, para 7.14.
51 J. Gornall, 'The price of silence', *BMJ* 2009:339.
52 R Francis, Report of the Mid Staffordshire NHS Foundation Trust Public Inquiry.
53 Ibid., p. 1458.
54 *The Mail Online*, 13 March 2013.
55 Francis, *Freedom to speak up*, para 9.10.

commentators have been equivocal,[56] with suggestions it has led to only limited change.[57] Moreover, while some healthcare cases have been litigated these are simply the tip of the iceberg: in a case with a strong claim the parties would be encouraged to settle rather than going to tribunal. Arguably, use of the legislation at tribunal demonstrates organisational failure – it shows the raising of concerns has not been respected within the institution.

Healthcare claims successful at hearing are less than 5%:[58] the vast majority of claims are either settled at ACAS, are withdrawn, or are privately settled.[59] Indeed, Gobert and Punch[60] comment that for the honest and well-meaning whistleblower the Act may be seen as 'a trap': not only are many organisations effective at intimidating perceived troublemakers, but finding new employment for the whistleblower – even if they are ultimately vindicated – may prove very difficult indeed. It remains to be seen whether the new provisions aimed at addressing blacklisting in the NHS will remedy this situation.

There is also a perception that, although ground-breaking in its time, the legislation is now dated and has been overtaken by approaches developed in other jurisdictions. Blueprint has argued that set against international standards of whistleblower protection the PIDA provisions fall far short.[61] Enforcing the legislation is also a problem. The introduction in 2013 of fees for claimants bringing employment tribunal proceedings led to a significant drop in the number of cases.[62] The cost of upfront lawyer fees may prove a considerable deterrent to taking a case forward. Measures inhibiting access to justice in this way, and deterring whistleblowers, may result in the NHS having less opportunity to learn from its mistakes.

Safer spaces for speaking up

In the face of the overwhelming evidence of quality and safety deficits, improving the safety and quality of health services will require making full use of the detailed knowledge of front-line staff. However, sometimes the messages conveyed by front-line staff are unwelcome, contentious and challenging to managerial and/or policy discourses. As a result, staff have sometimes felt compelled to take their concerns elsewhere – to more senior staff within the organisation, or to outside agencies, politicians or the media. The consequences of such actions only rarely

56 D. Lewis, 'Resolving whistleblowing disputes in the public interest: is tribunal adjudication the best that can be offered?' *Industrial Law Journal* 2010, 42(1):35–52.

57 J Ashton, '15 years of whistleblowing protection under the Public Interest Disclosure Act 1998: are we still shooting the messenger?', *Industrial Law Journal* 2015, 44(1):29–52.

58 PCAW, 2013.

59 Ashton '15 years of whistleblowing'.

60 J. Gobert and M. Punch, 'Whistleblowers, the public interest, and the Public Interest Disclosure Act', *Modern Law Review* 2000, 63(1):25.

61 Wolfe et al., 'Breaking the silence: strengths and weaknesses in G20 whistleblower protection laws', *Blueprint for free speech*, October 2015, p. 15–17.

62 Francis, *Freedom to speak up*, para 2.2.9; subsequent legal challenge led to these fees being overturned in 2017.

see the prompt remedying of the concerns reported: all too often concerns are ignored and rejected (with varying degrees of actual refutation), and there may be severe personal repercussions for those raising the concerns.

At the heart of this lies the essential ambiguity and contestability of many of the most important concerns central to healthcare failings: resources and staffing levels; the distribution and structuring of care services; the application of clinical judgement in the face of uncertainty; the appropriate management of risk; and the assessment of professional competencies. Given this, separating legitimate professional concerns from distracting, poorly-founded complaints is challenging indeed.

The legal frameworks to support such disclosures, and protect the discloser, such as the ERA and PIDA, and the more recent work round the Healthcare Safety Investigation Branch (HSIB), have struggled to reflect the ambiguity and contestability at the heart of reporting concerns in healthcare. It is also clear that many of those reporting concerns do not see themselves as whistleblowers (and hence having specific legal protections) until after the full weight of their organisation is thrown at rejecting their concerns and challenging their motives, competence and (sometimes) sanity. Indeed, it may be observed that once we are in the realms of protected disclosure and legal safeguards then we are far removed from earlier, upstream, opportunities for responsive organisational change.

An emerging typology of organisational spaces

It is clear that we need to create better, safer organisational spaces for staff to voice concerns in ways that create engaged dialogue rather than management resistance; it is *not* clear that this can effectively be done simply through statute. Given the foregoing discussions, Figure 5.1 shows a possible way of understanding two key dimensions of the organisational environment: the willingness of front-line staff to speak up, and the willingness of organisational actors to listen and respond. Each of these are affected by wider norms, communicated by policy, procedures and cultures, for example those that positively encourage voice, or those that signal clearly a hostility to unwelcome news.

Too often, organisations reside in the bottom left-hand quadrant, where staff are unwilling to speak out and more powerful organisational actors are unwilling to hear troublesome messages. Such a dynamic can be heavily self-reinforcing. In contrast, where speaking up has been encouraged, or even mandated – for example, by the recent Francis review[63] – unless the local organisational dynamic is also changed then those speaking up may be freshly vulnerable. Notwithstanding the legal safeguards of PIDA, those giving voice often pay a heavy price. A longer-term goal of policy should be to transition from bottom-left to top-right in the diagram, to create a virtuous dynamic of local learning that would obviate the need for powerful but cumbersome legal safeguards. Such a goal will only be reached through careful work at many levels within whole health systems, and cannot be

63 Ibid.

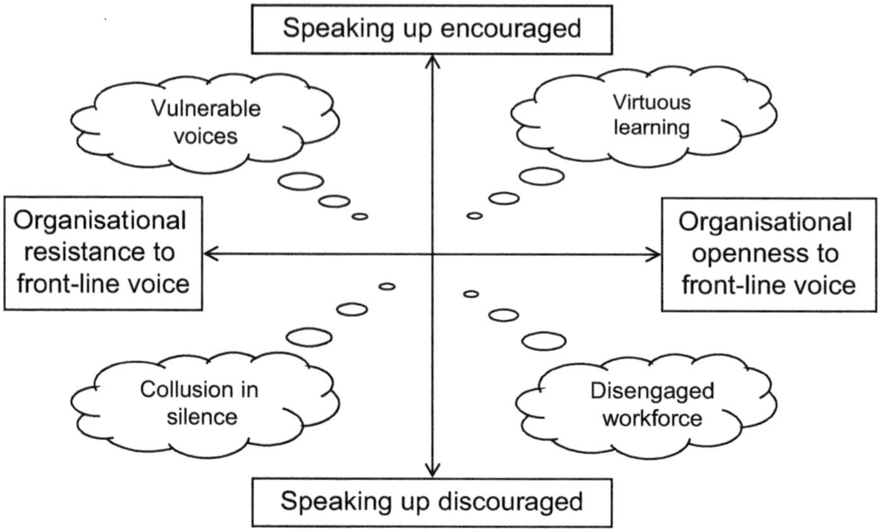

Figure 5.1 Employee voice and organisational listening

mandated by policy diktat or ensured through legislative change, although both may play important supporting roles. Thus, while reform is needed in all parts of the system, better local support for front-line voice and sustained managerial support for effective hearer action are key.

Funding acknowledgement

The research was funded by the National Institute for Health Research (NIHR) Health Services and Delivery (HSDR) programme.[64] The views and opinions expressed therein are those of the authors and do not necessarily reflect those of the HSDR programme.

References

Alford, C. F., *Whistleblowers: broken lives and organizational power*, Ithaca: Cornell University Press, 2001.

Ashton, J., '15 years of whistleblowing protection under the Public Interest Disclosure Act 1998: are we still shooting the messenger?', *Industrial Law Journal* 2015, 44(1): 29–52.

Blenkinsopp, J. and Edwards, M. S., 'On not blowing the whistle: quiescent silence as an emotion episode', in Zerbe, W. J., Charmine, E. J. Härtel and Ashkanasy, N. M. (eds), *Emotions, ethics and decision-making (research on emotion in organizations)*, volume 4, Emerald Group Publishing Limited, 2008.

64 Grant number 14/04; project title 'Understanding employee whistleblowing in health care'; applicants Russell Mannion, Ross Millar, Huw Davies, Jean McHale, John Blenkinsopp and Martin Powell.

Bowers, J., *Whistleblowing law and practice* 2nd edition, Oxford: Oxford University Press, 2012.

Braithwaite, J., Matsuyama, Y., Mannion, R. and Johnson, J., *Healthcare Reform, Quality and Safety: Perspectives, Participants, Partnerships and Prospects in 30 Countries*, Abingdon: Ashgate Publishers, 2015.

Breakey, Peter. 'Whistleblowing protection', *New Law*, 7715, 23 September 2016.

Chikudate, N. 'Collective myopia and disciplinary power behind the scenes of unethical practices: a diagnostic theory on Japanese organization', *Journal of Management Studies* 2002, 39(3):289–307.

Department of Health, *An organisation with a memory*, London: The Stationery Office, 2000.

Francis, R., *Report of the Mid Staffordshire NHS Foundation Trust Public Inquiry*, London: The Stationery Office, 2010.

Francis, R., *Report of the Mid Staffordshire NHS Foundation Trust Public Inquiry*, The Mid Staffordshire NHS Foundation Trust, 2013.

Francis, R., *Freedom to speak up: an independent review into creating an open and honest reporting culture in the NHS*, London: The Stationery Office, 2015.

Gobert, J. and Punch, M., 'Whistleblowers the public interest and the Public Interest Disclosure Act', *Modern Law Review* 2000, 63(1):25.

Gornall, J., 'The Price of Silence', *BMJ* 2009; 339.

Jones, A. and Kelly, D., 'Whistle-blowing and workplace culture in older peoples' care: qualitative insights from the healthcare and social care workforce', *Sociology of Health and Illness* 2014, 36(7):986–1002.

Keil, M. and Robey, D., 'Blowing the whistle on troubled software projects', *Communications of the Academy of Management* 2001, 44(4):87–93.

Kennedy, I., *The Report of the Public Inquiry into children's heart surgery at the Bristol Royal Infirmary 1984–1995. Learning from Bristol.* Report no. CM 5207(I), 2001.

Kohn, L. T., Corrigan, J. and Donaldson, M. S., *To err is human: building a safer health system*, Washington, DC: National Academy Press, 2000.

Lewis, D., 'Resolving whistleblowing disputes in the public interest: is tribunal adjudication the best that can be offered?' *Industrial Law Journal* 2010, 42(1):35–52

Mannion, R. and Davies, H. T., 'Cultures of silence and cultures of voice: the role of whistleblowing in healthcare organisations', *International Journal of Health Policy and Management* 2015.

Mannion, et al., 'Understanding the knowledge gaps in whistleblowing and speaking up in healthcare: narrative reviews of the research literature and formal inquiries, a legal analysis and stakeholder interviews', 2017. HSDR forthcoming.

McDonald, S. and Ahern, K., *Journal of Professional Nursing Management* 2000, 4(8):503–5.

McHale, J. V., 'Whistle blowing in the NHS', *Journal of Social Welfare and Family Law* 1992; 363.

Medical Protection Society (MPS), *Whistleblowing doctors afraid to speak out*, London: MPS, 2012.

Milligan, F., Wareing, M., Bhandol, J., Pappas, Y., Randhawa, G. and Preston-Shoot, M., *Supporting nursing, midwifery and allied health professional students to raise concerns with the quality of care: a systematic literature review*. Council of Deans of Health (Commissioned Report) 2016.

Near, J. P. and Miceli, M. P., 'Organizational dissidence: the case of whistle-blowing', *Journal of Business Ethics* 1985, 4:1–16.

NHS Staff Survey 2015, London: NHS England, 2016.

Okuyama, A., Wagner, C. and Bijnen, B., 'Speaking up for patient safety by hospital-based health care professionals: a literature review', *BMC Health Services Research* 2014, 14:61.

Park, H., Blenkinsopp, J., Oktem, M. K. and Omurgonulsen, U., 'Cultural orientation and attitudes towards types of whistle-blowing: a comparison of Turkey, South Korea and the UK', *Journal of Business Ethics* 2008, 82(4):929–39.

Teo, H. and Caspersz, D., 'Dissenting discourse: exploring alternatives to the whistleblowing/silence dichotomy', *Journal of Business Ethics* 2011, 104(2):237–49.

Vandekerckhove, W., Brown, A. J. and Tsahuridu, E., 'Managerial responsiveness to whistleblowing: expanding the research horizon', in Brown, A. J., Lewis, D., Moberly, R. and Vandekerckhove, W. (eds), *International handbook of whistleblowing research*, Cheltenham, UK: Edward Elgar, 2014.

Wolfe, S., Worth, M., Dreyfus, S. and Brown, A., 'Breaking the silence: strengths and weaknesses in G20 whistleblower protection laws', *Blueprint for free speech*, October 2015.

World Health Organization (WHO), *Patient safety: making health care safer*. Geneva: World Health Organization, 2017.

6 Patient safety, the 'safe space' and the duty of candour

Reconciling the irreconcilable?

Jean V. McHale

Introduction

Addressing medical errors in the National Health Service (NHS) is an area where there have long been concerns raised as to the impact of both internal organisation factors and also external factors upon attempts to effectively identify and resolve such issues.[1] Over many years it has been claimed that the investigation of medical errors and adverse incidents in the NHS has been fundamentally inhibited by the hostile environment which existed. In 2010 when the Mid Staffordshire Public Inquiry was announced by Andrew Lansley, the then Secretary of State for Health, he commented that there was:

> a culture of fear in which staff did not feel able to report concerns; a culture of secrecy in which the Trust board shut itself off from what was happening in its hospital and ignored its patients; and a culture of bullying which prevented people from doing their job properly.[2]

Recent initiatives discussed elsewhere in this volume, for example, in relation to whistleblowing following Sir Robert Francis' Report, *Freedom to speak up*, in 2015 are attempting to encourage staff to come forward and disclose concerns although many question marks remain as the work of Mannion et al. demonstrate.[3] In additional to internal factors some see the external impact of adversarial litigation processes as a deterrent undermining effective

1 See, for example, C. Vincent et al., *Medical accidents*, Oxford University Press, 1993; M. M. Rosenthal, L. Mulcahy and S. Lloyd-Bostock (eds), *Medical mishaps: pieces of the puzzle*, Open University Press, 1999; V. A. Sharpe and A. I. Faden, *Medical harm: historical, conceptual and ethical dimensions of iatrogenic illness*, Cambridge University Press, 1998; A. Merry and A. McCall-Smith, *Errors, medicine and the law*, Cambridge University Press, 2001; O. Quick, 'Outing medical errors: questions of trust and responsibility', *Medical Law Review* 2006, 14(1):22; J. Tingle and P. Bark (eds), *Patient Safety, Law Policy and Practice*, Routledge, 2011; O. Quick, *Regulating patient safety: the end of professional dominance?* Cambridge University Press, 2017.

2 Hansard 9 June 2010, column 333.

3 Sir Robert Francis, |*Freedom to speak up: an independent review into creating an open and honest reporting culture in the NHS* (2015).

identification of harms and the ability to learn lessons, and consequently reduce the prospect of future harm.[4]

This chapter focuses on the question of investigating matters where things have gone wrong in relation to patient safety and specifically in the context of two recent initiatives which can be seen potentially playing an important role in this area in the future. First, is the introduction of a duty of candour in England making provision for information to be routinely and frankly disclosed in the case of adverse incidents – the enactment of both a statutory duty of candour and also of a professional duty of candour applicable to both doctors and nurses. This paper examines the rationale for the development of this duty of candour, and what it entails, and explores some of the practical challenges for its implementation. Secondly, the paper then considers the evolution of what is known as the 'safe space' in England and its potential impact through the Health Service Safety Investigation Bill 2017. The concept of a safe space has been introduced with reference to developments in the air accident industry. It is the idea of an environment where an investigation can take place without fear of adverse implications from information being disclosed and utilised in other contexts adversely impacting of the investigation itself. This can be seen in principle as a means of facilitating free and frank discussion and effective investigations. However, this paper argues that the construction of the safe space itself may cause some major problems for justice and accountability where adverse clinical harms have been caused, and moreover it can be seen to be sharply at odds with the duty of candour itself. It suggests that the introduction and development of both a duty of candour and a safe space is unlikely to be something which can be effectively reconciled.

A question of veracity and the duty of candour

The introduction of a statutory duty of candour has followed the Francis Report into Mid Staffordshire NHS Trust. However, in fact it is not a new concept and its consideration preceded Francis by many years. In *Lee v South West Thames RHA* Sir John Donaldson commented *obiter* that 'some thought should be given to what is the duty of disclosure owed by a doctor and a hospital to a patient after treatment'.[5] Subsequently in *Naylor v Preston* in 1987 Sir John Donaldson stated that:

> I personally think that in professional negligence cases, and in particular medical negligence cases, there is a duty of candour resting on the professional

4 The malpractice 'crisis' has long been debated and there have been calls for example for the introduction of alternative dispute resolution structures in healthcare but this to date has not been taken forward in England; see for example C. Ham, R. Dingwall, P. Fenn and D. Harris *Medical negligence, compensation and accountability*, London: Kings Fund Institute 1988; P. Hoyte, 'Unsound practice: the epidemiology of medical negligence', *Medical Law Review* 1995, 3:53; Chief Medical Officer, *Making Amends: a consultation paper setting out the proposals for reforming the approach to clinical negligence in the NHS*, Department of Health 2003; NHS Redress Act 2006; A. M. Farrell and S. Devaney, 'Making amends or making things worse?' *Legal Studies* 2007, 27(4):630.

5 [1985] 1 WLR 845

> man. It is but one aspect of the general duty of care arising out of the patient/medical practitioner or hospital authority relationship.[6]

This statement was, however, simply *obiter* and, thus, not binding on subsequent courts. Subsequently support was given to a candour duty in an article in the *BMJ* by Jean H. Ritchie QC and Sally C. Davies, then a consultant haematologist and later to become Chief Medical Officer.[7] The prospect of the introduction of a duty of candour was considered by Kennedy and Grubb in the first edition of *Principles of Medical Law*. They stated that:

> It may be ethically appealing, but in the context of the trench warfare of medical negligence, it would not be regarded by those who advise doctors as a duty but rather an act of folly.[8]

Public attention was drawn to the case for a duty of candour by litigation which led to the call for 'Robbie's Law'.[9] Robbie Powell, a 10-year-old boy, fell ill in December 1989 with severe stomach cramps and vomiting. What followed was a catalogue of misinformation, miscommunication and negligence. He was seen by different GPs and hospital staff on several occasions. Although one of the doctors treating him in hospital suspected Addison's disease, this information was not communicated to his parents and the disease was not diagnosed. Instead, his parents were, over a period of time, either advised not to worry or were given inappropriate treatment. On 16 April 1990, his condition worsened. A doctor was called who advised them that if Robbie vomited or deteriorated further he should be admitted to hospital. The next day, Robbie's parents called for a home visit. Dr Flowers, a GP, attended. Robbie had collapsed, and fallen temporarily unconscious with blue lips and dilated pupils. Dr Flowers initially said there was no cause for concern and left. She was called out later that day. On that occasion, she said he could be admitted to hospital, but she refused to call out an ambulance. Robbie's parents, themselves, took Robbie to hospital. On arrival, he was put on a life-support system in intensive care. He, then, suffered two cardiac arrests and died that night.

After Robbie's death, evidence emerged that Addison's disease had been suspected as long ago as December 1989. It was asserted that medical notes were altered to remove references to Addison's disease and other letters substituted. The parents realised that the notes had been deliberately falsified. While this led to an initial hearing by the Medical Services Committee, no pertinent questions were raised about the cover-up and the Committee only made one finding against

6 *Naylor v Preston AHA* [1987] 2 All ER 353.

7 J. Ritchie, and S. Davies, 'Professional negligence: a duty of candid disclosure?', *BMJ* 1995, 310:888–9.

8 I. Kennedy and A. Grubb (eds), *Principles of medical law* 1st edition, Oxford: Oxford University Press, at para 3.141.

9 See for example the discussion in O. Quick, 'Regulating and legislating safety: the case for candour', *BMJ Quality & Safety* 2014, 23:614–18.

Dr Flowers, the minimum possible reprimand. They made no reference to allegations of falsifications of records.

His parents, subsequently, brought an action in negligence and also asserted psychiatric harm consequent upon the events which led to his death, having witnessed the death and in relation to the failure to disclose information concerning what had happened. Robbie's father, William Powell, was unable to work for 25 years and was diagnosed with post-traumatic stress disorder. Robbie's mother had to take medication for over two decades.[10] Mr Powell then brought further proceedings claiming damages in relation to psychiatric injury which he said he suffered due to the actions of Dr Boladz, a GP. Dr Boladz, it was claimed, removed and falsified medical records concerning Robbie's death. It was claimed that the substitution of false documents constituted negligence. Dr Boladz owed a duty of care to Mr Powell. Secondly, a claim was brought of trespass to the person under *Wilkinson v Downton*, the tort enabling an action to be brought for intentional infliction of nervous shock.[11] Finally, it was argued that there had been a breach of the tort of conspiracy to injure by unlawful means regarding the economic loss he had suffered through an appeal which was made unsuccessfully to the Secretary of State.

At first instance, the claimants were unsuccessful. The Court of Appeal dismissed the appeal. It held that there was not a sufficient relationship of proximity between Dr Boladz and Powell to create a duty of care. The duty of care was owed to the patient, not to the relatives to whom bad news had been conveyed. In situations in which the relatives were also patients of the doctor a duty of care would only arise in relation to treatment which they themselves had been given. Here, while Mr Powell was a patient of Dr Boladz, any duty would only relate to the latter's treatment of him. A reasonable person could not in the circumstances have foreseen that the substitution of documents which took place would result in injury. Secondly, there was not liability under *Wilkinson v Downton*. For liability to arise, a statement would need to have been made which was known to be false, with the intention of causing the subsequent injury. Here, Dr Boladz did not have sufficient foresight such as being able to appreciate what the consequences of his action would be. Thirdly, the tort of unlawful conspiracy was not applicable as Dr Boladz's unlawful act was not aimed at the claimant and it was not reasonably foreseeable that he would be injured. In response to the ruling of the Court of Appeal in 1997 Dr Brian Goss of the British Medical Association General Medical Services Committee was quoted in *GP* magazine on 11 July 1997 as stating that 'GPs could now put a gloss on the cause of death without fear of litigation.'[12]

10 *Powell v Boladz* [1998] Lloyds Rep Med 116. (1998) 39 BMLR 35.

11 [1897] 2 QB 57.

12 Quoted on AvMA website www.avma.org.uk/policy-campaigns/duty of candour/robbies-law/ (accessed 16 March 2018).

After the case was rejected in the domestic courts, the Powell family brought their case before the European Court of Human Rights (ECtHR, or the Court).[13] It was held to be inadmissible:

> As the law stands now doctors have no duty to give parents of a child who died as a result of their negligence a truthful account of the circumstances of the death, or even to refrain from deliberately falsifying records.

The Court noted that, while there was an arguable case following Lord Donaldson that a common law duty was placed on the doctors not to falsify medical records, nonetheless, there was no binding decision of the courts as to the existence of such a duty. Before the court it was argued that Articles 2, which protects the right to life; 8, which protects individual privacy and decision-making autonomy; and 10, that of freedom of expression of the European Convention on Human Rights (ECHR or the Convention) meant that they should have been given 'a truthful and accurate account of the circumstances surrounding the death' and, thus, by definition this meant that there should be no deliberate falsifying of records and provision of false information. However, the ECtHR rejected the argument that the decisions of the lower courts effectively gave the clinicians immunity. They recognised that actions do exist for acts and omissions through the tort of negligence. Furthermore, if evidence had been deliberately falsified there could be a criminal law prosecution and also a prosecution for perverting the course of justice. The Court noted that the claim that evidence had been covered up related to the evidence of documents seen by a cleric, the Revd Thomas, and that this was in the face of strong denials from the clinicians. It was held that this part of the claim was manifestly unfounded. A claim was made that there was no effective remedy in respect of a breach of Article 13 of the Convention (which requires effective remedies to be given). They argued that existing remedies under domestic law were not sufficient either on their own or cumulatively to guarantee them an effective remedy. The hearing undertaken by the Medical Services Committee was not sufficient because this is an internal professional disciplinary body created by the NHS to hear complaints from patients about alleged acts of medical negligence. This hearing took place before the alleged cover-up and, subsequently, they were not able to raise questions about it at that committee nor to effectively appeal, nor were they able to take effective advantage of their appeal to the Welsh Office. Further allegations in relation to the effectiveness of this investigation related to the conduct of the Welsh Office, undertaking false statements in Parliamentary questions regarding location of medical records. They also criticised a police inquiry which had focused on the prospect of a gross negligence manslaughter prosecution rather than allegations

13 In *William and Anita Powell v UK* ECHR 4 May 2000 45305/99; and see W. Powell, 'Robbie's Law: lack of candour. The impact on patients and their families', *Journal of Patient Safety and Risk Management* 2014, 20(1):4.

of falsification of records. The family consequently agreed that the negligence action was the only effective means of safeguarding their rights. The ECtHR took the view that the essence of the case was that they had been unable to bring a separate civil law action for damages, but the Court took the approach that in any event they would have been unable to do so due to the fact that there was no arguable basis in domestic law for invoking such a right. It was, thus, held that in these circumstances they cannot be said either to have an arguable claim for the purposes of Article 13 ECHR.

Subsequent to the Powell case, support for a duty of candour within the NHS was given in a serious of reports. In the Bristol Royal Infirmary Inquiry Report Professor Sir Ian Kennedy proposed the introduction of a duty of candour.[14] The Report stated that:

> A duty of candour, meaning a duty to tell a patient if adverse events have occurred, must be recognised as owed by all those working in the NHS to patients.[15]

Support for such a duty was also contained in the Donaldson Report *Making Amends* in 2003.[16] However, successive governments did not take this forward. It was not until the recommendations in the Mid-Staffordshire Inquiry Report that there was a decisive driver for change. In his Mid Staffordshire Inquiry Report, Sir Robert Francis recommended that statutory obligation should be introduced to establish a duty of candour.[17] This was to apply in a situation where healthcare providers believed that treatment given to a patient resulted in death/serious injury they were to inform the patient or another 'authorised person' of this as soon as reasonably practicable. In addition they should provide explanations where reasonably requested by patients. In addition an obligation would be placed on doctors, nurses and other registered healthcare professionals in a situation where they believed/suspected that the healthcare provider had caused death or serious injury to report this as soon as reasonably practicable. Failure to provide such information should give rise to a remedy on the part of the patient. Interestingly, however, the Report did state that in itself the provision of such information would not be admission of civil or criminal liability.[18]

This new duty would also operate alongside existing duties. So, for example, the Care Quality Commission (CQC) has the obligation in inspections of hospitals to consider whether there are hospital systems which:

14 The report of the public inquiry into children's heart surgery at the Bristol Royal Infirmary1984–1995, *Learning from Bristol* Cmnd 52071 (2001). See further on the Bristol Inquiry, O. Quick, 'Disaster at Bristol: explanations and implications of a tragedy', *Journal of Social Welfare and Family Law* 1999, 21:307.

15 Ibid., p. 441.

16 Chief Medical Officer, *Making amends. A consultation paper setting out proposals for reforming the approach to clinical negligence in the NHS*, London: Department of Health, 2003.

17 Interestingly Sir Robert Francis was also one of the counsel at the Bristol Royal Infirmary Inquiry.

18 Recommendation 181.

> Inform(s) (patients) or others acting on their behalf, if an adverse event, incident or error has occurred in their care, treatment or support that has caused or may result in harm.[19]

These requirements are also included in the standard contract between NHS clinical providers and commissioners. In addition, since 2010 obligations have been placed on hospitals to report serious untoward incidents to the CQC without delay where patients have died as a result of such circumstances which cannot be reasonably attributed to the condition of the patient and there has been an untoward incident which has harmed patient or shortened lifespan.[20]

The Government accepted the recommendation of Sir Robert Francis. Following the Mid Staffordshire Report, section 81 of the Care Act 2014 now provides the Secretary of State with power to make regulations concerning the duty of candour. The provision states:

> In section 20 of the Health and Social Care Act 2008 (regulation of regulated activities), after subsection (5) insert –
>
> (5A) Regulations under this section must make provision as to the provision of information in a case where an incident of a specified description affecting a person's safety occurs in the course of the person being provided with a service.

The Explanatory Notes to the Legislation provide that:

> This duty will mean that such providers will be required to ensure that patients and service users are told when something unexpected or unintended occurs in the course of their care or treatment, helping to ensure that honesty and transparency are the norm in every organisation overseen by the CQC.

This provision now has to be read in conjunction with regulation 20 of the Health and Social Care Act 2008 (Regulated Activities) Regulations 2014. This places an obligation on registered persons to 'act in an open and transparent way' regarding care and treatment.[21] As soon as reasonably practicable once it becomes apparent that a 'notifiable safety accident' has occurred,[22] the relevant person, e.g. the individual or their relatives, should be informed that the incident has taken place and also give 'reasonable support' to that person:[23]

19 CQC 2010.

20 National Health Service (CQC) Regulations 2009 SI 2009, No 3112, regs 13 and 19; and see C. Newdick and C. Danbury, 'Culture, compassion and clinical neglect: probity in the NHS after Mid Staffordshire', *Journal of Medical Ethics* 2013, p. 958.

21 Reg 1(1).

22 Reg 1(2).

23 Reg 2(a)(b).

> (3) The notification to be given under paragraph (2) (a) must –
>
> (a) be given in person by one or more representatives of the [registered person],
>
> (b) provide an account, which to the best of the [registered person's] knowledge is true, of all the facts the [registered person] knows about the incident as at the date of the notification,
>
> (c) advise the relevant person what further enquiries into the incident the [registered person] believes are appropriate,
>
> (d) include an apology, and
>
> (e) be recorded in a written record which is kept securely by the [registered person].
>
> (4) The notification given under paragraph (2)(a) must be followed by a written notification given or sent to the relevant person containing –
>
> (a) the information provided under paragraph (3)(b),
>
> (b) details of any enquiries to be undertaken in accordance with paragraph (3) (c),
>
> (c) the results of any further enquiries into the incident, and
>
> (d) an apology.
>
> 5) But if the relevant person cannot be contacted in person or declines to speak to the representative of the [registered person] –
>
> (a) paragraphs (2) to (4) are not to apply, and
>
> (b) a written record is to be kept of attempts to contact or to speak to the relevant person.
>
> (6) The [registered person] must keep a copy of all correspondence with the relevant person under paragraph (4).

It is too early to comprehensively examine what the impact of this provision will be, although, as we shall see below, there is some evidence as to initial problems. Essentially, it does signify a need to be open and transparent in the provision of information. At the same time, it should be noted that this is no general whistleblowing provision and it relates very much to specific disclosures for specific purposes.

Along with the new statutory duty there is also a professional duty of candour recognised by the medical profession and nursing regulatory bodies, the General Medical Council (GMC) and Nursing and Midwifery Council (NMC), who have now produced joint guidance on this issue.[24] This emphasises that patients must

24 General Medical Council/Nursing and Midwifery Council, *Openness and honesty when things go wrong: the professional duty of candour*. London: GMC/NMC, 2015.

'be fully informed' about their care.[25] The statements in relation to information provision reflect existing law concerning consent to treatment. It stipulates that it is relevant where something has gone wrong and harm has resulted.[26] Onus is placed on the health professional or on someone in their team to speak to the patient; the guidance notes that 'the most appropriate team member will usually be the lead or accountable clinician'.[27] This should be done as soon as possible, and, moreover, GMC/NMC guidance states that:

> You should share all you know and believe to be true about what went wrong and why, and what the consequences are likely to be. You should explain if anything is still uncertain and you must respond honestly to any questions. You should apologise to the patient.[28]

Where patients do not want more information, this option should still be raised with the patient. Their wishes should be respected 'as far as possible' and this decision by the patient should be recorded.[29] It is also the case that individuals are not expected to take responsibility for things which are not their fault but there is an expectation that an individual will receive an apology from an appropriate team member. This could lead to interesting and difficult dynamics in relation to who provides the apology if a range of different people's actions have contributed to the harm caused.[30] The guidance states that patients expect three things in relation to an apology. Firstly, what happened; secondly, actions which can be taken to address harm caused; and, thirdly, what actions will be taken to prevent a third person from being harmed.[31] Critically, it stresses that such an apology does not constitute an admission of legal liability.[32] It may also amount to evidence of insight at a professional practice panel.[33] While it is suggested that a formulaic response to apologising is not being encouraged, the guidance does provide some structured criteria in relation to apologies such as comprehensible information, delivered in a manner respecting of privacy/dignity as appropriate, and suggests that a personalised approach can be 'more meaningful' rather than a 'generalised expression of regret'.[34] The guidance also notes the need to be open and honest in relation to those close to the patient if the patient has died or harm of such a severe nature has been suffered such that they are unlikely to regain decision making capacity.[35] Emphasis, again, is placed on appropriate sensitivity being

25 Ibid., para 6.
26 Ibid., para 8.
27 Ibid., para 9.
28 Ibid., para 11.
29 Ibid., para 12.
30 Ibid., para 15
31 Ibid., para 13
32 Ibid., para 14.
33 Ibid., para 14.
34 Ibid., para 16.
35 Ibid., para 17.

used and appropriate support being given.[36] The guidance makes reference to the 'near miss' (defined as being 'an adverse incident that had the potential to result in harm but did not do so').[37] Professional judgement is to be exercised as to whether patients are told,[38] but, also, if information is not disclosed, it could damage patient trust and confidence.[39] Such questions of judgement are likely to prove exceedingly challenging for clinical teams in the future. The guidance makes express reference to the need to encourage 'a learning culture by reporting errors'.[40] It is stated that:

> When something goes wrong with patient care, it is crucial that it is reported at an early stage so that lessons can be learnt quickly and patients can be protected from harm in the future.[41]

Healthcare organisations are required to have policies in relation to the reporting of adverse incidents and near misses.[42] What is clear is that for a duty of candour to operate effectively support from the organisation is critical and, as it states, if this is not forthcoming concerns should be raised with management.[43] The guidance recognises the need for health professionals to be protected if they blow the whistle.[44] Senior health professionals are also placed under an obligation to encourage openness, learning and improvement[45] and have systems in place to identify failure and investigate concerns in relation to colleagues.[46] This, again, illustrates that health professionals in such a situation have a dual role – as health professionals with responsibility in relation to their professional code and, also, as employees who are managers. However, how realistic it is to expect healthcare professionals to undertake such a professional duty has been questioned. For example, it has been argued that nurses have not had the necessary training to implement such a duty in practice.[47]

The statutory duty of candour, along with the doctors' and nurses' professional duty of candour, demonstrates a sea-change in approach since the decision in *Powell*. Quick has suggested that '[i]t sends a strong signal to organisations and individuals about acceptable behaviour and is more likely to attract attention and affect behaviour than is the case in relation to existing guidelines and documents'.[48] But while, yes, it does send out signals and, in theory, provides a

36 Ibid., paras 18 and 19.
37 Ibid., para 20.
38 Ibid., para 20.
39 Ibid., para 21.
40 Ibid., para 22 onwards.
41 Ibid., para 22.
42 Ibid., para 23.
43 Ibid., para 26.|
44 Ibid., para 27.
45 Ibid., para 29.
46 Ibid., para 30.
47 A. Kleebauer 'Many health staff lack training to carry out duty of candour effectively', *Nursing Standard* 2014, 29(37):9.
48 Quick, 'Outing medical errors', p. 158.

good means of facilitating accountability in practice, the early experience of the duty of candour appears rather less a source of optimism. Hough has questioned how effective this has been. He noted that, according to the Public Accounts Select Committee in 2015, 12,000 avoidable deaths, 10,000 serious incidents and a total of 1.4 million 'incidents' were reported in the NHS with some 174,872 written complaints.[49] He commented that:

> These figures would suggest a huge number of letters of apology being sent out each week. That seems extraordinarily unlikely to have happened. I have yet to meet a client who has received such a letter.[50]

A report published in August 2016 by Action against Medical Accidents (AvMA) reviewing CQC inspections of 90 Trusts highlighted major concerns as to Trusts which were failing to address the duty of candour or who were superficial in the manner in which they had did so. The report noted that, even where implemented and reports had been made, there were no examples of any Trusts having provided a response as to how to improve.[51] It suggested that evidence indicated that not only was implementation inconsistent across England itself, but it was likely to be inconsistent across NHS bodies.[52] The report also highlighted the fact that the CQC was unaware of the number of specific reports detailing non-compliance which it had received from the public. This lack of CQC responsiveness is very concerning and raises questions of the appropriateness of extending the CQC role still further in relation to the National Guardian given existing problems in related areas. In September 2016, there were media reports of a case of a cancer patient who had undergone surgery on her kidneys due to a cancerous tumour.[53] During the procedure, blood supply was cut off from two arteries which was not part of the surgery. Her family were not told, nor was the coroner informed, that there was a surgical error at time of death or later until this was subsequently raised by the family's solicitor. Following the AvMA report, Robbie Powell's father, Will Powell, noted the problems with the existing legal position and stated that what is needed is a free-standing duty of candour going beyond the existing approach.[54]

While, as noted above, there is a professional duty in place in relation to the GMC and NMC, the scope, operation and effectiveness to date of this particular

49 C. Hough 'Patient power: the duty to explain post Montgomery and the statutory duty of candour', *Clinical Risk* 2016, 22(1–2):6.

50 Ibid.

51 H. Blythe, *Regulating the Duty of Candour. A report by Action against Medical Accidents on CQC inspection reports and regulation of the duty of candour*, AvMA 2016. www.avma.org.uk/?download_protected_attachment=Regulating-the-duty-of-candour.pdf (accessed 16 March 2018). For further discussion around concerns of use of a duty of candour see Y. Birks, 'Duty of candour and the disclosure of adverse events to patients and families', *Journal of Patient Safety and Risk Management* 2014, 20(1):19.

52 Ibid., p. 15.

53 M. Paduano, 'Family not told of cancer op error at Coventry hospital' (BBC News, 15 September 2016). www.bbc.co.uk/news/uk-england-coventry-warwickshire-37365233 (accessed 18 March 2018).

54 AvMA, 2016b.

duty of candour has also been questioned. As Oliver has noted, this is only guidance relating to nurses and doctors and it is the case that other professionals as well as NHS managers can play an important part in determining care conditions but are not necessarily the subject of registration or ethical codes.[55] A further point he makes about this guidance is that while the emphasis is on apology in relation to individual failings this is not in relation to apologies for systems failings or indeed the failure of other individuals. He also notes that, while the guidance states that it 'is not intended for circumstances where a patient's condition gets worse due to the natural progression of their illness', yet 'it is precisely these circumstances that often distress patients' families and can create the conditions for complaint.'[56] Moreover, as he comments, while an apology does not constitute an acceptance of liability, it remains questionable as to whether healthcare professionals will accept that this is, in fact, the case. He stresses that support must be given to professionals by the organisation. In addition, he notes 'for faults at the organisational or system level, the organisation or systems leaders should apologise including the health secretary himself'.[57]

It is clear that for the duty of candour, whether the statutory obligation or that which applies to doctors and nurses to work effectively, there needs to be much more effective engagement overall by NHS bodies. This links, generally, to the question of the need for an effective culture of transparency and openness where concerns can be raised.[58] Nonetheless, both statutory and professional duties of candour do at least provide one step down that road. Which is why the developments to be explored in the second part of this paper in relation to the introduction and operation of a 'Safe Space' in the NHS can be seen as so perplexing and potentially something which could critically undermine movements forward in relation to trust and transparency.

The safe space and the Health Service Safety Investigation Bill

The duty of candour and related developments in the area of raising concerns from the *Freedom to speak up* report work in favour of openness and transparency.[59] Longer term, they may facilitate dialogue between healthcare professionals and also with patients. But, alongside this trend, there is also the concern that where matters are investigated that these can be seen in an adversarial context with, of course, reputational and other consequential damage. The rise of litigation and consequent costs is also regarded as a major concern for the NHS. Thus, there were and remain tensions between the movement toward enhanced disclosure and what was perceived as being the best means of identifying harm.

55 D. Oliver, 'The hardest word: managers and leaders should say sorry too', *British Medical Journal online* 2015, 351.
56 Ibid.
57 Ibid.
58 See e.g. Mannion et al., Chapter 5 in this volume.
59 Francis, *Freedom to speak up*.

Concerns existed that the investigation, itself, might fuel litigation, rather than, ultimately, provide an effective means of addressing safety problems. Currently, NHS investigations were subject to a Senior Incidents Framework which sets out three levels of investigation: concise internal investigations; comprehensive internal investigations, which include those with an independent element; and independent investigation. In addition, there are other ways in which investigations can be undertaken, for example by healthcare regulatory bodies and by coroners.[60] Investigations in other serious cases can, of course, be undertaken by the police or may result in civil action or through a statutory inquiry under the Inquiries Act 2005.

Following the Public Accounts Select Committee report and the *Freedom to speak up* report, the Government, in its response 'Learning Not Blaming', accepted the recommendation of the need to establish a new independent safety investigations branch. This led to the establishment of an Expert Advisory Group in 2015 which published its advice in May 2016. The Department of Health decided to follow the approach of an independent investigatory body. It established the Health and Safety Investigations Branch.[61] On its face this can be seen as a good idea. A body which is perceived to be distanced from the NHS can facilitate accountability and public and professional trust in what can be an exceedingly fraught area. However, it is certain that aspects of the way in which this body is proposed to undertake its investigations are now coming under very critical scrutiny and are the subject of expressed concern and, as is suggested here, may prove a retrograde step.

In 2015 the Public Administration Select Committee, in its report 'Investigating Clinical Incidents in the NHS', took the approach that, if an investigation was undertaken by the new healthcare investigation body, then its body

> must offer a safe space; strong protections to patients, their families, clinicians and staff, so that they can talk freely about what has gone wrong without fear of punitive reprisals.[62]

Here, the model was that of the Air Accident Investigation Branch (AAIB).[63] There is a statutory framework and a 'safe space' approach which is operational. Critically here there is a duty placed upon the AAIB not to share information which has been obtained during an investigation unless such material has been

60 J. V. McHale and J. Laing (eds), *Principles of Medical Law* 4th edition, Oxford: Oxford University Press, 2017, paras 1.85–1.96, 1.125–1.131.

61 Established under directions given to it by the Secretary of State for Health under section 7 of the National Health Service Act 2006.

62 Public Administration Select Committee, *Investigating Clinical Incidents in the NHS*, 2015; see also in relation to the air accident model C. Macrae and C. Vincent. 'Learning from failure, the need for independent safety investigations in healthcare', *Journal of the Royal Society of Medicine* 2014, 107(11):439–43.

63 Department of Health *Providing a Safe Space in healthcare safety investigations*, London: Department of Health, 2016, 3.17.

requested by a High Court order or in relation to specific circumstances through an EU regulation in the context of criminal activity. This approach has proved attractive to the Department of Health. In March 2016, the Secretary of State for Health, Jeremy Hunt, stated that he intended to bring forward measures to implement a safe space approach and this was followed in October 2016 by the Department of Health Safe Space Consultation.[64] Jeremy Hunt noted that this approach was drawing upon work which had been done in the area of air accident investigation and this would allow the investigator to say to staff involved in the incidents:

> This investigation is not to attribute blame. The information you give me as part of the investigation will not be passed on to those not involved in the investigation unless there is a high court order or if the information you provide demonstrates to me there is an active and ongoing threat to patient safety represented by the practice or actions of one or more individuals that requires action.[65]

The key features of air accident investigation highlighted by the Department of Health are that there is clear articulation as to why the investigation is being undertaken and that this is not an issue for apportioning blame. Regulations provide that the Secretary of State for Transport, operating through the AAIB, is statutorily prohibited from disclosing certain classes of material save where there is a court order.[66] The Court, in disclosing, is to assess interests of justice as compared with adverse impact on investigations which are being currently undertaken or which will be undertaken in the future.[67] Superficially, this does indeed appear to be attractive. However, on closer examination, a number of major concerns become obvious.

In the Department of Health Consultation document on the safe space in 2016 the Department, itself, noted that there were challenges in relation to a safe space approach. Firstly, as it notes, there is the question of the inherent variation across the NHS.[68] This, in practice, is a huge challenge given the increasingly diverse forms of healthcare delivery and range of providers, including wholly NHS, or private sector providers operating under an NHS badge. A closed hospital unit is very different than a broader hospital or community setting. There are also, potentially, considerable practical problems in relation to the interface between private sector care provision under the NHS badge and standard NHS services. A full systems-type approach may be possible within a relatively discrete organisation. However, major potential problems can arise in a situation in which the private sector is involved in the delivery of care provision.

64 Ibid.

65 Department of Health, *Providing a Safe Space.*

66 Civil Aviation (Investigation of Air Accidents and Incidents) Regulations 1996, regulation 18.

67 Department of Health, *Providing a Safe Space*, para 5.9; the Civil Aviation (Investigation of Air Accidents and Incidents) Regulations 1996.

68 Department of Health, *Providing a Safe Space*, para 2.6.

To what extent can and should private sector providers be given the same immunity from disclosure as the rest of the NHS simply because they are operating as a contractor to the NHS process? It is submitted that this raises problematic questions of accountability, which are not addressed satisfactorily within the safe space consultation process.

The consultation document stressed that there was a strong connection between what it termed 'psychological safety' and a 'culture of learning within an organisation'.[69] It refers to research suggesting that teams work best under what are conditions of psychological safety.[70] The consultation notes that there is a not an effective culture to raise concerns and it makes reference to Sir Robert Francis' report on whistleblowing, *Freedom to speak up*.[71] A safe space is seen a means of facilitating a learning culture so that staff feel supported to raise concerns. The document identifies this, as a means of facilitating confidentiality, a safe space can 'complement and mutually reinforce a culture of learning'.[72] The consultation does, however, also note that this cannot be seen as independent from the obligation on senior staff to also facilitate such a culture. But, there are clear and possibly irreconcilable tensions between facilitating confidentiality and a learning culture. If something is fundamentally confidential then to disclose it broadly will necessarily adversely impact on professional reputations in any event. But, if it is a matter where there needs to be shared learning, then how can this be seen as truly something which will need to be maintained as confidential?

Linked to this the consultation noted the need, expressed in previous documents, for a culture of learning, and the danger of cover-ups and people not being blamed for genuine mistakes.[73] The adverse impact of investigations on staff was also highlighted and how this also can lead in effect to health professionals becoming less compassionate in their practice.[74] In addition it was said that families felt cut out of investigations and they were strongly of the view that the Healthcare Safety Investigations Branch (HSIB) should be independent. These clearly are very valid concerns. But they do not, by themselves, translate out from an independent body to, then, necessarily say that you should move towards what effectively operates as a closed investigation model. In fact, the very opposite could be said. The fact that light and fresh air is not shining in on investigations can lead to the risk that mould can develop and the very process itself can, ultimately, fundamentally undermine what is intended to be addressed. Rather than trust and accountability, there is a risk of this being seen as a 'secret court' where decisions are made behind closed doors and where families ultimately feel fettered in attempting not simply to establish the truth of what went wrong in their particular case, but also contribute to shared knowledge as to how this could broadly impact over the longer term.

69 Department of Health, *Providing a Safe Space*, para 3.8.
70 See e.g. A. Edmondson, 'Psychological safety and learning behaviour in work teams', *Administrative Science Quarterly* 1999, 44(2):350–83.
71 Francis, *Freedom to speak up*.
72 Department of Health, *Providing a Safe Space*, para 3.15.
73 Ibid., para 3.23.
74 Ibid., para 3.24

A further major problem with this initiative is as to what information may be disclosed even if a safe space process is in operation. As noted above, there is already a range of legal investigatory processes. The Directions of the HSIB state that the Chief Investigator should inform bodies including the health service regulator and professional regulatory bodies if it becomes aware of 'evidence of a serious, continuing risk to patient safety', then goes on to state that s/he 'subject to this sub-paragraph must not volunteer to take further part in the actions that such a body or bodies may subsequently take'.[75] It, then, provides that they:

> must seek to agree with professional regulatory bodies and other investigatory bodies which have statutory powers to require information, suitable protocols respecting the safe space principle in relation to the exercise of those statutory powers.
>
> must seek to agree with those bodies with which the Authority has a mutual duty of co-operate under section 290 of the Health and Social Care Act 2012 suitable protocols respecting the safe space principle which are to apply as between the Authority and those other bodies in discharging that duty.[76]

The HSIB are to produce protocols in relation to this which it is envisaged will feed into primary legislation.[77] This clearly raises major challenges. Yes, issues need to be raised but, then, precisely what concerns will be subject to a confidential safe space investigation and which will not be? How will this effectively operate to ensure transparency? There are, surely, very real concerns here as to exactly what will fall between the gaps.

In their response to the Safe Consultation, the Department of Health noted the concerns, but they have nonetheless decided to press ahead. The HSIB is due to undertake investigations involving the safe space principles in accordance with the NHS Trust Development body and is now to be established on a full statutory basis.

In September 2017, the UK government introduced the draft Health Services Safety Investigations Bill. The HSIB would be re-established as an independent organisation, the Health Services Safety Investigations Branch (HSSIB), under the Bill.[78] It would have the task of investigating 'qualifying incidents'. This would apply where these took place either during the provision of NHS services[79] or 'at premises where those services were provided'. The role of the HSSIB is 'exercisable for the purpose of addressing risks to the safety of patients by facilitating the improvement of systems and practices in the provisions of NHS

75 The National Health Service Trust Development Authority (Healthcare Safety Investigation Branch) Directions 2016, para 6(4)(c).

76 The National Health Service Trust Development Authority (Healthcare Safety Investigation Branch) Directions 2016, para 6(4)(d).

77 Department of Health, *Providing a Safe Space*, 4.36.

78 S. 1.

79 S. 2(1).

services'.[80] Critically, however, the Bill separates investigation from other broader liability questions. So, section 2(3) provides that:

> the functions conferred by subsection (1) is not exercisable for the purpose of the HSSIB assessing or determining
>
> (a) blame
> (b) civil or criminal liability or
> (c) whether action needs to be taken in respect of an individual by any panel, committee or tribunal of a regulatory body.

Nonetheless, it does provide that the HSSIB will be able to disclose certain relevant information or publish reports and send drafts of these reports to a range of statutory regulatory bodies such as the GMC, NMC and Health and Care Professions Council.[81] It will be required to publish criteria used for determining what is investigated, and what principles and processes are used to determine and undertake investigations.[82] The Bill states that processes must include patients and their families 'if and so far as reasonable and practicable'.[83] On the face of it, this seems a good provision – facilitating patient involvement – but here the devil will be in the detail as to what does in practice constitute 'reasonable' and 'practical'. There is an obligation placed on the HSSIB to consult the Secretary of State and also 'any other persons the HSSIB considers appropriate'[84] when drawing up such criteria. The HSSIB is to publish documents which will state how the investigative processes will operate in practice[85] and, importantly, s. 3(9) states that:

> A document published under subsection (8) must be in such terms that it is capable of being easily understood by the persons mentioned in subsection 1(d)(v) and the HSSIB must ensure that the document is easily accessible to such persons.

In addition, an obligation is placed on the HSSIB to publish a list of investigations in terms of where they are being conducted, where discontinued and where completed.[86] Interestingly, the HSSIB is to be required to consider representations from the Secretary of State and from other persons they consider appropriate as to whether or not to investigate.[87] This, surely, raises some question marks over the independence of the body itself from the NHS, and how this provision is interpreted in practice should be subject to close scrutiny.

80 Ibid.
81 S. 2(5).
82 S. 3(1)(2).
83 S. 3(3).
84 S. 3(6).
85 S. 3(8).
86 S. 3(10).
87 S. 4.

Specific powers are given to the HSSIB in relation to the conduct of investigations including powers to enter premises and undertake inspections.[88] In situations in which there is opposition from the organisation being investigated, then a notice can be given to the body/persons saying why action needs to be taken and when and the Chief Investigator is given power to apply to the Justices of the Peace for a warrant to authorise the taking of actions.[89] Powers are also given to the investigator to require provision of such things as information, equipment and documents.[90] Bodies from whom information can be obtained include NHS Foundation Trusts, Special Health Authorities, the CQC, the Health Research Authority, and the National Institute for Health and Care Excellence.[91] Provisions are included for penalty notices to be issued in relation to non-compliance with notices issued by the HSSIB.[92] The HSSIB will have the role of giving assistance in relation to dissemination of information in relation to best practice, developing standards and giving advice in relation to guidance and training.[93] NHS Trusts will also be able to apply to be accredited to undertake investigations and this will be subject to review by the HSSIB.[94] The statutory prohibitions on disclosure which are set out in section 28 of the draft Bill, apply to the HSSIB and accredited Trusts. Section 28(2) provides that the 'HSSIB or the accredited Trust must not disclose to any person any information, document, equipment or other item which is held by it in relation to the investigation'.

Section 28(3) goes on to state that this does not, however, apply to information which is in the public domain. There are, however, also a series of exemptions to the prohibition set out under section 29. These include where that information is potentially evidence of an offence, information can be disclosed to the police.[95] It can also be disclosed where it can provide evidence of continuing risk to patient safety or the HSSIB/Trust considers it serious.[96] There are also powers to disclose to a range of bodies including NHS Foundation Trusts, NHS Commissioning Board, Special health authorities providing oversight over NHS Trusts, the Care Quality Commissioner, Monitor, the Health and Safety Executive and the Secretary of State.[97] Information can also be disclosed to NHS Foundation Trusts, the NHS Clinical Commissioning Board or Clinical Commissioning Groups where this may provide evidence of the commission of an offence; continuing risk to patient safety, which is considered serious; or in relation to misconduct by any individual providing NHS services.[98] In addition if the accredited NHS Trust is undertaking an

88 S. 5.
89 S. 6(4)
90 S. 7.
91 S. 7(12).
92 S. 9.
93 S. 16.
94 S. 20–26.
95 S. 29(3).
96 S. 29(4).
97 S. 29(5).
98 S. 29(9).

investigation, the HSSIB has broad powers to require it to disclose information to the HSSIB.[99] So it is clear that safe space is not intended to inhibit police investigations, NHS investigations nor, indeed, unduly, regulatory investigations. However, in relation to patients and their relatives, access is to be restricted save where an application is made to the High Court for disclosure of that information under section 30. Therein lies the rub. The real emphasis appears less on a closed safe space environment – as a massive amount of information potentially could be disclosed through the exceptions set out in section 29. In addition, access to information which could be used directly by patients and their relatives, e.g. for litigation purposes, appears to be what is targeted. This raises questions about whether what is at stake here is as much about deterring litigation concerning the NHS as that of encouraging dialogue.

As noted above, the draft Bill raises a whole series of important questions in relation to NHS accountability and access to patient information. Yes, there are clear advantages in terms of team learning and benefit both to individual healthcare professionals and to practice itself. However, this could work in favour of preserving substandard practice unless it was linked expressly to other sanctions being utilised against the healthcare professionals where harm was caused – the very thing, though, that the safe space process itself will work against. An independent agency, itself, is, however, something to be welcomed, but, as noted above, the impact of section 4 and the need to consider representations (e.g. from the Secretary of State) as to whether the body should investigate at all is somewhat concerning. The real issue here is likely to be the scope of the exceptions under section 29 and how, ultimately, the HSSIB and the investigating Trust interpret them, along with applications under section 30 to the High Court and how these are, also, interpreted.

Conclusions and the future

This paper has explored two initiatives which have recently been taken forward in the NHS. On the one hand, the duty of candour. The whole concept is one of being frank and open with patients, the notion of patients and their relatives being treated with respect, and also ensuring ultimately transparency and accountability of the organisation. On the other hand is the idea of safe space. Here, the idea is that transparency has its limits, that by making certain aspects of the process less transparent through the control over the subsequent use of information you may be better able to make individuals come forward and ultimately speak up and raise concerns. Candour and safe space are, as we have seen, very uncomfortable bedfellows.

As noted above, early evidence indicates that the operation of the statutory and professional duties of candour itself is somewhat problematic. What will be important here is consequent education and training of healthcare professionals on an ongoing basis. There will clearly also need to be cultural acceptance and also organisational and professional support in the future to enable such disclosure

99 S. 29(10).

to be made. Much remains to be achieved. In relation to safe space, this seems rooted in a problematic assumption. Air accidents and NHS incidents are two very different factual scenarios and, while comparators may indeed be useful, transplanting concepts across such diverse areas should be approached with extreme caution.[100] The notion of an independent HSSIB, by itself, is a praiseworthy one and, indeed, its creation – save for aspects such as safe space and the ongoing role of the Secretary of State for Health etc. – is one to be welcomed. The critical thing is to ensure it is able to maintain independence in the future. Moreover, boundaries between its work and those of other regulatory bodies will require very careful monitoring to ensure that matters do not fall between the cracks. There are quite major powers given to the HSSIB and investigating Trusts to disclose information under section 29. It is far less of a closed investigative process than appears at first sight and could potentially allow quite a lot of information obtained in this way to be utilised in the NHS. Of course, it can be said that a lot of this is inevitable. If there is information giving rise to major concerns in relation to patient safety and this was not fed back and not acted upon, this could adversely impact on patient health and the effective operation of the NHS and, of course, itself lead to litigation in the future. But for NHS 'outsiders' (patients and their families), it appears that this process will become more difficult and, consequently, far more expensive, with applications needed to the High Court. This is a regrettable move and one which ultimately will work against trust and transparency.

Moreover, there is the question as to whether, while there are concerns to reduce litigation costs involving the NHS, that the introduction of safe space might actually increase them if it leads to disputes with patients and their families as to how information can and should be used, with consequent multiple applications to the courts in relation to specific cases. Fundamentally, what the safe space concept challenges is a commitment to open justice and accountability in health service investigations – a commitment which, itself, is surely inherent in the whole notion of a duty of candour. Candour and safe space do seem truly irreconcilable. It appears that, while with the statutory and professional duties of candour, we may have gone a few steps forward to assist in breaking down barriers and opening up healthcare and adverse incidents to scrutiny, the safe space concept is dragging us several paces back.

Funding Acknowledgement

Part of this research was funded by the National Institute for Health Research (NIHR) Health Services and Delivery (HSDR) programme. The views and opinions expressed therein are those of the author and do not necessarily reflect those of the HSDR programme.

100 P. Walsh '"Safe space" proposals could alter relationships between patients and the NHS – for the worse', *HSJ*, 5 December 2016.

'Grant number 14/04; project title "Understanding employee whistleblowing in health care"; applicants Russell Mannion, Ross Millar, Huw Davies, Jean McHale, John Blenkinsopp and Martin Powell.'

References

Birks, B., 'Duty of candour and the disclosure of adverse events to patients and families', *Journal of Patient Safety and Risk Management* 2014, 20(1):19.

Blythe, B., *Regulating the duty of candour: a report by Action against Medical Accidents on CQC inspection reports and regulation of the duty of candour*, (AvMA2016). www.avma.org.uk/?download_protected_attachment=Regulating-the-duty-of-candour.pdf (accessed 16 March 2018).

Chief Medical Officer, *Making amends. A consultation paper setting out proposals for reforming the approach to clinical negligence in the NHS*, London: Department of Health, 2003.

Department of Health, *Providing a safe space in healthcare safety investigations*, London: Department of Health, 2016.

Edmondson, A., 'Psychological safety and learning behaviour in work teams', *Administrative Science Quarterly* 1999, 44(2):350–83.

Farrell, A. M. and Devaney, S., 'Making amends or making things worse?' *Legal Studies* 2007, 27(4):630.

Francis, Sir Robert QC, |*Freedom to speak up. An independent review into creating an open and honest reporting culture in the NHS*, 2015. www.gov.uk/government/publications/sir-robert-francis-freedom-to-speak-up-review (accessed 16 March 2018).

General Medical Council/Nursing and Midwifery Council, *Openness and honesty when things go wrong: the professional duty of candour*. London: GMC/NMC, 2015.

Ham, C., Dingwall, R., Fenn, P. and Harris, D., *Medical negligence, compensation and accountability*, London: Kings Fund Institute, 1988.

Hough, C., 'Patient power: the duty to explain post Montgomery and the statutory duty of candour', *Clinical Risk* 2016, 22(1–2):6.

Hoyte, P., 'Unsound practice: the epidemiology of medical negligence', *Medical Law Review* 1995, 3:53.

Kennedy, I. and Grubb, A. (eds), *Principles of medical law*, 1st edition, Oxford: Oxford University Press.

Kleebauer, A., 'Many health staff lack training to carry out duty of candour effectively', *Nursing Standard* 2014, 29(37):9.

Macrae, C. and Vincent, C., 'Learning from failure, the need for independent safety investigations in healthcare', *Journal of the Royal Society of Medicine* 2014, 107(11):439–43.

McHale, J. V. and Laing, J. (eds), *Principles of medical law* 4th edition, Oxford: Oxford University Press, 2017.

Merry, A. and McCall-Smith, A., *Errors, medicine and the law*, Cambridge, UK: Cambridge University Press, 2001.

National Health Service (CQC) Regulations SI 2009, No 3112, regs 13 and 19.

Newdick, C. and Danbury, C., 'Culture, compassion and clinical neglect: probity in the NHS after Mid Staffordshire', *J Med Ethics* 2013.

Oliver, D., 'The hardest word: managers and leaders should say sorry too', *British Medical Journal online* 2015, 351.

Paduano, M., 'Family not told of cancer op error at Coventry hospital', BBC News, 15 September 2016. www.bbc.co.uk/news/uk-england-coventry-warwickshire-37365233 (accessed 18 March 2018).

Powell, W., 'Robbie's Law: lack of candour. The impact on patients and their families', *Journal of Patient Safety and Risk Management* 2014, 20(1):4.

Quick, O., 'Disaster at Bristol: Explanations and Implications of a Tragedy', *Journal of Social Welfare and Family Law* 1999, 21:307.

Quick, O., 'Outing Medical Errors: Questions of Trust and Responsibility', *Medical Law Review* 2006, 14(1):22.

Quick, O., *Regulating patient safety: the end of professional dominance?* Cambridge, UK: Cambridge University Press, 2017.

Quick, O., 'Regulating and legislating safety: the case for candour', *BMJ Quality & Safety* 2014, 23:614–18.

Report of the Public Inquiry into children's heart surgery at the Bristol Royal Infirmary 1984–1995, *Learning from Bristol* Cmnd 52071, 2001.

Ritchie, J. and Davies, S., 'Professional negligence: a duty of candid disclosure?', *BMJ* 1995, 310:888–9.

Rosenthal, M. M., Mulcahy, L. and Lloyd-Bostock, S. (eds), *Medical mishaps: pieces of the puzzle*, Buckingham, UK: Open University Press, 1999.

Sharpe, V. A. and Faden, A. I., *Medical harm: historical, conceptual and ethical dimensions of iatrogenic illness*, Cambridge, UK: Cambridge University Press, 1998.

Tingle, J. and Bark, P. (eds), *Patient safety, law policy and practice*, Abingdon, UK: Routledge, 2011.

Vincent, C., et al., *Medical accidents*, Oxford: Oxford University Press 1993.

Walsh, P., '"Safe space" proposals could alter relationships between patients and the NHS – for the worse', *HSJ*, 5 December, 2016.

7 Religious and cultural beliefs

The potential for patient safety to be compromised

Clayton Ó Néill

Introduction

Patient safety is the backbone to good healthcare provision. The World Health Organisation (WHO) describes patient safety as:

> . . . the prevention of errors and adverse effects to patients associated with health care. While health care has become more effective it has also become more complex, with greater use of new technologies, medicines and treatments. Health services treat older and sicker patients who often present with significant co-morbidities requiring more and more difficult decisions as to health care priorities. Increasing economic pressure on health systems often leads to overloaded health care environments.[1]

Patient safety is, thus, associated with stopping errors and preventing negative effects to patients. It is important to recognise that keeping patients safe involves lots of jigsaw pieces such as the actions of the doctors, the hospital protocols and guidance from regulatory bodies. Patient safety is compromised by equipment shortage,[2] escalating number of patients who have to be treated, disruptive patients, building issues, fatigue, medication errors, documentation errors, diagnostic errors, difficulties with discharge practice, workplace safety, sepsis, superbugs and cyber insecurity.[3] All doctors have a duty to act when they believe patients' safety is at risk, or that patients' care or dignity are being compromised.[4]

1 WHO, 'Patient Safety'. www.euro.who.int/en/health-topics/Health-systems/patient-safety/patient-safety (accessed 30 October 2017).

2 Steve Ford, 'Nurses warn patient safety is being compromised by equipment shortages', *Nursing Times*, 6 April 2010. www.nursingtimes.net/nurses-warn-patient-safety-is-being-compromised-by-equipment-shortages/5013217.article (accessed 27 October 2017).

3 'Top 10 safety issues for 2016', *Becker's Infection Control and Clinical Quality*, 12 January, 2016. www.beckershospitalreview.com/quality/10-top-patient-safety-issues-for-2016.html (accessed 27 October 2017).

4 GMC, *Raising and acting on concerns about patient safety* (GMC, 2012) sets out our expectation that all doctors will, whatever their role, take appropriate action to raise and act on concerns about patient care, dignity and safety. www.gmc-uk.org/Raising_and_acting_on_concerns_about_patient_safety___English_0617.pdf_48902813.pdf (accessed 27 November 2017).

This chapter questions whether and to what degree the expression of religious or cultural beliefs of patients can act as a threat to patient safety. The focus will be primarily on the United Kingdom (UK), but some references will be made to other jurisdictions.

We live in a new era, an era where patients feel that they have a sense of entitlement, an era where governmental bodies are under a duty to safeguard human rights, but also an era characterised by the ever-growing compensation culture. Cases are being taken under the tort of negligence every day, costing the National Health Service (NHS) billions. There is limited evidence, however, of cases based upon the religious or cultural beliefs of patients being brought in tort. Instead, these issues have mostly raised human rights concerns and action has been taken under the Human Rights Act 1998. The courts have been reluctant to use the language of patient safety. Instead, they have focused on human rights arguments and notions such as capacity and consent, *inter alia*. However, it is important to recognise the relevance of duty of care/breach of duty in the tort of negligence as well as the concept of informed consent following the recent Supreme Court case of *Montgomery v Lanarkshire Health Board*.[5] Obviously, there are consequences for hospital personnel in terms of patient safety. If they don't act in accordance with the autonomy of capacitated patients, there could be tortious or regulatory implications. Healthcare professionals have a responsibility to ensure patient safety, but, yet, allow for the autonomy of decision making. A conflict can exist between these two variables.

A lot of the literature comes from the perspectives of the systems that are put in place at a medical level by medical personnel, policy makers and technology experts, aimed at reducing human or technological error and subsequent harm to patients. There has, however, been little attention given to the role of patients themselves in contributing to the safety of their healthcare provision. Patients have a role to play within patient safety: they need to follow the regime of medication properly, they need to alert medical professionals to complications, they must reflect upon the decisions that they make and the consequences of those decisions, wise or unwise as they may be. Vincent and Coulter argue that most of the main reports dealing with patient safety pay insignificant attention to how patients contribute to their own safety, whether as individuals or collectively.[6] They argue that patients are often looked upon in a passive manner, as victims of mistakes. They recognise that an additional burden of responsibility ought not to be placed on patients who are particularly vulnerable. They state that '[w]hen patients are seriously ill it may be even more important to take their views and wishes into account, either by involving them directly or by using family members as surrogate decision makers'.[7] They identify a range of instances where patients can contribute to their own safety through 'provision of diagnostic information, participation in treatment

5 [2015] UKSC 11.

6 C. A. Vincent and A. Coulter, 'Patient safety: what about the patient?', *Qual Saf Health Care* 2002, 11:76–80.

7 Ibid.

decisions, choice of provider, the management and treatment of disease, and the monitoring of adverse events'.[8] For this to be successful, a culture needs to develop in which patients are supported in taking extra responsibility for their own care and safety. Additionally, in a subsequent article, they identify areas where patient input into their safety is productive.[9] Obviously, patient safety can be reduced by many worthwhile endeavours, such as double-checking and error procedures. Nevertheless, the human factor is an essential element in tackling cultural changes in order to enhance patient safety. This chapter argues that by further raising awareness of religious/cultural beliefs as an ingredient, this could improve and impact upon patient safety. Lee and Newberg explain that evidence exists whereby religion can have a positive influence on health. For example, religion can positively affect how patients cope with medical issues and can have a constructive impact upon lifestyle and disease morbidity.[10] The chapter will consider the relationship between the manifestation of religious or cultural beliefs and patient safety in the context of a number of different scenarios that potentially impact upon that safety, namely, ritual male circumcision, female genital mutilation (FGM) and the refusal of blood transfusions for religious reasons.

When we think of patient safety, we can visualise the Swiss cheese model of accident causation.[11] According to this model, the healthcare safety protocols can consist of many slices of cheese, which contain risks to patient safety. In every slice of cheese, different layers of defences against these risks are set out one behind each other. This means that a weakness in one defence should not allow for the development of any related risk because all of the other defences will come into play, so that one single point of weakness would not exist. These barriers act as defences against failure in medical procedures. The slices of cheese are, however, full of holes: some are large and some are small and they are situated in different parts of the cheese slices. These holes represent the weaknesses in the healthcare safety protocols and practices within the medical system. When the holes become aligned in such a way that a hazard can pass through the continuum of holes, then a failure or an error in the health system can occur, which can compromise patient safety. We can think of the expression of religious or cultural belief as being a variable which may or may not be represented as a hole in the cheese slice. How can we ensure that the expression of religious/cultural belief on the part of the patient does not lead to or become a factor in error in healthcare? In other words, the existence of holes in the cheese slices can add to the flavour and texture of the cheese – variety is a spice of life – so too, the entitlement to act in accordance with religious/cultural beliefs, even when such actions compromise individual safety, is a positive component of holistic healthcare provision, but should not become a determining factor in the causation of errors.

8 Ibid.

9 For example, reminding staff to wash their hands.

10 B. Y. Lee and A. B. Newberg, 'Religion and health: a review and critical analysis', *Zygon* 2005, 40:443–68.

11 James Reason, *Human Error*, CUP, 1990. Also see: Department of Health, *Report of an expert group on learning from adverse events in the NHS chaired by the Chief Medical Officer*, Department of Health, 2000, pp. 22–3.

One way of mitigating such errors is the provision of comprehensive guidelines that provide guidance to healthcare professionals as to how to deal with the manifestation of religious or cultural beliefs in healthcare decision making.

Guidelines on religious/cultural beliefs, patient safety and healthcare

In order to have a better understanding of the relationship between patient safety and the right to express one's religious or cultural beliefs, it is necessary to consider the relevant guidelines and protocols. The right of patients to manifest their beliefs in medical contexts is protected by medical guidelines. Broadly speaking, the General Medical Council (GMC) state that the beliefs of patients may cause them to 'ask for a procedure for mainly religious, cultural or social reasons' and subsequently refuse treatment that the doctor might regard as being beneficial.[12] Additionally, the NHS has produced guidelines for staff to better understand the needs of patients with particular religious or cultural beliefs. Firstly, the NHS recognises the legal requirements in the context of laws concerning discrimination, harassment and victimisation, as governed under the Equality Act 2010, as well as the role of Article 9 of the European Convention on Human Rights: freedom of thought, conscience and religion. The NHS validates the growing diverse mix of religious beliefs in the UK. This is set out in their report, entitled *Religion or belief. A practical guide for the NHS.*[13] In the context of palliative care, the NHS report states that healthcare professionals should be 'aware that an individual's level of compliance with their religious belief may well vary according to their perception of their illness, and that relatives and/or next of kin may have differing views on religion, practice and observance'.[14] The report states that there is a need to raise awareness of religious stereotyping and that staff should be aware of different beliefs and practices of individuals.

Therefore, in the context of the guidelines under which medical professionals work, there is cognisance taken of patients' religious and/or cultural beliefs. Notwithstanding the existence of guidelines that support this, there are, however, instances where the manifestation of religious belief might be perceived to impact negatively upon patient safety. One such instance is ritual male circumcision and attention is now drawn to that area.

Ritual male circumcision

Traditionally Jewish and Muslim parents wish for their children to be circumcised. However, the NHS does not routinely offer circumcision for non-medical

12 GMC, *Personal beliefs and medical practice*, 2013, para 9. www.gmc-uk.org/guidance/ethical_guidance/21177.asp (accessed 14 October 2017).

13 NHS, *Religion or belief. A practical guide for the NHS*, Department of Health, 2009/ www.clatterbridgecc.nhs.uk/application/files/7214/3445/0178/ReligionorbeliefApracticalguidefortheNHS.pdf (accessed 14 October 2017).

14 Ibid., p. 10.

reasons.[15] What is the response of the GMC to ritual male circumcision? In *Personal beliefs and medical practice*, they say that if a patient or parent wants (or wants their child) to be circumcised for religious or cultural reasons, the doctor should:

> discuss with them the benefits, risks and side effects of the procedure. You should usually provide procedures that patients request and that you assess to be of overall benefit to the patient. If the patient is a child, you should usually provide a procedure or treatment that you assess to be in their best interests. In all circumstances, you will also need the patient's or parental consent.[16]

Additionally, at paragraph 20, the GMC recognises the relevance of the *best interests* test, whereby assessing best interests also involves an assessment of the child's and/or his parent's religious or cultural beliefs. The guidelines state that doctors should get consent from the child if they have 'maturity and understanding to give it'. If this is not possible, parental consent should be granted. If, however, consent is not granted, as a result, for example, of a parental dispute, the doctor should state that he/she cannot undertake the circumcision unless authorised by the court.[17] (Note that, to date, in such circumstances, the courts have always stated that circumcision is against the child's best interests and that they should wait until the child is *Gillick* competent[18] before allowing for the circumcision).[19]

In the United States (US), circumcision is extremely common and, overall, it is regarded by many doctors as being 'relatively safe with a low overall complication rate'.[20] Most of the complications associated with circumcision are 'minor and can be managed easily'. However, Krill et al. point out that, even though it is quite uncommon, 'complications of circumcision do represent a significant percentage of cases seen by pediatric urologists' and these often result in surgical correction that is extremely costly to the US healthcare system.[21] They state that severe complications are relatively rare, but that, on occasion, it has resulted in death. They call for a 'thorough and complete preoperative evaluation, focusing on bleeding history and birth history' and argue that '[p]roper selection of patients based on age and anatomic considerations as well as proper sterile surgical technique are critical to prevent future circumcision-related adverse events'.[22]

15 Ibid., p. 28.
16 GMC, *Personal beliefs and medical practice*, para 18.
17 Ibid., para 20.
18 *Gillick v West Norfolk and Wisbech AHA* [1986] AC 112. *Gillick* competence is where a child under 16 can provide consent if he or she has 'sufficient understand and intelligence to enable him or her to understand fully what is proposed'. See p 189 of the judgment. Note that the courts may override the wishes of a *Gillick* competent child or his/her parents, if the courts feel that it is not in the child's best interests: *Re W* [1993] Fam 64.
19 E.g. *Re J* [2000] 1 FLR 571.
20 A. J. Krill et al, 'Complications of Circumcision', *Scientific World Journal* 2011, 11:2458–68.
21 Ibid.
22 Ibid.

Perera et al., in a US context, state that complications are uncommon.[23] They argued that:

> Strong evidence suggests circumcision can prevent human immunodeficiency virus/acquired immune deficiency syndrome acquisition in sub-Saharan African men. These findings remain uncertain in men residing in other countries. The role of adult nontherapeutic male circumcision in preventing sexually transmitted infections, urinary tract infections, and penile cancer remains unclear. Current evidence fails to recommend widespread neonatal circumcision for these purposes.[24]

The NHS, in their report, entitled *Religion or Belief. A practical guide for the NHS* drew attention to what they call a best practice model where, following concern about serious genital harm to boys as a result of unregistered practice, local parents were encouraged to send their babies to a clinic in Tower Hamlets, London.[25] The original unregistered practice involved the circumcision of boys aged about seven. This model attempted to provide regulation of an unregulated practice and, so, optimise patient safety. In theory, this is a practical and laudable step. In practice, parents signalled their satisfaction with it and recommended it to others. However, at an ethical level, there are some concerns because the circumcision is carried out on a voiceless and vulnerable infant. Those who were involved in this small study indicated that they thought that it was best to circumcise the child at an early stage in order to reduce pain and enhance safety.[26] It is difficult, however, to agree with the NHS that this well-intentioned action is best practice. While the physical safety of the infant may be less threatened due to the earlier circumcision, this practice is still injurious and any injury that is harmful compromises patient safety and should not be promoted by the NHS, particularly due to the lack of patient consent.

The NHS also gives an additional example of what they deem to be good practice, namely the development of a private male circumcision service in Bristol to cater for the growing Muslim community.[27] The NHS report states that, due to the lack of affordable safe circumcision services, families paid unregulated practitioners to carry out the circumcision. The report recognises that, to date, several cases have existed where the circumcision has resulted in genital damage.[28] Interestingly, in Bristol, feedback indicated that the Muslim community felt confused about the lack of safe circumcision services and this mistrust had a negative impact on how they responded to health improvement

23 C. L. Perera et al., 'Safety and efficacy of nontherapeutic male circumcision: a systematic review', *Ann Fam Med* 2010, 8(1):64–72.

24 Ibid., p. 64.

25 NHS, *Religion or belief*, p. 28.

26 Ibid. See Joan Cameron and Karen Rawlings Anderson, '"Circumcision", culture and health-care provision in Tower Hamlets, London', *Gender and Development* 1998, 3(1):48–54.

27 NHS, *Religion or belief*, p. 29.

28 Ibid.

programmes and health-enhancing initiatives.[29] Responding to this consultation, the Trust, in conjunction with the Department of Health's Pacesetters programme, worked with the Islamic community in order to 'develop an affordable, safe, private male circumcision service for parents who wish to have their child circumcised for social, cultural or religious reasons'.[30] Once again, however, it is questionable if the NHS should concern itself with medical procedures that bring harm to the child.

If we revert to the Swiss cheese model, we can now see a number of holes pertaining to the expression of cultural or religious beliefs and patient safety. Here is the circumcision of an infant who has not given informed consent, who has not the capacity to give this consent, who has not formed his own religious convictions that add to his sense of self-identity and self-definition. A procedure takes place that is irreversible and that can have, albeit in very limited instances, detrimental physical consequences. There is potential here for the alignment of these accident causative variables where lack of informed consent, lack of capacity, lack of maturity all have the potential to lead to a trajectory of potential tort. What is to stop the grown baby suing the hospital or the doctor for carrying out a procedure to which he did not consent and that resulted in harm to him? Some would argue that the harm that is created is negligible and that the importance of circumcision as a tribal marker to some religions, particularly Judaism, is stronger than concern for patient safety. The practice in Islam of waiting until the child is almost a teenager offers an improved pathway, in so far as this older child could be capable of consenting, thus providing the grounds for a more equitable paper trail. Some parents consider that that it is within the best interests of the child to be circumcised in accordance with parental wishes, in line with the traditional religious practices to which the parents are affiliated. However, a greater argument exists that circumcision causes physical harm and so comes under the mantle of patient safety. Circumcising a baby is an infringement of their bodily integrity and doctors should be discouraged from carrying out this procedure until the child is capable of consent. As it stands, this practice is allowable. However, when contention around ritual male circumcision has been taken to the courts, the decision has always been made that the carrying out of this procedure is not in the best interests of the baby/boy.[31] If the courts determine, following legal contention, that circumcision is not within the best interests of this child until they are *Gillick* competent, it is difficult to argue that it can be justifiable under normal daily practice.

Female genital mutilation

A more invidious compromising of patient safety exists in the form of female genital mutilation (FGM) and international compelling arguments have been made for its total banning, due to the significant harm that is meted out to a

29 Ibid.

30 Ibid.

31 E.g. *Re J* [200] 1 FLR 571.

young girl. It is estimated that across thirty countries, over 200 million women or girls have been subject to FGM. The most prevalent countries include Indonesia, Egypt and Ethiopia. Additionally, approximately 44 million of those who survive are under the age of 15. The practice is forbidden in 42 countries, including 24 African countries. In countries such as Sierra Leone, 90 % of women aged 15–49 have been subjected to FGM. It is estimated that the number of girls subjected to FGM in the US has tripled since 1990. The first prosecution took place in the US in 2017, despite legislation being enacted for 20 years. However, only 25 US states include laws that regard FGM as a crime.[32] Jones et al. state that uncertainty exists as to why FGM is still so persistent and there is recognition that the strategies to combat it have been, in many ways, ineffective. They say that even though FGM has been strongly condemned internationally, it can only be eliminated if 'practitioners are presented with a safe alternative that preserves their culture and, at the same time, protects the health and well being of women'.[33] They further argue that:

> . . . interventions for preventing FGM should be non-directive, culture-specific and multi-faceted to be of practical relevance. Such interventions should not only motivate change, but should also help communities to establish practical means by which that change can occur. Potentially effective prevention interventions targeted at local practitioners of FGM, parents, at-risk adolescents, health and social workers, governments, religious authorities, the civil society, and communities are presented.

This practice is disallowed in English law under the Female Genital Mutilation Act 2003. The NHS endorses the WHO's condemnation of FGM and recognises that where 'cases of FGM are presented, they should be treated as a child protection matter'.[34] However, a subterranean cultural practice exists where FGM is prevalent and increasing within some communities in the UK.[35] It is having a calamitous effect on patient safety,[36] but, notwithstanding the shared knowledge in the medical and social community that this practice exists and is being carried out, there are almost no prosecutions of FGM practitioners brought to the

32 Michelle Krupa, 'The alarming rise of female genital mutilation in America', CNN, 14 July, 2017. http://edition.cnn.com/2017/05/11/health/female-genital-mutilation-fgm-explainer-trnd/index.html (accessed 27 October 2017).

33 S. D. Jones et al., 'Female genital mutilation in developing countries: an agenda for public health response', *Eur J Obstet Gynecol Reprod Biol* 2014, 116(2):144–51.

34 NHS, *Religion or Belief*, p. 29.

35 Foundation for Women's Health, Research and Development (FORWARD), *Female genital mutilation: frequently asked questions: a campaigner's guide for young people*, (2012). Available at: www.gov.uk/government/uploads/system/uploads/attachment_data/file/332732/FGMfaq FORWARD.pdf (accessed 20 October 2017).

36 The effects of FGM include serious pain, shock, infections, problems associated with urination, menstrual problems, implications on sexual health, as well as psychological consequences. Note that different forms of FGM exist, ranging in severity. See WHO, 'Health risks of female genital mutilation'. www.who.int/reproductivehealth/topics/fgm/health_consequences_fgm/en/ (accessed 31 October 2017).

courts. It appears that sometimes those concerned with fostering group community relations are reluctant to engage with the cultural mores associated with this practice.[37] However, there is a very strong link between FGM and significant and tragic consequences for girls. More than many procedures, this has the potential to affect a huge worldwide population. If we take the idea that there is a responsibility on the part of the medical profession to ensure patient safety, then surely lack of action to facilitate prosecution is a derogation of that responsibility. The problem will not be resolved just at the medical level, however. The problem has to be resolved at societal, community, educational and cultural levels and should be led by coherent and holistic policy and practice.

Jehovah's Witnesses refusing blood transfusions

What are the legal consequences of allowing for the manifestation of religious belief of a patient in the knowing certainty actions or non-actions arising from this will result in harm or death to the patient? This question has particular relevance when it comes to adult Jehovah's Witnesses who refuse blood transfusions. A number of such cases have come before the courts. In the end, all of them, notwithstanding some nuances, have found in favour of the patient acting in accordance with their own will, as long as it was proven that there was no undue influence or duress and that the patient had capacity to refuse treatment.[38] According to Lord Donaldson in *Re T*, 'every adult has the right and capacity to decide whether or not he will accept medical treatment, even if a refusal may risk permanent injury to his health or even lead to premature death'.[39] In the context of children, a case in point was *Re E*,[40] where the Jehovah's Witness child was not allowed to refuse the transfusion but once he reached the age of 18, his refusal was accepted and he subsequently died. In *Re E*, Nolan LJ used the best interests test and further stated that '[a]n individual who has attained the age of 18 is free to do with his life what he wishes, but it is the duty of the court to ensure so far as it can that children survive to attain that age'.[41] This, of course, was a significant example of an instance where the religious belief of the patient compromised his own safety.

Patient safety is only one variable in this equation. Allowing an adult patient who has capacity to refuse treatment is a strict tenet of medical practice and, indeed, English law.[42] Conducting an unwanted blood transfusion on a capacitated adult

37 See Sandra Danial, 'Cultural relativism vs. universalism: female genital mutilation, pragmatic remedies', *The Journal of Historical Studies* 2013, 2(1):1–10.

38 See Clayton Ó Néill, 'Jehovah's Witnesses and Blood transfusions: an analysis of the legal protection afforded to adults and children in European/English Human Rights Contexts', *European Journal of Health Law* 2017, 24:1–22.

39 Lord Donaldson in *Re T* [1993] Fam 95.

40 *Re E* [1993] 1 FLR 386.

41 Also see *Re L* [1998] 2 FLR 810.

42 Note that further complications exist in relation to those who have 'borderline capacity' and vulnerable patients. See Emma Cave, 'Protecting patients from their bad decisions: rebalancing rights, relationships, and risk' *Medical Law Review* 2017, 25(4): 527–553.

patient would be an infringement of their autonomy and so patient safety has to be balanced with the issue of autonomy and consent. In incapacitated patients, who express religious beliefs, then the whole question of their best interests come into play. Thus, for the adult, capacity and consent are key factors. The situation is more complicated in the case of Jehovah's Witness children. There have been instances where such children have refused blood transfusions and many judges have said that it goes against their best interests, even if they could be regarded as *Gillick* competent. Therefore, they have consistently refused permission for a child to refuse the blood transfusion. The judge, in these instances, is trying to ensure patient safety and that no harm befalls the child. But is patient safety the only show in town, the only broker, the only arbitrating factor? The courts have been criticised for their overly paternalistic attitudes and for denying the *Gillick* competent child or a 16–17-year-old who satisfies the capacity test the right to refuse the blood transfusion. The advantage of this 'bright line' rule is legal certainty. The judge is, however, as often happens, between a rock and a hard place: the rock being the compromising of the safety of a child and the place being disrespecting the deeply-held belief of the child who is competent. This dilemma is never going to be easily resolved, and it would be facile to suggest that an equitable resolution can be arrived at. It is suggested here that there is still a need to give some weighting to the religious beliefs of the child. The age of the child should not be the sole determinant of capacity. Other variables exist which could help in determining the capacity to want to act in accordance with religious belief, such as maturity, depth of religious affiliation and the degree to which the expression of religious belief fulfils the innate and long-standing deeply-held and unwavering beliefs of the child. Of course, these factors are notoriously difficult to quantify, but weight should be allocated to them in the interests of giving regard to the deeply-held wishes of the child.

The Royal College of Surgeons (RCS) recently produced guidelines in response to the Supreme Court case of *Montgomery* where consent was clarified, entitled *Consent: supported decision making – a guide to good practice.*[43] These guidelines then indicate that doctors need to take reasonable steps to make sure that patients are informed of any material risks associated with treatment and that the patients should be told of any alternative treatments. The guidelines recognise that the principle in *Bolam* is still applicable.[44] These guidelines clearly state that there is now a move away from a 'paternalistic traditional model of consent' towards one that puts the patient first.[45] This means that surgeons need to change their attitudes when dealing with consent: 'they are no longer the sole arbiter of determining what risks are material to their patients'.[46] The RCS also

43 Royal College of Surgeons, *Consent: supported decision making – a guide to good practice*, Royal College of Surgeons, 2016.

44 *Bolam v Friern Hospital Management Committee* [1957] 2 All E.R: 'A doctor is not guilty of negligence if he has acted in accordance with a practice accepted as proper by a responsible body of medical men skilled in that particular art'.

45 Royal College of Surgeons, *Consent: supported decision making*, p. 3.

46 Ibid., p. 3.

explain that discussion needs to focus on the individual patient. Therefore, the practitioner needs to get to know the patient sufficiently in order to comprehend their values and views. This includes their beliefs or the fact that a surgeon may disagree with the patient's decision.[47] The difficulty that applies here is the degree to which, from a practical viewpoint, a surgeon can with validity assess the depth, sincerity and gravity of an individual's belief. The guidelines recognise that case law supports the rights of patients to refuse treatment, even if there are potentially fatal consequences. Surgeons ought to discuss potential implications of the patient's decision as well as the risks/benefits associated. Nevertheless, 'this should be aimed at helping the patient make an informed decision and should not influence the patient to take a course of action that is not in keeping with their wishes, even if this course of action has been proposed by the multidisciplinary team'.[48] When it comes to emergencies, however, the surgeon must proceed without consent or with limited information and act in the patient's best interests.[49]

The RCS subsequently, in 2016, introduced specific guidelines in relation to patients who refuse blood transfusions for religious reasons (e.g. Jehovah's Witnesses), entitled *Caring for patients who refuse blood*.[50] They recognise the fact that doctors are under a duty to safeguard 'physical wellbeing of patients' but also understand that this can conflict with the rights of patients to make healthcare decisions. According to the RCS:

> Surgeons are duty-bound to respect patients' religious freedoms and can feel uncomfortable refusing to treat patients because of restrictions stemming from a religious belief for fear of accusation of discrimination. . . Surgeons have the right to choose not to treat patients if they feel that the restrictions placed on them by the refusal of blood products are contrary to their values as a doctor. If a surgeon is not prepared to treat a patient who refuses blood they must refer them to a doctor who is suitably qualified and prepared to take on the patient knowing the circumstances of this refusal of blood.[51]

In emergency circumstances, where an immediate blood transfusion is required, the staff ought to act in accordance with the patient's best interests and try to 'communicate with them to keep them informed wherever possible'. This is in line with GMC guidance, whereby '[i]n an emergency, you can provide treatment that is immediately necessary to save life or prevent deterioration in health without consent'.[52]

47 Ibid., p. 10.
48 Ibid., p. 11.
49 Ibid., p. 11.
50 Royal College of Surgeons, *Caring for patients who refuse blood. A guide to good practice for the surgical management of Jehovah's Witnesses and other patients who decline blood*, Royal College of Surgeons, 2016.
51 Ibid., p. 8.
52 GMC, *Personal Beliefs and Medical Practice*, para 27.

What about a situation where the patient cannot give an informed decision? Should clinical judgement overrule the wishes of family members? Yes. However, the relatives are encouraged to provide evidence indicating that an advance decision exists. What about children? The RCS point to the fact that children can make valid legal decisions if they have the required capacity (e.g. under the Family Law Reform Act 1969 or if *Gillick* competent). Even though the main responsibility of surgeons is to ensure that the well being of children is ensured, 'every effort must be made to respect the beliefs of the family and avoid the use of blood or blood products wherever possible'.

Overall trends

If we consider what makes up the cases of a medical accident, we see that these are usually variables at system level. If religion is not to be a variable within the continuum of accident causation, then at system level and individual level, some certainty needs to exist. The relative importance of religious practice to the individual and the degree to which religious belief is a central tenet of existence can vary from patient to patient, from religious adherent to religious adherent, leading to difficulties in achieving this degree of certainty. To maximise the potential for achieving a level of surety, regulations that protect religious expression and balance patient safety must be well used and be subject to inspection and interrogation. Protocols should be agreed with hospital boards, shared with medical professionals and patients and subject to high-level leadership. There is a need to empower patients to have a greater understanding of both their right to express their religious or cultural belief as it applies to their medical care and equip them with the full knowledge of the consequences of any actions or non-actions that they take. All of this leads to a need for greater cohesion between medical, legal and societal systems, where patient rights and patient safety are all part of an agreed agenda.

The holy grail of patient safety is a Camelot-like context where care, concern, consent and capacity are hallmarks of best practice. The road to Camelot, however, is a stony one and can be beset by litanies of error. When errors happen, they usually do so because human beings make mistakes and systems can compound these mistakes due, sometimes, to lack of appropriate checking devices and procedures. When religious belief is a journeyman on this pathway, then the stones can be rockier and the pathway more torturous. There are instances where the manifestation of religious belief does result in compromising patient safety. But patient autonomy is key. A healthcare system that only aligns patient safety within very confined medical parameters would be one that, ultimately, negates patient autonomy. The exercise of this personal autonomy means that we can be the architects of our own medical downfall. As long as we have capacity, we have the autonomy to make medical decisions that may not be all that sensible, that may not be all that favourably balanced in terms of our own safety, but our autonomy is part of our self-identity and the right to express religious or cultural belief is one that needs the protection of the law and the support of medical personnel. Following a particular religion is, of course, not always a purely autonomous pathway. In many cases, the religious adherent is following the mandatory doctrine of his or her faith, which may leave no room for opting out.[53] Recognising the perceived conflict that can exist between the liberty of autonomous actions and the duties imposed on the individual who follows a particular religious belief, Calderwood Norton argues that '[a]n autonomy-based justification for religious freedom is not. . . inconsistent with recognising that a religious way of life can carry with it particular duties'.[54] It is clear that there are differences in the way religious adherents view the duties, obligations and freedoms that their religious practice imposes upon them. This, in turn, gives rise to the need for an individualised approach to patients when they make decisions based upon religious beliefs and when these decisions may have an impact upon their safety.

What is the impact of religious/cultural belief on patient safety and what are the instances where such belief compromises this safety?

Patient safety is a worldwide/global issue and, indeed, religion and its manifestation is also apparent at every corner of the world. The question is 'where does patient safety and religious/cultural expression intersect'? Obviously, religious expression is a human right, which is protected by a number of international conventions, but, at a practical level, this chapter has considered its real-life impact on patient safety, including the safety of children. Particular attention has been given to a number of scenarios where patient safety is potentially compromised by this religious or cultural expression: ritual male circumcision, FGM and refusal of blood transfusions by Jehovah's Witnesses.

If we accept that the patient is more than the sum of their parts, then it follows that their safety is more than the summation and inclusion of tangible and measurable nuts and bolts. Assuring the safety of the patient involves knowing something of the patient including, where relevant, their religious or cultural beliefs. There are generic variables associated with patient safety, but an individualistic approach is also required where the understanding of the make-up of an individual patient can result in a better understanding of her healthcare needs. Within the parameters of this individualism, the religious and cultural beliefs of the patient can be included. A number of medical guidelines and reports allude to the importance of recognising cultural and religious belief in terms of ensuring good patient care. At a practical level, procedures and protocols that set out what should be done when a particular medical treatment is either requested or refused as a result of religious belief should be agreed. At a second level, culturally, there has to be a non-judgemental openness that

53 See Sandel's account of the connections between religion, autonomy, choice, liberty and the duties imposed on the individual in manifesting their religious belief: Michael Sandel, 'Religious liberty – freedom of conscience or freedom of choice' *Utah LR* 1986, 597.

54 Jane Calderwood Norton, *Freedom of religious organizations* 1st edition, OUP, 2016, p. 28.

accepts the medical decisions made by patients with capacity when these decisions are based upon what might appear to be unreasonable religious/cultural belief. Equally, this openness must also, however, apply to a readiness to seek to prosecute those who flout the laws/violate human rights and compromise patient safety in the most extreme manner, such as in the case of FGM. There should not be fear of recognising cultural or religious practices that oppose the human rights of patients, as in FGM. In less menacing cases, the law of tort should be seen to apply.

Patient safety has to extend beyond the error and harm definitions to now encompass something a little bit further reaching than that. This concentration on error and harm in the safeguarding of patients on the part of healthcare professionals fails to take into account sufficiently the role of capacitated patients in their own medical care. We can accept as valid the previously given WHO definition of patient safety as 'prevention of errors and adverse effects to patients associated with health care'.[55] There are situations where a patient's own decisions based, as in this instance, for example, on religious/cultural belief, put them in the way of harm and this needs to be factored into these definitions. It is proposed here that an understanding of patient safety be extended to 'prevention of errors and adverse effects to patients associated with healthcare and decisions taken by healthcare personnel and/or patients'. The addition of this latter statement could have meritorious consequences in tort in so far as it provides recognition of the fact that the patient is an equal partner and, in some cases, a primary partner in the medical treatment offered and consented to. This broader perspective of patient safety would offer a more holistic view of the patient that recognises patient values and belief systems. This links in with the way in which tort now, in a post-*Montgomery* era, puts the opinions/consent of the patient first and rejects medical paternalism. A dialogical process is required that would ensure that this broader interpretation of patient safety is captured, understood and acted upon. No medical procedures that recognise religious/cultural belief and that bring about harm and so compromise patient safety may be given to a patient who lacks capacity to make specific decisions about their treatment and/or has not consented to the specific course of treatment. By recognising the role that patients play in the determination of their safety and by acting upon decisions made by the patient, based, in this case, on religious/cultural beliefs, the opportunity arises for a more open and shared dialogue between healthcare professionals and patients, leading to an even greater understanding of medical treatment and its consequences. This, surely, has the potential to lessen acrimony and contention and to reduce negligence claims that can emanate from situations where such contention exists. The broadening of the definition of patient safety comes from a philosophical base where value is given to the right of patients to act in accordance with their beliefs.[56]

55 WHO, 'Patient safety'.

56 The author would like to thank Professor Tom Lewis for commenting on an earlier draft of this chapter.

References

Beckers Hospital Review, 'Top 10 safety issues for 2016', *Becker's Infection Control and Clinical Quality*, 12 January, 2016. www.beckershospitalreview.com/quality/10-top-patient-safety-issues-for-2016.html (accessed 27 October 2017).

Calderwood Norton, Jane, *Freedom of Religious Organizations* 1st edition, Oxford: Oxford University Press, 2016.

Cameron, Joan and Anderson, Karen Rawlings, '"Circumcision", culture and health-care provision in Tower Hamlets, London', *Gender and Development* 1998, 3(1):48–54.

Cave, Emma, 'Protecting patients from their bad decisions: rebalancing rights, relationships, and risk', *Medical Law Review* 2017, 25(4): 527–553.

Danial, Sandra, 'Cultural relativism vs. universalism: female genital mutilation, pragmatic remedies', *The Journal of Historical Studies* 2013, 2(1):1–10.

Department of Health, *Report of an expert group on learning from adverse events in the NHS chaired by the Chief Medical Officer*, Department of Health, 2000.

Ford, Steve, 'Nurses warn patient safety is being compromised by equipment shortages', *Nursing Times*, 6 April 2010. www.nursingtimes.net/nurses-warn-patient-safety-is-being-compromised-by-equipment-shortages/5013217.article (accessed 27 October 2017).

Foundation for Women's Health, Research and Development (FORWARD), *Female genital mutilation: frequently asked questions: a campaigner's guide for young people*, 2012. www.gov.uk/government/uploads/system/uploads/attachment_data/file/332732/FGMfaqFORWARD.pdf (accessed 20 October 2017).

GMC, *Raising and acting on concerns about patient safety*, 2012. www.gmc-uk.org/Raising_and_acting_on_concerns_about_patient_safety___English_0617.pdf_48902813.pdf (accessed 27 November 2017).

GMC, *Personal beliefs and medical practice*, 2013, para 9. www.gmc-uk.org/guidance/ethical_guidance/21177.asp (accessed 14 October 2017).

GMC, *Personal beliefs and medical practice*, 2013, para 27. www.gmc-uk.org/guidance/ethical_guidance/21181.asp (accessed 27 October 2017).

Jones, S. D., et al., 'Female genital mutilation in developing countries: an agenda for public health response', *Eur J Obstet Gynecol Reprod Biol* 2014, 116(2):144–51.

Krill, A. J., et al., 'Complications of Circumcision', *Scientific World Journal* 2011, 11:2458–68.

Krupa, Michelle, 'The alarming rise of female genital mutilation in America', CNN, 14 July 2017. http://edition.cnn.com/2017/05/11/health/female-genital-mutilation-fgm-explainer-trnd/index.html (accessed 27 October 2017).

Lee, Bruce Y. and Newberg, Andrew B., 'Religion and health: a review and critical analysis', *Zygon* 2005, 40:443–68

NHS, *Religion or belief. A practical guide for the NHS*, Department of Health, 2009. www.clatterbridgecc.nhs.uk/application/files/7214/3445/0178/Religionorbelief ApracticalguidefortheNHS.pdf (accessed 14 October 2017).

Ó Néill, Clayton, 'Jehovah's Witnesses and blood transfusions: an analysis of the legal protection afforded to adults and children in European/English Human Rights Contexts', *European Journal of Health Law* 2017, 24:1–22.

Perera, C. L., et al., 'Safety and efficacy of nontherapeutic male circumcision: a systematic review', *Ann Fam Med* 2010, 8(1):64–72.

Reason, James, *Human Error*, Cambridge, UK: Cambridge University Press, 1990.

Royal College of Surgeons, *Caring for patients who refuse blood. A guide to good practice for the surgical management of Jehovah's Witnesses and other patients who decline blood*, Royal College of Surgeons, 2016.

Royal College of Surgeons, *Consent: supported decision making – a guide to good practice*, Royal College of Surgeons, 2016.

Sandel, Michael, 'Religious liberty – freedom of conscience or freedom of choice', *Utah LR* 1986, 597.

Vincent, C. A. and Coulter, A., 'Patient safety: what about the patient?', *Qual Saf Health Care* 2002, 11:76–80.

WHO, 'Health risks of female genital mutilation'. www.who.int/reproductivehealth/topics/fgm/health_consequences_fgm/en/ (accessed 31 October 2017).

WHO, 'Patient Safety'. www.euro.who.int/en/health-topics/Health-systems/patient-safety/patient-safety (accessed 30 October 2017).

8 Patient safety in Oman

Aisha Rashid Al Maqbali and Ahmed Al-Mandhari

Introduction

The Sultanate of Oman is an Arab country located on the south-eastern coast of the Arabian Peninsula. In 2014, the population of Oman was over 4 million. Oman has demonstrated great achievements in healthcare services. His Majesty Sultan Qaboos kept his promise in 1970 to prioritise on the development of the health of the country through the establishment of the Ministry of Health (MoH) in 1971.[1] This was recognised in a 191-country study by the World Health Organisation, when Oman was ranked first in the world for its levels of health and eighth for the overall performance of its health system.[2]

The increase in demand raised concerns about quality assurance in regard to the availability of healthcare. This influenced the MoH's health development plans and infrastructure development. The ultimate goal of quality assurance is to achieve the highest quality standards of care and thus achieve user satisfaction.[3] By implementing strategic plans and providing clear work pathways in the MoH, Oman achieved a dramatic transformation in its health status in a very short time span and its current health indicators are comparable with those of developed countries. In Oman, the MoH considers patient safety and quality of care as one of its priorities and urges all healthcare leaders and decision makers to conduct more training and awareness programs.[4]

Development of patient safety as a concept and as a practice in Oman

The concept of patient safety was most clearly introduced in Oman through the sixth five-year plan that was launched in 2001. The plan included three

1 Moeness Alshishtawy, 'Four decades of progress: evolution of the health system in Oman', *Sultan Qaboos University Medical Journal* 2010, 10(1):122–2. www.ncbi.nlm.nih.gov/pmc/articles/PMC3074664 accessed 6 July 2016.

2 WHO, *Health systems: improving performance*, WHO, 2000. www.who.int/whr/2000/en/, accessed 10 July 2016.

3 Alshishtawy, 'Four decades of progress'.

4 Samra Al Barwani, 'Our journey towards implementation of key performance indicators sets for hospitals in Oman', The International Society for Quality in Health Care, 32nd International Conference, Building Quality and Safety into the Healthcare System 2015, www.isqua.org/docs/default-source/qatar-info/ accessed 1 August 2016.

main actions to establish a culture of quality management. The first action was recruiting a consultant in quality management who initiated a training program, the purpose of which was to develop a national cadre that would lead the quality improvement programs across the regions. These have resulted in several interventions including establishing quality and patient safety supervisory bodies at the hospital, health services Directorate and the Ministry headquarter levels.[5] This helped in establishing quality management departments in the various regional hospitals, the first of which was established in 2007, and the Directorate General of Health Affairs. Further plans were also made in collaboration with the WHO-Eastern Mediterranean Regional Office (EMRO) by conducting projects that assessed the quality management system and identified areas for improvements.[6]

In 2009, the MoH implemented the National Performance Measurement sets for hospitals and invited an external Consultant in Hospital Performance Measurement Systems to review and provide guidance for improvement.[7] In 2013, the MoH introduced its 'Health Vision 2050' with major reforms of the healthcare system; directing its resources to hit targets in the curative, preventive and rehabilitative domains of the system. This was linked with the targets developed by the other providers in the country, such as Sultan Qaboos University Hospital (SQUH) and the Military Medical Services. During this period, a review of both the medical and the paramedical curriculums was conducted to improve the quality of graduates from these programs, as well as to increase the level of some programmes to Bachelors and Masters level. Also, this period witnessed the establishment of the Research Council which aimed to put strategic plans in place in regard to the country's need for research in the field of healthcare, thus supporting service development.[8]

The 'Health Vision 2050' is one of the major reforms of the MoH. Its main focus includes strengthening primary healthcare, in association with an increased awareness in Omani society through health promotion and inter-sectoral collaboration, and improving tertiary healthcare facilities. Furthermore, it aims at achieving the best value for money invested in the health sector, whilst improving accessibility to services by setting up 10,000 health centres in order to meet increasing demand from its growing population and expanded urbanisation. As one of the outcomes of this reform, the MoH announced the development of the Sultan Qaboos Medical City, which is expected to cost $1.5bn.[9]

5 Ahmed Al Mandhari, 'Oman' in Jeffrey Braithwaite, Matsuyama Yukihiro, Russell Mannion and Julie Johnson (eds) ***Healthcare reform, quality and safety: perspectives, participants, partnerships and prospects in 30 countries***', CRC Press, 2015.

6 Ahmed Al Mandhari, 'Visionary Plan For Quality And Patients Safety In Oman: Where Strategic And Operational Plans Meet', The International Society for Quality in Health Care, 32nd International Conference, Building Quality and Safety into the Healthcare System 2015. www.isqua.org/docs/default-source/qatar-info/, accessed 1 August 2016.

7 Al Barwani,'Our journey towards implementation of key performance indicators'.

8 Al Mandhari, 'Oman'.

9 Ibid.

Other healthcare providers, such as SQUH, have taken similar steps by inviting international experts to participate in the review process of the hospital strategic plan. For example, SQUH and College of Medicine and Health Sciences (COMHS) have worked together towards improving quality and patient safety by gaining accreditation from international bodies, such as Accreditation Canada International and the Association for Medical Education in the Eastern Mediterranean Region (AMEEMR). The main focus is to incorporate new strategies, in line with the 2050 vision, that will help in meeting the expanding demand for the teaching, research and clinical services of the hospital whilst ensuring the provision of high-quality services. This is coupled with the expansion in infrastructure in the hospital systems, such as facilities and human resources, as well as its administrative structure.[10]

The current reforms also encourage the private sector to invest in the system, through new 'medical cities' and the development of a number of small hospitals.[11] Although these facilities will serve the Omani population, the private sector seeks to attract patients from around the world, as medical tourism grows.[12]

Implementing patient safety into practice

Incident reporting

One of the key methodologies of the patient safety strategy in Oman is to gain an understanding of the causes and the consequences of an adverse incident. Therefore, setting up monitoring systems to facilitate such understanding and subsequently distributing the lessons learned across all healthcare facilities has been crucial.[13] There are two reporting methods followed in Oman.[14]

The first method used is the hospital incident report form. Most of the primary healthcare facilities depend on manual forms. However, some have taken up the more recent electronic reporting system. Almost all secondary and tertiary hospitals use the electronic forms. Despite the gradual introduction of the electronic system (Al Shifa System 3-plus),[15] over 80% of government and non-government facilities have now taken up and started to use. Through this system, all types of adverse incidents should be filled in by the staff involved in the incident and should be forwarded to the quality management team, where analysis of these incidents will take place.

10 Ibid.

11 For example, the International Medical City in Salalah is considered the largest private sector investment. It covers an area of 866,000 square metres which includes a healthcare complex, a healthcare resort, an educational facility, and a 530-bed multi-sociality hospital.

12 Al Mandhari, 'Oman'.

13 Itziar Larizgoitia, et al., 'WHO efforts to promote reporting of adverse events and global learning', *Journal of Public Health Research* 2013, 2.3:e29. *PMC* Web www.ncbi.nlm.nih.gov/pmc/articles/PMC4147748/, accessed 13 August 2016.

14 Ministry of Health, 'Incident/Accident Reporting', MoH04. health.gove.bz/www/attachments/368-Incident%20Policy.pdf, accessed 15 June 2016.

15 Ibid.

Oman has made great progress in this regard in the last ten years.[16] After implementing the electronic medical system, the number of reported incidents has increased. This can be related to many factors, including:

- i An increase in confidence in reporting incidents, given the secured nature of the system, which can only be accessed by authorised personnel. Thus, the identity of reporting staff remains confidential.
- ii The increased awareness of the policy of the reporting system and its importance to patient safety initiatives.
- iii The reports have become essential tools in legal investigations into adverse incidents.

Despite the improvement in the reporting system, the same incidents are still reported and repeated over time, both within and between healthcare facilities. This could represent a defect in the systems for communicating incident reports to other healthcare providers or in the way incidents are investigated and understood. Thus, the learning environment and incident reporting strategies are still a work-in-progress in Oman. Further development in this area could include adopting new strategies that have shown success in other countries, such as the alert system used in the United Kingdom.

The second important incident reporting system is the combination of patient satisfaction surveys and patients' (formal or informal) complaints. The information collected in this way provides important data to improve healthcare services. For example, patients and caregivers, at the level of the primary healthcare system, can complain directly to the unit Head or the Head of the health organisation, either through a verbal complaint or by filling in paper-based complaint formats.[17] The patient or the caregiver will be called for further clarification and updated about the progress of his/her incident. At the level of the secondary and tertiary healthcare, in addition to the suggestion boxes, there is a Patient Service Department which can receive complaints directly and try to resolve them on-site. In recent years, Oman has adopted the National Call Centre (NCC) system[18] which receives complaints and suggestions from the patients/relatives or the community regarding health services. The NCC system will direct the complaint to the health institute concerned to investigate the problem and to implement appropriate solutions. However, the NCC is not an independent, centralised investigative agency, nor is it involved in training or performance management; reports which are submitted locally will remain the responsibility of the local organisation.[19]

16 Khamis Al-Gharbi, et al., 'A case study of Al-Shifa: a healthcare information system in Oman', *International Journal of Social, Behavioural, Educational, Economic, Business and Industrial Engineering* 2014, 8(8):24432–48. http://waset.org/publications/9998985/a-case-study-of-al-shifa-a-healthcare-information-system-in-oman, accessed 2 July 2016.

17 There are suggestion boxes as well that are available in all healthcare facilities, so patients can fill in their complaints and they will be collected later by the responsible person for review and analysis.

18 Ministry of Health, 'The National Call Centre, Sultanate of Oman'. www.moh.gov.om/ar/call-center, accessed 7 July 2016.

19 Ibid.

Investigation of medical errors

In Oman, medical law is newly recognised and under development. The approach followed in Oman in regards to alleged errors includes the provision that claims will be submitted to one of the following channels: the hospital concerned, the Directorate General of the health services in the region or to the Minister/Under-Secretary's office. Then, the claim will be reviewed by the Regional Medical and Technical Committee (RMTC) to decide if there has been a medical error or not. If it is decided that no error occurred, the claim will be rejected. If, however, it is felt that there has been an error the claim will be directed, via the Under-Secretary's office, to the Higher Medical Committee (HMC) in the MoH. If the HMC decides that there is no medical error, the case will be dismissed. If the HMC accepts that an error has arisen, then the claimant will receive a payment from the compensation fund. The fund is generated through participation fees from all healthcare providers under the MoH (including both the public and private sectors). Alternatively, a claimant chooses to direct the complaint to the primary court or the public prosecutor. The former will direct it to the Under-Secretary's office. The findings of investigations and the curative and preventive recommendations are reported back to the MoH and other government healthcare institutions for implementation.[20]

Incorporating non-MoH sectors in patient safety in Oman

Other stakeholders are involved, in different ways, in patient safety. For example, at the macro levels, the MoH is invited on a regular basis to the discussions of the Shura Council, the elected lower house in the Oman parliamentary system.[21] The dialogue is based on questions raised by members of the Council on various healthcare issues, such as accessibility, safety, affordability, continuity and technical aspects. Similarly, the State Council invites decision makers from the MoH during its regular discussions of the healthcare system. Both are involved in reviewing the system's strategic planning and in directing resources to some of the health needs in the community.[22]

Challenges and opportunities

The MoH has faced many challenges over the last 40 years. One major obstacle has been to implement strategies to reduce communicable diseases, which is being tackled through national vaccination programs. Another key problem is responding to increased population growth, which has put strains on the available healthcare services. In 1970, there were only two hospitals, serving a population of 655,000. In comparison, in 2014, there were 67 hospitals serving 3,993,000. Whilst there is a need for large-scale, longitudinal studies to evaluate whether the

20 Al Mandhari, 'Oman'.

21 For general information, see www.shura.om/About-Us/About-the-Majlis.

22 Ibid.

increase in the number of facilities has improved the quality and safety of healthcare, the WHO have recognised that there has been a remarkable transformation in the health profile of the country, in no small part due to the near-universal access to primary healthcare.[23] However, this expansion carries its own problems: the rapid increase in staffing has led to a loss of accountability within care teams over responsibility for ensuring the delivery of quality health services. Further, the increase in primary care has not been reflected in tertiary, specialist services, where there remains a lag in staffing levels. [24] This creates fragmentation in the patient pathway through the healthcare system and can lead to disjunction in strategies aimed at improving the overall quality of the patient experience.

There remain a number of other challenges facing the MoH, all of which have implications for patient safety.[25]

Increases in costs of the Health Service

The estimated total governmental expenditure (Omani Rials) on the health services in 2014 was 12.9 billion, compared to 46 million in 1970. As per the health status indicators for 2013, MoH expenditure accounted for about 5.9% of the total government expenditures.[26] This cost is spent on recurrent and developmental expenses, unexpected complications and emergency situations, such as the outbreak of diseases. One of the strategies to overcome the increased cost is the use of advanced technical equipment that requires less human input, although, such technologies require costly short-term investment, as well as long-term training schemes to ensure that they are used effectively and efficiently.

Another strategy to manage the rising healthcare bill is identification of the reasons for 'frequent attenders' to, or health-seeking behaviours in, healthcare facilities in Oman. A study, covering the primary healthcare in a particular region in Oman in 2008, revealed that just 4% of patients were responsible for 18.6% of the total number of visits.[27] The majority of frequent attenders were female (57%) and it is more prevalent among the elderly (74%), people of a lower educational level (67.5%) and those who are divorced or widowed (76.7%). Also, frequent attenders reported a higher percentage of chronic illness/disease (74.7%) and more visits to other healthcare facilities (54.1%).[28] The increase of lifestyle-related diseases such as hypertension and diabetes puts pressure on health reforms in

23 WHO-EM, *Country cooperation strategy for WHO and Oman*, WHO, 2010. www.who.int/countryfocus/cooperation_strategy/ccs_omn_en.pdf. ; WHO, *The World Health Report 2008 – Primary Health Care (Now More Than Ever)*, WHO, 2008. www.who.int/whr/2008/en/, accessed 17 January 2018.

24 Al Mandhari, 'Oman'.

25 Oman Information Centre, 'New challenges to the healthcare system in Oman'. www.omaninfo.com/health/new-challenges-healthcare-system-oman.asp, accessed 24 July 2016.

26 Ministry of Health, 'Incident/Accident Reporting'.

27 Abdulaziz Al Mahrazi, et al., 'Prevalence and characteristics of frequent attenders to the Primary health care centers in Dakhliya region' (Master thesis, Oman Medical Speciality Board 2008).

28 Ibid.

terms of redirecting resources from other programs.[29] Such frequent visits represent a significant burden on healthcare workers, consuming time and resources. Community health education (discussed below) plays an important role in the management of this problem by raising awareness, and encouraging use, of preventive medicine and its role in the community.

Despite this, the cultural and economic stability, compared to many other countries in the region, represent positive forces for change in Oman. However, the health system is also facing reactionary external forces that have negative influences on these domestic reforms. One of these is the unstable political status of the Middle East, which discourages many skilled healthcare professionals from joining the healthcare systems in the Gulf Countries. Another factor is competing regional and international markets for skilled healthcare professionals which constrains the budget of the system.[30] This is complicated by the high dependence on expatriate medical personnel, which imports the challenges of differences in culture, medical practices and patient care. Furthermore, such personnel are subjected to high turnover, as there is a tendency to view their work in the Gulf as a transient learning experience, for international exposure, and later return to their home countries or to more developed markets for higher-paid jobs. Thus, as indicated earlier, the healthcare workforce in Oman is in a constant state of flux, affected by both investment in the system and overriding, regional political forces which buffet Oman.

Increase in community education

The increased demand and the increased cost are significantly correlated to high public expectations. These are all linked, at the same time, to levels of health education. The more knowledgeable patients are about the nature and extent of available health services, the more realistic expectations they will have, and hence the more satisfied they become. In Oman, there is a discrepancy between general levels of education and 'health education'. There is a prevailing cultural belief that doctors must be able to diagnose and treat all diseases, at the first point of contact. The aim of their visits to healthcare facilities is to obtain treatment only, not information or knowledge about their conditions and how to effectively manage them. Perhaps paradoxically, there is also a concern with being treated by a caring and empathic healthcare professional, rather than a skilled one. The MoH, then, finds itself struggling with the management of these expectations. One the one hand, there is a need to continue to dispel the long history of inadequate healthcare, prior to the 1970 reforms: in this way, the MoH has to continue to support the domestic and international narrative that Oman is now a world-leader in healthcare. On the other hand, the cultural power of this narrative is proving unduly burdensome on the realities of health provision. Increased health education is a strategy which can help with managing this tension. However, further research on this subject is needed to evaluate the current situation in Oman.

29 Ibid.
30 Al Mandhari, 'Oman'.

Impact of the media and perceptions of blame

The impact of the media on people, their expectations, their satisfaction, and the demands that they make of the healthcare system is another factor which acts as both challenge and opportunity for further patient safety development. It has a significant effect on policy-makers as well, in terms of motivating them to take quality issues into account, to proactively identify problems and try to correct, or prevent, them. Oman should learn from experiences in other countries. For example, in the UK, the public inquiry into the Mid Staffordshire NHS Foundation Trust in 2009 was conducted under the influence of a public outcry, led by a group of patients and their relatives who had experienced neglectful care at the Trust.[31] In Oman, there has been similar media response to patient complaints, albeit to a much lesser extent. Policy-makers are aware of these complaints and several visits are made to evaluate the system in some departments of the hospitals concerned. There is a need, however, to be mindful of the potential for the negative influence by the mass media, on the community, in magnifying adverse events. There are good policy reasons for maintaining confidentiality around incidents and incident investigation, particularly where there are concerns that public confidence in the system could be adversely affected by reportage. Significantly, the media portrayal of patient safety issues (or at least policy-makers' perceptions of this portrayal) can shape the ways that policies are formed and their implementation can (appear to) be defensive measures, rather than proactive attempts at improvement.

A closely linked issue is the fear, among healthcare professionals, of patient safety investigation leading to liability. A sensitivity towards this perceived 'threat' can have behavioural impacts, changing the way that practitioners interact with patients, and in the treatments options that they are willing to make available. Also, it is reflected in low incident reporting due to a fear of blame, and any resulting legal actions. The community perception of admitted medical errors shows a loss of trust in the healthcare facility or the healthcare providers working in that institution, and sometimes a mistrust of the whole system adopted by the healthcare organisation. Thus, the language in which the errors are explained to the patients should be more scientific and should focus on the system and not on people.

There is a need for the MoH to attempt to mitigate these fears, whilst ensuring that patient safety is a paramount concern of healthcare providers. As with managing public expectations of healthcare, training and education could help to dispel unrealistic or uninformed concerns, whilst increasing the transparency of investigation processes, among practitioners. The manner in which policies are drafted, investigations conducted and reports framed should reflect the systemic nature of patient safety, rather than the apportioning of blame between individuals within the wider healthcare team.

31 Robert Francis QC, *Report of the Mid Staffordshire NHS Foundation Trust Public Inquiry*, London: TSO, 2013. http://webarchive.nationalarchives.gov.uk/20150407084003/http://www.midstaffspublicinquiry.com/sites/default/files/report/executive%20summary.pdf, accessed 19 July 2016.

A significant shift would be towards a 'no blame culture'. All healthcare providers and the healthcare facility should work as one team with one aim: that is the patient, first and foremost. This involves being open with the patients and disclosing medical errors without undue fear of reprisals; but always involving patients in the treatment process in an attempt to foster a more balanced, respectful working relationship from the initial encounter. This is, in fact, the policy in Oman, but it is not widely distributed or applied in practice by healthcare practitioners, due to lack of communication and asymmetries in the level of health education between the two parties. Unfortunately, most of the time, there is an attitude of blame from the patient's side and a defensive attitude from the doctor's side.

Solutions and barriers

With a growing recognition of these patient safety problems, it is now the time to create and to implement further solutions for a safer healthcare system. But, the success of the suggestions in this chapter will ultimately be determined by how well caregivers work together as a team, how effectively they are communicating with each other and with the patients, and how the care delivery processes and supporting systems are designed.[32] There is a need to develop and maintain a culture that supports the concept of quality and patient safety among staff at all times, developing knowledge and skills of the staff, ensuring continuous provision of essential medications, attracting and retaining competent staff and creating and maintaining a trustful partnership with patients and community members. Furthermore, a clear vision by leaders will ensure that all those involved in service delivery are working towards a shared goal.

Another important aspect is developing professional bodies that help in protecting, promoting and maintaining the health and safety of community members by ensuring that doctors and paramedical staff follow appropriate standards of medical practice. The reforms are promising, with short, mid and long-term targets. Very effective human and material resources have been identified and stakeholders are working together to secure these resources. International experts from developed systems have been invited to review these reforms and positive critiques have been provided. The different domains of the reforms are planned to be completed on time. Overall, the improvements to be achieved by these reforms are expected to be seen by 2020.[33]

Conclusion

Healthcare reform is an essential step to be taken in order to improve patient safety. However, as ensuring success is challenging, healthcare reform must be done in a well-planned, fully informed manner. Oman's healthcare system has

32 WHO Collaborating Centre for Patient Safety Solutions, 'Patient safety solutions preamble – May 2007'. www.who.int/patientsafety/solutions/patientsafety/Preamble.pdf, accessed 13 July 2016.

33 Al Mandhari, 'Oman'.

undergone multiple reforms over the last 44 years. Improving quality and patient safety is at the heart of these reforms and targets identified have been achieved, as reflected in various quality and patient safety indicators which have involved improved accessibility, acceptability, efficiency, effectiveness, safety and efficacy. High-level leadership and political support have played a major role in making these reforms successful. However, lessons remain to be learned from less successful initiatives that the system has experienced. This can help Oman continually improve its strategies for future reforms.[34]

Oman intends to maintain the achievements in the healthcare system during the past four decades and to make progressive change for future quality outcomes.[35] But, to ensure that these improvements are sustainable, the challenges scoped in this chapter have to be considered in greater detail, drawing from appropriate mid- to long-term research. The healthcare system reforms in Oman face a number of competing forces and tensions, from within and without the country. Internally, the healthcare improvement agenda is influenced by the progressive pressures that arise from the strong political commitment to prioritising the health and the education sectors, by His Majesty Sultan Qaboos bin Said, which is reflected in many of his speeches.[36] Externally, Oman could use its position as a health leader in the Gulf, along with its own increasing economic and social stability, to coordinate more concerted regional efforts to improve commitments to health improvement.

References

Books and articles

Al Dhawi, Ali A. and West Jr, Daniel J., 'Challenging health care system sustainability in Oman', *Journal of Health Sciences Management and Public Health* 2006, 125. http://medportal.ge/eml/publichealth/2006/n2/2.pdf, accessed 25 July 2016.

Al-Gharbi, Khamis, Gattoufi, Said M., Al-Badi, Ali H. and Al-Hashmi, Ali, 'A case study of Al-Shifa: a healthcare information system in Oman', *International Journal of Social, Behavioral, Educational, Economic, Business and Industrial Engineering* 2014, 8(8): 2451–6.http://waset.org/publications/9998985/a-case-study-of-al-shifa-a-healthcare-information-system-in-oman, accessed 2 July 2016.

Al Mandhari, Ahmed, 'Oman', in Braithwaite, Jeffrey, Yukihiro, Matsuyama, Mannion, Russell and Johnson, Julie (eds) *Healthcare reform, quality and safety: perspectives, participants, partnerships and prospects in 30 countries*, Farnham, UK: CRC Press, 2015.

Alshishtawy, Moeness, 'Four decades of progress: evolution of the health system in Oman', *Sultan Qaboos University Medical Journal* 2010, 10(1):122–2. www.ncbi.nlm.nih.gov/pmc/articles/PMC3074664, accessed 6 July 2016.

34 Ibid.

35 Ali A. Al Dhawi, et al., 'Challenging health care system sustainability in Oman', *Journal of Health Sciences Management and Public Health*, 2006, 125. http://medportal.ge/eml/publichealth/2006/n2/2.pdf, accessed 25 July 2016.

36 Al Mandhari, 'Oman'.

Braithwaite, Jeffrey, Matsuyama, Yukihiro, Mannion, Russell and Johnson, Julie, *Healthcare reform, quality and safety: perspectives, participants, partnerships and prospects in 30 countries*, Farnham, UK: CRC Press, 2015.

Francis, Robert, QC, *Report of the Mid Staffordshire NHS Foundation Trust Public Inquiry*, London: TSO, 2013. http://webarchive.nationalarchives.gov.uk/20150407084003/http://www.midstaffspublicinquiry.com/sites/default/files/report/executive%20summary.pdf, accessed 19 July 2016.

Larizgoitia, Itziar, Bouesseau, Marie-Charlotte and Kelley, Edward, 'WHO efforts to promote reporting of adverse events and global learning', *Journal of Public Health Research* 2013, 2(3):2. www.ncbi.nlm.nih.gov/pmc/articles/PMC4147748, accessed 13 August 2016.

Online articles

Al Barwani, Samra, 'Our journey towards implementation of key performance indicators sets for hospitals in Oman', The International Society for Quality in Health Care, 32nd International Conference: Building Quality and Safety into the Healthcare System 2015, www.isqua.org/docs/default-source/qatar-info/, accessed 1 August 2016.

Al-Mandhari, Ahmed, et al., 'Reasons for consultation among patients attending primary healthcare centres in Oman', *Sultan Qaboos University Medical Journal* 2013, 13(2):248.

Al-Mandhari Ahmed, 'Visionary plan for quality and patients safety in Oman: where strategic and operational plans meet', *The International Society for Quality in Health Care,* 32nd International Conference, Building Quality and Safety into the Healthcare System 2015. www.isqua.org/docs/default-source/qatar-info/, accessed 1 August 2016.

Ministry of Health, 'Incident/Accident Reporting' (MOH04). health.gove.bz/www/attachments/368-Incident%20Policy.pdf , accessed 15 June 2016.

Ministry of Health, 'The National Call Centre, Sultanate of Oman'. www.moh.gov.om/ar/call-center, accessed 7 July 2016.

Oman Information Centre, 'New challenges to the healthcare system in Oman'. www.omaninfo.com/health/new-challenges-healthcare-system-oman.asp, accessed 24 July 2016.

WHO, *Country cooperation strategy for WHO and Oman 2010–2015*, 2010. www.who.int/countryfocus/cooperation_strategy/ccs_omn_en.pdf, accessed 15 June 2016.

WHO, *Health systems: improving performance*, 2000. www.who.int/whr/2000/en/, accessed 10 July 2016.

WHO, *Patient safety solutions preamble*, 2007. www.who.int/patientsafety/solutions/patientsafety/Preamble.pdf, accessed 13 July 2016.

Theses

Al Mahrazi Abdulaziz, Badriya Al-Abadi, Jokha Al-Abadi, Wafa Al-Fannah and Abdullah Al–maniri, 'Prevalence and characteristics of frequent attenders to the Primary health care centers in Dakhliya region' (Master thesis, Oman Medical Speciality Board 2008).

9 State adverse health incident reporting systems in the United States

An introduction and contextual discussion

Barbara A. Noah

Introduction

In 2000, the United States' Institute of Medicine (IOM) published its seminal report on patient safety, *To err is human: building a safer health system.*[1] Since then, there has been measureable progress in the reporting of adverse events and in the development of preventative patient health and safety systems, but preventable harms still occur with alarming frequency. Despite notable attention to the problem of patient safety since 2000, recent estimates suggest that medical errors and iatrogenic harm remain the third largest cause of death in the United States.[2] Overall, the progress to date is simply not good enough, although there have been notable successes with particular preventable adverse events.[3] One of the largest challenges to improvement lies with obtaining quality data on which to base an understanding of the magnitude and causes of the overall problem.

Lucien Leape defines medical error as "an unintentional act (either of omission or commission) or one that does not achieve its intended outcome."[4] The concept of medical error and patient safety and the opportunities for harm are broader than might be initially apparent. As a more recent U.S. report observes, patient safety "comprises more than just mortality; it also encompasses morbidity and subtler forms of harm, such as loss of dignity and respect. It involves more than inpatient care; it includes safety in every care setting. . ."[5] The U.S. National Patient Safety Foundation has concluded that significant gains in patient safety require a proactive systems approach, not merely piecemeal reactions to specific

1 Institute of Medicine, *To err is human: building a safer health system* (2000). Available at: www.nap.edu/catalog/9728/to-err-is-human-building-a-safer-health-system. (Accessed May 2017.)

2 Martin A. Makary and Michael Daniel, 'Medical error—the third leading cause of death in the US', *British Medical Journal* 2016, 353.

3 For an excellent case study on the prevention of blood infections associated with the placement of central lines, see P. J. Pronovost et al., 'Fifteen years after *To err is human*: a success story to learn from', *BMJ Qual. Saf.* 2015, 1–4.

4 Lucian Leape, 'Error in medicine', *JAMA*, 1994, 272:1851–7.

5 National Patient Safety Foundation, 'Free from harm: accelerating patient safety improvement fifteen years after *To err is human*', 2015, iv. Available at https://psnet.ahrq.gov/resources/resource/29554/free-from-harm-accelerating-patient-safety-improvement-fifteen-years-after-to-err-is-human. (Accessed 8 June 2017.)

types of risks.[6] In this context, coordinated, timely and accurate adverse event reporting systems will continue to play an essential role in future gains by providing current data on trends in patient safety.

The magnitude of the problem cannot be overstated. The United States Centers for Disease Control and Prevention (CDC) publishes annual data on causes of death with individual causes labeled based on death certificates that utilize an international coding system. However, the coding system does not include a classification for deaths that result from human error and systems failures.[7] According to the U.S. National Center for Health Statistics, the top two causes of death in the United States are heart disease and cancer respectively.[8] Deaths from adverse events associated with medical care constitute the third leading cause of death in the U.S., according to a recent analysis. The analysts calculated a mean rate of death from medical error using a series of studies published since the initial IOM Report and extrapolating these numbers to U.S. hospital admissions in 2013. But because the various studies included only hospital inpatient deaths from medical error, their analysis included a further extrapolation to all deaths (including outpatient and long-term care). Based on these calculations and the CDC numbers derived from death certificates, the authors concluded that medical error was the third leading cause of death in the U.S.[9] Even if the calculations are somewhat flawed, the overall conclusion suggests that medical error constitutes a major cause of death, even seventeen years after the publication of the IOM Report.

In addition to tracking medical errors that cause death, there has been an effort to identify other significant errors that result in morbidity as well as potential mortality. The term "sentinel event" refers to adverse health events that are "unambiguous (clearly identifiable and measurable), serious (resulting in death or significant disability), and usually preventable."[10] According to the Agency for Healthcare Research and Quality (AHRQ), the top sentinel events in the U.S. are as follows: wrong-site surgery; suicide (while in care); operative and post-operative complication; delay in treatment; medication error; and patient fall.[11] Of course, not all sentinel events arise from medical error and some medical errors that cause harm do not rise to the level of a sentinel event.[12]

6 Ibid.

7 Makary and Daniel,' Medical error', p. 1.

8 National Center for Health Statistics. Available at www.cdc.gov/nchs/fastats/leading-causes-of-death.htm. (Accessed 31 May 2017.)

9 Makary and Daniel, 'Medical error'.

10 Agency for Healthcare Research and Quality, *Patient safety primer: never events*, 2016. Available at https://psnet.ahrq.gov/primers/primer/3/never-events. (Accessed 12 June 2017.)

11 Ibid.

12 The Joint Commission, a private health institution accreditation organization, has announced its agreement with the IOM's views regarding the problem of medical errors and has published *Sentinel Event Policy and Procedures* which define these events and create mechanisms for the Joint Commission to work with hospitals that have experienced a sentinel event to protect the patient, improve systems, and prevent further harm. Available at www.jointcommission.org/sentinel_event_policy_and_procedures/. (Accessed 1 November 2017.)

This chapter will provide an overview of the responses to the IOM Report in the U.S., focusing particularly on adverse event reporting in the context of the U.S. health care delivery system with its tendency to encourage over-utilization of medical care. Specifically, it will examine the development and implementation of adverse event reporting systems in many of the U.S. states, the similarities and differences between various state reporting systems, and the effectiveness or limitations of various models in collecting relevant information and using this information to implement better preventative systems. It will then consider what patients themselves can do to prevent medical mishaps in their health care. The Joint Commission, an independent, not-for-profit organization that accredits and certifies nearly 21,000 health care organizations and programs in the United States, also runs a patient safety initiative called "Speak Up," which seeks to improve patient safety by involving patients and their families directly in the improvement of health care delivery.

The U.S. health care environment and its impact on the frequency of adverse events

A brief description of the U.S. health care delivery system will help promote understanding of the interplay between the health care culture in the U.S. and the causes and frequency of adverse events. The U.S. has a plethora of state and federal laws governing health care. State and federal health care laws fall into two basic categories: (1) health care reimbursement and insurance systems, and (2) laws governing practice, quality, licensing, and patients' rights. Layered over the 50 states' laws are various federal laws. The regulation of the practice of medicine, including promoting quality, and the laws governing provision of health care and health insurance are very decentralized and thus there is often no top-down mechanism for making improvements to quality of care, including matters of patient safety.

Health care quality in the U.S. suffers from the effects of our fragmented health care delivery system, lack of insurance coverage or of consistency in coverage, and a multi-payer private/public system. Preventable adverse events are of great concern, but it makes sense to keep in mind the logically preliminary source of poor health in the U.S., which is the lack of access to health care. There are wide variations in health insurance coverage among the states, which exert significant impact on those patients who are too young to be eligible for Medicare, the federal entitlement program that covers most people aged 65 and over. Most people under 65 with private insurance receive it as an employee benefit. Employers pay some of the cost and employees have pre-tax income deducted from each paycheck as a contribution to the cost. When employers purchase insurance for a large group, they receive some discount. Most employment in the US is "at will" meaning that employment can end at any time and with it insurance coverage for employees and their dependents. In addition, many employers do not provide health insurance as an employee benefit, particularly for hourly wage workers.

If employer-sponsored health insurance is not available, individuals may also purchase insurance directly, though they will pay higher costs and, until recently, could be denied coverage if they have a pre-existing condition. Until the enactment of President Obama's Patient Safety and Affordable Care Act (ACA) in 2010, only one state (Massachusetts) mandated insurance for all of its citizens—and provided the requisite financial subsidies to help lower-income residents afford to purchase health insurance. President Obama modeled the federal health insurance legislation on the Massachusetts program. The ACA ultimately was implemented with notable success, though it requires additional amendments to maximize its effectiveness and continue to reduce health care spending. Nevertheless, wide state-to-state variations in insurance coverage persist for individuals under the age of 65.[13] The ACA now faces threatened obliteration under the current federal administration, putting the substantial gains in coverage achieved by the ACA at risk. As of this writing, efforts to entirely repeal the ACA have failed, but the current federal administration has succeeded in upending insurance markets, sowing confusion about the status of the law, and otherwise disrupting the implementation of the ACA for 2018 so that losses in coverage are likely for individuals who are neither Medicare-eligible nor receiving insurance as an employee benefit.

The federal Medicare program is a broad entitlement program that covers all legal U.S. residents aged 65 and older and provides hospital insurance (Pt. A); Supplemental Medical Insurance (Pt. B) and pharmaceutical benefits (Pt. D) through a variety of mechanisms, along with co-insurance purchased by eligible program beneficiaries. Pt. A is funded primarily through payroll taxes. Pt. B is available to those who enroll and pay a Pt. B premium, and is funded through a combination of premium payments and tax-funded support.[14] Although there is plenty of room for improvement, particularly in the wise use of medical dollars, most Americans who receive care under Medicare are satisfied with the program.

The Medicaid program is a joint federal/state program that covers the "medically needy," a term which is defined differently by each participating state. It is

13 Before the implementation of the ACA, Massachusetts had 99.5% of its citizens covered through employee coverage, compulsory purchase rules, and subsidies to assist the purchase for low-income individuals, and Massachusetts continues to have nearly universal coverage. Other states, such as Texas and Florida, had very high numbers of uninsured individuals. Now, under the ACA, Texas still lags compared with Massachusetts and 22% of Texas citizens below the age of 65 lack health insurance of any kind and only 58% of Texans have employee-based coverage. Kaiser Family Foundation. Available at http://kff.org/other/state-indicator/adults-19-64/?currentTimeframe=0&selectedRows=%7B%22nested%22:%7B%22texas%22:%7B%7D%7D%7D&sortModel=%7B%22colId%22:%22Location%22,%22sort%22:%22asc%22%7D. (Accessed 31 May 2017.) Before the ACA was implemented, the latest data indicated that the U.S. government paid about 46% of total health care costs. Over 16% of U.S. residents (49.9 million) had no health insurance as of the end of 2010. Now, under the ACA, the latest numbers show the 2016 uninsured rate remains at an all time low with the uninsured rate at 11.9% for Americans 18–64 and 8.6% for all Americans. Kaiser Family Foundation. Available at http://kff.org/other/state-indicator/total-population/?currentTimeframe=0&sortModel=%7B%22colId%22:%22Location%22,%22sort%22:%22asc%22%7D. (Accessed 31 May 2017.)

14 Centers for Medicare and Medicaid Services. Available at www.cms.gov/Medicare/Medicare-General-information/MedicareGenInfo/index.html. (Accessed 31 May 2017.)

a welfare program, and thus eligibility is based primarily on economic need and coverage goes to very low-income individuals and their children. Not all low-income individuals are covered, however; Medicaid has in the past been described as covering the "deserving poor" which has been interpreted to include certain favored groups such as children of low-income households, the elderly, blind, and permanently and totally disabled individuals. Medicaid is financed and administered by federal and state governments together. State programs are subject to federal oversight in terms of eligibility, funding, and benefits.[15]

Once an individual has access to care via private insurance, Medicaid, or Medicare, the problem of preventable harm comes into play. In the U.S., the over-utilization of medical care and the concomitant risk of avoidable iatrogenic harm represents one particular area of concern that is susceptible to improvement. The U.S. health care system and health care delivery culture operate in ways that structurally encourage the provision of unnecessary tests, procedures, and medications.[16] It is well-documented that the risk of iatrogenic harm increases with the increased provision of care even as physicians themselves acknowledge that they are often providing unnecessary medical care.[17]

In the context of private insurance either purchased individually or provided as an employee benefit, the proliferation of "managed care" insurance structures originally was designed to streamline care with an eye to economic efficiency and to focus on preventative care in order to lower the costs of future serious and chronic illness. Prior to the implementation of managed care payment models, fee-for-service payment created perverse economic incentives that both encouraged physicians to provide more tests and treatments in order to increase income while at the same time spending valuable health care dollars without careful attention to the medical necessity or appropriateness of individual treatment decisions. In other words, fee-for-service reimbursement gave little attention to resource allocation. In contrast to old style fee-for-service payment, managed care usually requires pre-authorization for most tests and specialty care. Although the promised benefits of managed care in promoting preventative care have not fully

15 See: www.medicaid.gov/medicaid/. (Accessed 31 May 2017.) In addition to these two major federal government programs, there are several smaller but important federal programs that provide government-funded medical care. The State Children's Health Insurance Program (SCHIP) expands Medicaid coverage to cover children and mandates that states cover all children under age six whose family income falls below 133% of the poverty level and children under age 19 whose families have incomes up to 100% of the poverty level. SCHIP has rules that allow states that wish to provide coverage to children with higher family incomes to do so as well. The Veteran's Administration Tricare Program is a federally-administered and funded program of heath care for members of the military and veterans and their families. It has its own system of 1400 VA hospitals and clinics and provides care at very little cost to the recipients. Finally, the Indian Health Service provides health care in 600 facilities to 1.5 million Native Americans.

16 See, e.g. Allen Marshall, 'Unnecessary tests and treatment explain why health care costs so much', *Scientific America*, 29 November 2017. www.scientificamerican.com/article/unnecessary-tests-and-treatment-explain-why-health-care-costs-so-much/. (Accessed 27 March 2018.)

17 Heather Lyu et al., 'Overtreatment in the United States', *PLOS One*, 6 Sept. 2017. Available at http://journals.plos.org/plosone/article?id=10.1371/journal.pone.0181970. (Accessed 31 October 2017.)

materialized, it does have the benefit of eliminating some of the worst excesses of fee-for-service reimbursement.

Nevertheless, the fee-for-service reimbursement structure of the Medicare program continues to play an outsized role in the provision of unnecessary medical care in the U.S. The perverse incentives of fee-for-service payment systems incentivizes over-utilization of care and the data demonstrate the undesirable consequences.[18] Simply put, this payment structure means that the more treatments, tests, and procedures the patient receives, the more reimbursement the physician and/or hospital will receive.[19] As of 2015, Medicare covers approximately 55 million people, and any changes to the program will have a significant impact on both health care spending and quality.[20] Although there were some legislative efforts under the Obama administration and some general educational efforts to curb the excesses of fee-for-service payment in Medicare, the model remains the predominant approach to payment in this large population insurance program for those aged 65 and older.

More generally and apart from payment structures, the culture of health care in the U.S. tends to lead to frequent utilization of unnecessary tests, treatments, drugs, and procedures.[21] In the context of serious and possibly terminal illness, many people believe that more therapeutic care (such as tests, procedures, life-supportive measures and drug therapies) leads to longer life and improved physical well-being.[22] Another cause of over-utilization of medical tests and interventions

18 It is well documented that one-third of medical expenses for the last year of life are spent in the final month and that aggressive therapies and technologies in that final month account for nearly 80% of these costs. See Baohui Zhang et al., 'Health care costs in the last week of life: associations with end-of-life conversations', *Archives Internal Med*, 2009, 169:480, 482–4. Moreover, 30% of Medicare dollars spent go to care for the 5% of Medicare beneficiaries who die each year. *See* Amber E. Barnato et al., 'Trends in inpatient treatment intensity among Medicare beneficiaries at the end of life', *Health Serv. Res* 2004, 39:363, 363–4; see also Joan M. Teno, et al., Change in end-of-life care for Medicare beneficiaries: site of death, place of care, and health care transitions in 2000, 2005, and 2009, *J. Am. Med. Assn* 2013, 309:470, 473 tbl. 2 (noting that, in 2009, 29.2% of patients who died had received care in an ICU in the previous 30 days); Donald M. Berwick and Andrew Hackbarth, 'Eliminating waste in U.S. health care', *J. Am. Med. Ass'n*, 2012, 307:1513 (describing 6 categories of health care spending waste, including overtreatment such as use of surgery when watchful waiting is better and unwanted intensive care at the end of life, and estimating that wasteful spending in the overtreatment category accounts for between $158 billion and $226 billion in 2011).

19 Stephen F. Jencks et al., 'Rehospitalizations among patients in the Medicare fee-for-service program', *New Eng J Med*, 2009, 360:1418–28, (discussing the Medicare fee-for-service reimbursement system in the context of rates of rehospitalization for Medicare beneficiaries); Robert Steinbrook, 'The end of fee-for-service medicine? Proposals for payment reform in Massachusetts', *New Eng J Med* 2009, 361:1036–8 (discussing the incentives for over-utilization of medical services created by a fee-for-service payment system).

20 Centers for Medicare and Medicaid Services, *On its 50th anniversary, more than 55 million Americans covered by Medicare* (2015). Available at www.cms.gov/newsroom/mediarelease database/press-releases/2015-press-releases-items/2015-07-28.html. (Last accessed 13 July 2017.)

21 Barbara A. Noah and Neal R. Feigenson, 'Avoiding overtreatment at the end of life: physician-patient communication and truly informed consent', *Pace L. Rev* 2016, 36(3):101–64.

22 Sean Palfrey, 'Daring to practice low-cost medicine in a high-tech era', *New Eng J Med* 2011. Available at www.nejm.org/doi/full/10.1056/NEJMp1101392#t=article (commenting on the mistaken belief that "doing everything' is the best practice and the way to prevent harm'). (Accessed 12 June 2017.)

is the physician's fear of making a medical error or being accused of hastening death, with the accompanying prospect of malpractice litigation.[23] Although U.S. physicians tend to over-estimate the risk of litigation, the perceived threat has created a culture of defensive medicine.[24] All of this, coupled with the American tendency to believe that mortality is for other people,[25] puts pressure on physicians to deliver maximal care, even when that care itself can cause harm.

State-by-state adverse event reporting systems in the United States and evidence of progress

It is difficult to evaluate the level of improvement in patient safety since the publication of the IOM Report, and much of the problem in this evaluation lies with the lack of "robust mechanisms to routinely measure the problem."[26] Commentators suggest that serious adverse events remain underreported, in part due to confusion about which events should be reported.[27] In 2002, the U.S. National Quality Forum (NQF) published a list of 28 serious, preventable events with the goal of creating a standardized list of events for mandatory reporting by various entities, such as hospitals.[28] The NQF created this standardized list in order to bolster public accountability for adverse events, to foster the collection of consistent and useful data, and to reduce the reporting burden on health care professionals and facilities.[29]

The IOM Report advocated a national adverse event reporting system,[30] but it is unsurprising in the U.S. that such a system has not been implemented. There is cultural and political resistance to federal systems that might demand significant budgetary resources (even if the pay-off of such a system were to reduce costs), that might implicate individual privacy, or that might interfere with states' rights.[31] Health care providers apparently also opposed a national, mandatory

23 Nathan E. Goldstein et al., 'Prevalence of formal accusations of murder and euthanasia against physicians', *J Palliative Med* 2012, 15:334 (finding, based on survey data, that over half of respondents had been accused of euthanasia or murder by a patient or patient's family member within the previous five years and 4% of those surveyed had been formally investigated for hastening a patient's death).

24 Alan Meisel et al., 'Seven legal barriers to end-of-life care: myths, realities, and grains of truth', *J Am Med Ass'n* 2000, 284(19):2495–501 (explaining that physicians overestimate the risk of malpractice lawsuits and that poor communication by physicians about end-of-life issues increased the risk of litigation).

25 Barbara A. Noah, 'In denial: the role of law in preparing for death', *Elder Law Journal* 2013, 21:1–31.

26 Pronovost et al., 'Fifteen years after *To err is human*'.

27 K. W. Kizer and M. B. Stegun, 'Serious reportable adverse events in health care, advances in patient safety', *Advances in Patient Safety*, 2005, 4:339–52. Available at www.ncbi.nlm.nih.gov/books/NBK20598/. (Accessed 16 June 2017.)

28 Ibid. p. 341.

29 Ibid. pp. 348–9.

30 For another overview of state reporting systems that advocates for a national system of adverse event reporting, see Nathan West and Terry Eng, 'Monitoring and reporting hospital-acquired conditions: a federalist approach', *Medicare and Medicaid Research Review* 2014, 4:E1–E16.

31 The U.S. Constitution reserves to the states those powers that are not specially enumerated as federal powers. U.S. Constitution, Amendment X ('The powers not delegated to the United States by the Constitution, nor prohibited by it to the States, are reserved to the States respectively, or to the people.').

reporting system,[32] perhaps because of concerns that increasing public awareness of the rate of preventable adverse events would encourage more medical malpractice litigation, particular if data are publicly available.[33] Nevertheless, moving to a national reporting system or, at least, the collating of data from all of the extant state systems into a larger data set with a uniform list of mandatory reportable events, most certainly would provide a clearer picture of the nature and magnitude of the problem.[34] The ACA also includes multiple provisions aimed at improving patient safety, including efforts to standardize good medical practices by encouraging practice guidelines and evidence-based health care delivery and provisions to track adverse events in hospitals.[35]

Many of the most relevant laws governing adverse event reporting are drafted on a state-by-state basis, the primary exception being the U.S. Food and Drug Administration's (FDA) federal regulations concerning the reporting of adverse drug, device, and biologic product events via the Medwatch system.[36] In addition, there are other federal initiatives that track specific types of adverse events. For example, all 50 states have received federally-funded grants to reduce hospital-acquired infections (HAIs) and to offer training and other support to states, and the latest data demonstrate a reduction of many types of HAIs.[37] The Centers for Disease Control's National Healthcare Safety Network (NHSN) tracks health care-acquired infections via reports from participating health care institutions and provides educational support to institutions of various types regarding infection prevention.[38] The Centers for Medicare and Medicaid Services (CMS) also began to gather data on the frequency of hospital-acquired conditions (HACs) as defined by the Medicare program. Beginning with federal legislation enacted in 2005, Medicare regulations prohibit payments to hospitals and other health care facilities for treatment of various categories of HACs that Medicare deems to be preventable.[39] In response to the CMS initiative, a number of states with state-based adverse event reporting systems (as described below) also participate in the NHSN reporting program and seven states that have no other state reporting program participate in the NHSN program.[40]

However, none of the federal reporting or tracking programs truly carry out the IOM Report's recommendation for a unified, national adverse event

32 Kizer and Stegun, 'Serious reportable adverse events in health care', p. 346.

33 West and Eng, 'Monitoring and reporting hospital-acquired conditions', citing M. Mello et al., 'Fostering rational regulation of patient safety', *Journal of Health Politics, Policy and Law* 2005, 30(3):375–426.

34 Ibid. p. 348.

35 Barry R. Furrow, 'Regulating patient safety: the Patient Protection and Affordable Care Act' *U Pa L Rev* 2011, 159:101.

36 U.S. Food and Drug Administration, Questions and answers on FDA's adverse event reporting system (2016). Available at www.fda.gov/drugs/guidancecomplianceregulatoryinformation/surveillance/adversedrugeffects/. (Accessed 13 June 2017.)

37 Centers for Disease Control and Prevention, *National Healthcare Safety Network*. Available at www.cdc.gov/nhsn/about-nhsn/index.html. (Accessed 18 June 2017.)

38 Ibid.

39 West and Eng, 'Monitoring and reporting hospital-acquired conditions'.

40 Ibid. at E8 and Exhibit 3.

reporting system. As with the U.S. health care system more generally, adverse event reporting remains a fragmented product of various federal and state initiatives. Given the apparent lack of political will to implement a national adverse event reporting system, the process was left to the states to decide whether and how to create a system in the wake of the IOM's recommendations. As a result, there are state reporting systems in just over half of the states, but there is significant variation among these systems as to what is reportable and what information will be made available to the public or otherwise shared with stakeholders.

As of 2015, 27 states and the District of Columbia have implemented some form of adverse event reporting system: California, Colorado, Connecticut, District of Columbia, Florida, Georgia, Illinois, Indiana, Kansas, Maine, Maryland, Massachusetts, Minnesota, Nevada, New Hampshire, New Jersey, New York, Ohio, Oregon, Pennsylvania, Rhode Island, South Carolina, South Dakota, Tennessee, Texas, Utah, Vermont, and Washington. Nearly all the states' reporting systems are mandatory, with the exception of Oregon's reporting system, which is voluntary.[41]

There is also variation as to which entities are required to report. While all of the state systems require adverse event reporting from hospitals, four states also require reporting from ambulatory surgical centers, long-term care facilities, ambulatory clinics, and home health care providers.[42] Seventeen states collect reports from various other types of facilities including abortion clinics, birthing centers, substance abuse treatment centers, dialysis clinics, clinical laboratories, or pharmacies.[43] Reportable events also vary from state to state. A number of states have adopted the NQF's list of Serious Reportable Events, though some states use a modified version of this list and others have created their own lists of which events must be reported.[44] Unsurprisingly, the number of reports received varies considerably from state to state depending on the number and type of events that are included in states' lists of reportable events and the varied requirements as to which entities must report.

The big question is, of course, how do states make use of the data? States can pinpoint individual health care facilities with systemic problems that lead to errors and require that these facilities improve the relevant system. States also use cumulative data to develop and disseminate reports about common errors and best practices. Policy-makers (both governmental and private) also may use the data to make decisions as to how best to change problematic behavior or protocols.[45]

One important distinction between state systems centers around whether to make the reported adverse event data available to facilities and to the public.

41 Carrie Hanlon et al, 'Guide to state adverse event reporting systems, National Academy for State Health Policy' (Jan. 2015) (noting that Wyoming had a reporting system but that it has sunset). Available at https://psnet.ahrq.gov/resources/resource/29119/2014-guide-to-state-adverse-event-reporting-systems. (Accessed 12 June 2017.)

42 Ibid. at 6 (Colorado, the District of Columbia, Massachusetts and Tennessee).

43 Ibid. at 6 and appendix.

44 Ibid. at 6–8 and fig. 2.

45 Ibid. at 9 (adding that just under half of state systems use data to recommend facility-wide changes and for provider and facility education).

Most states share reported data with facilities, though a few state reporting systems have no mechanism for sharing information with health care facilities. Most states also share data publicly, with only five states keeping the data private. If a state does opt to make data public, there is the secondary question of whether to publish facility-specific information or data based on aggregated reports from all facilities of a particular type. In any event, aggregated data increases the likelihood that policy-makers can spot particular trends and address them.[46]

Of course, the whole idea behind these state adverse event reporting facilities is to use the data to educate providers and facilities in order to prevent, proactively, future harm from adverse events. Given the wide variation between state systems, it is difficult to draw conclusions about which systems work most effectively to react quickly to patterns of preventable harm and to take corrective action to reduce future harm. Experts in this subject acknowledge that it is challenging to measure the impact of various state systems in preventing future harm.[47] Nevertheless, there is some evidence of improvement as a result of state reporting schemes. Most of the state officials surveyed about their systems believe that the reports have encouraged communication, provided a basis for provider and institutional training to improve processes and prevent adverse events, and have increased awareness of patient safety issues.[48] A separate chapter in this volume provides an in-depth look at the success of Minnesota's adverse event reporting program.[49]

As to the overall "success" of various state adverse event reporting systems, those that require the broadest range of reportable events and those that share this information with the providers and the public are most likely to have a demonstrable impact on patient safety. Commentators also strongly urge coordination of adverse event reporting systems with other state initiatives to improve health care quality.[50] Any system is better than no system, and all of the representatives surveyed from the various states indicate that their state systems have improved awareness, encouraged a culture of transparency in health care, provided the basis for provider education and facility systems improvement, and allowed states to track trends.[51] Given the widespread geographic variation in health care outcomes in the U.S.,[52] state-by-state data is useful even if a national reporting system remains the optimal model.

46 Ibid. at 9 (providing additional details as to the types of public reports among the states that publish the data).

47 Ibid. at 14 (adding that most states have not formally evaluated their own reporting systems).

48 Even so, there is wide variation in how states estimate the impact of their adverse event reporting systems, with some states focusing on quantity and quality of reports, while others evaluate whether trends in particular adverse events demonstrate a reduction in specific types of harm. Ibid. at 14.

49 For an in-depth examination of the structure, implementation, and successes of one state's adverse event reporting system, please see Chapter 10 (describing the adverse event reporting scheme in Minnesota).

50 K. Sheedy et al., 'Adverse event reporting in Massachusetts and other states, status and trends in 2014', pp. 14–15. Available at www.betsylehmancenterma.gov/assets/uploads/blc-nashp-research.pdf. (Visited 15 June 2017.)

51 Ibid. p. 19.

52 B. L. Rosenberg et al., 'Quantifying geographic variation in health care outcomes in the United States before and after risk-adjustment', *PLOS One* 2016, 11(12):1–21.

It is difficult to explain why the state systems vary, although the explanation is most likely a political one. Within the complex and multi-layered "system" of U.S. health care delivery described above, individual states have a good deal of latitude in how they allocate resources to promote public health, including major areas of investment such as access to health care, availability of affordable health insurance, and data collection and record-keeping. Some states will, unsurprisingly, opt to invest less in the public's health than others, for political, ideological, or budgetary reasons.

There may also be a link between the average education level or the average income level of various states and the states' willingness to implement adverse event reporting systems, but this is merely speculation. It is worth noting that two of the more progressive areas of the country (e.g., the West coast and New England) have widespread adoption of adverse event reporting systems. All of the West coast states (Washington, Oregon, and California) and all of the New England States (Connecticut, Maine, Massachusetts, New Hampshire, Rhode Island, and Vermont) have adopted reporting systems. Other politically progressive states such as New York, Minnesota, and the District of Columbia also have such systems. But the adoption of these systems is not limited to "Blue States." Some of the more politically conservative states ("Red States") such as Kansas, Utah, and Texas also have adopted reporting systems.

The provision of health care to those who cannot otherwise afford insurance continues to be a politically divisive issue in the U.S. The enactment of the ACA in 2010 was a partial victory for liberals and progressives who seek coverage for all residents of the country and, in the current politically conservative administration, there is a strong political will to undo these significant gains in insurance coverage based on an ideology of individual responsibility for health. This broad battle of views will rage on for some time and likely will fold in other efforts to improve the quality of health care (as opposed to access) for all Americans. If the current administration succeeds in rolling back major portions of the ACA, it will be left to individual states to decide how much they wish to invest in the health of their citizens, whether in the form of access to care via affordable insurance, patient safety initiatives, or other public health mechanisms.

The patient's role in safety: the Joint Commission's "Speak Up" initiatives

In addition to state adverse event reporting initiatives, the Joint Commission, which is an independent, not-for-profit organization that accredits and certifies nearly 21,000 health care organizations and programs in the United States, began a patient safety program in 2002. The program, called "Speak Up," seeks to improve patient safety by involving patients and their families directly in the safe provision of health care. The Speak Up initiative has now been implemented in approximately 70 countries.[53]

53 The Joint Commission, *Facts about Speak Up*. Available at www.jointcommission.org/facts_about_speak_up/. (Accessed 21 May 2018.)

The program seeks to educate patients and families about how to prevent or avoid medical errors by providing them with information about steps that they can take to protect themselves. The program urges patients to:

> **S**peak up if you have questions or concerns.
>
> **P**ay attention to the care you get.
>
> **E**ducate yourself about your illness.
>
> **A**sk a trusted family member or friend to be your advocate (advisor or supporter).
>
> **K**now what medicines you take and why you take them.
>
> **U**se a health care organization that has been carefully checked out.
>
> **P**articipate in all decisions about your treatment.[54]

The detailed patient brochure includes additional, detailed suggestions about how patients and families can participate actively in their health care including helping to keep health care safe.[55] The program represents the flipside to efforts to improve quality of care and reduce error on a system-wide basis. Instead, the Speak Up initiatives seek to tackle the problem of adverse events on a patient-by-patient basis by educating patients and families about the problem of medical error and various ways to reduce the likelihood of an adverse event in any health care encounter.

More specifically, the brochure focusing on preventing errors in health care states that, "As a patient, you can make your care safer by being an active, involved and informed member of your health care team."[56] The brochure makes the following suggestions, among many others:

- Do not be afraid to ask about safety. If you are having surgery, ask the doctor to mark the area that is to be operated on.
- Do not be afraid to tell the nurse or doctor if you think you are about to get the wrong medicine.
- Do not be afraid to tell a health care professional if you think he or she has confused you with another patient.
- Notice whether your caregivers have washed their hands. Handwashing is the most important way to prevent infections. Do not be afraid to remind a doctor or nurse to do this.
- Know what time of day you normally get medicine. If you do not get it, tell your nurse or doctor.
- As a trusted family member or friend to be your advocate (advisor or supporter).

54 Ibid.

55 The Joint Commission, *Speak Up: help prevent errors in your care*, available at www.jointcommission.org/assets/1/6/speakup.pdf. (Accessed 29 October 2017.)

56 Ibid.

- Ask this person to stay with you, even overnight, when you are hospitalized. You may be able to rest better. Your advocate can help make sure you get the correct medicines and treatments.
- If you are given an IV, ask the nurse how long it should take for the liquid to run out. Tell the nurse if it does not seem to be dripping right (too fast or too slow).[57]

As aspirational advice, these Speak Up suggestions are excellent, though the responsibility and burden that the program places on patients and families often may prove excessive or simply unachievable. Many patients enter the health care system with low levels of "health literacy," that is, with limited ability to understand complex medical concepts and with limited ability and experience in navigating the fragmented and often confusing U.S. health care system.[58] Moreover, many patients and family members may hesitate to "speak up" for fear of alienating their health care providers by expressing a lack of trust in them. The information and educational asymmetry between many patients and their health care providers creates a hierarchical relationship in which many patients will feel both inferior and wary of demonstrating a lack of respect for their physicians and other health care providers. None of this commentary is intended to suggest that the Speak Up initiative lacks merit. On the contrary, its suggestions, when capable of being implemented, must surely prevent many potentially harmful medical errors.

Conclusion

The conglomeration of multiple overlapping adverse event reporting systems in the United States reflects this country's fragmented, inefficient, and inequitable health care finance and delivery system. Any attempts at major reform to adverse event reporting, such as a unified, streamlined federal system as the IOM envisions, will likely face serious political and practical obstacles. In spite of the system's gaps and failings, the efforts of many physicians, health care institutions, regulatory bodies, and other stakeholders deserve recognition for their roles in improving the safety of the U.S. system and substantially more governmental and budgetary support going forward.

References

Agency for Healthcare Research and Quality, *Patient safety primer: never events*, 2016. Available at https://psnet.ahrq.gov/primers/primer/3/never-events. (Accessed 12 June 2017.)

Barnato, Amber E., et al., 'Trends in inpatient treatment intensity among Medicare beneficiaries at the end of life', *Health Serv. Res* 2004, 39: 363–4.

57 Ibid.

58 Office of Disease Prevention and Health Promotion, 'Health Literacy Basics'. Available at https://health.gov/communication/literacy/quickguide/factsbasic.htm (accessed 29 October 2017.); see also Don Nutbeam, 'Health literacy as a public health goal: a challenge for contemporary health education and communication strategies into the 21st century', *Health Promotion International* 2000, 15:259–67.

Berwick, Donald M. and Hackbarth, Andrew, 'Eliminating waste in U.S. health care', *JAMA* 2012, 307:1513.

Centers for Disease Control and Prevention, *National Healthcare Safety Network*. Available at www.cdc.gov/nhsn/about-nhsn/index.html. (Accessed 18 June 2017.)

Centers for Medicare and Medicaid Services. Available at www.cms.gov/Medicare/Medicare-General-information/MedicareGenInfo/index.html. (Accessed 31 May 2017.)

Centers for Medicare and Medicaid Services, *On its 50th anniversary, more than 55 million Americans covered by Medicare* (2015). Available at www.cms.gov/newsroom/mediareleasdatabase/press-releases/2015-press-releases-items/2015–07–28.html. (Accessed 13 July 2017.)

Furrow, Barry R., 'Regulating patient safety: the Patient Protection and Affordable Care Act', *U Pa L Rev* 2011, 159:101.

Goldstein, Nathan E., et al., 'Prevalence of formal accusations of murder and euthanasia against physicians', *J Palliative Med* 2012, 15.

Hanlon, Carrie, et al., 'Guide to state adverse event reporting systems, National Academy for State Health Policy' (Jan. 2015). Available at https://psnet.ahrq.gov/resources/resource/29119/2014-guide-to-state-adverse-event-reporting-systems. (Accessed 12 June 2017.)

Institute of Medicine, *To err is human: building a safer health system*, 2000. Available at: www.nap.edu/catalog/9728/to-err-is-human-building-a-safer-health-system. (Accessed May 2017.)

Jencks, Stephen F., et al., 'Rehospitalizations among patients in the Medicare fee-for-service program', *New Eng J Med* 2009, 360:1418–28.

Kaiser Family Foundation. Available at http://kff.org/other/state-indicator/adults-19–64/?currentTimeframe=0&selectedRows=%7B%22nested%22:%7B%22texas%22:%7B%7D%7D%7D&sortModel=%7B%22colId%22:%22Location%22,%22sort%22:%22asc%22%7D (Accessed 31 May 2017); and http://kff.org/other/state-indicator/total-population/?currentTimeframe=0&sortModel=%7B%22colId%22:%22Location%22,%22sort%22:%22asc%22%7D. (Accessed 31 May 2017.)

Kizer, K. W. and Stegun, M. B., 'Serious reportable adverse events in health care, advances in patient safety', *Advances in Patient Safety*, 2005, 4:339–52. Available at www.ncbi.nlm.nih.gov/books/NBK20598/. (Accessed 16 June 2017.)

Leape, Lucian, 'Error in medicine', *JAMA* 1994, 272:1851–7.

Lyu, Heather, et al., 'Overtreatment in the United States', *PLOS One* 2017. Available at http://journals.plos.org/plosone/article?id=10.1371/journal.pone.0181970. (Accessed 31 October 2017.)

Makary, Martin A. and Daniel, Michael, 'Medical error—the third leading cause of death in the US', *British Medical Journal* 2016, 353.

Marshall, Allen, 'Unnecessary tests and treatment explain why health care costs so much', *Scientific America*, 29 November 2017. www.scientificamerican.com/article/unnecessary-tests-and-treatment-explain-why-health-care-costs-so-much/. (Accessed 27 March 2018.)

Meisel, Alan et al., 'Seven legal barriers to end-of-life care: myths, realities, and grains of truth', *JAMA* 2000, 284(19):2495–501.

Mello, M., et al., 'Fostering rational regulation of patient safety', *Journal of Health Politics, Policy and Law* 2005, 30(3):375–426.

National Center for Health Statistics. Available at www.cdc.gov/nchs/fastats/leading-causes-of-death.htm. (Accessed 31 May 2017.)

National Patient Safety Foundation, 'Free from harm: accelerating patient safety improvement fifteen years after *To err is human*'. 2015, iv. Available at https://psnet.ahrq.gov/

resources/resource/29554/free-from-harm-accelerating-patient-safety-improvement-fifteen-years-after-to-err-is-human. (Accessed 8 June 2017.)

Noah, Barbara A., 'In denial: the role of law in preparing for death', *Elder Law Journal* 2013, 21:1–31.

Noah, Barbara A. and Feigenson, Neal R., 'Avoiding overtreatment at the end of life: physician-patient communication and truly informed consent', *Pace L. Rev* 2016, 36(3):101–64.

Nutbeam, Don, 'Health literacy as a public health goal: a challenge for contemporary health education and communication strategies into the 21st century', *Health Promotion International* 2000, 15:259–67.

Office of Disease Prevention and Health Promotion, 'Health Literacy Basics'. Available at https://health.gov/communication/literacy/quickguide/factsbasic.htm. (Accessed 29 October 2017.)

Palfrey, Sean, 'Daring to practice low-cost medicine in a high-tech era', *New Eng J Med* 2011. Available at www.nejm.org/doi/full/10.1056/NEJMp1101392#t=article. (Accessed 12 June 2017.)

Pronovost, P. J., et al, 'Fifteen years after *To err is human*: a success story to learn from', *BMJ Qual. Saf.* 2015, 1–4.

Rosenberg, B. L., et al., 'Quantifying geographic variation in health care outcomes in the United States before and after risk-adjustment', *PLOS One* 2016, 11(12):1–21.

Sheedy, K., et al., 'Adverse event reporting in Massachusetts and Other states, status and trends in 2014'. Available at www.betsylehmancenterma.gov/assets/uploads/blc-nashp-research.pdf. (Accessed 15 June 2017.)

Steinbrook, Robert, 'The end of fee-for-service medicine? Proposals for payment reform in Massachusetts', *New Eng J Med* 2009, 361:1036–8.

Teno, Joan M., et al., 'Change in end-of-life care for Medicare beneficiaries: site of death, place of care, and health care transitions in 2000, 2005, and 2009', *JAMA* 2013, 309:470, 473, tbl. 2.

The Joint Commission, *Facts about Speak Up*. Available at www.jointcommission.org/facts_about_speak_up/. (Accessed 21 May 2018.)

The Joint Commission, *Sentinel event policy and procedures*. Available at www.jointcommission.org/sentinel_event_policy_and_procedures/. (Accessed 1 November 2017.)

The Joint Commission, *Speak Up: help prevent errors in your care*, available at www.jointcommission.org/assets/1/6/speakup.pdf. (Visited 29 Oct. 2017.)

U.S. Food and Drug Administration, *Questions and answers on FDA's adverse event reporting system* 2016. Available at www.fda.gov/drugs/guidancecomplianceregulatoryinformation/surveillance/adversedrugeffects/. (Accessed 13 June 2017.)

West, Nathan and Eng, Terry, 'Monitoring and reporting hospital-acquired conditions: a federalist approach', *Medicare and Medicaid Research Review* 2014, 4:E1–E16.

Zhang, Baohui, et al., 'Health care costs in the last week of life: associations with end-of-life conversations', *Archives Internal Med*, 2009, 169:480, 482–4.

10 Adverse health events in Minnesota

Rachel Jokela

Introduction

In 2003, the Minnesota State Legislature passed the Adverse Health Care Events (AHE) Law, requiring hospitals and, later, ambulatory surgical centers to report to the Minnesota Department of Health (MDH) whenever one of 27 serious adverse health events occurred. The law was modified during the 2007 legislative session to add a 28th reportable event, and again in 2013 to add four new events and modify or delete others to make 29 reportable events (Appendix A).

Since the inception of the Minnesota AHE Reporting Law 14 years ago, the field of patient safety, as well as the health care environment, has changed significantly. At its core, the AHE system strives to balance learning and accountability. MDH and its partners believe that in order to encourage facilities to continue to share data and learnings throughout Minnesota, hospitals and surgical centers

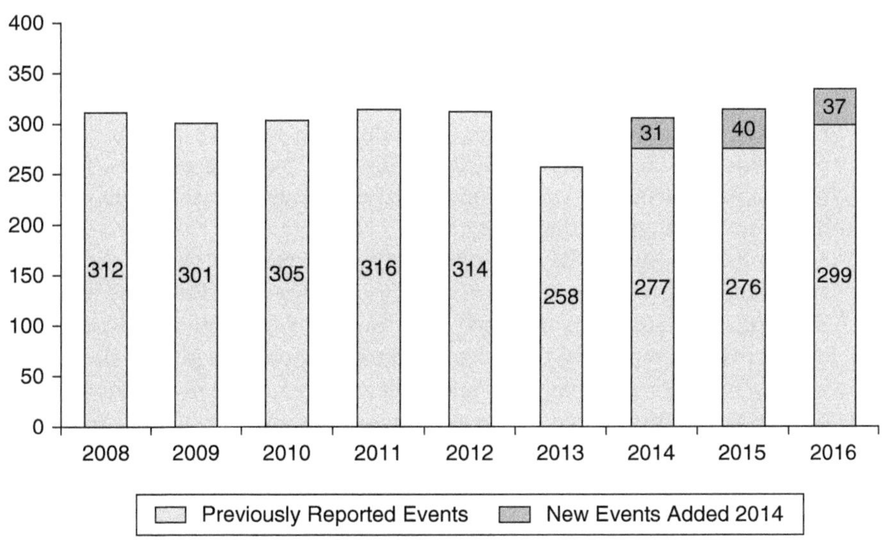

Figure 10.1 Reported adverse health events 2008–2016

need to see the value in the system, which includes receiving support to identify root causes and identify action steps to proactively prevent future events from occurring. Since 2003, over 2,800 events have been reported through the adverse events system (Figure 10.1). However, while counting the frequency with which adverse health events occur and reporting the results publicly is part of the law, it is the focus on improving systems and learning that is of the utmost importance to sustainable improvements in patient safety.

In 2014, for the 10-year evaluation of the program, MDH convened a series of focus groups with patient safety managers, conducted a survey of staff from reporting hospitals and ambulatory surgery centers, and worked with the Minnesota Hospital Association (MHA) and Stratis Health (the Medicare Quality Improvement Organization in MN) to further analyze data from both an epidemiological and statistical perspective over the 10 years of the reporting system. Throughout the evaluation, areas of success were identified as well as areas for future improvement. Key findings from the 10-year evaluation and the three years of data collected since that evaluation, include:

- The AHE law was a catalyst for patient safety throughout the state. It has helped to bring patient safety to the forefront, increased awareness, and led to focused patient safety improvement activities.
- As the system has evolved, facilities have been asked to submit much more robust data and root causes than at the inception of the system. This has led to more in-depth analysis of events and the ability to identify focused improvement opportunities to address specific issues.
- Hospitals and surgical centers reported that the AHE system works well in the current health care environment in Minnesota and would like the same commitment to transparency, learning and public reporting spread to all settings of care, including: cosmetic surgery centers, long term care facilities and clinics.
- Facilities have put many policies/procedures to improve patient safety in place since 2003, including policies to disclose events to patients/families, regular assessment of organizational culture, and sharing AHE data with the board and throughout the facility.
- The number of deaths has declined overall since the first year of the system and events that result in serious injury are on a downward trend as well.
- The registry system was designed as a learning system and analysis of the data across the reporting years demonstrates this primary goal of the system is being met. For example, after Safety Alerts are issued, typically the number of reported events related to the alert increase as awareness about reporting and preventing those types of events has increased. Then numbers begin to decline as identified practices are implemented across the state.
- Although event information is shared between hospitals that have voluntarily agreed to share their data in a de-identified manner and key learnings are incorporated into statewide improvement initiatives, facilities are interested in continuing to proactively expand their ability to learn from each other.

- Some facilities still struggle to engage physicians/surgeons and other staff members in certain safety initiatives (usually surgical safety), and would like assistance developing physician/surgeon champions to build support for safety initiatives.

Impact of the reporting law

During the 10-year evaluation of the program there was a focus on patient safety best practices that have been implemented since the inception of the system, the degree to which the reporting law has led to broader changes within facilities, and the priority patient safety takes at facilities. The ultimate question with regards to the AHE system is whether or not it has made patient care safer in Minnesota, and met its goal of supporting a system of learning and transparency that will lead to fewer adverse events and lower levels of harm

Are we safer?

Patient safety is a complex and evolving concept, one that is measured in many different ways by individual facilities and state/national organizations. Examples of safety measures include: the rate of reportable adverse health events, the lack of health care acquired infections, or performance relative to state or national goals (to name a few). As a result, many facilities find it challenging to answer the question of how best to measure the extent to which they are making progress, particularly in the area of adverse events.

Survey data analysis

During the organizational survey in 2010 respondents were asked if they felt that Minnesota was safer than it was at the start of the reporting system in 2003. A strong majority of survey respondents (94 percent) reported that they felt their facility was somewhat safer or significantly safer than in 2003 (Figure 10.2). In 2008, during the five-year evaluation of the reporting system, MDH asked the same question of reporting facilities. The percentage of respondents that reported feeling "significantly safer" in 2013 is four times higher than the level reported in 2008; the percentage of respondents stating a neutral response has declined sharply as well.

Adverse events data analysis

While one way to measure the level of safety in Minnesota health care is to look at qualitative data such as the survey responses and focus group answers, another way is to look at event specific data such as rates of events and level of harm to patients from these events. Analyzing this type of quantitative data is a challenge for the AHE system as a whole, as it only captures a relatively small subset of events and some definitions have changed over time, making it difficult to interpret increases or decreases in numbers.

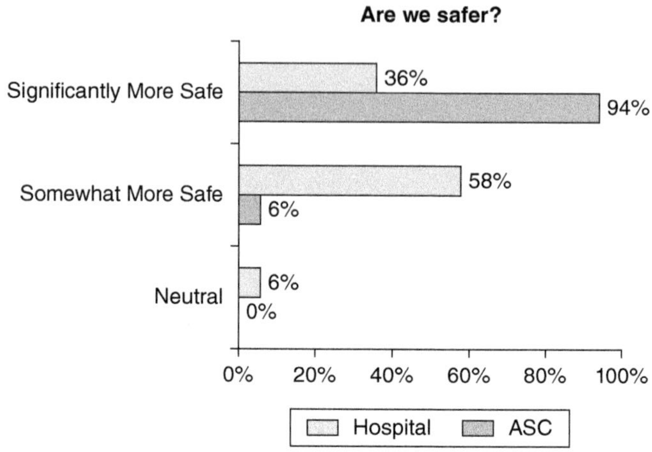

Figure 10.2 Survey data: are we safer?

Prior to the implementation of the law, there was no statewide system for assessing how frequently these events happened, making it hard to retroactively compare where we are now with where we were then. While some individual facilities tracked their own adverse or serious events, there was no law in place requiring reporting of events publicly or collectively. This also made quantifying the progress of the first 10 years of the system somewhat of a challenge. However, the data does show some patterns of progress that are highlighted in this section.

Level of harm

Under the reporting law, some event categories are reportable regardless of level of harm (e.g., retained objects or wrong body part procedures). Other categories, such as falls or medication errors are only reportable if the event results in a patient death or serious injury. Still other events have evolved over the life of the reporting law, such as the addition of the reporting of falls resulting in serious injury in 2008 (prior to 2008, only falls resulting in a patient death were reportable).

Regardless of the changes to the reporting system, reportable events resulting in death of a patient have been reported consistently throughout the years since 2004, making it possible to analyze trends over a full decade of reporting. Analysis of the number of deaths from reportable adverse events per year shows that the overall number of deaths associated with AHEs has varied from year to year, but has declined as a whole (Figure 10.3).

Trends associated with events resulting in serious injury are harder to quantify with the addition of falls associated with serious injury in 2008 (which increased the number of reports from 2008 forward). However, when looking at the data from the years since that category was expanded, there was a slow, yet steady downward trend in the number of events reported with serious injury until 2014, when that number began to rise. However, this rise in events resulting in serious injury also correlates to the decline in number of deaths (Figure 10.4).

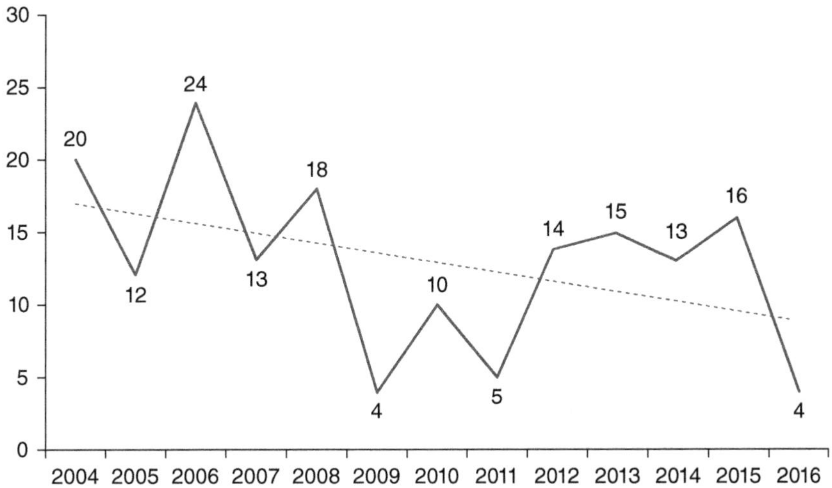

Figure 10.3 Number of deaths associated with adverse events

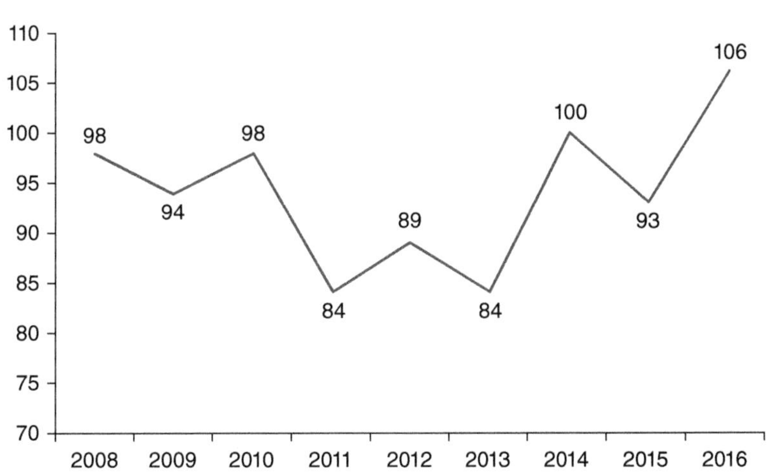

Figure 10.4 Number of serious injuries resulting from adverse events

Pressure ulcers

Since 2003, pressure ulcers have been the most commonly reported event, and are reportable regardless of level of harm to the patient. A definitional change in 2007 added "unstageable" pressure ulcers to the list of reportable events and since those types of pressure ulcers are more frequent, the number of events increased substantially at that time (Figure 10.5).

Staff from Minnesota health care facilities often state that through the MHA "SAFE SKIN" Call to Action (a set of best practices and accompanying toolkit to assist organizations with reducing pressure ulcers), they have put best practices in place to prevent many types of pressure ulcers, but are still struggling with critically ill patients, often those in intensive care units. Typically, these patients' conditions are tenuous and may prevent staff from repositioning them to relieve pressure.

In the past several years, MDH and its partners have worked to develop a turning clock that is a visual reminder to staff when turning a patient and greatly minimizes not only the time spent in the supine position, but also the time spent sitting in a chair with pressure on the coccyx as well. Furthermore, a best practice was added to the MHA SAFE SKIN Call to Action gap analysis that asks hospitals to put policies in place to use "micro turns" on patients who are too hemodynamically instable to be turned in a traditional manner, but also need to have some movement to avoid pressure injuries.

Retained foreign objects

Overall numbers of retained foreign objects (RFO) have remained relatively stable throughout the last 13 years, however, there is a slight decrease on a linear

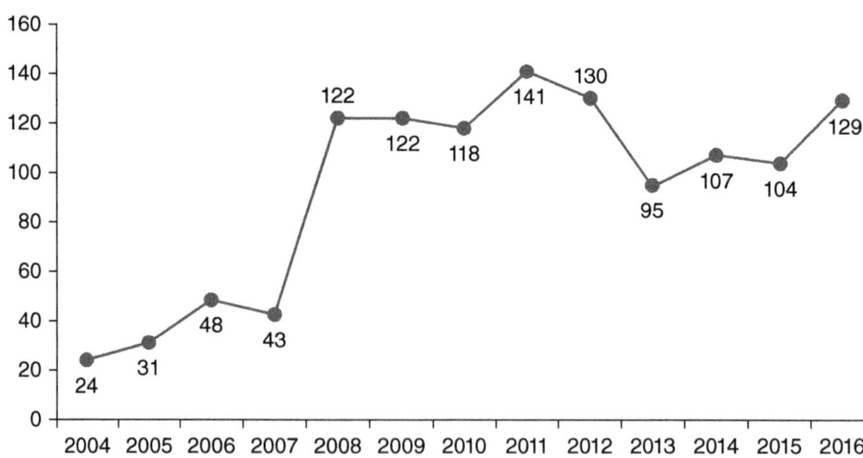

Figure 10.5 Reportable pressure ulcers

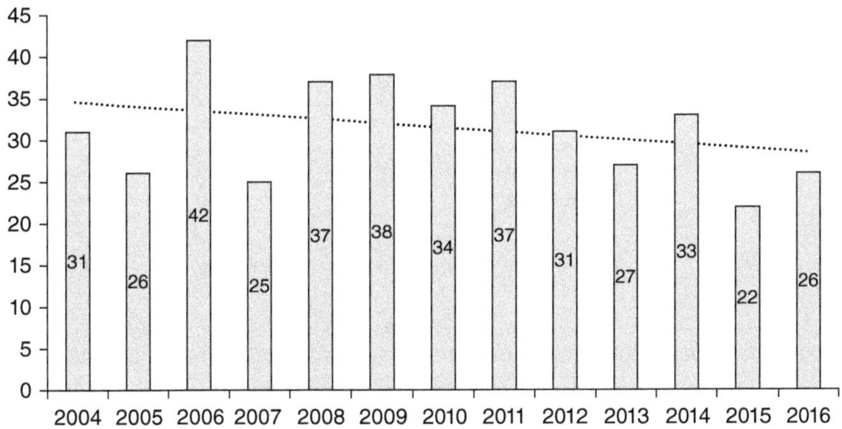

Figure 10.6 Retained Foreign Objects

trend line (Figure 10.6). Even without vast improvement in overall numbers, much work has been done through the MHA "SAFE COUNT" Call to Action on best practices for counting and accounting for all items used during surgical or invasive procedures.

Looking specifically at vaginal packing (sponges, or gauze intentionally placed during a surgical procedure with the intent to remove before discharge), in the early years of the reporting system, there were many of these cases reported in labor and delivery (L&D). In response to those findings, MHA developed the SAFE COUNT Call to Action to address the issues surrounding accounting for items in L&D. After this campaign began, there was a sharp decline in the number of retained foreign objects found in L&D and in 2011 and 2012 there were no RFO in that area (Figure 10.7). This was regarded as a large success for a Call to Action campaign and SAFE COUNT was retired in 2012 with 97 percent of facilities reporting having implemented all of the best practices. However, in 2013, there were two cases of retained objects in L&D, causing MDH and its partners to ask facilities to review the SAFE COUNT practices to ensure best practices remain in place.

Due to the increase in retained objects in gynecological surgery, MHA developed "SAFE ACCOUNT 2.0" in 2013 to address new issues of vaginal packing in gynecological surgery. This campaign was rolled out in 2013 with over 100 MN facilities participating and reporting data on their rates of implementation of best practices on a quarterly basis. After the dissemination of the SAFE ACCOUNT 2.0 gap analysis, there was a sustained decrease in retained packing in gynecological surgery.

Figure 10.7 RFO (vaginal packing) by location 2003–2016

There are other types of RFO as well, such as small miscellaneous items, soft goods, unretrieved device fragments, whole device/instruments, and whole sharp needles. Prior to 2013, the Patient Safety Registry did not collect this information. Additional data fields were put into the registry in 2014 that allowed for analysis of which type of object was retained on this level of granularity. This has been helpful in tailoring education and resources toward which types of objects are most commonly retained. Most commonly these are pieces of needles or tips of instruments. In 2009, due to an increase in these types of events, MDH and its partners issued a Safety Alert to all Minnesota facilities around accounting for items being intact before and after surgical or invasive procedures. In the past several years, facilities have begun to see success in this area and the numbers of these types of reportable events are on the decline. This type of decline, seen after the issuance of a Safety Alert, demonstrates that the AHE system in Minnesota is one of learning and improvement, where the data can inform best practice development.

Biggest changes in facilities as a result of the law

During the 10-year evaluation, participants were asked to share the biggest changes in their facilities as a result of the AHE law. Some changes that have come about as a result of the law are difficult to quantify, but provide strong evidence of a shift in the focus of organizations toward safety. Even so, a clear theme that emerged through the evaluation is the idea that the law helped to focus attention on safety beyond what it might otherwise have been.

Focus group participants stated that the law has brought attention and awareness to events that in the past may have been seen as "inevitable" and are now seen as nearly always "preventable." This has shifted the emphasis away from accepting events such as pressure ulcers and falls as inevitable, to learning how events occur and implementing interventions to prevent them in the future. Focus group participants also stated that this is a significant shift from the "way of thinking" prior to 2003 and has been a gradual but profound cultural shift in the years since the inception of the reporting system. Participants stated that because the AHE process is standardized and required across all hospitals and ambulatory surgical centers, it has introduced a level of rigor and structure, where employees understand the process to report and how to work toward preventing these events. Many participants remarked how this standardized approach has resulted in a higher quality of care for patients and how patient safety and evidence-based best practices have become a community standard in Minnesota and allow all facilities to consistently report and improve patient safety.

Root Cause Analysis investigations

One component of the AHE law requires facilities to perform a Root Cause Analysis (RCA) after each reportable event and report those findings to the state through the registry system. An RCA is a method of problem solving that attempts to identify the root causes of events, typically looking deeper than human error and identifying systems issues. Many focus group participants reported having broadened the use of RCA beyond reportable events and say that the AHE law has helped facilities to look at all their events (or near misses) in terms of identifying patterns and trends and being able to mitigate risks. Participants reported that this practice was not common in 2003 and has allowed for a more robust investigation of events and near misses.

Learning from events

Analysis of reported events across the lifespan of AHE reporting demonstrates a system of learning and improvement. As trends are identified in the data, aggregate information from the event information, including findings from the RCAs and action plans, are communicated to hospitals and ambulatory surgical centers in the form of Safety Alerts and/or incorporated in best practice recommendations, such as MHA Calls to Action.

Figure 10.9 illustrates this system of learning and improvement for pressure ulcers, in which trends were identified and communicated, awareness increased resulting initially in an increase in reports related to the type of event involved, and best practices were implemented resulting in a gradual decrease in the specific type of events being targeted.

In October 2007, unstageable pressure ulcers were formally added to the list of reportable pressure ulcers. Prior to that time, the vast majority of pressure ulcers were either Stage III or IV ulcers. The sharp increase in reported

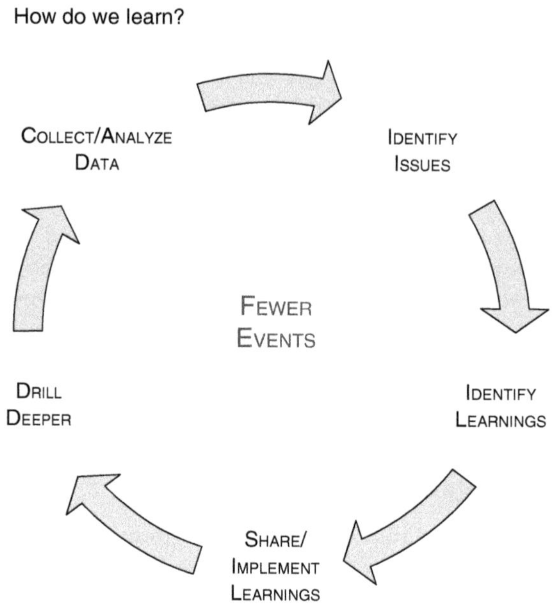

Figure 10.8 How do we learn?

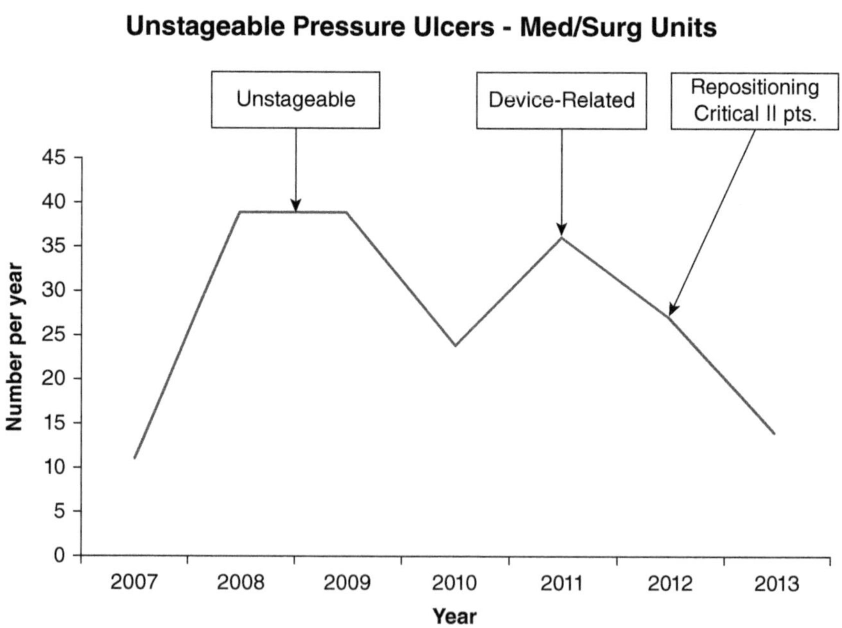

Figure 10.9 Number of unstageable pressure ulcers – med/surg units

unstageable pressure ulcers in 2008 reflects that change. At that same time, Minnesota facilities began participating in the statewide initiative, SAFE SKIN, to collectively implement best practices to prevent pressure ulcers. Following the statewide implementation, there was a decrease in pressure ulcers.

Several years later, ongoing review of reported events identified a number of pressure ulcers resulting from medical devices such as oxygen tubing, endotracheal tubes and cervical collars. In 2010, these findings were communicated to facilities, which raised awareness of this issue, and after best practices were put into place around the state, another decrease was noted (Figure 10.9).

Learnings from these events were used as a foundation for best practice recommendations and were incorporated into the next iteration of the statewide initiative, MHA "SAFE SKIN 2.0," which began in early 2011. Since inception of this initiative, facilities report success with reducing pressure ulcers in those that are critically ill and may have contraindications to traditional turning methods.

Sharing of information

Since the inception of the reporting law, MDH and its partners have held countless education and training events for reporting facilities on such topics as falls, pressure ulcers, safe surgical practices, suicide risk assessment and prevention, and RCA. This education is based on the learnings that come from the reported events in the Patient Safety Registry and is a crucial element in supporting the program's goal to create a learning health care system.

Overview of resources provided through the AHE system include (this list is not exhaustive):

- MHA Calls to Action on five topics with an average of 110 hospitals participating per campaign with accompanying web-based and in-person education sessions.
- Twenty-Two Safety Alerts on topics such as: implant verification, fall injury risk and suicide prevention.
- Semi-annual RCA training(s) done throughout the state since 2007.
- An online RCA toolkit with resources compiled nationally and at a local level.
- Regional training/education sessions on safe surgical practices and how to audit pre-surgical Time Outs.
- Suicide prevention trainings led by national topic experts.

Many participants in the focus groups and survey stated that one of the most valuable parts of the AHE program is the training and resources that have been made available, in particular the MHA Calls to Action. In these campaigns, developed in response to data submitted through the adverse events system, facilities agree to implement a series of evidence-based best practices and to report quarterly on their progress. Participants described feeling supported in their patient safety efforts with this education and training as well as hundreds of resources and multiple toolkits that have been made available online for all facilities.

This approach of training/education and sharing all resources publicly has helped facilities by allowing them to use those resources instead of creating their own tools at individual facilities, which is time consuming and can be cost prohibitive. Health care organizations also report a benefit to attending training and education with other facilities throughout the state and sharing learnings and best practices with one another in person. These in-person opportunities can sometimes be the most beneficial to them, providing innovative and "outside the box" ideas.

Reporting and review process

In the nearly 14 years that the adverse events reporting system has been in place, it has evolved from a basic web-based reporting tool and review process to a much more comprehensive system that involves complete reviews of reported events, a higher level of granularity of data that is required for each event, and alerts and campaigns based on best practices and other issues identified through the reporting and review process.

The reporting and review process is designed in a way that requires facilities to input basic information about the event (patient de-identified) but also requires the submission of a root cause, contributing factors and corrective action plan. Through the years, MDH has worked with reporting facilities to refine the web-based system and make its use as intuitive as possible, including changes to make its use easier and quicker and to add additional categories for data collection in order to accommodate changing practice.

RCA and corrective action plans

One of the pillars of the AHE system is that facilities investigate their events by completing a RCA. MDH has been collecting data on the type of root causes identified by facilities for each event since the inception of the law.

Root cause categories have shifted and changed slightly over the years, but overall have remained mostly consistent. The percentage of times that facilities choose "Communication" as the root cause of an event has steadily decreased over time, while the percentage of times that facilities had a finding of no root cause or contributing factor has increased. This is partially due to the complex nature of events that are currently reported into the system.

The Communication category includes all forms of communication, such as: verbal, electronic, communication of test results, etc., and is often reported as communication of important information to the incorrect person, lack of communication of important information, or lack of team work during a stressful situation.

Many facilities in Minnesota are now performing teamwork training for all staff as a way of preventing communication errors and increasing a culture of patient safety. Much of this work came out of the Minnesota Alliance for Patient

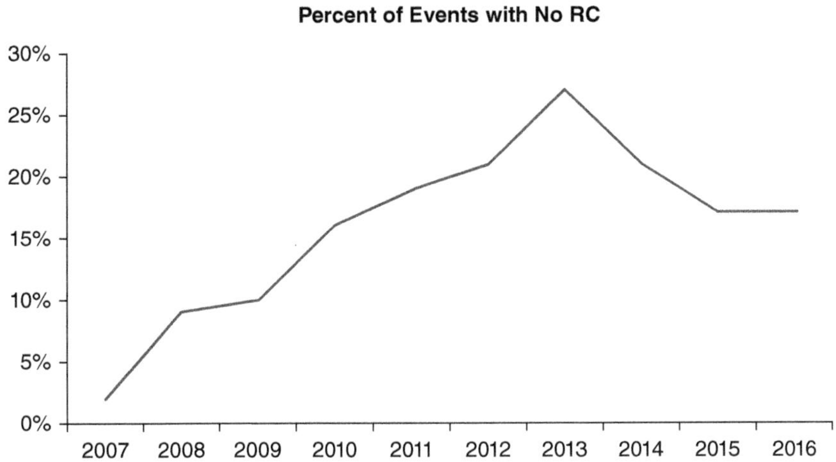

Figure 10.10 Percentage of reported adverse events with no identified root cause

Safety's "SAFE CULTURE" roadmap in 2012, which MDH helped to develop. Also of note is an increase in facilities choosing "Rules/Policies/Procedures" as a root cause; since the first few years of the reporting system, this is often reported as lack of a policy/procedure or an ineffective policy/procedure in place.

As noted above, facilities are increasingly reporting an inability to identify a root cause or contributing factor for their events. In 2007 (the first year this data was mined through the registry), only 2 percent of events had no identified root cause, whereas in 2013 over a quarter of events were reported without an identified root cause or contributing factor. The vast majority of events with no root cause or contributing factor were pressure ulcers and falls.

Through the AHE system, facilities are required by law to complete a RCA; however, those findings may conclude there was no root cause (system breakdown) or contributing factor (any possible factors that could have played a role aside from system breakdowns)—or that the event could not have been prevented. The challenge with the issue of preventability is to assure that facilities are looking at all possible avenues for improvement, rather than looking at preventability, and working to reduce risk as much as possible. The fact that these types of events with no identified root cause or contributing factors was increasing (Figure 10.10) was of note and in the last several years, MDH worked with facilities to increase the rigor with which they recognize and strive to reduce risks and look for opportunities for improve safety. Some of this was accomplished by changes that were made to the Patient Safety Registry itself. A more robust root cause is now required, as well as submission of any and all contributing factors that are identified. The MDH review team also changed from reviewing events for completeness (prior to 2016) to reviewing events for proper identification of root cause/contributing factors, strength of, and proper linkage of, the corrective action plan to the root cause, as well as the types of measurement that are being used to measure the success of the corrective action plan.

Now that the review team is reviewing events in a new way, this has opened up new avenues for the review team to offer assistance to facilities. If a facility is identified as needing assistance with identifying a root cause, putting a corrective action in place, or finding accurate ways to measure the impact of that corrective action plan, the review team reaches out and provides that assistance. The review team consists of trained health care personnel with a background in process improvement and patient safety. The assistance that is offered to the facilities can come in the form of telecommunication or in-person training or assistance.

Recommendations and evolution of the system

The majority of stakeholders from hospitals and surgical centers, as well as long term care organizations, reported during the 10-year evaluation that they would like to see the same commitment to transparency and public reporting (similar to this system) expanded to include clinics and long term care facilities in Minnesota. Current reporting facilities feel very strongly that the AHE system and its commitment to learning and transparency has been a catalyst for change and has made the care patients in those settings receive much safer. Reporting facilities (specifically ambulatory surgical centers) also feel that expanding a similar system to other settings would "even the playing field" in some cases. For example, ambulatory surgery centers that are licensed by MDH are subject to the reporting law; however, the majority of cosmetic surgery centers in Minnesota are not licensed by MDH and therefore are not subject to the law. Surgery centers feel that this would offer an opportunity to further health care safety in the state if the reporting system were to include cosmetic surgery centers. In addition, clinics that are licensed under a hospital are required to report under the AHE law; however, independent clinics are not currently required to report.

In the past several years, MDH has convened discussions with stakeholders, including state regulators, long term care associations, hospitals, clinics, surgery centers and other invested parties, to discuss the idea of expanding a similar AHE system across all settings of care in the state. Movement toward expanding to other settings is complex and involves many stakeholders and, therefore, may be a lengthy process, but all partners are committed to continuing the discussion. Two topics that MDH has begun work on that have a shared interest with long term care are the prevention of controlled substance diversion and the prevention and mitigation of patient violence toward staff. MDH has formed multi-stakeholder groups for both of these topics and work is underway to develop and disseminate best practices and training on them.

Hospitals and surgical centers have been on a journey with MDH and its partners though the AHE system for 14 years now. Progress toward eliminating

AHEs has been made; however, the work continues and will be an ongoing process, defined by new types of events, evolving best practices, and shared learnings throughout the state. Facilities have committed time and resources and are seeing progress. They should be proud of the work that they have invested in improving patient safety and quality in Minnesota and therefore providing a higher level of care to their patients. However, patient safety is a continuous process in Minnesota and MDH and its partners are committed to ensuring that the progress from the first years of the reporting system continues to advance.

Some next steps for MDH and its partners to move patient safety forward in Minnesota are:

- Developing new methods, tools or resources for data sharing across facilities. This includes sharing learnings from events as well as near misses.
- Working with the Minnesota Board of Medicine, medical schools and other stakeholders to educate resident physicians on patient safety and quality, even before they begin practicing.
- Working with all stakeholders, including physicians, to encourage adoption of best practices in patient safety
- Working with experts statewide to reduce the incidence of controlled substance diversion in health care settings
- Working with law enforcement and health care facilities to create and adopt best practices for the prevention and mitigation of patient violence in hospitals and other health care settings.

Appendix A

Reportable events as defined by law

Below is a list of the events that hospitals and licensed ambulatory surgical centers are required to report to the Minnesota Department of Health.

The language is taken directly from Minnesota Statutes, section 144.7065.

Surgical events

1. Surgery or other invasive procedure performed on a wrong body part that is not consistent with the documented informed consent for that patient. Reportable events under this clause do not include situations requiring prompt action that occur in the course of surgery or situations whose urgency precludes obtaining informed consent;
2. surgery or other invasive procedure performed on the wrong patient;
3. the wrong surgical or other invasive procedure performed on a patient that is not consistent with the documented informed consent for that patient. Reportable events under this clause do not include situations requiring prompt action that occur in the course of surgery or situations whose urgency precludes obtaining informed consent;
4. retention of a foreign object in a patient after surgery or other invasive procedure, excluding objects intentionally implanted as part of a planned intervention and objects present prior to surgery that are intentionally retained; and
5. death during or immediately after surgery or other invasive procedure of a normal, healthy patient who has no organic, physiologic, biochemical, or psychiatric disturbance and for whom the pathologic processes for which the operation is to be performed are localized and do not entail a systemic disturbance.

Product or device events

1. Patient death or serious injury associated with the use of contaminated drugs, devices, or biologics provided by the facility when the contamination is the result of generally detectable contaminants in drugs, devices, or biologics regardless of the source of the contamination or the product;
2. patient death or serious injury associated with the use or function of a device in patient care in which the device is used or functions other than as intended. Device includes, but is not limited to, catheters, drains, and other specialized tubes, infusion pumps, and ventilators; and
3. patient death or serious injury associated with intravascular air embolism that occurs while being cared for in a facility, excluding deaths associated with neurosurgical procedures known to present a high risk of intravascular air embolism.

Patient protection events

1 A patient of any age, who does not have decision-making capacity, discharged to the wrong person;
2 patient death or serious injury associated with patient disappearance, excluding events involving adults who have decision-making capacity; and
3 patient suicide, attempted suicide resulting in serious injury, or self-harm resulting in serious injury or death while being cared for in a facility due to patient actions after admission to the facility, excluding deaths resulting from self-inflicted injuries that were the reason for admission to the facility.

Care management events

1 Patient death or serious injury associated with a medication error, including, but not limited to, errors involving the wrong drug, the wrong dose, the wrong patient, the wrong time, the wrong rate, the wrong preparation, or the wrong route of administration, excluding reasonable differences in clinical judgment on drug selection and dose;
2 patient death or serious injury associated with unsafe administration of blood or blood products;
3 maternal death or serious injury associated with labor or delivery in a low-risk pregnancy while being cared for in a facility, including events that occur within 42 days post-delivery and excluding deaths from pulmonary or amniotic fluid embolism, acute fatty liver of pregnancy, or cardiomyopathy;
4 death or serious injury of a neonate associated with labor or delivery in a low-risk pregnancy;
5 stage 3, 4 or unstageable ulcers acquired after admission to a facility, excluding progression from stage 2 to stage 3 if stage 2 was recognized upon admission;
6 artificial insemination with the wrong donor sperm or wrong egg;
7 patient death or serious injury associated with a fall while being cared for in a facility;
8 the irretrievable loss of an irreplaceable biological specimen; and
9 patient death or serious injury resulting from the failure to follow up or communicate laboratory, pathology, or radiology test results.

Environmental events

1 Patient death or serious injury associated with an electric shock while being cared for in a facility, excluding events involving planned treatments such as electric countershock;
2 any incident in which a line designated for oxygen or other gas to be delivered to a patient contains the wrong gas or is contaminated by toxic substances;
3 patient death or serious injury associated with a burn incurred from any source while being cared for in a facility;
4 patient death or serious injury associated with the use of or lack of restraints or bedrails while being cared for in a facility.

Potential criminal events

1 Any instance of care ordered by or provided by someone impersonating a physician, nurse, pharmacist, or other licensed health care provider;
2 abduction of a patient of any age;
3 sexual assault on a patient within or on the grounds of a facility; and
4 death or serious injury of a patient or staff member resulting from a physical assault that occurs within or on the grounds of a facility.

Radiologic events

1 Death or serious injury of a patient associated with the introduction of a metallic object into the MRI area.
2 For more information about Minnesota's Adverse Health Events Reporting Law, or to view annual reports or facility-specific data, go to www.health.state.mn.us/patientsafety

Appendix B

Background on Minnesota's Adverse Health Events Reporting Law

In 2003, Minnesota became the first state in the nation to establish a mandatory AHE reporting system that included all 27 serious reportable events identified by the National Quality Forum and a public report that identified adverse events by facility. The law covers Minnesota hospitals and licensed outpatient surgical centers.

Momentum toward a system for mandatory adverse event reporting began with the publication of the Institute of Medicine (IOM) report "To Err is Human" in 2000. While the issue of medical errors was not a new one for health professionals, Americans reacted strongly to the idea that preventable errors could contribute to the deaths of up to 98,000 people per year. The public and media attention that followed the report's publication started a national conversation about the reasons why such errors occur. A primary focus of the discussions was the concept of systemic causes for errors.

In the past, discussions of medical errors often focused on identifying and punishing those who had caused the error. While individual accountability for behavior that could put patients at risk is very important, the IOM report confirmed that most errors were not the result of the isolated actions of any one care provider, but rather of a failure of the complex systems and processes in health care. Given that knowledge, the old "blame and train" mentality, wherein individual providers were blamed for mistakes and provided with training in the hopes of preventing future slip-ups, has to make way for a new approach that encompasses a broader view of accountability and learning from errors or near misses.

Every facility has processes for dealing with individual providers who exhibit dangerous or inappropriate behavior or who knowingly put patients at risk. Disciplining, educating or dismissing an individual provider will always be an option in those cases. But the focus of the reporting system is on using focused analysis of events to develop broader opportunities for education about patient safety and best practices – solutions that can be applied across facilities. Responses focused on an individual provider may or may not prevent that provider from making a mistake again, but changing an entire system or process to eliminate opportunities for error, whether by building in cross-checks, establishing a "stop the line" policy, or using automation to prevent risky choices, will help to keep all patients safer.

From the beginning, the reporting system has been a collaborative effort. Health care leaders, hospitals, doctors, professional boards, patient advocacy groups, health plans, MDH, and other stakeholders worked together to create the reporting law, with a shared goal of improving patient safety. The vision for the reporting system is of a tool for quality improvement and education that provides a forum for sharing best practices, rather than a tool for regulatory enforcement.

In 2007, the AHE Reporting Law was modified to include a 28th event and to expand the definitions of certain other events. The most significant change was an expansion of reportable falls to include those associated with a serious disability in addition to those associated with a death. At the same time, the pressure ulcer category was expanded to include "unstageable" pressure ulcers.

In 2012, the AHE Reporting Law was modified to expand the definitions of several events, re-categorize several events, delete two events and add four additional events. The four new events were:

- The irretrievable loss of an irreplaceable biological specimen;
- Patient death or serious injury resulting from the failure to follow up or communicate laboratory, pathology, or radiology test results;
- Death or serious injury of a neonate associated with labor or delivery in a low-risk pregnancy;
- Death or serious injury of a patient associated with the introduction of a metallic object into the MRI area.

At the same time the "serious disability" language was changed to "serious injury." The reporting of these new events began on October 7, 2013.

11 The role of regulatory frameworks in Latvian patient safety culture

Evija Palceja and Agnese Bankava

Introduction

The improvement of patient safety is undoubtedly based on moral, ethical and, at the same time, economic considerations. Therefore, ensuring safety is the primary responsibility of both individual healthcare workers and the healthcare system in general. The Organisation for Economic Co-operation and Development (OECD) draws attention to the cost of errors and failures, the causes of the damage, and the ability to reduce them effectively.[1] It has been 17 years since the American Medical Institute's publication, entitled *To err is human*, and significant changes in patient safety have been put in place, by shifting from blaming and punishing healthcare professionals, to a systematic approach to failures and mistakes. Unwanted events arise from the complexity of the healthcare system, where treatment and care depend on many factors, not only on the competence and diligence of healthcare providers. Moreover, the World Health Organisation (WHO) points out that the culture of punishment is a significant barrier to patient safety. Anticipation of accusations contributes to concealment. Fear of criticism and subsequent punishment does not allow for rational analysis of the causes of an incident.[2] It is this newly developed patient safety culture that is the biggest challenge for the European Union (EU) Member States, including Latvia. The complexity of the implementation of effective patient safety measures, protocols, and practices, underpinned by an agreed and positive culture, is due to the interdisciplinary nature of this process: it is inextricably linked to other sectors, such as politics, social sciences, economics and law.[3] As a result, it is not possible to develop a modern approach to patient safety solely from the perspective of the healthcare system.

1 L. Slawomirski, A. Auraaen, N. Klazinga, 'The economics of patient safety. Strengthening a value-based approach to reducing patient harm at national level', OECD, 2017. Grant N.DI161105.

2 WHO, *Definitions of key concepts from the WHO Patient Safety Curriculum Guide*, 2011. Available: www.who.int/patientsafety/education/curriculum/course1a_handout.pdf

3 Z. Linde Priekšizpētes ziņojums par Eiropas Savienības pacientu drošības politiku. Pacientu drošības politika piecās Eiropas Savienības dalībvalstīs: Apvienotajā Karalistē, Nīderlandē, Dānijā, Lietuvā un Igaunijā. Rīga: 2010. Available: www.biodrosiba.lu.lv/fileadmin/user_upload/lu_portal/projekti/biodrosiba/ZLinde_Pacientu_drosiba.pdf.

The *Reporting and Learning System* is one of the key elements of risk management in many high-risk businesses, including within the framework of patient safety. For example, in aviation, the reporting system is strengthened by a regulation on the reporting, analysis and follow-up of occurrences in civil aviation, which also provides for protection of individuals involved in the incident against penalty sanctions.[4] There are European level recommendations for patient safety. Many EU actions support Member States' implementation of their own national and regional strategies for patient safety. Providing safe healthcare is, however, the responsibility of each Member State.[5] The Committee of Ministers of the Council of Europe recommends that governments of Member States promote the development of a non-punitive reporting system for patient safety incidents in order to enhance patient safety by learning from such incidents.[6] However, these recommendations have not been strong enough to initiate changes or new approaches in the Latvian legislation and clinical practice.

Although Latvia has been a Member State of the EU since 2004 and an OECD member since 2016, patient safety in Latvia, on a national level, was only updated in 2016 following the conference entitled *Patient safety in clinical practice: realities and challenges in the 21st century*. This conference bought together more than 500 healthcare professionals and professionals from related areas, including lawyers and patient organisations.[7] The Children's Clinical University Hospital, which had four years of experience in developing a patient safety system, provided an impetus for this conference.

In April 2017, the Ministry of Health published the conceptual report, *On the Reform of the Healthcare System*, in which the Ministry of Health pointed out the most important issues of patient safety: Latvia lacks a constructive approach and a common understanding of patient safety and quality management in the health sector. Other countries' experience, standards and good practice are not sufficiently used, and the medical institutions do not have enough support in addressing quality and patient safety issues.[8] Several important patient safety features have already been introduced in Latvia, and conclusions have been formed in

4 Regulation (EU) No 376/2014 of the European Parliament and of the council, 3 April 2014, on the reporting, analysis and follow-up of occurrences in civil aviation. EUR-Lex. Available: http://eur-lex.europa.eu/legal-content/LV/TXT/?uri=CELEX%3A32014R0376.

5 Communication from the Commission to the European Parliament and the Council on Patient Safety, including the prevention and control of healthcare-associated infections {COM (2008) 837 final} {SEC(2008) 3004} {SEC(2008) 3005}. Available: http://eur-lex.europa.eu/legal-content/en/TXT/?uri=CELEX:52008DC0836.

6 Council of Europe, Committee of Ministers, 'Recommendation of the Committee of Ministers to member states on management of patient safety and prevention of adverse events in health care', 2006, Rec 7. Available: https://search.coe.int/cm/Pages/result_details.aspx?ObjectID=09000016805ae8b5.

7 VSIA, 'Bērnu klīniskā universitātes slimnīca'. Pacientu drošība klīniskajā praksē- realitāte un izaicinājumi 21.gadsimtā. Available at: www.bkus.lv/lv/content/pacientu-drosiba-kliniskaja-prakse-realitate-un-izaicinajumi-21gadsimta.

8 Veselības ministrija, Konceptuālais ziņojums 'Par veselības aprūpes sistēmas reformu' 2017). Available at: www.vm.gov.lv/lv/aktualitates/zinojums_par_veselibas_aprupes_sistemas_reformu/.

relation to the implementation of patient safety as a system. Significant challenges to this process are faced by Latvia and attention is now drawn to these challenges.

Patient safety discussion and system development in Latvia

On 29 September 2005, the first patient safety working group of the Member States of the EU was convened, which stated that the Member States should take primary responsibility for patient safety.[9] In 2007, the working group concluded that patient safety is most effective and should be promoted at the level of each Member State as well as at EU level. The EU Patients' Safety Working Group called on each Member State to take concrete measures at national level to develop a positive patient safety culture, to promote education and training for healthcare professionals and all other employees, to establish effective reporting and learning mechanisms, and to develop and improve compensation mechanisms for the consequences of unwanted events.[10] Following the calls made by this group, in 2008, the Commission of the European Communities drafted a communication from the Commission to the European Parliament and the Council on Patient Safety, including the prevention and control of healthcare-associated infections, which included patient safety features. It highlighted the Luxembourg Declaration, which stated that the fundamental principle of patient safety is that it is necessary to develop a system that identifies the scale and causes of undesirable events, with the aim of effectively channelling resources for solutions and active searches.[11]

However, these EU documents are of a purely advisory nature. Therefore, Latvia was not obliged to integrate patient safety into legislation or patient care actions. Pharmacovigilance, hemovigilance, medical device vigilance systems, infection control systems, high education standards for healthcare professionals, mandatory requirements for healthcare institutions and their structural units, and various treatment monitoring systems were in place in Latvia. They did not include an integrated understanding of errors and their causes. However, the legal framework for healthcare and patient safety was strengthened through Directive 2011/24/EU of the European Parliament and of the Council on the application of patients' rights in cross-border healthcare[12] (referred to as the Patients' Rights Directive). The Directive obliged the Member States to introduce, by 25 October 2013, two essential elements of patient safety in national legislation: (1) a system for reimbursement of health damage and (2) a system for protecting the rights of healthcare workers.

Latvia has fulfilled these obligations and has introduced the regulatory enactments required to comply with the requirements of the Patients' Rights Directive,

9 European Commission, *High Level Group on health services and medical care*. Minutes of the meeting of the High Level Group on 29 September 2005. Available at: http://ec.europa.eu/health/ph_overview/co_operation/mobility/docs/highlevel_2005_015_en.pdf.

10 WHO, *A brief synopsis on patient safety*, 2010. Available at: www.euro.who.int/__data/assets/pdf_file/0015/111507/E93833.pdf.

11 VSIA, 'Bērnu klīniskā universitātes slimnīc'.

12 Directive 2011/24/EU of the European Parliament and of the Council of 9 March 2011 on the application of patients' rights in cross-border healthcare. *Official Journal of the European Union*, nr.L88/45, 4 April 2011.

namely the establishment of a *Treatment Risk Fund*, which provides patients with the opportunity to receive compensation for healthcare damage, and has established a competent state institution for the development of patient safety policy and the provision of methodological support for patient safety, as well as incorporating a patient safety reporting and learning system into the regulatory enactments. The additional impact on patient safety in Latvia was also due to the fact that, on 1 July 2016, Latvia joined the OECD.[13]

The legal responsibilities of Latvia oblige practitioners to carry out specific actions to support the safety of patients at state level. In this context, the role of the Children's Clinical University Hospital in the development of the patient safety system in Latvia is to be noted. This hospital has been actively involved in the experience exchange programme of the European Hospital and Healthcare Federation (HOPE),[14] where the topic of patient safety has relevance.

Patient safety Reporting and Learning System in Latvia

Patient safety training programmes are a relatively recent initiative in Latvia, with a national training strategy only being developed since 2017. The patient safety training programme modules, largely derived from the WHO *Patient Safety Curriculum Guide* and the recommendations of the European Commission Working Group on Patient Safety and Quality Care, are targeted at managers and clinical leaders,[15] clinicians,[16] and nurses.[17]

13 Convention on the Organisation for Economic Co-operation and Development. Available at: www.oecd.org/general/conventionontheorganisationforeconomicco-operationanddevelopment.htm. The OECD emphasises that patient safety has a major impact on the economy, focusing on the cost of errors and failures, the causes of harm, and the ability to reduce them effectively. The OECD points out that, in OECD countries, 15% of hospital spending and activities are diverted to treatment errors. The OECD also explains that patient safety can also be seen in the broader economic context, through the loss of capacity and productivity of patients and their relatives. The OECD emphasises that many unwanted events can be systematically addressed through better policies and best practices at costs below the cost of the damage. Therefore, at a national level where resources are limited, activities that have the highest added value should be implemented by investing in system-level initiatives, in initiatives such as professional education and training, safety standards and basic information infrastructure. Patient safety experts participating in an OECD survey on best practices for patient safety also show importance of no-fault medical negligence legislation.

14 European Hospital and Healthcare Federation. Available at: www.hope.be;

15 For managers and clinical leaders: risks and patient safety into practice – 21 acad. hours (960 min) with subtopics on introduction in patient safety; human factors; learning from incidents: root-cause analysis, 5 Whys, contributing factors, barrier analysis. practical training: proactive risk analysis – risk matrix; FMEA, SWIFT; international patient safety goals; good practices in surgery and anaesthesia, medication, effective communication across settings, patient identification; reporting and patient safety culture.

16 Human Factors in Clinical Practice – 5 acad. hours (225 min) seminar with practical exercises (patient safety incidents from hospital practice) in small working groups. 2–3 training groups yearly.

17 Presentations and discussions on patient safety topics (45 to 90 min.) according to internal patient safety incidents and newly developed safety standard operating procedures: effective communication – SBAR, safe medication, patient identification, safe surgery, patient evaluation (PEWS, Aldrete Score etc.), reporting and learning, human factors in reported incidents – findings from root-cause analysis.

To illustrate an example of how patient safety training has had a positive effect on practice, the practices of Riga Children's University Hospital may be highlighted. Their quality and patient safety team has started to apply patient safety training processes, with the goal of helping other hospitals develop and implement patient safety systems. This hospital has succeeded in motivating and engaging employees in the process of improving patient safety and achieving an increase in patient safety. The motivation for action is based on the principle: 'collecting information on adverse events now will help us to avoid severe patient safety incidents in the future'.

One of the main disadvantages of motivated reporting of adverse events and serious adverse events at both the national and medical institutions level is the lack of confidence that reporting will not lead to punishment. Historically in Latvia, there has been no legal protection for those who report adverse events. In contrast, the protection of information received through reporting has also been established by other countries. For example, legislation in Ireland stipulates that the information found in the reporting system (both mandatory and voluntary) is strictly confidential, protected from legal disclosure and not subject to the Freedom of Information legislation.[18] However, despite a cultural distrust of the investigatory process, the AB: Not the correct name of the University Children's Hospital has achieved an increase in patient safety reports, from 77 in 2013 to 373 in 2017.

As of October 2017, amendments have been made to Latvian regulatory enactments, which have made the introduction of reporting–learning systems in medical institutions obligatory. At the moment, it is premature to evaluate whether the amendments made to the legislation will support patient safety in Latvia, but with these amendments, very important actions have been carried out there with a view to introducing a patient safety system in line with the other national positions. With this in mind, the study of legal norms, problem analysis and change is of vital importance for the development of patient safety in Latvia.

Patient safety and the labyrinth of liability

The introduction of patient safety 'is a great challenge as human nature is characterised by a need to find somebody to blame and to believe that penalising will prevent the next error'.[19] Yet, an environment where adverse events can be analysed within an atmosphere free of penalties and reproach is an important precondition for the development of patient safety. It is, therefore, important that patient safety must be seen also in the context of legal liability, by assessing whether the legislative acts could promote patient safety in Latvia. Unfortunately, in Latvia, there are serious problems related to liability issues in

18 Commission on Patient Safety and Quality Assurance, *Building a culture of patient safety*, Dublin: Department of Health and Children, Dublin, 2008. Available at: http://health.gov.ie/wp-content/uploads/2014/03/en_patientsafety.pdf.

19 Z. Straume, *Pacientu drošības konference*. Available at: www.bsf.lv/lv/jaunumi/2016/pacientu drosibas-konference;

medical law and Latvia is only at the stage of identifying the related problems. Thus, there is still a long way ahead before the liability issues in the context of patient safety will be clarified.

The WHO has noted that the concept of patient safety is related to the 'quality of healthcare'; however, these two concepts are not synonymous.[20] Patient safety is the fundamental philosophy of improving quality.[21] The International Covenant on Economic, Social and Cultural Rights, the European Social Charter, the Treaty on the Functioning of the European Union and the Patient Rights Directive all clearly state that a responsibility and obligation on States exists to ensure quality healthcare.[22]

However, the Latvian Law on the Rights of Patients stipulates that, in general, it is the attending physician who is responsible for the justification, purposefulness, continuity, quality and results of the entire treatment of a patient.[23] Therefore, responsibility for the quality and results of a patient's treatment fully and exclusively lies with the attending physician, regardless of the fact that the quality of treatment may depend on the circumstances in which care is provided, including the actions of other professionals involved in the provision of healthcare.

A physician's actions, carried out in the framework of a patient's medical treatment, must not only accord with external legislative acts, but also with the internal regulations of the medical treatment institution, employment or professional service agreement and instructions issued by the head of the medical treatment institution. Yet, this personal liability sits uneasily with the Latvian Medical Treatment Law, which regulates at the level of medical treatment *institutions*, defined so as to include doctors' practices, state and local government health institutions and commercial companies offering health services. This creates great disparity and uncertainty as regards the moment at which liability attaches, either to the medical institution or to the medical practitioner providing care through that institution. The authors are of the opinion that there is an urgent need for clarity as to the subject of liability for deficiencies in the treatment process. Failure to provide such clarity is likely to contribute towards a culture of fear of litigation and to foster an environment of extreme caution in the provision of care. Further, the authors contend that liability should attach more readily to medical institutions, reflecting the fact that patient safety is an issue running through the entire healthcare system. However, as will be detailed in the next section, personal liability for health professionals is entrenched in the Latvia legal system.

20 WHO, *Conceptual framework of an international patient safety event classification: final technical report*, 2009. Available at: www.who.int/patientsafety/taxonomy/icps_full_report.pdf;

21 WHO, *Quality of care: patient safety*, No. WHA55.18. World Health Assembly, Ninth plenary meeting, 18 May 2002. Available at: http://apps.who.int/gb/archive/pdf_files/WHA55/ewha5518.pdf?ua=1.

22 International Covenant on Economic, Social and Cultural Rights (ICESCR). Available at: www.humanrights.lv/; European Social Charter, available at https://rm.coe.int/168048b059; Treaty for the Functioning of the European Union. Available at http://eur-lex.europa.eu/legal-content/EN/TXT/?uri=celex%3A12012E%2FTXT.

23 Pacientu tiesību likums: L. R. likums. 'Latvijas Vēstnesis' Nr.205 (4191), 30.12.2009.

Legal liability of a medical practitioner

Being responsible for the quality of medical treatment, a medical practitioner in Latvia may be subject to various types of legal liability, i.e. disciplinary liability, administrative liability, civil liability or criminal liability. Medical practitioners are, undoubtedly, to be held liable in accordance with the procedure stipulated in the legislative acts for failure to observe legislative acts, an administrative violation or criminal offences.[24] However, when it comes to holding medical practitioners liable, issues arise, due to legal provisions which contain undefined legal concepts.[25]

Errors in healthcare can be viewed from two different perspectives – individually and systemically. The individual approach envisages that an individual person is responsible for the medical error which has taken place. This results in 'putting to shame, blaming and penalising'. Whereas the systemic approach envisages that it is in the human nature to make a mistake and that errors can be expected even in the best of organisations. Errors are considered to be consequences of systemic factors rather than of ill-intentioned actions of people. The systematic approach believes that the human nature to make errors cannot be changed but that circumstances can be changed in order to create obstacles and minimise the possibilities for people to make mistakes. What is important is to find out why there has been an error and how to prevent such a possibility in the future rather than to find out who made the mistake.[26] Patient safety is based on the systemic approach, and, in the field of patient safety, an error is an unexpected action (performed or not) or action which fails to deliver the expected result.[27] Unfortunately, the understanding of errors in the field of healthcare in Latvia fails to correspond to the understanding of errors in the field of patient safety, and is based on the individual approach. While there are several representatives of the legal sector in Latvia who recognise that errors in the field of medical treatment are not a rare phenomenon and cannot be avoided, they point out, however, that persons should be held liable for errors that have occurred during a process of medical treatment.[28] Rožkals has noted that:

24 Latvijas Administratīvo pārkāpumu kodekss: L. R. likums. '*Ziņotājs*' nr.51, 20.12.1984; *Krimināllikums*: L. R. Likums. "Latvijas Vēstnesis" nr.199/200 (1260/1261) 08.07.1998, '*Ziņotājs*' nr.15. 04.08.1998.; Criminal offences may arise, for example, for using medical technologies in medical treatment which have not been approved by an institution authorised according to the stipulated procedure, for performing unauthorised abortion, or for unauthorised provision of narcotic drugs and psychotropic substances.

25 These provisions are: section 45 (1) of the Latvian Administrative Violations Code, which lays down that, for violations in the field of healthcare, a medical practitioner or a head of a medical treatment institution are to be held administratively liable; and Section 138 (1) of the Criminal Law, which lays down that, for the failure to fulfil the professional duties of medical practitioners or for negligent fulfilment of such duties, a medical practitioner is to be called to criminal liability.

26 A Öhrn, Measures of patient safety – studies of Swedish reporting systems and evaluation of an intervention aimed at improved patient safety culture, Sweden: Linköping University, 2011. Available: http://liu.diva-portal.org/smash/get/diva2:460214/FULLTEXT01.pdf;

27 L. L. Leape, 'Error in medicine', *JAMA* 1994. Available: www.uphs.upenn.edu/gme/pdfs/Leape_Error%20in%20Medicine_JAMA.pdf;

28 R. Rožkalns, 'Kas ir kļūdaina ārstniecība', *Jurista Vārds*, nr. 41(792), 2013.gada 8.oktobris; S Ašnevica-Slokenberga, (ed), *Medical Rights*, Riga: Tiesu Namu Agentura, 2015; L. Dzērve, 'Tiesāšanās ar ārstiem ir specifiska un ilgst gadiem'. Available at: www.lsm.lv/lv/raksts/vide-un-zinatne/dzive/tiesashanas-ar-arstiem-ir-specifiska-un-ilgst-gadiem.a82881/;

> [I]n the case of erroneous medical treatment by a medical practitioner, civil liability, criminal liability, administrative liability, as well as disciplinary liability may arise. In order to assess whether a medical practitioner should be held liable, the court must find answers as to whether the respective medical treatment has been erroneous, as well as whether the patient has suffered harm directly as a result of such a medical treatment.[29]

Equally, Lieljuksis has pointed out that 'in Latvia, liability is envisaged for a medical practitioner in the case of failure to observe legislative acts and healthcare errors due to unprofessional conduct, negligence and carelessness in the field of healthcare'.[30] Lieljuksis points to errors, due to unprofessional conduct, negligence and carelessness, by thus narrowing down the errors of a medical practitioner, for which he/she can be held liable, but he does not claim that the medical practitioner should not be held liable for errors which have occurred during the process of medical treatment. He also fails to explain in more detail the errors that are due to unprofessional conduct, negligence and carelessness. Olsena notes that 'a concept of a common understanding must be developed in the justice system as to what are medical errors, what they consist of, by whom and how they are assessed'.[31] Olsena also argues that a medical practitioner is to be held liable for errors in the process of medical treatment and that it is only the type of liability that the medical practitioner should be subjected to which needs to be examined. Unfortunately, none of the above representatives of the legal sector has viewed and examined the errors from the perspective of causes, and they have only taken a single view that the errors are made by specific medical practitioners, and these medical practitioners must be held liable for such errors.

The legislative acts of the Republic of Latvia fail to define what errors are in the medical treatment process. The term 'medical error', however, has been used, for example, in the Criminal Procedure Law.[32] In most cases, incidents do not occur due to a physician or a nurse being a bad professional and a careless, perfunctory or negligent employee. Individual errors in the field of healthcare are only one of the circumstances that affect the occurrence of specific consequences. The knowledge, skills and personality of the practitioner all impact upon their performance of health tasks. But, other external facts are by no means less important: the nature of the task to be performed, the environment in which the task is carried out, the technologies which are available and organisational factors (such as team communication, shift rotas and staffing levels).

29 Rozkalns, ibid.

30 Q. A. Lieljuksis, 'Responsibility of a medication practitioner', in Ašnevica-Slokenberga, *Medical Rights*.

31 Olsena, as quoted in Dzērve, 'Tiesāšanās ar ārstiem ir specifiska un ilgst gadiem'.

32 This law stipulates that an expert-examination by a commission of experts is usually performed in order to examine an error of a medical practitioner in providing medical treatment, thus placing such errors at the same level with a failure of a medical practitioner to perform their professional duties or with negligence for which criminal liability is envisaged.

There are, then, a number of serious problems in assessing the liability of medical practitioners, not only in the context of patient safety but also in the framework of legislative acts currently applicable in Latvia:

1 Neither the legislative acts, nor the legal literature offers any explanation as to what is a healthcare violation or a negligent performance of a medical practitioner's professional duties, which makes legal assessment of medical practitioners' actions difficult.
2 Expert examinations and opinions are made by expert physicians who are not specialised in the respective field.
3 Expert opinions are justified neither with legal sources, nor medical literature; this, however, does not prevent holding medical practitioners liable.
4 When medical practitioners defend their rights and appeal the decisions that are taken regarding liability, neither the Health Inspectorate, nor the courts assesses the opinions as part of the evidence of the case and, instead, they assess the evidence on the basis of the expert opinion's findings.

We would like to point out that significant changes are necessary to the assessment of liability of medical practitioners: opinions should be prepared by expert physicians specialising in the respective field. These opinions must contain a justification of the medical practitioners' liability, i.e. legal provisions from which specific duties of a medical practitioner arise in the specific actual circumstances, as well as legal scientific and medical scientific literature recognised in practice. Expert opinions should be assessed as part of the evidence in the context of holding medical practitioners liable. Guidelines must be drawn up for assessing liability of medical practitioners taking into account, as far as possible, the understanding of patient safety as regards the liability of persons involved in healthcare.

Role of the Treatment Risk Fund in the patient safety culture in Latvia

The legal framework for healthcare in Latvia entails the necessity to comply with a number of key laws including the Medical Treatment Law, the Law on the Rights of Patients and the Latvian Administrative Violation Code. With the EU Patients' Rights Directive a legally binding obligation to implement the elements of the patient safety strategy has now come into force in Latvia. This Directive stipulates that the Member States are obliged to ensure that systems of professional liability insurance, or a guarantee or similar arrangement that is equivalent or essentially comparable as regards its purpose, are in place. The fundamental principles laid down in the Directive do not search for a person to blame and penalise but, instead, focus on the elimination of the harm caused to the patient or on due compensation.

The Treatment Risk Fund (TRF) has been considered to be a good basis for the development of a patient safety culture within that context. The TRF was established in Latvia on 25 October 2013 as a new patients' rights defence institute with a systemic approach.[33] The TRF is broadly aligned with the requirements of the Patients' Rights Directive and aims to allow patients to defend their rights and receive compensation, according to out-of-court procedures. The TRF established an administrative process where medical practitioners are able to limit the risk attached to their professional activity and the possible consequences thereof.[34]

We have conducted an analysis of the TRF in order to determine its role in patient safety culture. A number of key points are worth raising. First, it is difficult for patients to receive compensation for harm in cases where no causal link is found between the harm and the action or failure to act by a medical practitioner during the medical treatment process. Second, it is difficult for patients to receive compensation in cases when other persons involved in the medical treatment process have caused the harm. Third, not only are medical practitioners partially unprotected in the framework of their professional activity, and at risk of being called to administrative or criminal liability after an examination of a patient's compensation claim, but the TRF even increases that possibility. Ultimately, the TRF fails to promote a patient safety culture founded on the concept of collective responsibility for providing high-quality healthcare. This is at odds with the Patients' Rights Directive, which does not envisage the occurrence of liability of a particular person. Rather, what is important is that healthcare has been provided and, during that process, harm has been caused.[35]

What should be done to change the situation? Firstly, the Law on the Rights of Patients should be amended in accordance with the Directive on the application of patients' rights, stipulating that a patient is entitled to compensation for harm caused as a result of the provided healthcare (and not due to action or failure to act by a medical practitioner or due to conditions). A much more difficult task will be changing the mentality in the field of patient safety towards a policy that is reflected in legislative acts and that fails to comply with the common principles of patient safety in Europe: the TRF and assessment of compensation claims should be clearly separated from the institution (Health Inspectorate) which is authorised and obliged to penalise medical practitioners. Accordingly, it is recommended that the TRF operational rules should be reassessed and take into account more actively and more visibly the fundamentals of patient safety. The issue of insurance and liability needs to be clarified further. The rules of the

33 Ministru kabineta noteikumu "Ārstniecības riska fonda darbības noteikumi" projekta sākotnējās (ex-ante) ietekmes novērtējuma ziņojums (anotācija). Available: http://tap.mk.gov.lv/.

34 R. Muciņš, 'The Nature and Legal Aspects of the Treatment Fund', 2013, 41(792) *Jurista Vārds*, 11.

35 The 'without guilt' (no fault) system envisages that nobody looks for a physician or another service provider to be blamed for the harm done to a patient in order to pay out compensation. Instead the patient receives the compensation for the harm caused during healthcare using the administrative system where the patient fills out a form and after verification and finding of the harm (and not action or failure to act or guilt), the patient is paid the compensation. This system 'without guilt' envisages in-depth examination of causes of the harm without blaming anybody, and implementing improvements so that such harm would not be caused in the future by thus improving patient safety. The EU too supports the system, 'without guilt', and it this system encourages the introduction of a culture of patient safety and the implementation of activities that improve patient safety.

TRF should reaffirm that the medical treatment process involves not only medical practitioners but also a wide array of supporting medical staff and health experts, such as pharmacists.

Conclusion

As pointed out by Pēteris Apinis, President of the Latvian Medical Association:

> Latvia is amongst the countries where distorted legislation and unprofessional legal proceedings prevent the analysis of errors. Namely, a physician can be penalised for an error, imposed an actual imprisonment, prosecuted and his/her career and life can be destroyed. In countries where an error can become a reason for criminal liability, errors are being concealed; there is no discussion about errors; no patholo-anatomical conferences take place so no opportunity is given to learn from one's mistakes. Helping others in a better way is being prevented. Moreover, an error does not mean carelessness, negligence, sloppiness, but mainly means a complex clinical picture, side-effects caused by medicines or reduction of the picture of the main disease.[36]

It is noted that the complaint system provides information about healthcare quality and identifies deficiencies therein. Compensation systems compensate for the harm caused to a person. However, in practice, these systems fail to ensure improvement of healthcare quality.[37] Contradiction between the law of tort and patient safety undermines the efforts to improve quality. Fear of being held legally liable reduces the interest in patient safety measures and objectives.[38] The objective of patient safety and medical liability reforms is to improve healthcare and foster patient safety. It is essential to combine medical liability with patient safety and healthcare quality, reducing at the same time the differences between penalising individuals and lack of penalising focusing on patient safety.[39]

While the implementation of reporting and learning systems in the Member States is not stipulated as legally binding, we repeatedly note that, in accordance with the Patients' Rights Directive Member States are obliged to ensure that systems of professional liability insurance, or a guarantee or similar arrangement that is equivalent or essentially comparable as regards its purpose, are in place for treatment provided on their territory. However, as it has been concluded in this document, in Latvia, medical practitioners are not protected against liability in terms of compensation for harm caused. Protection from liability in terms

36 P. Apinis, 'Veselības aprūpes reforma'. Available: http://apollo.tvnet.lv/zinas/peteris-apinis-veselibas-aprupes-reforma/787459.

37 C. Clancy, 'Patient safety and medical liability reform: putting the patient first', *Patient Safety and Quality Heathcare* 2010, September/October Available: https://archive.ahrq.gov/news/newsroom/commentaries/putting-patients-first.html.

38 D. M. Studdert, M. M. Mello and T. A. Brennan, *Medical malpractice. Health policy report.* Available at: https://cdn1.sph.harvard.edu/wp-content/uploads/sites/487/2012/10/HPR_final.pdf.

39 Clancy, 'Patient safety and medical liability reform'.

of information concerning any medical practitioner obtained within the process is necessary to eliminate fears and to encourage medical practitioners to report patient safety cases.[40] Latvia also needs to introduce in its legislation a provision for protection from liability of the whistle-blower. It should also determine that any information concerning any medical practitioner, obtained as a result of the reporting process, can be used only in the framework of the Reporting and Learning System.

References

Apinis, P., Veselības aprūpes reforma. Available: http://apollo.tvnet.lv/zinas/peteris-apinis-veselibas-aprupes-reforma/787459.

Ašnevica-Slokenberga, S. (ed), *Medical rights*, Rīga: Tiesu namu aģentūra, 2015.

Clancy, C., 'Patient safety and medical liability reform: putting the patient first', 2010, September/October. Available: https://archive.ahrq.gov/news/newsroom/commentaries/putting-patients-first.html.

Dzērve, L., 'Tiesāšanās ar ārstiem ir specifiska un ilgst gadiem'. Available: www.lsm.lv/lv/raksts/vide-un-zinatne/dzive/tiesashanas-ar-arstiem-ir-specifiska-un-ilgst-gadiem.a82881/.

European Commission. High Level Group on health services and medical care. Minutes of the meeting of the High Level Group on 29 September 2005. Available: http://ec.europa.eu/health/ph_overview/co_operation/mobility/docs/highlevel_2005_015_en.pdf.

European Hospital and Healthcare Federation. Available: www.hope.be/.

Kohn, L. T., Corrigan, J. M. and Donaldson, M. S. (eds), Committee on Quality of Health Care in America. *To err is human: building a safer health system*, Washington, D.C.: Institute of Medicine, National Academy Press, 2000.

Leape, L. L., 'Error in medicine', *JAMA* 1994. Available: www.uphs.upenn.edu/gme/pdfs/Leape_Error%20in%20Medicine_JAMA.pdf.

Lieljuksis, Q. A., 'Responsibility of a medication practitioner', in Ašnevica-Slokenberga, S. (ed), *Medical Rights*, Rīga: Tiesu namu aģentūra, 2015.

Linde, Z., 'Priekšizpētes ziņojums par Eiropas Savienības pacientu drošības politiku. Pacientu drošības politika piecās Eiropas Savienības dalībvalstīs: Apvienotajā Karalistē, Nīderlandē, Dānijā, Lietuvā un Igaunijā'. Rīga: 2010. Available: www.biodrosiba.lu.lv/fileadmin/user_upload/lu_portal/projekti/biodrosiba/ZLinde_Pacientu_drosiba.pdf

Ministru kabineta noteikumu "Ārstniecības riska fonda darbības noteikumi" projekta sākotnējās (ex-ante) ietekmes novērtējuma ziņojums (anotācija). Available: http://tap.mk.gov.lv/.

Ministru kabineta noteikumu projekta 'Grozījumi Ministru kabineta 2009.gada 20.janvāra noteikumos Nr.60 'Noteikumi par obligātajām prasībām ārstniecības iestādēm un to struktūrvienībām'' sākotnējās ietekmes novērtējuma ziņojums (anotācija). Available: http://tap.mk.gov.lv.

Muciņš, R., Ārstniecības riska fonda būtība un tiesiskie aspekti. Jurista Vārds. 2013. 8.oktobris, nr.41..

Öhrn, A., 'Measures of patient safety – studies of Swedish reporting systems and evaluation of an intervention aimed at improved patient safety culture', Sweden: Linköping

40 L. T. Kohn, J. M. Corrigan and M. S. Donaldson (eds), Committee on Quality of Health Care in America, *To err is human: building a safer health system*, Washington D.C.: Institute of Medicine. National Academy Press, 2000.

University, 2011. Available: http://liu.diva-portal.org/smash/get/diva2:460214/FULLTEXT01.pdf.

Rožkaln, R., Kas ir kļūdaina ārstniecība. Jurista Vārds. Nr.41(792) 2013.

Slawomirski, L., Auraaen, A. and Klazinga, N., 'The economics of patient safety. Strengthening a value-based approach to reducing patient harm at national level. OECD. 2017. Grant N.DI161105.

Straume, Z., Pacientu drošības konference. Available: www.bsf.lv/lv/jaunumi/2016/pacientu-drosibas-konference.

Studdert, D. M., Mello, M. M. and Brennan, T. A., *Medical malpractice. Health policy report.* Available: https://cdn1.sph.harvard.edu/wp-content/uploads/sites/487/2012/10/HPR_final.pdf.

Treaty for the Functioning of the European Union. Available: http://eur-lex.europa.eu/legal-content/EN/TXT/?uri=celex%3A12012E%2FTXT.

Veselības ministrija, Konceptuālais ziņojums 'Par veselības aprūpes sistēmas reformu'. 2017. Available: www.vm.gov.lv/lv/aktualitates/zinojums_par_veselibas_aprupes_sistemas_reformu/.

VSIA, 'Bērnu klīniskā universitātes slimnīca'. Pacientu drošība klīniskajā praksē- realitāte un izaicinājumi 21.gadsimtā. Available: www.bkus.lv/lv/content/pacientu-drosiba-kliniskaja-prakse-realitate-un-izaicinajumi-21gadsimta.

World Health Organisation, *A brief synopsis on patient safety*, 2010. Available: www.euro.who.int/__data/assets/pdf_file/0015/111507/E93833.pdf.

World Health Organisation, *Conceptual framework of an international patient safety event classification: final technical report.* 2009. Available: www.who.int/patientsafety/taxonomy/icps_full_report.pdf.

World Health Organisation, *Definitions of Key Concepts from the WHO Patient Safety Curriculum Guide*, 2011. Available: www.who.int/patientsafety/education/curriculum/course1a_handout.pdf.

World Health Organisation, *Quality of care: patient safety.* No. WHA55.18. World Health Assembly. Ninth plenary meeting, 18 May 2002. Available: http://apps.who.int/gb/archive/pdf_files/WHA55/ewha5518.pdf?ua=1.

Regulations:

Convention on the Organisation for Economic Co-operation and Development Available: www.oecd.org/general/conventionontheorganisationforeconomicco-operationand-development.htm.

International Covenant on Economic, Social and Cultural Rights (ICESCR). Available: www.humanrights.lv/.

Consolidated version of the Treaty on the Functioning of the European Union. Available: http://eur-lex.europa.eu/legal-content/EN/TXT/?uri=celex%3A12012E%2FTXT.

European Social Charter. Available: https://m.likumi.lv/doc.php?id=255041.

Regulation (EU) no 376/2014 of the European Parliament and of the council, 3 April 2014, on the reporting, analysis and follow-up of occurrences in civil aviation. EUR-Lex. Available: http://eur-lex.europa.eu/legal-content/LV/TXT/?uri=CELEX%3A32014R0376.

Directive 2011/24/EU of the European Parliament and of the Council of 9 March 2011 on the application of patients' rights in cross-border healthcare. Official Journal of the European Union Nr.L88/45, 04.04.2011.

Council of Europe. Committee of Ministers. Recommendation Rec(2006)7 of the Committee of Ministers to member states on management of patient safety and prevention of adverse events in health care. 2006. Available: https://search.coe.int/cm/Pages/result_details.aspx?ObjectID=09000016805ae8b5.

Communication from the Commission to the European Parliament and the Council on Patient Safety, including the prevention and control of healthcare-associated infections {COM(2008) 837 final} {SEC(2008) 3004} {SEC(2008) 3005}. Available: http://eur-lex.europa.eu/legal-content/en/TXT/?uri=CELEX:52008DC0836.

Latvijas Administratīvo pārkāpumu kodekss: LR likums. '*Ziņotājs*', nr.51, 20.12.1984.

Krimināllikums: L. R. likums. "Latvijas Vēstnesis", nr.199/200 (1260/1261) 08.07.1998., '*Ziņotājs*' Nr.15. 04.08.1998.

Pacientu tiesību likums: L. R. Likums. 'Latvijas Vēstnesis', nr.205 (4191), 30.12.2009.

12 Patient safety in Thailand

Piyawan Limpanyalert

Introduction

Thailand has increasingly recognised patient safety as a crucial healthcare issue. Special efforts have been undertaken to improve the healthcare system to ensure the delivery of quality services. Patient safety is, fundamentally, a dimension of healthcare which fulfils the needs of both service providers and users. The Ministry of Public Health (MoPH), healthcare professional councils and other responsible agencies in the healthcare system (public and private), communities and civil societies are becoming involved in collaboratively creating a better and safer healthcare system.

In Thailand, the Healthcare Accreditation Institute Public Organisation (HAI) has legislative responsibility for quality improvement and accreditation of health care organisations. Thus, the HAI has been both a driver and an active participant in the patient safety movement. This chapter begins by sketching the patient safety profile of Thailand, drawing upon available empirical data. It then provides an account of the HAI's initiatives for promoting patient safety in the country, including (i) tools and mechanisms to promote *patient safety in hospitals* and (ii) programmes and mechanisms to promote *patient safety in the healthcare system*. The chapter concludes by sharing the lessons that have been learned through the patient safety movement and identifies a number of factors critical for the success in promoting patient safety in Thailand, but also elsewhere in the world.

Thailand's patient safety profile

Traditionally, national statistics on patient safety in Thailand have been limited. Nevertheless, since 2006, there has been an effort to build a national data collection system. The MoPH surveyed adverse events (AEs) across the country, finding 207,073 AEs reported from 389 hospitals.[1] The top three AEs were medical error, problems with communication and the care process. Community hospitals had more AEs than provincial and central hospitals in all risk areas.

Thailand has had a system to review patient complaints, and a compensation scheme, since 2004. Data from the National Health Security Office showed that, in 2016, the Office paid relief money to 885 patients and/or their families who

1 Ministry of Public Health, 'Risk Management Manual: Promoting safety in Hospital', Nonthaburi: Ministry of Public Health, 2013. (Unpublished Thai manuscript.)

suffered from undesirable consequences of medical practices, with an average of USD 7,200 per case,[2] a figure which has risen 40 times in the last 10 years. The top three medical departments that were complained against were Obstetrics and Gynaecology (36.8%), Surgery (14.9%) and Internal Medicine (10.5%). To some extent, compensation can relieve the financial burdens incurred by some patients and families as a result of medical errors. However, the determinant of medical error is an evaluation of the standard of care which the patient received, assessed from a clinical perspective focus. This raises an underlying question about whether the patient experience of safety is fully realised through a system of compensation for medical liabilities. Arguably, only a more proactive, systemic approach towards patient safety can address the complexities of quality and safety in healthcare. Thailand has begun to implement a more holistic approach through a variety of patient safety initiatives.

Patient safety initiatives

The HAI has carried out numerous initiatives, including the development of tools and mechanisms for promoting patient safety in hospitals and the healthcare system. In 2012 the HAI established the Community of Practice, a knowledge-exchange mechanism, in four high-risk areas (Emergency Room, Labour Room, Operating Room and Intensive Care Unit) to engage experts and healthcare workers in sharing their experiences and examples of good practice guidelines. In 2013 the HAI set up a monitoring system, through the Thailand Hospital Indicators Project to benchmark healthcare outcomes.

Despite these efforts, improvement in patient safety has been slow; Thailand still has problems of AEs and medication errors. The engagement of all stakeholders and participants is essential to improve patient safety. In order to tackle this issue, the Engagement for Patient Safety Programme was initiated in 2014. Consequently, the Patient and Personnel Safety policy was recently issued by the MoPH as a result of this engagement.

Quality tools and mechanisms to promote patient safety in hospitals

The HAI's initial work on patient safety focussed on quality improvement in hospitals. It encourages quality assurance through hospital accreditation alongside the use of quality tools/mechanisms such as quality review activities, the adoption of the Thailand Patient Safety Goals and Trigger Tools.

Hospital accreditation

The HAI has been using hospital standards to drive quality improvement since 1997. The HAI, in performing its function as an accrediting body, promotes quality improvement and patient safety using self-assessment and self-improvement, along with external evaluation and recognition as an incentive. The accreditation programme takes a three-step grading approach to hospital

2 National Health Security Office, *Annual report of National Health Security Office 2015*, Bangkok, 2016 (Thai manuscript).

accreditation (HA) recognition.[3] For *Step One*, in applying for HA, healthcare organisations have to identify and review their risk profiles and determine an agreed approach to minimisation of key risk areas. Healthcare practitioners are encouraged to embed quality review activities into routine activities. In order to be eligible for *Step Two* recognition, the HAI encourages them to improve their systems to meet the HA standards including the risk management system, infection control system, medication management system, the system of safe environment of care, and patient care processes. After they had improved and produced quality and safe outcomes, they would be awarded with *Step Three* recognition. As of October 2017, the percentage of fully accredited hospitals is now 55%, and nearly 10% are at the second step of HA recognition; indicating that nearly 65% of all hospitals in Thailand have developed some form of risk management system.

Patient safety, therefore, has been significantly enhanced through the introduction of a risk management system and an accreditation process. Patient safety is a fundamental component that HAI surveyors must assess during their visits for hospital accreditation. Hospital staff are guided on developing incident report systems. Data on AEs in a hospital, their root cause analysis and opportunities for improvement are discussed during the surveyors' visit.

Thailand patient safety goals: SIMPLE

In 2008 the HAI, in collaboration with key stakeholders, developed the 'SIMPLE' guidebook on patient safety goals.[4] SIMPLE is an acronym of six key issues that should be highlighted when promoting patient safety. These are:

S = Safe surgery

I = Infection control

M = Medication and blood safety

P = Patient care process

L = Line, tubing and catheter and laboratory

E = Emergency response.

'Thailand Patient Safety Goals' is an attempt to ensure that all healthcare organisations have a set of shared safety priorities and a practical safety guideline for major risk areas. These goals were developed using survey data, academic data and related guidance documents from within and outside the country. These were also consistent with the directions of the World Health Organisation's (WHO) Global Patient Safety Challenges[5] and Patient Safety Solutions.[6]

3 Healthcare Accreditation Institute, *3-step to HA recognition*, Thailand, 2002 (Thai manuscript).

4 HAI, *Patient safety goals: SIMPLE*, Nonthaburi: Thailand 2008 (Thai manuscript).

5 For information on the Global Patient Safety Challenges see www.who.int/patientsafety/medication-safety/en/.

6 www.who.int/patientsafety/topics/solutions/en/

Within the SIMPLE framework, each healthcare organisation is able to pursue their patient safety interests or needs by setting their own safety goals and establishing practical guides, then implementing and evaluating these in their operations. Healthcare organisations are also encouraged to use quality tools for learning and improving their system for safety, such as using 'root cause analysis' to analyse the causes of AEs, and the Trigger Tool to identify major risks from medical records for review.

Trigger Tool

Setting up an effective incident report system in a hospital usually takes time. Under-reporting is generally a challenge, either because hospital staff do not recognise the importance of this data for quality improvement, or when they are involved in any AEs, they may be afraid of 'punishment' in the form of litigation. Trigger Tools were initially developed by the Institute for Healthcare Improvement, an international quality improvement agency, to sample medical records to proactively identify AEs which have not been reported, rather than waiting for reports from the incident report system.[7] The HAI adapted this international tool to fit the national context, and introduced the Trigger Tool to the hospitals that underwent the quality improvement journey in 2007.

Programmes and mechanisms to promote patient safety in the healthcare system

The HAI broadened its patient safety work outwards from the hospital level to the whole health care system. The MoPH issued a 10-year plan for coordinating the movement on patient safety (see Table 12.1). In addition, the HAI also supported the development of the 'Thailand Hospital Indicator Project' and the 'Community of Practice' to empower health professionals. Moreover, realising that quality of healthcare and patient safety requires engagement by all stakeholders within and outside the health sector, an 'Engagement for Patient Safety' project was therefore initiated.

Long-term plan for promoting patient safety

In the systematic development of the 10-year plan for ongoing improvement of patient safety in Thailand, the setting of targets was done with cooperation from all sectors. Consequently, various movements/mechanisms for patient safety were integrated into the plan. Many organisations have collaboratively launched various programmes and projects for improving the quality of care and patient safety. Proposed actions during 2015–2024 are summarised in Table 12.1.

7 www.ihi.org/resources/Pages/Tools/IHIGlobalTriggerToolforMeasuringAEs.aspx

Table 12.1 Action plan for the decade of improving quality of care and patient safety

The Decade of Improving the Quality of Care and Patient Safety		
Phase 1 (2015–2017)	*Phase 2 (2018–2021)*	*Phase 3 (2022–2024)*
• Raise awareness and clarify understanding about patient safety among health personnel and general public. • Develop tools, mechanisms, systems, bodies of knowledge, and models. Piloting on voluntary basis in various participatory forms of the implementation about patient safety. • Establish a network of organisations, agencies and people. Build up the leading teams in various aspects of patient safety for driving the movements as a whole. • Have a patient safety goal (or target) in place at national level. • Initiate a systematic research and develop a policy recommendation for improvement in phase 2. • Propose and participate in the movements at the ministerial and regional levels. • Duration = 3 years.	• Educational Institutions integrate the teaching of patient safety in their curriculum, covering all institutions. • Scale-up the implementation of "Hospital for Patient Safety" as a policy covering all healthcare organisations. • Special interest group drives a move on patient safety covering all regions of health providers. • Have a system to evaluate and monitor incident reporting database; have an indicator system to compare the quality of clinical outcomes at the national level. • Have a structure for the improvement of patient safety in healthcare organisations; and have a legal protection for quality-improvement data. • Propose and participate in the movements of patient safety at the global level. • Duration = 4 years.	• Create safety innovations in healthcare system. • Ensure the inclusiveness of patient safety covering health promotion, treatment, prevention and rehabilitation. • All people are engaged in the improvement of health service system. • Healthcare organisations awarded with healthcare accreditation have quality and patient safety outcomes for publicizing in public media. • Have a system for giving feedback and awarding the recognition by general public. • Have the outcomes from systematic research regarding quality and patient safety at national level. • Serve as the prototype of outcome-oriented model for driving the movement on patient safety; and have a safety culture at the global level. • Duration = 3 years.

Thailand Hospital Indicator Project

In 2007, the HAI and the Medical School Consortium launched the Thailand Hospital Indicator Project, aimed to develop a set of indicators for comparing the quality of key processes and outcomes in medical school hospitals so that hospital staff can identify areas for improvement and learn from good practices. Initially, 84 indicators were developed, of which seven reflect patient safety (for example, rate of ventilator-associated pneumonia, rate of catheter-associated urinary tract infection). The definition of terms and data collection methods were collaboratively discussed and then written down in the data dictionary for use as a reference book. The project was further extended to cover indicators that suit the requirement of smaller hospitals, such as provincial hospitals and community hospitals. Now, 179 indicators are included and 362 hospitals are voluntarily enrolled in this project.

'Community of Practice' for high-risk areas

In 2012, the HAI focussed its efforts on the acquisition of knowledge, the sharing of common experiences, and the horizontal alignment of safety networks. This was carried out by setting up a Community of Practice (CoP), an exchange forum that will serve as a platform for shared learning. CoPs were established in four high-risk operation units: (i) Emergency Room (ER), (ii) Labour Room (LR), (iii) Operating Room (OR), and (iv) Intensive Care Unit (ICU).

CoPs are groups of people with shared professional interests and experiences, gathering together as a group or 'knowledge domain'. CoP members share experiences in order to develop good practices to prevent risks, which can be varied between institutions to suit contextual needs. The underlying knowledge base was derived directly from practitioners' experiences of their field of work (tacit knowledge) and was supplemented with academic expertise (explicit knowledge) from each specialty area. The knowledge acquired could be applied, extended, or scaled up as a research project on a topic of common interest. For example, CoP LR decided to initiate a study on postpartum haemorrhage; CoP ER decided to study the triage of patients; CoP OR decided to study surgical safety checklists, and CoP ICU decided to present the experiences of success related to sepsis. On this latter project, CoP ICU found that responsible staff were unable to provide care for patients with sepsis in accordance with international standards. Consequently, utilising the tacit knowledge of practitioners, adjustments were made to adapt care processes so as to be more practically appropriate for the existing contexts. Once this tacit knowledge was communicated and exchanged, experts were engaged to synthesise, review and develop this data and, ultimately, the findings provided a new Thai sepsis guideline.

CoP networks were expanded to various regions throughout the country, and later incorporated into the Engagement for Patient Safety Project to more systematically develop policy from practice.

Engagement for Patient Safety project

There are several challenges within the health system for the improvement of patient safety. These include reporting errors and AEs, the safety culture, safety practices of health professionals, effective communication and coordinated care among health professionals, and lack of whole system solutions, to name just a few. Thailand has learned to appreciate that it is essential to have the engagement of all relevant stakeholders, particularly patients and health professionals, communities and actors beyond the health sector, in building safer health care systems and for creating and sustaining a culture of safety at all levels of the healthcare system. The Engagement for Patient Safety project was thus initiated, and the HAI was the main coordinating body for its implementation.

As the patient safety issue is complex, the HAI decided to apply Wasi's concept of 'The triangle that moves the mountain'[8] which emphasises the pursuance of social changes that could affect a larger number of people. Under this concept, three aspects must be pursued simultaneously: (1) knowledge, (2) social movement and (3) policy link.

Under the umbrella of the Engagement for Patient Safety project, three main programmes were developed: (1) Patient Safety Education Programme; (2) Patients for Patient Safety Programme; and (3) Hospitals for Patient Safety and Patient Safety Policy Programme.

The three programmes were driven simultaneously, serving as a push for the adoption of related policies that would be proposed in a bottom-up fashion. Meanwhile, the policies adopted at global level would be driven in a top-down scheme. The strategies used for pursuing the engagement included *Share* (listen, exchange and learn); *Chain* (establish the networks of parties involved); *Shape* (develop a practical guideline consistent with the given contexts); and *Change* (implement, monitor and evaluate).

1. Patient Safety Education Programme

The HAI applied the WHO *Patient safety curriculum guide: multi-professional edition*[9] in developing three key objectives:

(1) To integrate the WHO *Multi-professional patient safety curriculum guide* into undergraduate and postgraduate training of healthcare professionals in Thailand.
(2) To encourage and facilitate collaboration and networking among healthcare professional education institutions.
(3) To collaborate with the WHO and disseminate the WHO's resources to educators and trainers, and facilitate the integration of patient safety in their teaching.

8 Prawase Wasi, 'The triangle that moves the mountain'. .www.bloggang.com/viewdiary.php?id=samrotri&month=01-2007&date=14&group=11

9 World Health Organisation, *Patient safety curriculum guide, multi-professional edition*, Geneva, Switzerland, 2011.

The HAI employed four principles – Share, Chain, Shape and Change – in applying this guide:

> *Share:* This step uses listening and information sharing to build relationships, mutual respect and care with all stakeholders. Meetings, workshops, focus group discussions and questionnaires were organised for sharing and learning the experience from leaders and multi-professionals of the health professional education institutions. It was revealed that 94% of people supported the integration of patient safety into a regular training course but only 9% of healthcare professional education institutions had it.
>
> *Chain:* This approach encourages and facilitates collaboration through building networks among various stakeholders. This was achieved by establishing networks for patient safety education. For example, a committee consisting of representatives from multi-professional organisations was set up to formulate action plans; a working group comprising representatives from education institutions was also set up to translate and review the WHO *Patient safety curriculum guide* to Thai language; and the CoP of patient safety education was established.
>
> *Shape:* It is a process for creating and shaping achievements in a way that is specific and suitable for each health professional education institution. Participants embraced the concept of a patient safety curriculum, had a shared vision and purpose, created a mechanism for collaboration and actively participated in drafting, pilot testing and adapting the *Curriculum guide* to Thai context. Ownership is very important in engagement at this stage.
>
> *Change:* The protocols for monitoring and evaluation of the *Curriculum guide* is adopted. These included changes in knowledge, skills, competency and mind-set of the trainees, developed specifically for safer care. These tools are available for regular and wide application in assessing patient safety education in undergraduate and postgraduate training. This approach is responsive for the changes based on the results of information systems and research.

The results of this initiative are as follows: (1) the *Curriculum guide* was translated into the Thai language; (2) 133 health professional educational institutions participated, which were divided into five working groups: namely doctors, dentists, pharmacists, medical technologists and nurses; (3) eight professional education regulators (such as the Consortium of Thai Medical Schools, the Medical, Dental, Pharmacy, and Nursing and Midwifery Councils of Thailand) signed a collaborative agreement to integrate patient safety into professional education/training and established the Patient Safety Education Committee; (4) 150 trainers were developed from the 'training of the trainers' programme; (5) a resource centre to collect all related documents, training guidelines and materials was established by the HAI; (6) a project on inter-professional education on patient safety is now piloting at three universities.

The key achievements of this programme were: (1) the scaling up of patient safety in health professional educational programmes, from only 39 education institutes to 133 institutes at present; (2) the guidelines developed for implementation in various disciplines, which had been adapted to suit each educational institute; (3) all health professional councils are accountable for and engaged with their respective health professional education and practice to ensure competent practitioners for safer care; and (4) teaching-learning aids were developed by the learners themselves, which would enable the training to be more effective, given that the students have ownership of the issues and understand them well.

2. Patients for Patient Safety

Patient engagement and empowerment are key factors that contribute to sustainable and improved patient safety. In August 2014 the HAI, in collaboration with the WHO, organised a capacity-building workshop and established the Patients for Patient Safety (PFPS) Thailand Network as a mechanism to collaborate with patients and families. Volunteer participants and HAI established a patient-led working group and a national network of patients and patient organisations to drive patient safety initiatives.

PFPS Thailand is building a patient-led, national network of patients and patient organisations to lead a patient safety movement. Its vision is to enhance public participation in the healthcare system's development for safety and equity, with evidence-based policies and common understanding of all partners. Additionally, the strategic objectives are: to raise public awareness of rights and responsibilities for health and safety in healthcare; to educate the public on healthcare safety; to promote better understanding between providers and clients; to promote safe health care in healthcare organisations and community; and to encourage collaborative movement among all stakeholders for safer healthcare.

Thailand's Patient Safety Champions and Network established a working group to advocate, facilitate and incorporate the patient, family and community voice into all levels of the health care system. The group developed PFPS tools, such as the 'Reminding Card', to guide patients on what to ask and tell when visiting the doctor. The PFPS team developed a patients' experience survey tool in 2015 for determining ways to further improve quality and safety of healthcare from clients' perspective. The study showed that 47.8% of patients were 'most concerned' and proposed immediate improvements with regards to involvement in the decision-making around their own care. However, 70.1% of the patients were 'most satisfied' with doctors giving a physical examination prior to diagnosis.[10] Thailand PFPS activities were publicised in the WHO 'PFPS Newsletter'.[11]

10 Healthcare Accreditation Institute, *Reporting of patient experience for healthcare system development*, Thailand 2016 (Thai manuscript).

11 World Health Organisation, *PFPS News, Patients for Patient Safety*, 2016, Spring. www.who.int/patientsafety/patients_for_patient/newsletters/en/.

3. Hospitals for Patient Safety and Patient Safety Policy

Improvement was driven through policy-related movements, simultaneously, in two directions. The first direction involved the establishment of 'bodies of knowledge'. This was a 'bottom-up' approach to policy development, influenced by the learning exchange process among the selected healthcare organisations, to summarise the acquired information as a practical guide for policy recommendations.

The second direction was the 'top-down' approach to determine strategies for improving patient safety in healthcare system at national and international levels. This was carried out by the development of a guideline consistent with that of WHO, so that global/regional patient safety policy could be adapted for use in the country.

(A) HOSPITAL FOR PATIENT SAFETY

This was the establishment of a space for learning exchange among healthcare organisations, with the aim of developing mechanisms to ensure the 'safety of healthcare system'. Its goal is to ensure that the participating healthcare organisations pursue quality improvement in a programme for producing safety outcomes for the service providers and clients, in line with HA standards.

148 healthcare organisations voluntarily participated in this programme. The director of each organisation sent the executive and operational personnel responsible for a specifically defined work or system to join improvement activities and a learning exchange forum with other hospitals and experts in various fields through a knowledge management process (with an aim to ensure improvement in line with HA standards). They had to send 'key patient safety indicator outcomes' into the information system continuously for three consecutive years. The framework for improvement covered three categories (organisation management, improvement of work related to patient safety, and improvement among high-risk operation units) and involved 11 CoPs (Table 12.2).

The implementation of this programme was done using the 3-P concept:

- *Purpose*. The purpose was to ensure patient safety, a reliable and safe healthcare system available at all times and everywhere for everybody.

Table 12.2 Hospitals for Patient Safety frameworks for improvement

Framework for Improvement	*CoP Involvement*
Organisational Management	CoP Organisation; CoP Human Resource; and CoP Customer.
Work Relating to Patient Safety	CoP Risk Management System; CoP Medication Management System; CoP Infection Control System; and CoP Environment System.
High-risk Operation Units	CoP ER; CoP LR; CoP OR; and CoP ICU.

- *Process*. The process used was the knowledge management process driven through 11 CoPs. The learning exchange activities were organised over the period of three years as a face-to-face conference for the members in central areas; and as a distance conference through telecommunication systems for all other members in rural areas.
- *Performance*. The performance outcomes were measured by 32 indicators for patient safety, as defined in the Thailand Hospital Indicator Project (see above). The safety culture was assessed by a 'Safety Culture Survey', modified from the Hospital Survey on Patient Safety Culture of the United States Agency for Healthcare Research and Quality.[12] The incident report of each healthcare organisation was linked to a central system. It was an outcome-oriented improvement comparable with the level of Advanced HA standards[13].

All 148 healthcare organisations (around 10% of all hospitals) were located widely across all 12 regions of health providers and covered all levels of healthcare settings. They worked together to drive the movement on patient safety in a networking scheme. More than 120 experts from various fields and professional organisations served as the resource persons in the learning exchange activities of 11 CoPs. Public health personnel also participated in 11 CoPs throughout the country. At each CoP face-to-face conference, more than 300 persons attended; and at each distance conference, 1,500 persons across the country attended. More than 100,000 persons participated in the diagnosis and assessment of safety culture in healthcare organisations over the period of 3 years.

A new guide was developed for the practice and review of the Thailand Patient Safety Goals. These were adapted to be consistent with the actual practice and the changes; and were further developed for incorporating in the National Patient and Personnel Safety Goals. A 'National Reporting and Learning System' was developed using the software programme developed by the 80 hospital members of CoP Risk Management. A tool for assessing patients' experience was developed by healthcare workers working with expert patients from the PFPS project. The quality communicators were developed for facilitating the collaborative work that needed to be carried out by healthcare organisation and communities. The use of an 'Organisation Diagnosis' tool would be scaled up to make it a requirement before an improvement plan could be set up for each healthcare organisation across the country.

(B) PATIENT SAFETY POLICY

Policy advocacy was a movement corresponding to the global trend and was carried out by participating in international assemblies as a Member State or an expert on patient safety. In 2015, Thailand actively took part in drafting a proposal of Patient Safety Resolution for consideration at the 68th session of the Regional

12 Hospital Survey on Patient Safety Culture. Agency for Health Research and Quality, Rockville, MD USA. www.ahrq.gov/professionals/quality-patient-safety/patientsafetyculture/index.html.

13 Healthcare Accreditation Institute (Public Organisation), *Advanced HA criteria, 2013*. www.ha.or.th/Backend/fileupload/A%20HA/Attach/Advanced%20HA%20Criteria%202013_update%20140602.pdf

Committee of the WHO South-East Asia Region. The proposed resolution requests all parties to pay special attention to patient safety, and view it as the main mechanism for ensuring access to quality healthcare service in a sustainable manner. Consequently, the Regional Committee of WHO South-East Asia Region adopted the resolution SEA/RC68/R4 on 'Patient safety contributing to sustainable universal health coverage', urging all Member States, including Thailand, to translate the 'Regional Strategy for Patient Safety in the WHO South-East Asia Region'[14] into actions, implementation, monitoring and evaluations.

In order to enable countries to understand their own patient safety-readiness in implementing the above-mentioned Regional Strategy on Patient Safety, WHO-Regional Office for South-East Asia developed a tool, 'Country Self-Assessment on Patient Safety Situation', for assessing the situation of patient safety at the country level. The HAI was the main coordinating body for carrying out Thailand's

Table 12.3 Patient and Personnel Safety Strategy 2018–2022

Thailand's Patient and Personnel Safety Strategy 2018–2022
Vision: Thailand has quality and safe healthcare service
Goal: To ensure patient and personnel safety through the implementation of 5 key strategies.
Strategy 1: Prepare health personnel by enhancing their capability and raising their awareness about quality and safety. Human resource management is an important issue. If health personnel are empowered as aforementioned; it would be the starting point for the sustainable improvement of the service system.
Strategy 2: Establish collaboration with the network of civil society and the organisations involved in the healthcare system. This strategy will lead to a change, the engagement of all sectors, and mutual understanding, and thus will lead further to the reduction of conflicts.
Strategy 3: Develop supporting systems necessary for ensuring the quality and safety in the healthcare system. This strategy will boost the actual practice among related parties. That is the reason why this strategy has served as the origination of "Patient and Personnel Safety Goals," in which the key issues are prioritized and aligned for finding a shared approach for risk prevention that all parties will act together.
Strategy 4: Set up the systems for reporting, learning, and measuring the quality and safety outcomes of healthcare service. This is for learning and setting up a system to prevent the repetition of an incidence. National Reporting and Learning System will be connectable to any systems required for learning from errors, which is currently being emphasized by other countries as an essential approach for developing a preventive system. Patient safety reporting issue is important; and proper understanding and good attitude are required for this development.
Strategy 5: Increase the efficiency of the overseeing and nurturing of the healthcare system. This strategy would lead to sustainability as well as the supports and oversight based on proper understanding and clear information, and with the consideration about clinical governance.

14 World Health Organisation – Regional Office for South-East Asia. *Regional strategy for patient safety in the WHO South-East Asia Region (2016–2025)*. New Delhi, India: WHO-SEARO, 2015.

self-assessment on patient safety situation in 2016. The committee designated for this purpose consisted of people from various sectors to ensure the adoption of tangible strategies for driving the movements. The results of the assessment were presented to the Public Health Minister and other key stakeholders on 16 September 2016.

Based on the results of Thailand's self-assessment, the following key points were identified for further improvement of patient safety:

1) Establishing the engagement of patients, community and society in patient safety improvement.
2) Establishing the incidence reporting system for AEs at the national level.
3) Strengthening patient safety regarding the medication management system; and conducting research on patient safety to serve as evidence-based support for necessary improvement in relevant areas.
4) Encouraging the health professional education institutions to emphasise the integration of 'Patient and Personnel Safety' in their education curriculum.[15]

Patient and Personnel Safety Strategy

The results of Thailand's self-assessment had raised awareness of the importance of patient safety. However, the national safety improvement approach has since been extended from covering the patients alone, to also promoting and protecting healthcare personnel safety. This has most recently been enshrined in the 'Patient and Personnel Safety Strategy' or '2P Safety' (Table 12.3).

Furthermore, a working group was set up to develop the National Reporting and Learning System, which will serve as a surveillance system for AE reporting, as well as providing a platform for learning to continue to drive forward systemic improvements in patient safety policy and practice.

The above strategies will serve as a key mechanism for improving the healthcare system in a participatory manner, which always take into account the service providers and clients simultaneously. This is the way to create and sustain this kind of balance.

Conclusion: lessons learned

From vast and extensive experiences in driving the movements on patient safety and quality of health care and the '2P Safety' strategy, Thailand has learned a number of key lessons:

- *Strong leadership*: Leaders play a key role in driving the movements. Committed and competent leaders are crucial at the national and the health care organisation level. It is beneficial to develop a core group of leaders to lead and facilitate the movements at various levels, groups and/or programmes.

15 Healthcare Accreditation Institute (Public Organisation), *Thailand self-assessment on patient safety situation*, Nonthaburi, Thailand, 2017.

- *Clear goal*: A clear goal is required to mobilise action. A coordinator or a main coordinating agency is needed for driving the movements and to coordinate with all sectors on a continual basis.
- *Horizontal and vertical approach*: A two-pronged approach is required to drive the movement. The horizontal approach is aimed at transforming and empowering hospital staff to operate and appreciate its benefits for patient and staff's safety. Meanwhile, the vertical movement is aimed at gaining support from concerned authorities within and outside the country. Clear policy direction and adequate financial support are critical for the movements' success.
- *Collaboration between practitioners and experts*: CoP provides a learning-sharing platform for health professionals and experts on patient safety. Practical realities and patient safety issues defined for establishing safety culture and 'bodies of knowledge' were developed together. Thus, collaboration of health professionals and experts should be augmented for a sustainable safety culture in the health system.
- *Information technology*: There were a large number of CoPs operating throughout the country. Thus, information technology played a critical role in facilitating the exchange of knowledge between the communities. GIN (web-based) conferences were organised for various distant CoPs. Use of information technology for promoting patient safety, particularly for raising public awareness and engagement, will need to be further harnessed.
- '*All engagement*': A more holistic view for systematic improvement in quality and safety can be obtained from working together with all healthcare stakeholders within and outside the health sectors, including patients, families and communities. Engagement of all helps to facilitate an improvement in a sustainable manner and helps in reducing conflicts. Clients' engagement is crucial in ensuring clients' perspectives are correctly reflected; and listening is key to engaging patients and their families.

The author would also like to propose a number of key factors which have been critical for Thailand's success in implementing a wide-ranging programme of patient safety interventions:

- *Public awareness*: Patient safety has become one of the targeted quality outcomes expected by service providers and clients.
- *Political commitment and support*: Clear policy directions in terms of improving quality of healthcare and patient safety and 2P Safety were given by the MoPH. In addition, the executive management of healthcare institutions and healthcare professionals showed commitment to patient safety.
- *Networking and alliance*: Networking and alliance of health professionals, experts, clients and other stakeholders in CoPs, Patients for Patients Network and others helps to facilitate the work towards achieving common goals for patient and personnel safety.
- *WHO technical tools*: WHO technical tools such as 'country self-assessment on patient safety situation' and the WHO *Patient safety multi-professional curriculum* are supportive and were successfully adapted to use in the country.

- *HAI's reputation*: The HAI's extensive experience and expertise in quality improvement are well recognised and supported by healthcare organisations.

In summary, many patient safety initiatives and interventions have taken place in Thailand during recent years. A concerted effort is being made to prioritise patient safety, through the implementation of a cohesive strategy. There has been a distinct approach towards integrating the experiences of healthcare practitioners and patients into the international and national policy agenda, to formulate strategies which are suitable for implementation in the specific contexts of the Thai healthcare system and within particular healthcare settings. Whilst ongoing evaluation of these initiatives is most certainly required, there is much that other countries could learn from the Thai experience to date.

References

Agency for Health Research and Quality, 'Hospital survey on patient safety culture', Rockville, MD: US. www.ahrq.gov/professionals/quality-patient-safety/patientsafety culture/index.html.

Healthcare Accreditation Institute (Public Organisation), *3-steps to HA recognition*, Thailand, 2002 (Thai manuscript).

Healthcare Accreditation Institute (Public Organisation), *Patient safety goals: SIMPLE*, Nonthaburi, Thailand, 2008 (Thai manuscript).

Healthcare Accreditation Institute (Public Organisation), *Advanced HA Criteria*, HAI, 2013. www.ha.or.th/Backend/fileupload/A%20HA/Attach/Advanced%20HA%20 Criteria%202013_update%20140602.pdf.

Healthcare Accreditation Institute (Public Organisation), *Reporting of patient experience for healthcare system development* Thailand, 2016 (Thai manuscript).

Healthcare Accreditation Institute (Public Organisation), *Patient and Personnel Safety Strategy*, Nonthaburi: Thailand, 2017 (Thai manuscript).

Healthcare Accreditation Institute (Public Organisation), *Thailand Self-Assessment on Patient Safety Situation*, Nonthaburi: Thailand, HAI, 2017.

Ministry of Public Health, (Draft) 'Risk Management Manual Promoting safety in Hospital', Nonthaburi: Ministry of Public Health, 2013. (Unpublished Thai manuscript.)

National Health Security Office, 'Annual report of National Health Security Office 2015', Bangkok, 2016 (Thai manuscript).

Wasi, P., 'The triangle that moves the mountain'. www.bloggang.com/viewdiary.php?id=samrotri&month=01-2007&date=14&group=11&gblog=11.

World Health Organisation, *Patient safety curriculum guide: multi-professional edition*, Geneva, Switzerland: WHO 2011.

World Health Organisation – Regional Office for South-East Asia, *Regional Strategy for Patient Safety in the WHO South-East Asia Region (2016–2025)*, New Delhi: India: WHO-SEARO 2015.

World Health Organisation, 'PFPS News: Patients for Patient Safety – Spring 2016'. www.who.int/patientsafety/patients_for_patient/newsletters/en/.

13 Patient safety in Uganda

Kay Seden and Regina Kamoga

Introduction

November 2015 saw the first World Health Organisation (WHO) Patients for Patient Safety (PFPS) country workshop in Uganda. Here, key stakeholders such as healthcare workers, researchers, health ministers and patients, alongside representatives from the WHO, discussed sources of local patient safety issues and national policy, and shared raw experiences of healthcare-related errors with great honesty. This heralded a new chapter for patient safety initiatives and research in Uganda, placing the fundamental concepts and issues firmly at the door of the Ministry of Health, in a local and global context.

Uganda is a low-income country, under the World Bank terminology, and has a mostly rural population. There are many issues affecting patient safety that are specific to Uganda and, indeed, specific to sub-Saharan Africa. Here we discuss the healthcare landscape in Uganda, with relation to patient safety, and the rapidly expanding opportunities to improve health outcomes and patient engagement. We will explore, in-depth, the example of medication safety in the setting of the antiretroviral programme for HIV treatment, which has undergone a rapid and successful scale-up in Uganda. Patient rights and healthcare ethics in Uganda will be discussed, alongside the legal and policy frameworks that govern them.

The healthcare landscape in Uganda: what affects patient safety?

In Uganda, the life expectancy at birth was 62 in 2015, which has increased by 15 years since 2000, according to WHO data.[1] The per capita expenditure on health fell below 50 USD (US dollars) in 2013,[2] but rose to 133 USD in 2014. Almost half of the population are under 15 years of age, and only 15% of the population live in urban areas.

1 World Health Organisation-Africa Regional Office, *Uganda factsheet of health statistics 2016*, 2016. www.aho.afro.who.int/profiles_information/images/f/fb/Uganda-Statistical_Factsheet.pdf, (accessed 26 June 2017).

2 WHO, *Uganda: WHO statistical profile – country statistics and global health estimates by WHO and UN partners*, 2015. www.who.int/gho/countries/uga.pdf?ua=1 (accessed 26 June 2017).

The prevalence of HIV is thought to be 7.3% in the general population, 9.1% in adolescent girls,[3] and 35–37% in sex workers.[4] HIV/AIDS was the leading cause of death, killing 61.4 thousand people in 2012. While other infectious diseases such as malaria and diarrhoeal conditions contribute significantly to causes of death, the rate of recorded deaths from stroke and ischaemic heart disease are increasing. The mortality rate in children under five years was 55 per 1000 live births in 2015, which represents a significant decrease since 2000.[5] Uganda is therefore a country in gradual transition; while infectious diseases represent a significant burden, non-communicable conditions which are prevalent in high-income countries, and associated with older age, are increasing.

Uganda has diverse ethnic and social groupings, with a wide range of customary laws and practices, which may influence their healthcare-seeking behaviour. While the availability of healthcare services may be rising, with the scale-up of HIV services, decentralisation of health centres to rural settings, and a growing array of missionary hospitals and private services, these services may be out of financial reach for many people. Privatisation of aspects of public services in the 1980s has caused attrition in the quality of, for example, publicly funded hospitals. Patients may access care using health insurance, pay privately, or like the majority of patients, access government-owned facilities. Health insurance premiums are beyond the means of the majority, and are purchased privately or through employment contracts. Although a consultation or hospital stay at a government facility should be free, medicines, some equipment, and lab investigations incur charges, especially when essential medicines are not in hospital stock and need to be bought by patients from private pharmacies. This can mean that a stay in a public hospital is unaffordable for many Ugandans. Patients may attend hospitals for care, but leave if they cannot afford basic tests and treatment, often, sadly, with life-threatening but entirely treatable conditions. Unofficial payments may be requested by public hospital staff to treat patients promptly, often as a result of insufficient staff remuneration. Low salaries may lead in some cases to poor motivation and often 'brain drain' from public to private services. Unlike neighbouring Tanzania, Uganda has no legislation to control the prices of private healthcare or medication sales.[6]

Decentralisation and Scale-up

Alongside cost, low density of healthcare workers and healthcare facilities outside larger towns may also reduce healthcare-seeking behaviours. Doctors may prefer to work in centres with better facilities, such as in the capital Kampala, rather than

3 United Nations Uganda, *Press release on HIV situation in Uganda*, 23 February 2017. www.un-ug.org/press-releases/press-release-hiv-situation-uganda-february-23-2017 (accessed 26 June 2017).

4 UAC, 'An AIDS free Uganda, My responsibility: documents for the National HIV and AIDS Response, 2015/2016–2019/2020', 2015.

5 WHO-ARO, *Uganda factsheet of health statistics 2016*.

6 Ben Kiromba Twinomugisha, *Fundamentals of health law in Uganda*, South Africa: Pretoria University Law Press, 2015, Chapter 3.

working in rural communities long term. This may lead to brain drain, leaving rural hospitals and clinics with a high turnover of doctors, and lack of senior support. Task-shifting, a strategy used in low-income countries to rapidly scale up health services, means that lower cadre healthcare workers, or even lay volunteers, are trained to take on roles traditionally undertaken by doctors, nurses or pharmacists. Task-shifting is particularly used in district health centres and centres which provide HIV care, whose services needed to be scaled up rapidly. While effectively enabling more people to be reached by healthcare services, task-shifting may lead to simplification of care, which would ideally be overseen by experts. Protocol-driven care may be necessary, due to training and knowledge restrictions of lower cadre health workers; and also due to reduced availability of medicines, equipment or facilities.

Village health teams, also referred to as community or lay health workers, are part of the Ministry of Health service provision structure in Uganda. They are often volunteers, or paid basic expenses. They are the backbone of the Ministry's health promotion; mobilising and educating communities to take health action by preventing diseases and treating simple illnesses at home. They educate the community about safe use of medicines and hand hygiene. The communities refer to them as their first 'doctor', although their training may be very basic. There is need to further build their capacity to enable them have the necessary knowledge and skills to deliver health services effectively.

Health literacy

The health literacy levels in Uganda are generally low which can result in issues such as use of inappropriate medication, poor healthcare-seeking behaviour, seeking alternative healthcare from traditional practitioners and failure to adhere to treatment instructions. Low health literacy may adversely affect the ability of patients to actively participate in decisions about their care. It is also associated with worse health outcomes and higher costs.[7]

The Joint Commission white paper *'What did the doctor say?' Improving health literacy to protect patient safety* asserts that 'The safety of patients cannot be assured without mitigating the negative effects of low health literacy'.[8] Hence, there is a pressing need for empowerment of individuals, groups and communities, so that they can become health literate, allowing them to acquire knowledge and skills to understand, access and use health information for positive health outcomes.

Traditionally, a paternalistic relationship exists between doctors and patients in Uganda. During the 2015 WHO PFPS Uganda workshop, many patients reported that they were not given information about their treatment, or that their questions were not answered or welcomed.[9] Health worker–patient relationship is

7 Community Health and Information Network (CHAIN), 'Gaps and challenges in contemporary health promotion and health communication in Uganda', 7 February 2014.

8 The Joint Commission, *'What did the doctor say?' Improving health literacy to protect patient safety*, Illinois, USA: 2007.

9 WHO Patients for Patient Safety country workshop – Uganda. 3–5 November 2015, Makerere University Guest House, Kampala, Uganda.

a key component of patient safety. The relationship is impacted by literacy levels, low health literacy, and lack of knowledge about patient rights. Many patients feel it is impolite to ask questions and may lack self-esteem or confidence to engage as an equal partner with health workers. They may also lack trust in the healthcare system, due to previous bad experiences, or the experiences of friends or relatives.

Health workers may perceive patients as receivers of care, with no autonomy. Patients may not be consulted when critical decisions or medical procedures are being planned or undertaken, raising issues about informed consent. Effective communication between the health worker and patient is vital to the diagnostic and therapeutic process. It forms the basis for the health worker–patient relationship. The communication gap is still big, as one patient shared:

> 'When I ask a question the doctor just looks at me without answering.'[10]

Another important aspect is the working relationships between doctors and other cadres of health workers such as nurses and midwives. There is a tendency for doctors to disregard and under-utilise information given by nurses and midwives, yet this is often vital patient information. It is critical that other health workers are supported, respected and recognised in order to improve the quality of services and patient safety, and for the provision of balanced, holistic care. In a session with doctors and nurses organised by the Community Health and Information Network (CHAIN) on medication safety, a nurse shared how her clinical notes were crossed out of a patient file by the doctor, despite the fact that these notes could potentially have prevented a medical error.[11]

Ugandan healthcare law and protection of patient rights

The first textbook on Ugandan healthcare law was published in 2015,[12] and 'Health and the Law' is part of the syllabus for Ugandan law students. Health law in Uganda is derived from the Constitution, principal legislation, subsidiary legislation, case law, international law and customary law, with the Constitution taking precedence over all other laws in the country. Violations of health rights or medical malpractice complaints may be challenged in courts of law.

There are a broad array of statutes relevant to the protection of health.[13] Most of these contain a provision empowering the relevant Minister to make regulations for attaining the objectives of the particular law. As health laws are

10 CHAIN, Public hearing on 'Promoting medication safety', 16 April 2014, Kampala, Uganda.

11 CHAIN, Workshop for Healthcare Professionals on 'Promoting medication safety', 22 January 2014, Mulago Hospital, Kampala, Uganda.

12 Kiromba Twinomugisha, ***Fundamentals of health law in Uganda.***

13 Public Health Act, Cap 281; Mental Treatment Act, Cap 279; Food and Drugs Act, Cap 278; Venereal Diseases Act, Cap 284; the Water Act, Cap 152; National Medical Stores Act, Cap 207; National Drug Policy and Authority Act, Cap 206; National Environment Act, Cap 153; the Medical and Dental Practitioners Act, Cap 272; the Nurses and Midwives Act, Cap 274; and the Allied Health Professionals Act, Cap 268.

decentralised, local governments may pass by-laws or regulations for the promotion of health in their jurisdiction, which must conform to the Constitution.[14]

The Uganda Human Rights Commission, established by the Constitution, plays a role in protecting health rights, including monitoring the government's compliance with its obligations under international law. The Commission has a Right to Health Unit, which handles complaints regarding health rights issues. The Commission has powers of the High Court. Unlike the courts, the procedure before the Commission is informal and is likely to incur fewer fees. This informal procedure is important given the high levels of illiteracy and poverty in the country, where the costs for instituting legal proceedings are usually high.[15] The Initiative for Social and Economic Rights has produced information leaflets introducing the Right to Health Unit, aimed at community health advocates. It outlines the responsibilities of the government, and legal protection linked to the right.[16]

International treaties are another important sources of health law in Uganda. The most significant of these are the International Covenant on Economic, Social and Cultural Rights (ICESCR), which provides for 'the right to the highest attainable standard of physical and mental health',[17] and the Convention on the Elimination of All Forms of Discrimination against Women (CEDAW).[18] Other treaties, which contain provisions critical for the protection of health include the Convention on the Rights of the Child (CRC);[19] the Convention on the Rights of Persons with Disabilities (CRPWD),[20] the African Charter on Human and Peoples' Rights (ACHPR),[21] the African Charter on the Rights and Welfare of the Child (ACRWC),[22] and the Protocol to the African Charter on Human and Peoples' Rights on the Rights of Women in Africa (Women's Protocol).[23]

14 Kiromba Twinomugisha, *Fundamentals of health law in Uganda*, p. 7.

15 Ibid.

16 Initiative for Social and Economic Rights, *Introduction to the right to health in Uganda: a handbook for community health advocates.* www.iser-uganda.org/images/downloads/A16_10_04_ISER_Booklet_design_layout.pdf (accessed 28 June 2017).

17 International Covenant on Economic, Social and Cultural Rights, entry into force 3 January 1976. www.ohchr.org/EN/ProfessionalInterest/Pages/CESCR.aspx, Article 12.

18 The Convention on the Elimination of All Forms of Discrimination against Women, adopted in 1979. www.un.org/womenwatch/daw/cedaw, article 12.

19 Convention on the Rights of the Child, entry into force 2 September 1990. www.ohchr.org/EN/ProfessionalInterest/Pages/CRC.aspx; see Articles 23 and 24, particularly Art. 24((2)(e): 'To ensure that all segments of society, in particular parents and children, are informed, have access to education and are supported in the use of basic knowledge of child health and nutrition, the advantages of breastfeeding, hygiene and environmental sanitation and the prevention of accidents.'

20 Convention on the Rights of Persons with Disabilities, adopted on 13 December 2006. www.un.org/development/desa/disabilities/convention-on-the-rights-of-persons-with-disabilities.html.

21 African Charter on Human and Peoples' Rights, came into effect on 25 January 2005. www.achpr.org/instruments/achpr/, Article 16: (1) 'Every individual shall have the right to enjoy the best attainable state of physical and mental health'; (2) States parties to the present Charter shall take the necessary measures to protect the health of their people and to ensure that they receive medical attention when they are sick.

22 African Charter on the Rights and Welfare of the Child, adopted July 1979. www.achpr.org/instruments/child/.

23 Protocol to the African Charter on Human and Peoples' Rights on the Rights of Women in Africa, adopted June 1995. www.achpr.org/instruments/women-protocol/.

The regional Treaty for the Establishment of the East African Community (EAC) undertakes to cooperate in the areas of the prevention and control of communicable and non-communicable diseases, management of health delivery systems, drug polices, harmonisation of national health policies, exchange of information, and promotion of research.[24] A number of initiatives have also been developed in the area of health such as the East African Community HIV and AIDS Prevention and Management Act, 2012.[25] However, the right to health is not explicitly provided for in the Bill of Rights of the Constitution of the Republic of Uganda, and there is no law that specifically deals with the right to health. There have been few attempts by patients or patients' families to challenge the state over violations of health rights.[26]

Professional regulation

Healthcare professionals such as doctors, nurses, pharmacists, dentists and midwives are regulated by professional bodies and councils, which are established by statute. These bodies, as in many countries, are designed to regulate ongoing professional education, competency and fitness to practise. These bodies also usually maintain registers of practitioners, and investigate misconduct. However, misconduct is often not clearly defined. The Pharmaceutical Society of Uganda, for example, is governed by the Pharmacy and Drugs Act. This Act calls on the Society to develop a pharmacist code of conduct; however, the most recent document is a draft copy from 2013.[27]

Traditional birthing assistants and traditional herbalists still practise widely in Uganda, and are not specifically regulated.

Patient rights

The 2009 Patients' Charter, issued by the Ugandan Ministry of Health Quality Assurance Department, outlines patient rights and responsibilities, and the responsibilities of healthcare workers. The document's objectives are to empower health consumers to demand high quality healthcare, to promote the rights of patients and to improve the quality of life of all Ugandans and finally eradicate poverty nationwide.[28]

24 The Treaty for the Establishment of the East African Community, entered into force on 7 July 2000. www.eala.org/uploads/The_Treaty_for_the_Establishment_of_the_East_Africa_Community_2006_1999.pdf.

25 East African Community HIV and AIDS Prevention and Management Act, adopted 2012. www.kelinkenya.org/wp-content/uploads/2017/04/EAC-HIV-ACT-2012.pdf.

26 Kiromba Twinomugisha, ***Fundamentals of health law in Uganda***.

27 Pharmaceutical Society of Uganda, ***Draft Pharmacists' Code of Conduct***, September 2013. http://psu.or.ug/files/downloads/DRAFT_PSU_COD http://psu.or.ug/files/downloads/DRAFT_PSU_CODEofCONDUCT.pdf EofCONDUCT.pdf (accessed 8 July 2017).

28 Republic of Uganda Ministry of Health, Department of Quality Assurance, Patients' Charter, October 2009. http://unhco.or.ug/library/?did=11.

The Charter encourages patients to take an active role in their health, and healthcare decisions, citing empowerment, information, education and interaction with healthcare workers as the way to achieve this. Importantly, the Charter introduces the concept of accountability, and the promotion of accountability among healthcare workers, led by empowered patients. Although not technically enforceable by law, the Patients' Charter may introduce themes and familiarise patients, healthcare workers and ministers with concepts of healthcare legislation, paving the way to full legal protection of healthcare rights, in the Ugandan setting.[29] Although not legally binding, courts may refer to policy documents, such as the Patient Charter.

The Charter comes with a caveat. It is subject to the provisions of any law operating within the Republic of Uganda and to the financial means of the country. In most settings, paternalism and prescriptive relationships between healthcare workers and patients are still the norm. Over-stretched services, where healthcare workers see upwards of 50 patients per day, clearly have less scope for patient concordance and active involvement. At the WHO PFPS workshop, patient representatives felt that lack of patient involvement in care was additionally an issue of doctor training and attitude.[30]

Patient advocacy and non-government organisations

In Uganda, patient advocacy groups and non-government organisations (NGOs) play an important role in promoting patient-centred healthcare and patient safety and rights. These often focus on specific disease areas including cancer, epilepsy, hepatitis, sickle cell anaemia, HIV/AIDS and mental health. Others, such as CHAIN, cover issues affecting access to healthcare services, and also health promotion and disease prevention initiatives. These groups work at community and national level, and are often well connected with, for example, the Ministry of Health and international organisations. They are well placed to raise awareness on prevention, treatment and care, and advocate for issues including: access to medicines, increased healthcare budget, and maternal and child health. Representatives from these organisations often sit on technical working groups in the Ministry, where they bring issues affecting patients to the decision-making table. Between 2011 and 2017, CHAIN has engaged and raised awareness with over 500,000 patients, families and communities on the safe use of medicines, injection safety, hand hygiene and the importance of health literacy through media, sports, music, dance and drama workshops, public hearings, dialogues and community outreach programmes.

CHAIN promotes health literacy as one of its core activities with the aim of improving the health and welfare of the nation through increased health literacy levels. CHAIN has worked with patient organisations to design and implement health literacy campaigns tailored to different types of health needs of patients (cancer, heart disease, epilepsy, HIV/AIDS etc). Dialogues with government

29 Kiromba Twinomugisha, *Fundamentals of health law in Uganda*, p. 13.

30 CHAIN Workshop for Healthcare Professionals, 'Promoting medication safety'.

ministries and departments have been organised, on implementing health literacy programmes, and community-owned resources, including the media, have been engaged in health literacy campaigns targeting the grass root communities and the general public.

A network of patient safety champions was established following the PFPS workshop in Uganda. Community safe medicine advocates and village health teams are currently working in health facilities and at the community level to raise awareness about patient safety issues. These teams are established in the community and aim to develop a critical mass of empowered patients who can demand higher-quality and safer care.

Medication safety: an in-depth example drawing on experience from antiretroviral treatment provision

In countries such as Uganda, the rapid scale of antiretroviral (ARV) services has been successful, meaning that more people are accessing healthcare services than before. Further, healthcare services may be scaled up alongside ARV clinics, increasing availability. As mentioned above, task-shifting and decentralisation of care played a fundamental role in reaching more people with life-saving medicines, however, little is known about the impact on patients or costs to health systems of medication safety issues. ARV treatment is life-long and involves multiple drugs that have a high risk of drug–drug interactions (DDIs), which can lead to toxicity or affect drug efficacy. HIV prevention, care and treatment is protected by the (somewhat outdated) Public Health Act, and several policy documents.

Lack of community medicines regulation may pose significant risk to patients in all sectors of care. In Uganda, patients may freely access medicines from pharmacies and drug stores, often with little restriction. This has serious implications for antimicrobial resistance, a key campaign for the WHO in 2016–17. Patients often buy antibiotics for a cough, or flu-like symptoms which are usually viral and do not respond to antibiotics; it is common for patients to treat fever with antimalarials. Inappropriate durations of treatment, inappropriate dosing and the antimicrobials used may all precipitate antimicrobial resistance, leaving fewer options available to treat future patients with infections. Antimicrobial use should therefore be overseen by a medical professional, after appropriate assessment of the condition. Pharmacists are bound by a code of conduct, which stresses that pharmacists must: 'Ensure the health of the patient is their primary focus' and '[e]ncourage the rational and proper use of medicines'.[31] However, pharmacists may supervise pharmacies remotely, and many 'supervise' more than one pharmacy concurrently. This is justified by the lack of pharmacists and high demand for pharmacy services. Conversely, rapid empirical treatment with antibiotics or antimalarials before diagnosis may save lives in more remote districts, where diagnostic tests are unavailable or time consuming, and medical professionals may be sparse. Rigorous training is therefore necessary for pharmacists or community health volunteers, in the safe and appropriate use of antimicrobials to safeguard their use in future patients.

31 Pharmaceutical Society of Uganda, *Draft Pharmacists' Code of Conduct.*

Medication safety issues, and indeed any patient safety issues, are not always linked to lack of policy or regulation. In developing countries, world-class guidelines may be written, approved and disseminated. However, guideline implementation and accountability for implementation are often lacking. This may relate to lack of health-worker training, or lack of institutional infrastructure with which to implement them. For example, newer guidelines may recommend closer monitoring of patients taking ARVs, which patients or healthcare providers may not be able to afford, or thorough counselling of patients, which time constraints ors' lack of human resources do not realistically allow.

Importantly, while many clinics providing HIV care do not provide routine monitoring for renal function or anaemia, which are known side effects of the commonly used ARV regimens, it is not yet known whether routine monitoring could be cost-effective in reducing healthcare utilisation such as hospital admission for renal failure or blood transfusion for severe anaemia.

New guideline recommendations may significantly precede the availability of newer, safer ARVs. For example, the 2016 consolidated guidelines for prevention and treatment of HIV in Uganda consider recent evidence and reflect the current WHO ARV guidelines. However, the alternative treatments now recommended for patients who have significant adverse events to first-line regimens are minimally available and would require extra monitoring in most cases.

Currently available antiretrovirals for first-line regimens in Uganda, and other low-income countries, comprise drugs which are the most susceptible to DDIs, and with the highest propensity to cause adverse drug reactions, of all the globally available ARVs. Unfortunately, low-income countries are the least able to consistently monitor patients, switch regimens due to toxicity, or tailor treatment to individuals.[32]

All licensed medicines must demonstrate safety, as well as efficacy, in order to be approved for use, which should include evaluating DDIs with drugs which are commonly used concurrently. When data are available to inform a particular DDI, studies may have sampled populations that differ significantly to those sampled globally. For example, African patients are more likely to carry genetic differences, which lead to higher exposure to the first-line ARV efavirenz, which has been linked to central nervous system side effects, such as dizziness and memory impairment.[33] Studies which take into account ethnicity and even known genetic differences, are not usually required for drug licensing.[34] In Uganda,

32 Kay Seden, Marta Boffito and Saye Khoo, 'Drug interactions and the role of pharmacokinetic trials in guiding choices in first-line HIV therapy in low-income and middle-income countries', *Current Opinions in HIV and AIDS* 2017, 12(4): 377–82.

33 W. Stohr, D. Back, D. Dunn, et al., 'Factors influencing efavirenz and nevirapine plasma concentration: effect of ethnicity, weight and co-medication', *Antiviral Therapies* 2008, 13(5):675–85; Verena Gounden, Chantal van Niekerk, Tracy Snyman, Jaya A. George, 'Presence of the CYP2B6 516G> T polymorphism, increased plasma Efavirenz concentrations and early neuropsychiatric side effects in South African HIV-infected patients', *AIDS Research and Therapy* 2010, pp. 7, 32.

34 Seden, Boffito and Khoo, 'Drug interactions and the role of pharmacokinetic trials'.

43% of patients taking efavirenz reported currently experiencing a side effect classified as a nervous system disorder or psychiatric disorder.[35]

Traditional medicines

Traditional and herbal medicines are unregulated in Uganda, and are commonly purchased from pharmacies, drug stores, markets, the road side, or made at home. Traditional medicines are often unlabelled, which means patients and other healthcare workers often do not know the contents. In other countries, such herbal products have been found to be adulterated with prescription drugs.[36] In Uganda, over 103 herbal components used in HIV patients were identified by traditional healers.[37] In western Uganda, 46.4% of patients had used herbal medicines alongside ARVs; 39.8% reported using herbal medicines daily. Almost none of these patients had reported their use of herbal medicines to their ARV prescriber, suggesting also that prescribers do not ask about traditional medicine use. The most frequently used herbs were aloe vera (25%) and *Vernonia amygdalina* (21%).[38] Aloe vera has been found to inhibit the action of metabolic enzymes, which may lead to an increase in blood exposure of many ARVs, raising concerns about toxicity.[39] Various other commonly used herbs may also affect the metabolism of other drugs, including ARVs.[40]

Although *in vitro* studies and case reports suggest potentially significant interactions, appropriate DDI studies in patients or healthy subjects taking herbal medicines at realistic doses, alongside ARVs, are rare.[41] In the absence of such data, clinicians lack evidence with which to caution patients on safe herbal use,

35 Kay Seden, Daniel Kiiza , Eva Laker, et al., 'High prevalence and long duration of nervous system and psychiatric adverse drug reactions in Ugandan patients taking efavirenz 600mg daily', 18th International Workshop on Clinical Pharmacology of Antiviral Therapy (Chicago, 14–16 June 2017). .www.natap.org/2017/Pharm/Pharm_17.htm.

36 E. Deconinck, T. Cauwenbergh, J. L. Bothy, et al., 'Detection of sibutramine in adulterated dietary supplements using attenuated total reflectance-infrared spectroscopy', *Journal of Pharmaceutical and Biomedical Analysis* 2014, 100:279–83; K. Skalicka-Wozniak, M. I. Georgiev and I. E. Orhan, 'Adulteration of herbal sexual enhancers and slimmers: the wish for better sexual well-being and perfect body can be risky', October 108(Pt B) *Food and Chemical Toxicology* 2017, 355–64.

37 M. Lamorde, J. R. Tabuti, C. Obua, et al., 'Medicinal plants used by traditional medicine practitioners for the treatment of HIV/AIDS and related conditions in Uganda', *Journal of Ethnopharmacology* 2010, 130(1):43–53.

38 S. J. Lubinga, A. Kintu, J. Atuhaire and S. Asiimwe, 'Concomitant herbal medicine and antiretroviral therapy (ART) use among HIV patients in western Uganda: a cross-sectional analysis of magnitude and patterns of use, associated factors and impact on ART adherence', *AIDS Care* 2012, 24(11):1375–83.

39 A. Djuv and O. G. Nilsen, 'Aloe vera juice: IC(5)(0) and dual mechanistic inhibition of CYP3A4 and CYP2D6', *Phytotherapeutic Research* 2012, 26(3):445–51.

40 N. E. Thomford, C. Awortwe, K, Dzobo, et al., 'Inhibition of CYP2B6 by medicinal plant extracts: implication for use of efavirenz and nevirapine-based highly active anti-retroviral therapy (HAART) in resource-limited settings', *Molecules* 2016, 21(2). doi: 10.3390/molecules21020211. PubMed PMID: 26891286; E. Cordova, L. Morganti, and C. Rodriguez, 'Possible drug–herb interaction between herbal supplement containing horsetail (Equisetum arvense) and antiretroviral drugs', *Journal of the International Association of Providers of AIDS Care* 2017, 16(1):11–13.

41 M. M. Calderon, C. L. Chairez, L. A. Gordon, et al., 'Influence of Panax ginseng on the steady state pharmacokinetic profile of lopinavir-ritonavir in healthy volunteers', Pharmacotherapy 2014, 34(11):1151–8.

or alternatively issue patients with a blanket ban on using herbals alongside their ARVs, which may potentially lead to patients not discussing their medicines use with ARV prescribers.

Prescribing and dispensing

Pharmacists are often not involved in the dispensing process, and are usually absent in village settings. Prescribing guidelines for inpatients and outpatients are rigorously and clearly set out in the ministry's *Uganda Clinical Guidelines.*[42] Although these guidelines are robust, they are rarely adhered to, outside of centres of excellence. Lack of prescriber time or accountability are likely causes.

In busy clinics, pharmacy technicians often do not have time to counsel every patient, or even every new patient on the use of their medicines, and whether they understand how to take them. Commonly dispensed medicines are often pre-packed and labelled, with little information for patients; although, as noted previously, many patients cannot read. Medicine bags may be dose-labelled '1x1' which means take one tablet once daily, although this unclear to many patients. Patients may be too intimidated to ask questions of busy staff. In rural centres, village health teams may supply medicines, although they have little medical knowledge.

Medicine availability and integrity

As mentioned above in the case of ARVs, the most recent medicines and medical technology are either absent, or take time to reach Uganda, and sub-Saharan Africa in general, due to cost. The WHO issues a model list of essential medicines. The core list presents a list of minimum medicine needs for a basic healthcare system, listing the most efficacious, safe and cost-effective medicines for priority conditions.[43] In rural settings, and sometimes in larger towns, some medicines may not be available, particularly in public hospitals and clinics. Although ARVs are free to patients, being supplied mostly via foreign aid, other medicines needed by patients may be unavailable, necessitating private purchase, which is often not affordable.

The Ugandan National Drug Authority (NDA) frequently issues alerts to health centres about counterfeit drugs which may have reached clinic shelves. The Quality Control Department also offer a laboratory service to test suspected counterfeit or adulterated medication. There is a 'fraud hotline' telephone number on their website.[44]

42 Ministry of Health, *Uganda Clinical Guidelines*, Kampala: Uganda 2016.

43 WHO, *19th WHO Model List of Essential Medicines*, Geneva, Switzerland 2015.

44 Uganda National Drug Authority Quality Control Department, www.nda.or.ug/ug/smenu/8/Quality-Control-Department.html (accessed 8 July 2017).

Underused reporting systems

Pharmacovigilance reporting systems collect data on side effects experienced by patients or conditions detected by healthcare workers, which are thought to be related to medicines. Collation of these adverse drug reactions (ADRs) nationally enables 'safety signals' to be detected, and interventions to improve the safety of medicines implemented. In Uganda, the NDA developed an international standard reporting system, currently online, which feeds in to the WHO Programme for International Drug Monitoring database, which comprises 150 countries. However, many practical difficulties may lead to minimal reporting of ADRs in countries such as Uganda. Initially, a paper-based reporting system led to logistic and financial difficulties in transporting completing forms. The electronic system may not be functional in remote village locations, where government hospitals often lack internet connection. Again, oversubscribed facilities with low density of medical doctors or pharmacists will face time constraints. Where task-shifting has left community health workers on the front line, expertise and awareness of pharmacovigilance may be lacking.

Conclusions: the future of patient safety issues in Uganda

Some feel that the available pieces of legislation, for example the Public Health Act and the Mental Treatment Act, are outdated or inadequate in ensuring protection of the right to health.[45] Review of these Acts, and incorporation of the right to health in the Constitution, would pave the way to true accountability in healthcare and protection of patients. Similarly, while healthcare law is taught in Ugandan law schools, patient safety must be incorporated into the training and education of all cadres of healthcare workers.

Malpractice litigation, or litigation for violation of rights, is rare in Uganda. This may be because patients are unaware of their rights, unaware of regulating professional bodies, and unaware of the courts. Notwithstanding the fact that many patients and their families may not be empowered or confident to challenge problems in the health system, when they experience it, in this hierarchical society. The majority of patients/families would also not be able to afford litigation expenses.

Patients and the public should have greater awareness of the Uganda Human Rights Commission and its role in monitoring the government's adherence to international treaties concerning health rights. To do this, patients need greater knowledge about their rights, and those outlined in the Patients' Charter. The Patients' Charter becoming legislation would protect patient rights by law. It would normalise patients' rights to information about their health, different treatment options, and the costs involved, enabling patients to make informed decisions about their healthcare.

There is, then, a need for patients, families and health professionals to work together, to engage and empower patients to effectively manage their own care and make behavioural changes, in a non-tokenistic manner. Further provision of free

45 Kiromba Twinomugisha, *Fundamentals of health law in Uganda*, p. 34.

services, such as malaria treatment, basic tests in public hospitals, and availability of essential medicines and emergency care would vastly improve safety for those unable to afford private care, whether via affordable insurance for all, or via public services.

The second National Development Plan 2015/16–2019/20 sets Uganda's medium term strategic direction, development priorities and implementation strategies.[46] The plan aims to address the key challenges facing Uganda's health system but also sets out priorities and key areas on which to focus health investment in the medium term, for both public and private partners, in order to optimally contribute to the attainment of both the health sector goals and the national goals as outlined in the National Development Plan. The goal of this plan is to accelerate movement towards universal health coverage (UHC) with essential health and related services needed for promotion of a healthy and productive life, over a five-year period. UHC is planned to ensure that all people receive essential and good quality health services without suffering financial hardship. Implementing the Uganda National Minimum Health Care Package continues to be the core strategy for achieving maximum outcomes in the health sector development plan. A stronger focus has been placed on health promotion and disease prevention using a multi-sectoral approach. Plans to increase the highly skilled health sector workforce, alongside UHC, would make a profound difference to the healthcare landscape in Uganda; however, the outcomes are not yet realised.

It is important that family, patient and community are engaged for a number of reasons. 'Patients and their caregivers see things that busy healthcare workers often do not'.[47] Patients and their families are experts on their own needs and values and can make the work of health workers easier. Unfortunately the Ugandan healthcare system is not currently prepared to optimally promote participation, due to constraints on time, resources and health worker training. Health workers should provide a conducive environment to enable patients and their families to participate. Patient engagement that is based on mutual respect and open and honest communication not only improves the relationships between patients, families and healthcare providers but enables the health workers to discover, understand and address the patient's physical and emotional needs. Professionals would, therefore, able to provide care that is focused on the person as an individual, in the context of family and community, rather than on the disease.

Patient safety research is a relatively new global field. Due to the current lack of accountability of healthcare workers, and the lack of empowerment of patients, research into medical errors in Uganda is sometimes controversial. Health centres and healthcare workers may be reluctant to take part in a setting where errors are not discussed openly and objectively. Perseverance into researching patient safety questions may help to normalise accountability and 'fair blame' cultures in health centres, strengthening the concept that errors should be used to educate and strengthen systems.

46 Ministry of Health, 'Health Sector Development Plan 2015/16–2019/20'. http://health.go.ug/content/health-sector-development-plan-201516-201920.

47 A response in the CHAIN Workshop for Healthcare Professionals 'Promoting medication safety'.

References

African Charter on Human and Peoples' Rights, came into effect on 25 January 2005. www.achpr.org/instruments/achprAfrican Charter on the Rights and Welfare of the Child, adopted July 1979. www.achpr.org/instruments/child/.

Calderon, M. M., Chairez, C. L., Gordon, L. A., et al., 'Influence of Panax ginseng on the steady state pharmacokinetic profile of lopinavir-ritonavir in healthy volunteers', Pharmacotherapy 2014, 34(11):1151–8.

CHAIN, Public hearing on 'Promoting medication safety', 16 April 2014, Kampala, Uganda.

CHAIN, Workshop for Healthcare Professionals on 'Promoting medication safety', 22 January 2014, Mulago Hospital, Kampala, Uganda.

CHAIN, 'Gaps and challenges in contemporary health promotion and health communication in Uganda', 7 February 2014.

Convention on the Rights of the Child, entry into force 2 September 1990. www.ohchr.org/EN/ProfessionalInterest/Pages/CRC.aspx.

Convention on the Rights of Persons with Disabilities, adopted on 13 December 2006. www.un.org/development/desa/disabilities/convention-on-the-rights-of-persons-with-disabilities.html.

Cordova, E., Morganti, L. and Rodriguez, C., 'Possible drug–herb interaction between herbal supplement containing horsetail (Equisetum arvense) and antiretroviral drugs', *Journal of the International Association of Providers of AIDS Care* 2017, 16(1):11–13.

Deconinck, E., Cauwenbergh, T., Bothy, J. L., et al., 'Detection of sibutramine in adulterated dietary supplements using attenuated total reflectance-infrared spectroscopy', *Journal of Pharmaceutical and Biomedical Analysis* 2014, 100:279–83.

Djuv, A. and Nilsen, O. G., 'Aloe vera juice: IC(5)(0) and dual mechanistic inhibition of CYP3A4 and CYP2D6', *Phytotherapeutic Research* 2012, 26(3):445–51.

East African Community HIV and AIDS Prevention and Management Act, adopted 2012. www.kelinkenya.org/wp-content/uploads/2017/04/EAC-HIV-ACT-2012.pdf.

Gounden, V., van Niekerk, C., Snyman, T. and George, J. A., 'Presence of the CYP2B6 516G> T polymorphism, increased plasma Efavirenz concentrations and early neuropsychiatric side effects in South African HIV-infected patients', *AIDS Research and Therapy* 2010, pp. 7, 32.

Initiative for Social and Economic Rights, *Introduction to the right to health in Uganda: a handbook for community health advocates.* www.iser-uganda.org/images/downloads/A16_10_04_ISER_Booklet_design_layout.pdf (accessed 28 June 2017).

International Covenant on Economic, Social and Cultural Rights, entry into force 3 January 1976. www.ohchr.org/EN/ProfessionalInterest/Pages/CESCR.aspx, Article 12.

Kiromba Twinomugisha, Ben, *Fundamentals of health law in Uganda*, South Africa: Pretoria University Law Press, 2015.

Lamorde, M., Tabuti, J. R., Obua, C., et al., 'Medicinal plants used by traditional medicine practitioners for the treatment of HIV/AIDS and related conditions in Uganda', *Journal of Ethnopharmacology* 2010, 130(1):43–53.

Lubinga, S. J., Kintu, A., Atuhaire, J. and Asiimwe, S., 'Concomitant herbal medicine and antiretroviral therapy (ART) use among HIV patients in western Uganda: a cross-sectional analysis of magnitude and patterns of use, associated factors and impact on ART adherence', *AIDS Care* 2012, 24(11):1375–83.

Ministry of Health, 'Health Sector Development Plan 2015/16–2019/20'. http://health.go.ug/content/health-sector-development-plan-201516-201920.

Ministry of Health, *Uganda Clinical Guidelines*, Kampala: Uganda 2016.

Pharmaceutical Society of Uganda, *Draft Pharmacists' Code of Conduct*, September 2013. http://psu.or.ug/files/downloads/DRAFT_PSU_CODEofCONDUCT.pdf (accessed 8 July 2017).

Protocol to the African Charter on Human and Peoples' Rights on the Rights of Women in Africa, adopted June 1995. www.achpr.org/instruments/women-protocol/.

Republic of Uganda Ministry of Health, Department of Quality Assurance, Patients' Charter, October 2009. http://unhco.or.ug/library/?did=11.

Seden, K., Boffito, M. and Khoo, S., 'Drug interactions and the role of pharmacokinetic trials in guiding choices in first-line HIV therapy in low-income and middle-income countries', *Current Opinions in HIV and AIDS* 2017, 12(4): 377–82.

Seden, K., Kiiza, D., Laker, E., et al., 'High prevalence and long duration of nervous system and psychiatric adverse drug reactions in Ugandan patients taking efavirenz 600mg daily', 18th International Workshop on Clinical Pharmacology of Antiviral Therapy (Chicago, 14–16 June 2017). www.natap.org/2017/Pharm/Pharm_17.htm.

Skalicka-Wozniak, K., Georgiev, M. I. and Orhan, I. E., 'Adulteration of herbal sexual enhancers and slimmers: the wish for better sexual well-being and perfect body can be risky', October 108(Pt B) *Food and Chemical Toxicology* 2017, 355–64.

Stohr, W., Back, D., Dunn, D., et al., 'Factors influencing efavirenz and nevirapine plasma concentration: effect of ethnicity, weight and co-medication', *Antiviral Therapies* 2008, 13(5):675–85.

The Convention on the Elimination of All Forms of Discrimination against Women, adopted in 1979. www.un.org/womenwatch/daw/cedaw.

The Joint Commission, *'What did the doctor say?' Improving health literacy to protect patient safety*, Illinois, USA: 2007.

The Treaty for the Establishment of the East African Community, entered into force on 7 July 2000. www.eala.org/uploads/The_Treaty_for_the_Establishment_of_the_East_Africa_Community_2006_1999.pdf.

Thomford, N. E., Awortwe, C., Dzobo, K., et al., 'Inhibition of CYP2B6 by medicinal plant extracts: implication for use of efavirenz and nevirapine-based highly active antiretroviral therapy (HAART) in resource-limited settings', *Molecules* 2016, 21(2). doi: 10.3390/molecules21020211. PubMed PMID: 26891286.

UAC, 'An AIDS free Uganda, My responsibility: documents for the National HIV and AIDS Response, 2015/2016–2019/2020', 2015.

Uganda National Drug Authority Quality Control Department, www.nda.or.ug/ug/smenu/8/Quality-Control-Department.html (accessed 8 July 2017).

United Nations Uganda, *Press release on HIV situation in Uganda*, 23 February 2017. www.un-ug.org/press-releases/press-release-hiv-situation-uganda-february-23-2017 (accessed 26 June 2017).

WHO-ARO, *Uganda factsheet of health statistics 2016.*

WHO Patients for Patient Safety country workshop – Uganda. 3–5 November 2015, Makerere University Guest House, Kampala, Uganda.

WHO, *Uganda: WHO statistical profile – country statistics and global health estimates by WHO and UN partners*, 2015. www.who.int/gho/countries/uga.pdf?ua=1 (accessed 26 June 2017).

WHO, *19th WHO Model List of Essential Medicines*, Geneva, Switzerland 2015.

14 Patient safety in Nigeria

An emergent concept

Cheluchi Onyemelukwe

Introduction

Patient safety is an emerging concept in Nigeria. Nigeria is Africa's most populous country with a population of about 180 million persons. Despite its chequered economic and political history, it remains a regional powerhouse with much influence in the African continent. Its significant population is one of the key reasons why effective patient safety policy, practice and infrastructures are essential. Issues of quality have often been raised, yet they remain at a nascent stage in regard to both policy and practice. The protection of patients from iatrogenic harms is a matter that deserves much more attention than it is currently getting in Nigeria. Although there was a spike of attention to patient safety concerns, particularly with regard to sanitation and hygiene in health facilities and infection control in the aftermath of the Ebola epidemic's brief appearance in Nigeria in 2014, there has not been sustained attention to patient safety.[1]

Available funding from domestic, international and non-governmental sources are largely focused on health care provisioning as compared to quality assurance and patient safety. While there is often more interest in, advocacy for, and ensuing legislation on universal health coverage (that is access to care and managing the cost implications) there is only just beginning to be interest in the quality of care provided as part of such coverage. Thus, for example, while the Nigeria Demographic and Health Survey[2] provides reliable information on a variety of health matters, patient safety is not yet one of those. Many instances of medical negligence and resulting iatrogenic harms are reported anecdotally, but there is not yet any established requirement for collecting data on patient safety and harms that occur in the health care setting. Nor has there been much systemic analysis or narrative of patient safety infrastructure in the country. Discrete pockets of initiatives are, however, in place at different organisations and I describe some of these in the subsequent pages.

1 See for example, W. Adebimpe, 'Knowledge, attitude, and practice of use of safety precautions among health care workers in a Nigerian tertiary hospital, 1 year after the Ebola virus disease epidemic', *Annals of Global Health* 2016, 82(5):897–902.

2 National Population Commission and ICF International, *Nigeria Demographic and Health Survey 2013*, Abuja: Nigeria, and Rockville, Maryland: USA: NPC and ICF International, 2014.

From a policy perspective, the recently enacted National Health Act portends a good beginning for quality improvements generally, and hopefully, patient safety. Prior to this law, the common law of negligence was the dominant means of enforcement of patient safety standards from a legal perspective. However, even with the enactment of the National Health Act, health care standards as contained in policies may vary on the basis of whether or not the facility is a public or private institution, is a tertiary or a primary health care facility or whether it is governed primarily by state or federal law. The imperative of patient safety remains, as yet, unembraced at different levels of health care delivery.

Increasingly, new initiatives are emerging to deal with issues of patient safety. Some of these initiatives are being developed by discrete organisations and within pockets of health institutions. Perhaps more interesting are the emerging technologies and applications that are being deployed to improve and assist patient safety. These are also being given a boost through advocacy via social media platforms. The move towards digitisation of records and increased use of information technology must also be noted. While only at the early stages, these new developments have the potential to bring improvement to patient safety in Nigeria.

In this paper, I examine the emerging patient safety policy in Nigeria, through an investigation of recent legislation, regulations, policy guidelines and the institutions which enforce such policy. Limited resources are a major challenge to patient safety practice and the development of essential infrastructure. However, it is also crucial to manage the limited available resources in a manner that enhances patient welfare. Increase in the use of digital technology and social media and the emerging understanding of their power, particularly in patient safety matters, have the potential to enhance patient safety practice and policy in the country through better community engagement. Furthermore, the state of patient safety in Nigeria, as will be described in this chapter, indicates the need for more concerted attention to issues of patient safety, including through clarifying patient safety policy and targets. There is a need to develop a comprehensive agenda for patient safety in Nigeria.

The state of patient safety in Nigeria

The Nigerian health system is an assortment of public and private health facilities operating within a federal system, where the Federal Government primarily manages tertiary institutions while state governments are in charge of general hospitals. Primary health care centres operate at the local level and may be publicly or privately managed. Patient safety is an issue of great concern in each of these health facilities in Nigeria, as it in most countries around the world. The concept of patient safety requires the prevention, reduction or minimisation of the risk of avoidable and unnecessary harm associated with health care to an acceptable minimum,[3] with emphasis on prevention of errors, systematic learning from previous errors, effective

3 WHO, *Conceptual framework for international classification for patient safety*. www.who.int/patientsafety/taxonomy/icps_full_report.pdf.

use of current knowledge, and development of a culture of safety that encompasses health care professionals, facilities, institutions, national systems and patients.[4] Some key goals of patient safety are to ensure quality, reduce harms and engender trust.

As suggested elsewhere,[5] a systematic review of the literature on various patient safety issues (for example, what is the rate of health care associated infections, antibiotic resistance, medical or surgical error, length of stay in hospitals, patient disability, patient complaints mechanisms), or the health and safety of health care providers may be helpful in beginning to establish a baseline of information. Thus, although comprehensive, nation-wide data is lacking, there are discrete, institutional-drawn data that indicate that the problem of unsafe care in Nigerian health facilities. Studies done on health care associated infections in various institutions in Nigeria indicate that the prevalence of health care-associated infections is high, with figures as high as 60 per cent in some facilities.[6] Other studies have shown a total hospital acquired infections (HAI) cumulative incidence in Nigerian surgical wards ranging from 5.7% to 45.8%.[7] A recent study, the Health Care Quality Index, which measured Health Access Quality (HAQ) globally gave Nigeria an aggregate score of 39 out of a possible 100 on the indicator of adverse medical treatment in the period between 1999 and 2015.[8]

High levels of surgical complications, overcrowding in health facilities, contaminated urethral catheters, poor hand hygiene, and lack of infection control committees in many private health facilities are some of the factors causing the high rates of hospital infections, with the attendant consequences of illness, longer stay in the hospital, financial costs, disability and even death.[9] Poor surveillance capabilities have also been noted.[10] Medicine supply chains remain plagued with counterfeit medicines, though much effort has been made by the regulatory agencies in this regard. Other factors that affect patient safety such as poor injection safety management and compliance with related policy[11] inadequate effective

4 P. H. Mitchell, 'Defining patient safety and quality care – patient safety and quality', in Agency for Healthcare Research and Quality, *Patient safety and quality: an evidence-based handbook for nurses*, Rockville, Maryland, USA: AHRQ, 2008.

5 R. Harrison, A. Wai Seung Cohen and M. Walton, 'Patient safety and quality of care in developing countries in Southeast Asia: a systematic literature review', *International Journal for Quality in Health Care* 2015, 27(4):240–54.

6 O. A. Nnamdi and K. C. Okoli, et al., 'Health professionals' knowledge about relative prevalence of hospital-acquired infections in Delta State of Nigeria', *The Pan African Medical Journal* 2016, 24:148. www.panafrican-med-journal.com/content/article/24/148/full/.

7 S. Bagheri Nejad, 'Health-care-associated infection in Africa: a systematic review', *Bulletin of the World Health Organization* 2011, 89:757–65. doi: 10.2471/BLT.11.088179.

8 GBD, Healthcare Access and Quality Collaborators, [Healthcare Access and Quality Index based on mortality from causes amenable to personal health care in 195 countries and territories, 1990–2015: a novel analysis from the Global Burden of Disease Study 2015', 2017, *The Lancet*. http://thelancet.com/pdfs/journals/lancet/PIIS0140-6736(17)30818-8.pdf.

9 Nnamdi, Oli and Okoli, et al., 'Health professionals' knowledge about relative prevalence of hospital-acquired infections'.

10 Bagheri Nejad, 'Health-care-associated infection in Africa'.

11 A. I. Obi and A. J. Ofili, 'Injection safety practices among medical doctors in a tertiary health institution in south southern Nigeria', *IOSR Journal of Dental and Medical Sciences* 2013, 8(1):42–9; G. B. Gadzama, S. B. Bawa, Z. Ajinoma, M. M. Saidu and A. S. Umar, 'Injection safety practices

trauma facilities,[12] and poor patient understanding of matters such as antibiotic resistance[13] have been noted in the literature. Studies also suggest that while health professionals may know what to do, they do not often implement appropriate prevention controls,[14] and that there is poor knowledge of medical ethics amongst doctors,[15] amidst other patient safety related challenges. Prescription errors are also not uncommon, and often exist hand in hand with a lack of quality assurance mechanisms.[16] Poor laboratory infrastructure is also a factor in misdiagnosis, the rates of which are significant.[17] Patient safety is also sometimes compromised by patients' failure to adhere to treatment, sometimes resulting from belief systems and cultural tradition in a context that remains culturally conservative.

Aside from these data, news reports[18] and anecdotal information strongly suggest that medical errors and incidents are high. Although such information may not provide sufficient support for policy change or reform, such anecdotal information cannot be dismissed lightly. Such information influences patient perception and helps cause distrust in the health care system. In particular, there is a general, pervading sense that public health facilities cannot be trusted to deliver quality care and to ensure patient safety.[19] Such distrust is one of the key reasons why Nigeria's medical tourism statistics are very high,[20] with political leaders and high- to middle-income patients seeking treatment abroad. Furthermore, a perception of high levels of adverse events may cause a reluctance to access even free and essential health services, such as immunisation.[21]

in a main referral hospital in Northeastern Nigeria', *Nigerian Journal of Clinical Practice* 2014, 17:134–9. www.njcponline.com/text.asp?2014/17/2/134/127420.

12 F. A. Onyekwulu and S. U. Anya, 'Pattern of admission and outcome of patients admitted into the Intensive Care Unit of University of Nigeria Teaching Hospital Enugu: a 5-year review', *Nigerian Journal of Clinical Practice* 2015, 18:775–9. www.njcponline.com/text.asp?2015/18/6/775/163291.

13 WHO, *Antibiotic resistance: Multi-Country Public Awareness Survey*, Geneva: WHO, 2015. http://apps.who.int/iris/bitstream/10665/194460/1/9789241509817_eng.pdf?ua=1

14 K. J. Awosan, et al., 'Knowledge of radiation hazards, radiation protection practices and clinical profile of health workers in a teaching hospital in Northern Nigeria', *Journal of Clinical and Diagnostic Research* 2016, 10(8):LC07–LC12. O. Aluko, et al, 'Knowledge, attitudes and perceptions of occupational hazards and safety practices in Nigerian healthcare workers', *BMC Research Notes* 2016. 9(71).

15 J. O. Fadare, et al., 'Knowledge of medical ethics among Nigerian medical doctors', *Nigerian Medical Journal* 2012, 53(4):226–30.

16 M. Kehinde Babatunde, et al., 'Prevalence and pattern of prescription errors in a Nigerian kidney hospital', *Ghana Medical Journal* 2016, 50(4):233.

17 C. A. Petti, 'Laboratory medicine in Africa: a barrier to effective health care', *Clinical Infectious Diseases* 2006, 42(3):377–82; B. H. Oladeinde, et al., 'Biorisk assessment of medical diagnostic laboratories in Nigeria', *Safety and Health at Work* 2013, 4(2):100–4.

18 WHO, *Patient safety in Nigeria is deplorable*, May 17, 2017. www.thisdaylive.com/index.php/2017/05/11/who-patients-safety-in-nigeria-deplorable/.

19 F. N. Chukwuneke, 'Medical incidents in developing countries: a few case studies from Nigeria', *Nigerian Journal of Clinical Practice* 2015, 18(7):20–4. www.njcponline.com/article.asp?issn=1119-3077;year=2015;volume=18;issue=7;spage=20;epage=24;aulast=Chukwuneke. The author observes that, 'The public hospitals in Nigeria have a greater percentage of death rate and unreported malpractice incidents.'

20 See the National Health Policy, 2016, p. 8.

21 U. Muhammad Lawan, et al., 'Pattern of adverse events following immunization in nourished and malnourished infants in Kano, North-Western Nigeria', *Sahel Medical Journal* 2016, 19(3):131.

The impact of inadequate hospital facilities is of particular importance.[22] Access to health care services is strongly linked with the quality of health services in the Nigerian context. With great disparities between the income classes in respect of access, there are also major differences in the quality of care experienced by lower and higher-income groups, thus making patient safety an equity issue. Health facilities in urban areas and in the more affluent areas generally provide better equipment, more specialists, may have more courteous staff, and engage patients more than in the lower-income areas, including rural regions. The dependence on user fees and low penetration of health insurance exacerbates this problem. As observed elsewhere, 'There are everyday emergencies that have ended in fatality because of the down payment required before treatment even in public hospitals'.[23] The 'no bed syndrome' is well recognised, particularly in densely populated areas like Lagos State. With a population of about twenty million persons, Lagos State has only two teaching hospitals, some general hospitals and several private hospitals. Many emergencies are unattended to, with patients being turned away because there are no beds.

Research conducted for this paper amongst health professionals working in teaching hospitals identified other systemic issues that pose a challenge for the improvement of patient safety. Many hospitals have infection control committees, but they do not meet regularly and do not have specific funding allocated to them. In some facilities, there are monthly mortality meetings but often no formal mechanism for recording or managing medical errors and adverse events.[24] Shortage of staff, personnel who are not well motivated as a result of poor working conditions, and strikes in the health sector are also challenges that filter down into effective management of patient safety. Some of the above concerns are captured in a situation analysis provided in the National Health Policy noting with respect to health services in Nigeria that:

> The quality of health services is generally poor and does not instil confidence in the people. This has led to some people seeking care outside the country or bypassing primary and secondary facilities to seek health care at tertiary institutions. Competence in diagnosis and management of clinical illnesses is disproportionate, while adherence is to clinical guidelines is low. Even where the quality may be high, the perception of the service users may not correlate with the actual quality of care delivered. These may be due to poor attitude of health workers, lack of clarity of standards and protocols as well as inadequate implementation of these guidelines and other regulations. While States' Ministries of Health issue licences to ensure that facilities comply with standards, monitoring of quality of services provided by the private sector is limited. There is a lack of institutional framework that regulates quality and standards. While the National Health Act provides that facilities are required to obtain a Certificate of Standards, the requirements for this certificate are not provided in the Act. Regulations that would provide for these requirements have not yet been enacted.[25]

22 S. B. Garko, et al., 'Duration of hospital stay and mortality in the medical wards of Ahmadu Bello University, Kaduna State Annals of African Medicine', *Annals of African Medicine* 2003, 2(2):68–71.

23 Chukwuneke, 'Medical incidents in developing countries'.

24 I undertook informal interviews of health professionals working in government hospitals.

25 The National Health Policy, 2016, p. 8.

The lack of comprehensive national data on medical errors, health care associated infections and adverse events is also a major systemic challenge in Nigeria. Research suggests a high rate of medical error and adverse events,[26] and yet there is no central mechanism for collecting information on those outside of individual health facilities. Thus, while data exists in discrete pockets, we lack comprehensive information on issues that have been identified in other climes. This indicates, amongst other things, that health policy has not given due consideration to patient safety and that it has not yet become a 'front burner' issue for the different entities working in the Nigerian health context: from government, international donors to civil society organisations. It also suggests that the magnitude of the problem is not really known, the root causes are yet to be identified, and that it is not being dealt with in an adequate manner. The need for such information can therefore not be overemphasised. The development of a patient safety policy and strategy must be based on adequate information. The absence of such systematic information is based, in part, on a lack of resources to put in place adequate surveillance systems.[27]

Limited resources – financing, human resources for health, infrastructure, amongst others – are clearly an important consideration. Improvement in infrastructure and investments in capacity building for health care practitioners, both of which will likely have a significant positive impact on patient safety in the country, require resources. Poor funding has led to continuous strikes amongst health care professionals in Nigeria, increasing patient safety concerns. As noted elsewhere, even considering the limited resources available to the country, not enough is devoted to health care. What limited resources are devoted to health care also have to be shared between key health challenges such as HIV/AIDS, malaria and non-communicable diseases (NCDs). Yet even within these challenges, quality and safety of care provided to ameliorate them remain important matters.

The aggregation of these factors – strong data-driven evidence in discrete pockets of patient safety problems, anecdotal information, high rates of medical tourism – make patient safety a burning issue. The key question is, then, what policy steps are being taken to manage patient safety issues in Nigeria? How do these translate into action in health facilities in the country?

Patient safety policy in Nigeria

The National Health Policy (2016) is Nigeria's primary policy on health. One of the social values that it adopts as a fundamental principle is the recognition of every Nigerian possessing 'the right to the highest attainable level of health as a fundamental right of every Nigerian which includes access to timely, acceptable, affordable health care of the highest quality and international best practice'.[28]

26 Chukwuneke, 'Medical Incidents in Developing Countries'.

27 WHO, 'Health-care-associated infection in Africa: a systematic review', *Bulletin of the World Health Organization* 2011, 89:757–65.

28 National Health Policy, 2016: Social Values, p. 17.

To further emphasise this point, one of the six Guiding Principles enunciated in the Policy is that 'Government shall ensure quality health care at all levels.' Thus universal health coverage is a key policy thrust and the Policy now recognises quality as an integral part of access.

For the first time, Nigeria's National Health Policy identifies patient safety clearly as a component of health service delivery. The policy objectives to be translated into programming include the strengthening of accountability and governance, service delivery units, referral systems, and ensuring timely and reliable laboratory investigations to enhance accurate diagnosis, and to 'improve the quality of health services and ensure ***patient safety*** at all levels of the health system.'[29] This marks the first time that quality and safety are recognised in these specific terms. This is largely due, no doubt, to increased international interest in quality issues in health care articulated as 'patient safety' and to the increasing patient safety concerns amongst the Nigerian populace, which affects care uptake in the country and medical tourism outside of the country. The specific initiatives to implement these general objectives include the implementation of the service charter, SERVICOM, which provides amongst other things complaints channels and the improvement of clinical governance. While the implementation plan for the policy is still in the process of being developed, the clear policy statement on patient safety indicates that it is likely to get more attention from policy implementers and programming.

There are several other allied policies focused on specific relevant patient safety issues. These include the National Guidelines on Maternal and Perinatal Outcomes, National Policy on Injection Safety and Health Care Waste Management,[30] the National Quality Assurance Policy 2016 (concerned with, amongst other things, the dispensing of medicines to consumers), Injection Safety and Health Care Waste Management Policy (2007), National Health Care Waste Management Policy (2013), National Health Care Waste Management Guidelines (2013), the NESREA (National Environmental Standards and Regulations Enforcement Agency) Gazette, and the National Infection Prevention and Control Policy (2013).[31] These many policies highlight the lack of systemic data to inform policy action and the lack of coordination of existing laws; but there is no evidence that these gaps and weaknesses are then systematically addressed.Several of the policies contain targets to be met in regard to

29 National Health Policy, 2016, p.27.

30 O. Okezie Enwere and K. Chiekulie Diwe, 'Knowledge, perception and practice of injection safety and healthcare waste management among teaching hospital staff in south east Nigeria: an intervention study', *Pan African Medical Journal* 2014, 17:218; Gadzama, Bawa, Ajinoma, Saidu and Umar, 'Injection safety practices in a main referral hospital in Northeastern Nigeria'; A. Onyemocho, J. I. Anekoson and E. O. Pius, 'Knowledge and practice of injection safety among workers of Nigerian Prison Service health facilities in Kaduna State', *American Journal of Public Health Research* 2013, 1(7):171–6. doi: 10.12691/ajphr-1-7-5.

31 H. Galadanci, W. Künzel, O. Shittu, et al., 'Obstetric quality assurance to reduce maternal and fetal mortality in Kano and Kaduna State hospitals in Nigeria', *International Journal of Gynecology and Obstetrics* 2011, 114(1):43, 238. https://aidsfree.usaid.gov/sites/default/files/2016.8.1_aidsfree_nigeria_health_worker_training_manual_tagged.pdf.

specific patient safety issues. For example the 2007 Injection Safety and Health Care Waste Management Policy identifies the need for safe management of health care waste and the need to enhance occupational safety, and sets specific timelines for certain activities, including the need for enactment of relevant legislation required for effective health care waste management policy implementation by 2008. It requires that every health care facility establishes an infection control and waste management committee and has in place a registered Environment Health Officer in charge of waste management in the hospital; that every teaching hospital, specialist hospital or other similar health care facility with more than 200 beds provides a modern incinerator and has a contract with a registered health care waste or sewage collector who also has a disposal contract with a disposal facility.[32] At this time, it is safe to state that these targets have not been achieved, nor is there any publicly accessible information on efforts to ensure that they are. There is, as yet, no legislation on health care waste management which would provide sanctions and give legal teeth to the policy recommendations. Discussions with key personnel at major government and private health facilities in teaching hospitals reveal uneven implementation of these policy directions.

While there is therefore no single, comprehensive policy on patient safety, there are several policies and guidelines at the national level with implications for patient safety. These contain many helpful provisions, but implementation is arguably lacking. For example, while the existing policies seek to manage the over-prescription of injections, there continues to be such over-prescription and inattention to safety procedures. Further, there are other patient safety issues that are not addressed at all, for instance, patients' rights and awareness and reporting requirements across a variety of patient safety issues.

Patient safety and law in Nigeria

Patient safety is complicated by the organisation of health services in Nigeria's constitutional and federal arrangements. The Constitution specifies the legislative authority of each tier of government (Federal, State, and local governments) to a certain degree. Certain aspects of health are captured in the Exclusive List (occupational health, drugs and poisons, professional regulation), matters over which only the Federal Government can legislate. Others are provided for under the Concurrent List. All other areas of health are not addressed, thus falling under the residual list and therefore allowing the States considerable authority. Although the Constitution does not specifically delineate responsibilities for managing health facilities, practically speaking, health facilities have been managed along federal lines for a long time. In practice, health care facilities are arranged along federal lines, with the Federal Government having authority over tertiary institutions like the teaching hospitals, the States managing general hospitals which provide secondary care and overseeing primary health facilities which the

32 See Article 4 of the Injection Safety and Health Care Waste Management Policy 2007.

local governments are expected to be responsible for, but also teaching hospitals being affiliated with state universities. Outside of these government arrangements, there are many private health facilities offering care, at different levels.

What this means is that patient safety frequently depends on where a patient is receiving care and how much attention the controlling tier of government, or the private entity, has paid to safety issues. And a lot depends on the facilities themselves, especially when they are privately managed. Patient safety standards therefore tend to be uneven, and in some cases, not at all clear.

From a legal perspective, patient safety issues (including such concepts as medical error, quality of care adverse events, and safety) have been managed through the use of the common law of negligence. While there are several reported cases on negligence in the health care setting, Nigeria cannot be considered a particularly litigious context, with very few cases reaching the courts. The reasons are not hard to decipher: a prevailing 'doctor knows best' attitude; patients' lack of knowledge of rights; religious beliefs and other socio-cultural beliefs; long delays in getting judgement; the reluctance of health professionals to act as expert witnesses; and limited resources to pursue cases that may last for several years. A fault-based negligence system also makes cases of negligence difficult to prove, especially in view of the complicating factors such as lack of knowledge on the part of patients. Even so, negligence law is well recognised and the courts have sometimes given judgements in favour of patients. The upshot of the ubiquity of these constraining factors is a lack of accountability. In my experience, as a lawyer practising health law in Nigeria, there is evidence that this may be beginning to change as a result of patients becoming more aware of their rights, including through the advocacy efforts of several civil society groups working in this area and the burgeoning use of social media.

The Codes of Ethics of various professional bodies in health are subsidiary legislation, being made under powers given under the laws establishing them: the Medical and Dental Council's Code of Medical Ethics for Medical and Dental Practitioners; the Pharmacists Council's Code of Conduct, the Nursing and Midwifery Council's Code of Conduct. Within these codes of conduct, patient safety is clearly recognised as crucial. The Code of Medical Ethics for Medical and Dental Practitioners in Nigeria recognises the central importance of patient safety and the management of medical errors. Accessing 'medical' treatment from uncertified providers remains a serious challenge, leading to avoidable patient death and injury. Efforts by the councils through their Inspectorate Departments are yet to eliminate it. Similar challenges are found in medicines supply with much effort being made by the National Administration for Food and Drug Control (NAFDAC) to limit the sale of counterfeit medicines. The effective implementation of the Codes, recognised as subsidiary legislation, and therefore having the force of law, remains essential.

Under our current health insurance arrangements, one of the key goals of the social health insurance scheme, the National Health Insurance Scheme, is the provision of good quality health services.[33] Zonal offices throughout the country

33 Section 1 of the National Health Insurance Scheme Act, 1999.

have the task of inspecting facilities to ensure good quality of service delivery.[34] A Standards Committee is established by the National Health Insurance Scheme Act to make recommendations for quality services amongst providers and health maintenance organisations. Quality assurance is also undertaken by the health maintenance organisations which are given the responsibility of setting up mechanisms to ensure quality service from health providers under the Scheme.[35] Health insurance schemes are also emerging at the State level and have similar provisions.[36]

Recent legislation such as the National Health Act and various state health insurance laws contain provisions on quality assurance, patients' rights, and safety mechanisms. The National Health Act establishes as one of its aims the provision of the best possible health services at an affordable cost for all residents of the country.[37] To achieve this, the Act establishes the National Tertiary Health Institutions Standards Committee, which will establish minimum standards for tertiary institutions in the country.[38] Tertiary health institutions are the highest level of health facilities providing specialised care, teaching medical students and typically conducting research. They receive referrals from the secondary facilities, although in practice one of the major challenges of the health care system is that even basic health issues that should be dealt with at the lowest level of care, that is the primary care facilities, usually show up for the first time at the tertiary facilities thus overburdening them.

Under the National Health Act, the National Tertiary Health Institutions Standards Committee has inspecting, accreditation and reporting functions, with accountability to the Federal and State Governments. The Committee is also required to provide information on tertiary health services to the public annually.[39] Although patient safety is not specifically mentioned, it stands to reason that the 'minimum standards' would comprise quality and safety. Should the Committee perform its functions as expected, information on patient safety and welfare should become more readily available than has hitherto been the case, at least in tertiary health care. The Committee was inaugurated by the Minister of Health in February 2017. It remains to be seen how well the functions will be executed.

The National Health Act also requires, amongst other things, that a Certificate of Standards must be obtained by every facility.[40] Without being in possession of such a Certificate of Standards, a health institution is not permitted to provide health services, construct or modify a health establishment, acquire health technology or increase the number of beds in such a facility. A health facility is required to obtain the Certificate of Standards from the appropriate body of government. Within the States, this may be the Hospital Inspectorate Departments or a specialised agency established for the purposes of monitoring quality and standards. For tertiary

34 Ibid., Section 22.
35 Ibid., Section 20.
36 See, for example, the Lagos State Health Management Scheme Law, 2015.
37 Section 1 of the National Health Act.
38 Ibid., Section 9.
39 Ibid., Section 10.
40 Ibid., Section 13.

institutions, the National Tertiary Institutions Standards Committee earlier described is the authority which shall provide the Certificate of Standards, acting through the Federal Ministry of Health. Failure to obtain a Certificate of Standards as required by the Act is a criminal offence, rendering the guilty party liable to 500,000 naira (equivalent of about £1000) or two years' imprisonment or both.[41]

The Certificate of Standards is an innovative mechanism which, if utilised effectively, will have some positive impacts on patient safety. Three years after the National Health Act came into effect, however, the Certificate of Standards has not become operational. The Act does not specify the content of the Certificate of Standards. Furthermore, health being a residual matter, to a large extent states have flexibility for adopting the National Health Act and for instituting the requirements for the Certificate of Standards within their own institutions. At the time of writing, no state has adopted the Certificate of Standards.

In addition, the Act provides for referrals in situations where a health facility does not have the requisite infrastructure or personnel to attend to a patient.[42] All health establishments are required to comply with the quality requirements and standards set by the National Council on Health, Nigeria's highest policy decision making body on health comprising the Federal Minister of Health and the Commissioners of all States. These standards may relate to human resources, technology, equipment, hygiene, premises, health services delivery, safety and the manner in which patients are accommodated and treated.[43] This provision creates a space for the National Council on Health to create specific standards, perhaps articulated in a National Patient Safety Policy. Created under powers conferred by the National Health Act, such policy would have the indirect force of law, which would bind all institutions, public and private.

Further, the Act articulates the rights and responsibilities of patients and health providers, being the first national legislation to do so. The rights of patients include the right to emergency treatment, a serious issue that has led to the death of many Nigerians in the past. It is now a criminal offence for a facility to refuse to provide emergency treatment, at least at the national level.[44] Patients have the right to provide informed consent to treatment with full knowledge of the benefits and risks of treatment.[45] Patients also have the right to information about the full range of services provided by the health establishment, the right to view information on their rights in the establishment and the right to complain about services.[46] Health facilities are also required to keep health records and to provide such records to patients when needed. They are also required to maintain confidentiality of patient information.[47] These may all seem basic, but issues have arisen in these respects and continue to arise. There continues to be a lack

41 Ibid., Section 14.
42 Ibid., Section 17 and 18.
43 Ibid., Section 19.
44 Ibid., Section 20.
45 Ibid., Section 23.
46 Ibid., Section 24.
47 Ibid., Sections 25–27.

of awareness of these rights and patients often suffer harm as a result. For health care providers, the Act requires health establishments to implement measures to minimise injury or damage to the person or property of a health care provider, prevent disease transmission, and provide protection from verbal, physical and sexual abuse from a non-psychiatric patient.[48] This is particularly important as other relevant legislation such as the Labour, Safety, Health and Welfare Bill, which would protect the safety of health care personnel, are yet to be passed.

The National Health Act is federal law, which would require adoption by States. At the present time, no State has clearly adopted the Act. Even so, some States have taken active steps to improve quality and safety in facilities within their authority. Lagos State is a key example. Lagos State's Health Sector Reform Law enacted in 2006, for instance, makes provision for quality control committees to be established in State-owned and operated facilities.[49] It contains similar provisions to the National Health Act on the rights of patients,[50] but does not make the refusal of emergency care a criminal offence.[51]

The Lagos State Health Sector Reform Law also establishes the Health Facilities Monitoring and Accreditation Agency (HEFAMAA).[52] HEFAMAA's objectives are 'to set up necessary standards for both public and private hospitals and other health institutions, improve the quality and efficiency of health care services to the patients by setting adequate standards and ensure strict compliance with same'.[53] The inclusion of both kinds of facilities provides the same protection to patients, regardless of whether they seek care in the public or private sector. The Agency has powers to, amongst other things, 'enforce compliance for the improvement of health services to patients'.[54] Schedules 3 and 4 of the Law contain the items required in every health facility. HEFAMAA is responsible for accrediting, inspecting, monitoring and licensing all health facilities, in order to ensure that all the requisite equipment is in place and that the premises are such as would be conducive for the provision of health care. Its functions also include the checking of credentials of health care practitioners, oversight of the Quality Drug Assurance Laboratory, disseminating specific performance indicators by way of information to the public from data made available by the Research and Statistics Department at least quarterly, and ensuring actual compliance of the performance indicators.[55] In recent years, HEFAMAA has undertaken these tasks and has, in several cases, shut down hospitals.[56] Even so, there is very little data on its work in the public sphere, notwithstanding the specific requirement of the law in respect of HEFAMAA's obligation to disseminate

48 Ibid., Section 21 and 22.
49 Section 39(5) of the Health Sector Reform Law, Lagos State.
50 See Schedule 2 of the Health Sector Reform Law, Lagos State.
51 Section 1 of Schedule 2 of the Health Sector Reform Law, Lagos State.
52 Section 45 Health Sector Reform Law, Lagos State.
53 Ibid., Section 47.
54 Ibid., Section 49.
55 Ibid., Section 48.
56 HEFAMAA, 'Lagos shuts 13 hospitals over quackery'. www.tetryte.com/hefamaa/lagos-shuts-13-hospitals-quackery/.

information to the public.[57] There is little research on its work, its effectiveness, and the impact of its service on the quality of health care provision. Its remit is also limited and does not include areas critical to patient safety such as infection control, hand washing monitoring, and data on length of hospitalisation and patient deaths etc.

In other States the Ministry of Health typically has a department (which may go by different nomenclatures, for example, Hospital Inspectorate, Health Management Board etc), which regulates hospitals, including private health facilities. In Ogun State, for instance, the Ogun State Health Management Law establishes the Ogun State Hospitals Management Board. The primary objective of the Board is 'the provision of effective, qualitative and quantitative health care services to the people of the State'.[58] These boards are involved in inspection of facilities. Many of their activities remain obscure and are not generally recognised even by the facilities over which they are expected to exercise authority.

In summary, there is a plethora of legal provisions at state and federal levels which aim to improve quality and which will, in turn, in all likelihood impact patient safety. Some of these create institutions which are required to manage quality but not many of their activities are documented or focus squarely on managing patient safety issues. The constitutional division of powers in the health sphere often means that quality depends on the institution, the tier of government in charge of it and the level of interest shown. There has not been a stringent requirement of data on adverse events, patients' deaths, or other quality indicators, resulting in limited public information. While court action through the torts of negligence or fundamental rights enforcements are other ways in which the law intervenes in patient safety in Nigeria, this avenue has not been pursued vigorously by patients for reasons identified here and in other literature. However, with the burgeoning use of technology as I describe below, this situation might be about to change.

Emerging solutions to the state of patient safety in Nigeria

For the first time, the National Health Policy has identified a need to ensure patient safety. This suggests a renewed attention to patient safety in the country. However, it is evident from the description and analyses of the state of patient safety, and patient safety policy and law, that much remains to be done to boost patient safety in the country. Still, the challenges should not be considered insurmountable. The major improvements recorded by the drug regulator, NAFDAC, in cleaning up the Nigerian markets of counterfeit drugs is proof that where there is a will, much can be accomplished. The use of media, incentives to staff of the regulator, the use of technology, and the pioneering work of the late Professor Dora Akunyili, the former Chair of NAFDAC who championed drug

57 Section 48(6) Health Sector Reform Law, Lagos State.

58 Ogun State Hospital Management Board, 'Brief on the Agency'. http://ogunstate.gov.ng/ohmb/.

safety and the cleaning up of corrupt practices, were very helpful in this regard.[59] Thus awareness, technology improvements and champions can help promote patient safety improvements.

The now universal use of the internet, social media and mobile phone technology presents an opportunity to further develop an effective patient safety framework that will save lives and prevent harm to patients. Technology has been used effectively in the pharmaceutical sector by NAFDAC to monitor medication safety through a coding system where a code is put on the packets of medicines and which purchasers can track by sending the code by text message for a response on its genuineness or otherwise. Although this has not completely eliminated the problem of counterfeit medicines in Nigeria, it has made an appreciable difference. The effective implementation of such a system by a regulator in Nigeria indicates that we can replicate similar ideas across the health care setting, on health care infections, measuring surgical complications, etc.

Technology is also emerging to support patient safety initiatives. From initiatives like patientsafety.org.ng, a website which encourages patients to tell their stories of interactions with health care facilities and practitioners, to applications that aim to provide ratings of hospitals, to apps that aim to make reporting of medical negligence easier, there is a growing appetite to utilise technology in encouraging patient safety. Lagos State has also collaborated with development partners to commence electronic auditing of maternal deaths.[60] Petitions on medical negligence can now be submitted to the Medical and Dental Council of Nigeria on their website. Many of these technology-based solutions are still in the developing stages and their effectiveness cannot be properly assessed at this time. Yet technology ought to remain a key strategy for patient safety improvement. The pervading prevalence of the internet, mobile phone usage and social media in Nigeria presents a viable, cost-effective, opportunity to increase patient education not only about their rights, but about disease prevention and management and what to expect in health care facilities. It also presents a relatively cost-effective tool for providing and linking complaints and feedback mechanisms in both public and private sectors.

Improving health information management systems is also another essential aspect of technology that must necessarily take prime position in managing patient safety in Nigeria. Much effort has been made in this regard, but it remains inchoate. The lack of comprehensive data is a key challenge that can only be addressed through the appropriate and effective use of technology.

Costs are a key consideration in the improvement of patient safety systems, and more so in a resource-constrained setting like Nigeria. Despite this, some health care organisations have developed standalone frameworks that are not linked with other efforts by the government or private sector. Moreover, initiatives have sprung up in the past decade to address issues of patient safety. Many of these initiatives have originated outside the government sphere but have, to some

59 A. E. Ehikwe, 'Social marketing communications for check-mating sales of fake and adulterated drugs in Nigeria', *British Journal of Marketing Studies* 2015, 3(7):30.

60 J. Leonard-Okafor, 'Maternal death review goes digital in Lagos', *Daily Trust*, www.dailytrust.com.ng/news/health/maternal-death-review-goes-digital-in-lagos/198947.html.

degree, partnered with government institutions. At the present time, some of the relevant initiatives being implemented include the establishment of the Society for Quality in Health Care in 2006, whose mission is to improve quality through education, collaboration, training and accreditation. The 'Pharmaccess Safecare' project aims to use rating, benchmarking and performance-based payout mechanisms to improve quality in health facilities in resource-constrained countries like Nigeria, and partners with government. Linkages between these initiatives and some government input may provide more comprehensive, broad-based support for patient safety in the country.

Patient safety in Nigeria requires champions. Issues such as HIV/AIDS, malaria, tuberculosis and maternal mortality or even health care financing have received some political commitment and resources. While the problems surrounding these are not yet eliminated, there is evidence of some progress. This is in part because these issues have champions. Patient safety issues in Nigeria require more visible champions to advocate for attention to the issue by government, international development agencies and non-governmental organisations involved in health care. Such advocacy should ideally engage different communities – the general populace, women (for maternal and child morbidity and mortality issues), members of the health professions, etc. The aim of advocacy should be to increase awareness, and generate more research, funding, and targeted interventions. Patient safety champions will lead advocacy for recognition of the impact of patient safety on health, mortality, medical tourism and other relevant issues. Matters such as overcrowding in health facilities, contaminated urethral catheters, poor hand hygiene, non-functional infection control committees in public health facilities and the absence of such committees in many private health facilities can be addressed effectively within such advocacy. The implementation of the National Health Act, National Health Policy and other relevant policy as well as the need for more comprehensive data can be addressed within such advocacy. Shifts in current organisational cultures of complacency will require champions from within the organisation who could advocate for effective implementation of mechanisms for identifying and managing error, etc. Champions can also be engaged from within the community, encouraging patients to use existing complaints and feedback mechanisms and empowering communities in which health facilities work to provide feedback on health service delivery, through ward health committees, for example.

From a legal perspective, more medical negligence suits, quicker court and disciplinary processes and patients' rights awareness creation will involve seeking out champions from the legal and medical professions. Implementing the requirements of law such as the Certificate of Standards provided for by the National Health Act is one step that could be taken immediately to improve patient safety. Building an evidence base should be a key aspect of the requirements for obtaining the Certificate of Standards – thus, for example, a health facility could be required to maintain certain specific records to be turned over to the government in each year as an eligibility requirement for the certificate. The establishment of accreditation bodies under the National Health Act is one avenue that may also help boost patient safety. Providing support to these bodies to engage effectively would be helpful. Requiring the implementation of infection control committees in hospitals as required under the Act is another important step. The implementation of the National Health Act is also an opportunity for the different levels of government and the private sector to develop relationships, including in the area of quality assurance, that will enhance patient safety in hospitals – private, public, Federal or State. The National Council of Health, which comprises States' and Federal Ministries of Health, has in the past recognised the need for the states to implement the National Health Act. Encouraging States to begin to implement relevant provisions of the Act, including areas of patient safety such as the Certificate of Standards, should be undertaken as an urgent matter.

Finally, a patient safety agenda is critical. While the National Health Policy specifies the need to attend to patient safety, there is need to develop a comprehensive and achievable agenda for patient safety in Nigeria. At the present time, there is a plethora of policy and laws that address various aspects of patient safety, yet pockets of patient safety issues remain unaddressed, including the need for research and evidence-based development. A clear articulation of a patient safety goals, strategy and implementation of such strategy at different levels of government and in public and private facilities, is essential at this time. This may be expressed within a single National Patient Safety Policy which will articulate government commitment. Such policy should address the issues of patient safety comprehensively drawing from existing policies and laws such as the National Health Act and other matters not specifically addressed in existing policy, develop interventions to address the issues, identify the role of private institutions, establish a platform for community engagement and patients' rights, identify funding mechanisms, promote clinical governance in all health facilities, and set achievable targets and timelines. There is a template for such a policy in the format developed by the World Health Organisation.[61] The template is based on addressing patient safety along the lines of the building blocks of the health system – leadership and governance, service delivery, human resources for health, health financing, health equipment, vaccines and medicines, and health information. Beyond the development of a patient safety agenda, implementation is essential. The research and analysis undertaken make it clear: it is time for patient safety issues in Nigeria to receive more concerted policy and practical attention.

References

Adebimpe, W. 'Knowledge, attitude, and practice of use of safety precautions among health care workers in a Nigerian tertiary hospital, 1 year after the Ebola virus disease epidemic', *Annals of Global Health* 2016, 82(5):897–902.

Aluko, et al., 'Knowledge, attitudes and perceptions of occupational hazards and safety practices in Nigerian healthcare workers', *BMC Research Notes* 2016. 9(71).

Awosan, K. J., et al., 'Knowledge of radiation hazards, radiation protection practices and clinical profile of health workers in a teaching hospital in Northern Nigeria', *Journal of Clinical and Diagnostic Research* 2016, 10(8):LC07–LC12.

61 WHO, *Guide for developing a national patient safety policy and strategic plan*, 2014. www.who.int/patientsafety/guide-for-developing-national-patient-safety-policy-and-strategic-plan_final.pdf.

Bagheri Nejad, S., 'Health-care-associated infection in Africa: a systematic review', *Bulletin of the World Health Organization* 2011, 89:757–65. doi: 10.2471/BLT.11.088179.

Chukwuneke, F. N., 'Medical incidents in developing countries: a few case studies from Nigeria', *Nigerian Journal of Clinical Practice* 2015, 18(7):20–4. www.njcponline.com/article.asp?issn=1119-3077;year=2015;volume=18;issue=7;spage=20;epage=24;aulast=Chukwuneke.

Fadare, J.O et al., 'Knowledge of medical ethics among Nigerian medical doctors', *Nigerian Medical Journal* 2012, 53(4):226–30.

Ehikwe, A. E., 'Social marketing communications for check-mating sales of fake and adulterated drugs in Nigeria', *British Journal of Marketing Studies* 2015, 3(7):30.

Gadzama, G. B., Bawa, S. B., Ajinoma, Z., Saidu, M. M. and Umar, A. S., 'Injection safety practices in a main referral hospital in Northeastern Nigeria', *Nigerian Journal of Clinical Practice* 2014, 17:134–9. www.njcponline.com/text.asp?2014/17/2/134/127420.

Galadanci, H., Künzel, W., Shittu, O., et al., 'Obstetric quality assurance to reduce maternal and fetal mortality in Kano and Kaduna State hospitals in Nigeria', *International Journal of Gynecology and Obstetrics* 2011, 114(1):43, 238. https://aidsfree.usaid.gov/sites/default/files/2016.8.1_aidsfree_nigeria_health_worker_training_manual_tagged.pdf.

Garko, S. B., et al., 'Duration of hospital stay and mortality in the medical wards of Ahmadu Bello University, Kaduna State Annals of African Medicine', *Annals of African Medicine* 2003, 2(2):68–71.

GBD, Healthcare Access and Quality Collaborators, 'Healthcare Access and Quality Index based on mortality from causes amenable to personal health care in 195 countries and territories, 1990–2015: a novel analysis from the Global Burden of Disease Study 2015', 2017, *The Lancet*. http://thelancet.com/pdfs/journals/lancet/PIIS0140-6736(17)30818-8.pdf.

Harrison, R., Wai Seung Cohen, A., and Walton, M., 'Patient safety and quality of care in developing countries in Southeast Asia: a systematic literature review', *International Journal for Quality in Health Care* 2015, 27(4):240–54.

HEFAMAA, 'Lagos shuts 13 hospitals over quackery'. www.tetryte.com/hefamaa/lagos-shuts-13-hospitals-quackery/.

Kehinde Babatunde, M., et al., 'Prevalence and pattern of prescription errors in a Nigerian kidney hospital', *Ghana Medical Journal* 2016, 50(4):233.

Lagos State Health Management Scheme Law, 2015.

Leonard-Okafor, J., 'Maternal death review goes digital in Lagos', *Daily Trust*, www.dailytrust.com.ng/news/health/maternal-death-review-goes-digital-in-lagos/198947.html.

Mitchell, P. H., 'Defining patient safety and quality care – patient safety and quality', in Agency for Healthcare Research and Quality, *Patient safety and quality: an evidence-based handbook for nurses*, Rockville, Maryland, USA: AHRQ, 2008.

Muhammad Lawan, U., et al., 'Pattern of adverse events following immunization in nourished and malnourished infants in Kano, North-Western Nigeria', *Sahel Medical Journal* 2016, 19(3):131.

National Health Act, 2014.

National Health Policy, 2016.

National Population Commission and ICF International, *Nigeria Demographic and Health Survey 2013*, Abuja: Nigeria, and Rockville, Maryland: USA: NPC and ICF International, 2014.

Nnamdi O. A. and Okoli, K. C., et al., 'Health professionals' knowledge about relative prevalence of hospital-acquired infections in Delta State of Nigeria', *The Pan*

African Medical Journal 2016, 24:148. www.panafrican-med-journal.com/content/article/24/148/full/.

Obi, A. I. and Ofili, A. J., 'Injection safety practices among medical doctors in a tertiary health institution in south southern Nigeria', *IOSR Journal of Dental and Medical Sciences* 2013, 8(1):42–9.

Ogun State Hospital Management Board, 'Brief on the Agency'. http://ogunstate.gov.ng/ohmb/.

Okezie Enwere, O. and Chiekulie Diwe, K., 'Knowledge, perception and practice of injection safety and healthcare waste management among teaching hospital staff in south east Nigeria: an intervention study', *Pan African Medical Journal* 2014, 17:218; A.

Oladeinde, B. H., et al., 'Biorisk assessment of medical diagnostic laboratories in Nigeria', *Safety and Health at Work* 2013, 4(2):100–4.

Onyekwulu, F. A and Anya, S. U., 'Pattern of admission and outcome of patients admitted into the Intensive Care Unit of University of Nigeria Teaching Hospital Enugu: a 5-year review', *Nigerian Journal of Clinical Practice* 2015, 18:775–9. www.njcponline.com/text.asp?2015/18/6/775/163291.

Onyemocho, A., Anekoson, J. I. and Pius, E. O., 'Knowledge and practice of injection safety among workers of Nigerian Prison Service health facilities in Kaduna State', *American Journal of Public Health Research* 2013, 1(7):171–6. doi: 10.12691/ajphr-1-7-5.

Petti, C. A., 'Laboratory medicine in Africa: a barrier to effective health care', *Clinical Infectious Diseases* 2006, 42(3):377–82.

WHO, 'Health-care-associated infection in Africa: a systematic review', *Bulletin of the World Health Organization* 2011, 89:757–65.

WHO, *Guide for developing a national patient safety policy and strategic plan*, 2014. www.who.int/patientsafety/guide-for-developing-national-patient-safety-policy-and-strategic-plan_final.pdf.

WHO, *Antibiotic resistance: Multi-Country Public Awareness Survey*, Geneva: WHO, 2015. http://apps.who.int/iris/bitstream/10665/194460/1/9789241509817_eng.pdf?ua=1.

WHO, *Patient safety in Nigeria is deplorable*, May 17, 2017. www.thisdaylive.com/index.php/2017/05/11/who-patients-safety-in-nigeria-deplorable/.

WHO, *Conceptual framework for international classification for patient safety*. www.who.int/patientsafety/taxonomy/icps_full_report.pdf.

15 A critical analysis of patient safety strategies in Kurdistan Region of Iraq (KRI)

Azhin Omer

Introduction

Patient safety is defined by the World Health Organisation (WHO) as 'the reduction of risk of unnecessary harm associated with health care'.[1] Although it is beyond the bounds of possibility to avoid medical errors, in developing countries, particularly in the Kurdistan Region in Iraq (KRI), medical errors are more common.[2] With about 25 million people, Kurds are one of the largest ethnic groups in the world without a state.[3] Kurdish people are living in different countries, including Turkey, Iran, Iraq, and Syria.[4] This chapter focuses on KRI, which is currently recognised as an autonomous region under the Iraqi constitution.[5]

KRI is subject to decades of successive civil and conventional armed conflicts, including the Iran–Iraq war (1980–8), Gulf War (1990 and 2003), civil war (1994–8), and the war against the so-called Islamic State (ISIS) (2014–present).[6] The existence of ongoing political instabilities has had a negative impact on medical and educational standards in KRI.[7] The first part of this chapter examines the characteristics of the current healthcare system, such as the existence of dual healthcare practices, healthcare financing, and the role of policy makers under clinical governance. The second part of this chapter critically analyses future strategies of patient safety, including the

1 M. Kathrin, et al., 'Global research priorities to better understand the burden of iatrogenic harm in primary care: an International Delphi exercise', *PLOS Medicine* 2013, 2.

2 WHO, *10 facts on patient safety*, 2014. www.who.int/features/factfiles/patient_safety/en/ (accessed 20 March 2014).

3 The Kurdish Heritage Foundation of America, 'Kurds and Kurdistan: facts and figures', *International Journal of Kurdish Studies* 1992, 5:161.

4 Ibid.; The Kurdish Heritage Foundation of America, 'Kurds and Kurdistan'. www.oswego.edu/~baloglou/anatolia/kurds.html (accessed 21 August 2017).

5 Ibid; Elizabeth Miller and Charles Buker, 'Legal education in Iraqi Kurdistan', *Stanford Lawyer*, 2015, 93. https://law.stanford.edu/stanford-lawyer/articles/legal-education-in-iraqi-kurdistan/ (accessed 20 July 2017).

6 F. M. Hasan, 'A quantitative analysis about the prevalence of PTSD after the chemical attack I Halabja/Kurdistan, Iraq', *European Psychiatry* 2010, 25(1):344.

7 A. Towfik-Shukur and H. Khoshnaw, 'The impact of health system governance and policy processes on health services in Iraqi Kurdistan', *BMC International Health and Human Rights* 2010, June, (8):1.

recommendations to implement an Incident Reporting System, the use of Health Information Systems to measure and improve patient safety, and the provision of education and training to improve healthcare performance.

The healthcare system structure of KRI

Iraq is one of those middle-income countries that, since the 1920s,[8] has developed health infrastructure: a total of 1,146 primary health centres, 1,185 health centres, and 229 hospitals are established for the purposes of providing medical treatment, preventing diseases and promoting health.[9] Following the political uprising in 1991, the KRI healthcare system is no longer governed by the Iraqi Ministry of Health, but by the Kurdistan Regional Ministry of Health, with the assistance of the Health Committee of Kurdistan Parliament.[10] KRI consists of three provinces, *Sulaymaniyah*, *Erbil* and *Duhok*, and the healthcare providers of each province are managed by local Departments of Health.[11] In KRI, General Practitioner (GP) medical centres do not exist to ensure access to healthcare prior to hospital admissions, to refer patients to specialists, and guarantee follow-up by monitoring patient health on regular basis.[12] As a substitute to health services by GPs, primary health centres, private clinics, and public hospitals are most commonly used by KRI patients as the *first* point of access to healthcare.[13]

Healthcare financing

Although KRI has enjoyed autonomous status since the political uprising of 1991, the Kurdistan Regional Government (KRG) is financially dependent on the 17% annual budget allocated by the Iraqi Central Government.[14] Out of the 17% national budget, 6% is allocated to finance the public health sector and free medical care is provided to over 6.5 million Kurds and political refugees.[15]

8 WHO, Report on the regional consultation on improving quality of care and patient safety in the Eastern Mediterranean Region, Jeddah Saudi Arabia, 2014, pp. 11–12.

9 WHO, *Iraq: Primary Healthcare*, 2017. www.emro.who.int/irq/programmes/primary-health-care.html (accessed 9 December 2017); IRFAD, *Healthcare in Iraq: Iraq healthcare system* (2014). www.irfad.org/healthcare-in-iraq/ (accessed 9 December 2017).

10 P N. Shabila, et al., 'Iraqi health system in Kurdistan Region: medical professionals' perspectives on challenges and priorities for improvements', *Conflict and Health*, 2010, 4:19. www.conflictandhealth.com/content/4/1/19 (accessed 25 March 2014).

11 Towfik-Shukur and Khoshnaw, 'The impact of health system governance and policy processes', pp. 1, 4; M. Moore, et al., 'The future of health care in the Kurdistan Region – Iraq: toward an effective, high-quality system with an emphasis on primary care', *RAND Health* 2014, 4(2):17, 19.

12 N. Goodwin, et al., Improving the quality of care in general practice: report of an independent inquiry by the King's Fund, London: The King's Fund 2011, p. 16.

13 Towfik-Shukur and Khoshnaw, 'The impact of health system governance and policy processes', p. 4.

14 S. Waladbagi, 'Private hospitals are the new face of medical services', *Kurdish Globe* 2011; The Kurdish Heritage Foundation of America, 'Kurds and Kurdistan: facts and figures', *Kurdish Studies: International Journal*, 1992. www.oswego.edu/~baloglou/anatolia/kurds.html (accessed 21 August 2017).

15 C. R. Anthony, et al. 'Strengthening health care in the Kurdistan Region of Iraq', *RAND Research Briefs* 2017, p. 1. www.rand.org/pubs/research_briefs/RB9990.html; Moore et al., 'The future of health care in the Kurdistan Region – Iraq', p. xvii.

Nevertheless, due to the lack of clear strategic policy directions, the budget is not allocated in accordance to the healthcare needs of the population. For instance, the province of Sulaimaniyah, with the largest population, receives only 15.7% of the healthcare budget, whilst Erbil and Duhok are receiving a total of 73% of the allocated healthcare budget.[16]

Furthermore, due to the political instabilities resulting from the attacks by ISIS, the relationship between the KRI Parliament and Iraqi Central Parliament is characterised by a standoff, whereby the Iraqi and KRI Ministries of Health (MoHs) do not collaborate sufficiently to address patient safety issues and improve the healthcare system.[17] Since 2014 restrictions have been imposed by the Iraqi Central Government on the allocation of the national budget and as a result, the current KRI healthcare system is severely underfunded.[18] One of the main causes of patient safety failures is an underfunded healthcare system, as currently in KRI, the delays in salaries have led to strikes by healthcare practitioners and hospital closures, causing major work pressure within the emergency departments. Each paramedic is expected to treat over 50 patients in less than 4 hours. As a result, consultation time with each patient is less than two minutes, which is not sufficient to ensure correct diagnosis of a patient's illness.[19]

It is important to highlight that the restrictions on the healthcare budget, as the result of political instabilities, also means the lack of medical supplies.[20,21] Recently the KRI MoH sought help from international health organisations, including the WHO, to provide medical supplies to over 1.3 million refugees who escaped violence by ISIS from other parts of Iraq and Syria.[22] Consequently, according to the KRI MoH, the allocated national budget is not sufficient to cover more than 40% of the healthcare needs in KRI.[23]

At the present time, the healthcare system of KRI consists of two types of primary healthcare centres (PHCs) including PHC main centres (which serve between 5,000 and 10,000 residents) and PHC sub-centres or branches (which serve up to 5,000 residents).[24] A wide range of human resources is employed in each PHC, including primary care physicians, nurses, dermatologists, specialists, dentists and pharmacists. Although, the KRI PHCs utilise diagnostic laboratories and pharmacies, the lack of the most basic and necessary medical equipment is regarded as one of the leading causes for patient

16 Towfik-Shukur and Khoshnaw, 'The impact of health system governance and policy processes', p. 3.

17 Ibid.

18 KRG Cabinet, 'Ministry of Health: more health services needed for IDPs', 29 September 2014, KRG. http://cabinet.gov.krd/a/d.aspx?s=040000&l=12&a=52300; Miller and Buker, *Legal Education in Iraqi Kurdistan*, p. 51.

19 Moore, et al., 'The future of health care in the Kurdistan Region – Iraq', p. 17.

20 KRG Cabinet, 'Ministry of Health: more health services needed for IDPs'.

21 Doctors of the World, *Access to healthcare in the UK*, 2015. www.doctorsoftheworld.org.uk/publications.

22 Miller and Buker, *Legal Education in Iraqi Kurdistan*, p. 1 .

23 Alexandra Di Stefano Pironti, Ministry of Health: more health services needed for IDPs, KRG, 2014.

24 Moore, et al., 'The future of health care in the Kurdistan Region – Iraq', p. 17.

safety failures.[25] Additionally, healthcare staff are poorly distributed across the healthcare providers of KRI. Currently, instead of 33 physicians, only 11 physicians are allocated to serve about 10,000 residents.[26] The lack of medical resources, and the poor distribution of medical staff, has the effect of preventing the provision of effective medical intervention within a reasonable time.

Due to the current political instabilities in Iraq, there are no guarantees for continuous budgetary allocation to the KRG by the Iraqi Central Government. As a patient safety strategy, the MoH found it necessary to propose the implementation of a health insurance scheme to improve the perceived financial issues. Additionally, the KRG funded research conducted by an international research organisation known as the RAND Corporation to explore the current health finance issues of KRI and the 'Accountable National Health Service' was strongly recommended.[27] Unlike the current health financing system of KRI, which is only based on public budget by the Iraqi Central Government,[28] the Accountable National Health Service aims to ensure funding allocation to the public health sector through national wage taxes.[29] Although, a health insurance scheme and the Accountable National Health Service were recommended as an alternative to the current publicly financed healthcare system, due to the lack of further research, the process of reform will be challenging for the MoH.

Dual healthcare practice

The phenomenon of Dual Practice (DP) is common in KRI amongst healthcare practitioners, whereby the majority of physicians are practising in both public and private health sectors. Physicians are entitled to establish private clinics once they have completed the Kurdistan Board of Medical Specialty (KBMS) course and registered with the National Doctors' Union.[30] The KRG employed RAND Corporation to research the impact of DP on the current healthcare system of KRI.[31] It was found that physicians spend most of their working in private clinics to generate more income.[32] The existence of DP has a negative impact on the scarce resources within the public healthcare providers. According to Towfik-Shukur, in KRI there is an unclear delineation between public and private sectors as he argued that '[p]rimary care physicians actually refer patients to their private evening practices and feed off the hospitals' public

25 Towfik-Shukur and Khoshnaw, 'The impact of health system governance and policy processes', p. 4.
26 Moore, et al., 'The future of health care in the Kurdistan Region – Iraq', p. 17.
27 C. R. Anthony, et al., 'Health sector reform in the Kurdistan Region – Iraq: financing reform, primary care, and patient safety', *RAND Health*, 2014. www.rand.org/pubs/periodicals/health-quarterly/issues/v4/n3/02.html (accessed 9 Jan 2018).
28 Moore, et al., 'The future of health care in the Kurdistan Region – Iraq', Executive Summary, p. xvii.
29 Ibid.
30 J. Hamanajm, 'Kurdistan Board of Medical Specialties', 2014. www.kbms.org/?page=aboutus (accessed 24 January 2018).
31 Anthony, et al., 'Health sector reform in the Kurdistan Region – Iraq'.
32 Ibid., p.37.

diagnostic services to augment their own business'.[33] This indicates that physicians are using the limited resources within the public healthcare providers for the benefit of their private clinics.[34]

In addition to the above, the law regulating the KRI private clinics fails to systematically monitor the safety of healthcare. It does not currently have an efficient licensing system for the purpose of assessing the competency of physicians practising under the private sector.[35] As a result, the MoH proposed various patient safety strategies such as reviewing the existing policies relating to DP and proposing to introduce a strict licensing system to prevent incompetent healthcare professionals from practising and setting up private clinics. Furthermore, the MoH has proposed to increase taxes on alcohol and tobacco and introduce a National Health Insurance Scheme. The idea is to encourage physicians to work in public healthcare providers only, by utilising the income from the taxes and insurance premium to increase physicians' monthly payments.[36]

Clinical governance

Clinical governance is a system through which health governors and clinical leaders are responsible for continuously improving health services and maintaining the quality of care by overseeing the functions of healthcare practitioners.[37] The existence of clinical guidelines, regulations and professional regulatory authorities contributes to the process of ensuring effective clinical governance. Firm reliance on clinical guidelines and regulations enables healthcare practitioners to act in accordance with the highest possible standards.[38] Nevertheless, under the current healthcare system of KRI, no effective mechanism is in place to guide and clarify the responsibilities of healthcare practitioners.

Clinical guidelines and regulations are successfully implemented through proficient regulatory authorities and the highest standards set under regulations are achieved through the process of overseeing the functions of healthcare practitioners; providing certification to competent healthcare practitioners and holding incompetent practitioners accountable for negligent treatments.[39] Unfortunately, under the KRI healthcare system, no independent professional regulatory authority exists, and the majority of the existing management team (including hospital directors) are not sufficiently qualified to direct healthcare practitioners effectively.[40]

33 Towfik-Shukur and Khoshnaw, 'The impact of health system governance and policy processes', p. 4.

34 Anthony, et al., 'Health sector reform in the Kurdistan Region – Iraq', p. 37.

35 Towfik-Shukur and Khoshnaw, 'The impact of health system governance and policy processes', p. 4.

36 Anthony, et al., 'Health sector reform in the Kurdistan Region — Iraq', p. 71.

37 L. J. Scally and G. Donaldson, 'Clinical governance and the drive for quality improvement in the new NHS in England', *British Medical Journal* 1998, 61–65.

38 S. Moloney, 'Medical misadventure: compensation, accountability and regulating standards of practice', *Medico-Legal Journal of Ireland* 2000, p. 2.

39 L. J. Donaldson and G. Scally, 'Clinical management and the drive for quality improvement in the NHS in England', *British Medical Journal* 1998, 1727; B. Keogh, *Review into the quality of care and treatment provided by 14 hospital trusts in England: overview report*, London: ISO, 2013.

40 Moore, et al., 'The future of health care in the Kurdistan Region – Iraq', pp. 14–15.

The absence of independent professional regulatory authorities has also resulted in the lack of an accountability system.

The rationale behind the absence of independent professional regulatory authorities is political interference. In this case, political parties are interfering with the practice of clinical leaders under the KRI healthcare system. Although Kurdistan Doctors Syndicates was established to regulate the functions of doctors, due to political interferences, the role of this syndicate was criticised by the Kurdistan Parliament Health Committee for failing to take action and solve medical failures.[41] Political interference is common in KRI as the political parties are in charge of the national budget, therefore healthcare providers are financially dependent on political parties. Political parties are interfering with the management of healthcare providers by employing those practitioners who share similar political views.[42] Towfik-Shukur and Khoshnaw claim that 'staff employment at the MoH and Departments of Health (DoH)s are mainly based on political affiliation'.[43] This has a negative impact on patient safety and it increases the risk of harm to patients as incompetent practitioners are being employed and allowed to practise in return for electoral votes.[44]

As a patient safety strategy, currently the MoH is assisted by the Health Committee of Kurdistan Parliament to implement health policies, including a job description to set up clinical standards and define the scope of practice for KRI healthcare professionals.[45] This attempt at introducing healthcare policy is in response to the findings from the research by the RAND Corporation in which it was strongly recommended that the MoH introduce clinical management protocols and clinical guidelines to ensure effective leadership within the healthcare providers of KRI.[46] Additionally, KRG Quality Health Council was recommended as an independent regional health regulatory authority with non-interventionist ideologies from political parties to ensure a safe environment for patients.[47] The Quality Health Council corroborates with local hospital leadership by clarifying the responsibilities with the aid of clinical management protocols and by promoting collective leadership through the development of communication strategies.[48] Moreover, during the International Congress on Reform and Development of the Health Care System in Kurdistan Region (2011), Shawis recommended the Medical Registration and Licensing Body to award a license to practise, register and certify competent medical practitioners and to hold incompetent practitioners to account.[49]

41 Kurdish News Network, 'Kurdistan parliament warns Kurdistan Doctors Syndicate', 2018.

42 S. C. Stokes, 'Clientelism' in C. Boix and S. C. Stokes (eds), *The Oxford Handbook of Comparative Politics*, Cambridge: Cambridge University Press, 2009, pp. 4–13.

43 Towfik-Shukur and Khoshnaw, 'The impact of health system governance and policy processes', p. 3.

44 Stokes, Clentelism', p. 5.

45 Towfik-Shukur and Khoshnaw, 'The impact of health system governance and policy processes', p. 1.

46 Moore, et al., 'The future of health care in the Kurdistan Region – Iraq'.

47 Anthony, et al., 'Health Sector Reform in the Kurdistan Region — Iraq'.

48 J. Allsop and M. Saks, Regulating the health professions, London: SAGE, 2002, pp. 22, 51; WHO, Report on the regional consultation, p. 11; Keogh, *Review*, p. 25.

49 R. N. Shawis, 'Kurdistan Regional Government – Iraq Ministry of Health medical registration and licensing body is a pre-requisite for good medical practice', KRG, 2011. www.duhokhealth.org/files/Lecture%202-%20Rang%20shawis-GMC%20PresentationNew%20Microsoft%20PowerPo.

Future strategies of patient safety for KRI

Subsequent to the political uprising of 1991 and the invasion of Iraq in 2003, the KRI has witnessed social and economic growth. As a result, numerous patient safety initiatives are undertaken, including the following: the collaboration with international research organisations to evaluate the current healthcare system; the review of the healthcare finance system; and the construction of new hospitals. Although it is a challenging process, it can be argued that this is the time to transform the current healthcare system and implement long-term patient safety strategies as the current KRI political situation is in a stage of evolution.[50] The introduction of the Incident Reporting System, the measurement of patient safety through a Health Information System and the improvement of safety via education and training are examples of future and long-term patient safety strategies for KRI. Each patient safety strategy will now be considered in further detail.

Implementing an Incident Reporting System for patient safety events

An Incident Reporting System is globally recognised as the cornerstone for safe practice within healthcare providers.[51] Under this system adverse events are reported for the purpose of learning lessons from mistakes and minimising future risks of harm to patients.[52] According to the WHO, an effective Incident Reporting System is in three stages. Firstly, healthcare practitioners are encouraged to report errors through the imposition of a duty.[53] Secondly, the reported failures are recorded and investigated by Local Health Boards.[54] Finally, the disclosed information is analysed and the causes of the failures are highlighted by patient safety teams in order to learn lessons and prevent future failures.[55]

Currently, an Incident Reporting System does not exist in the KRI healthcare system. The introduction of such a system would have numerous advantages, including the identification of tangible information about the root causes of patient safety failures. Additionally, the Incident Reporting System would allow the healthcare practitioners to contribute to the process of improving the healthcare system by identifying and reporting failures to clinical managing teams. However, the implementation and the enforcement of the Incident Reporting System under the KRI healthcare system could be complicated and, without doubt,

pdf 29 January 2018; Angela Yu, et al., *Patient safety 2030*, 2016, National Institute for Health Research, p. 23.

50 Di Stefano Pironti, *Ministry of Health*.

51 J. Legemaate, Exploring patient participation in reducing health-care-related safety risks, Geneva: World Health Organisation, 2013, p. 14.

52 T. Inglesby, 'Incident Reporting Systems', *Patient safety & Quality Healthcare* 2014. www.psqh.com/analysis/incident-reporting-systems-reporting-and-prevention/ (accessed 9 January 2018).

53 WHO, WHO draft guidelines for adverse event reporting and learning systems, 2005, p. 13.

54 Ibid., p. 35.

55 WHO, *Safer Primary Care*, 2014. www.who.int/patientsafety/safer_primary_care/en/ (accessed 20 March 2014); Allsop and Sacks, *Regulating the health professions*, p. 88.

would take years.[56] Prior to the introduction of such a system, the implementation process needs to be evaluated. It is important to emphasise that, due to the absence of clinical guidelines and regulations, strenuous efforts are required by healthcare practitioners to identify unacceptable practice. Additionally, KRI needs to introduce Local Health Boards to oversee the incident reporting process by imposing a duty on healthcare practitioners to report medical errors.[57]

In order to analyse the reported data, an electronic Health Information System needs to be introduced in KRI, and the reported data (including patients' medical information) needs to be uploaded into a database for further analysis. Electronic Health Information Systems are required to record the reported data and a Reporting and Learning Team should to be put in place to analyse the reported data and learn from mistakes. Moreover, a Reporting and Learning Team needs to be employed to analyse the reported data; identify root causes and common risks across the healthcare providers; and issue alerts in cases of major patient safety failures.[58] The MoH is required to produce regulations and guidelines to identify clinical standards. Health boards should oversee the reporting process.

Measuring and improving patient safety through a Management Information System

A Management Information System (MIS) is a system that stores and manages health-related information derived from various sources including patients' medical records, National Health Statistic Offices, health surveys and human resource records. MIS is regarded as the cornerstone for patient safety, as the health-related information can be used as an assessment tool to detect the patient safety failures and ensure better clinical oversight.[59] Similar to the third stage of the reporting system (considered above), the data recorded under the MIS can be analysed to identify risk factors and areas for improvement.[60] Moreover, the MIS provides the underpinning for decision making relating to the allocation of limited resources and ensures greater access to medical care within a reasonable time. MIS is regarded as a tool for assessing the use of medical resources, owing to the fact that it provides valuable information regarding the use of health resources including medication, medical equipment and healthcare practitioners.

Additionally, the MIS can also inform policy makers about the key indicators of risk of harm and the need to establish healthcare related policies. Although the KRI healthcare system is moving towards the modernisation of healthcare practice by introducing an electronic health record system in a number of

56 Towfik-Shukur and Khoshnaw, 'The impact of health system governance and policy processes', p. 5.

57 WHO, WHO draft guidelines, p. 13.

58 Ibid., p. 35.

59 WHO, *Health Information System: toolkit on monitoring health systems strengthening*, 2008. www.who.int/healthinfo/statistics/toolkit_hss/EN_PDF_Toolkit_HSS_InformationSystems.pdf. (accessed 30 January 2018).

60 Yu et al., *Patient safety 2030*, p. 24.

hospital departments, recording patients' medical information is not functionally standardised across all healthcare providers of KRI.[61] As evidenced in the research conducted by the RAND Corporation, it was concluded that 'a culture of data for action' does not exist in KRI. It was found that standardised forms of recording medical information and adverse events are not maintained for the purposes of identifying risks and hazards.[62] As a result, RAND recommended MIS for the purposes of monitoring health services in PHCs and identifying areas for improvement.

Between 2012 and 2013, MIS was piloted in 605 PHCs and from 2013 to 2015 the data from the pilot study was analysed. It was found that the Geographic Information System (GIM), which captures geographic data relating to the health of the population, was available in KRI. Additionally, the data from the pilot study revealed a number of facts relating to the healthcare system which can be used to improve the KRI healthcare system.[63] As the result, it can be argued that the MIS pilot study can have a positive impact on patient safety as it pinpointed the failures within the PHCs.[64] Although electronic health records under the MIS enhance the process of recording health-related information, the existing paper-based recoding system in KRI can be beneficial if well-conceived. For the purposes of guaranteeing 'a culture of data for action', the recorded data under the MIS need to be used to review mortality rates, patients' care, safety measures, and workforce.[65] Furthermore, a Data Analysis Team could be employed to monitor the data generated from the MIS and share it with the policy makers to establish effective health-related protocols for the healthcare system.[66]

Improving safety via education and training

Nowadays, due to medical and technological developments, health education and training are becoming indispensable.[67] Healthcare practitioners' knowledge is updated through education and training courses, including web-based e-learning programs by councils, associations and unions.[68] The provision of education and training has a number of advantages as sufficient knowledge and skills can lead to a safety culture: the risks of misdiagnosis, drug misuse and harm to patients are,

61 Towfik-Shukur and Khoshnaw, 'The impact of health system governance and policy processes', p. 4.

62 Moore et al., 'The future of health care in the Kurdistan Region – Iraq', pp. 17–18.

63 Ibid., p. 20. The first finding was about unequal standards amongst PHCs of the three provinces of Duhok, Erbil and Sulaymaniyah, whereby nursing training had its highest level in the province of Erbil. The second finding from the pilot study was related to the lack of a clear policy on the health services provided whereby not all KRI PHCs are capable of providing vaccinations and dental care.

64 D. A. Handel, et al., 'Using information technology to improve the quality and safety of emergency care', *Academic Emergency Medicine* 2011, 18(6):e45–51.

65 Keogh *Review*; Moore, et al., 'The future of health care in the Kurdistan Region – Iraq', pp. 17–18.

66 Yu, et al., *Patient safety 2030*, p. 24.

67 WHO, Guide for developing national patient safety policy and strategic plan, 2014, pp. 11, 28; H Legido-Quigley, et al., *Assuring the quality of healthcare in the European Union*, Geneva: European Observatory on Health Systems and Policies, 2008, p. 32.

68 Medical Protection Society, *Professionalism - what does it look like?* MPS, 2015; Allsop, and Saks, Regulating the health professionals, p. 154.

consequently, decreased.[69] There are, however, no effective mechanisms in place to ensure the successful implementation of new knowledge gained from education and training courses. As a consequence, the majority of PHCs are dependent on the practice of GPs with less than two years' experience, which is regarded as a major patient safety hazard and a system failure.[70] As a patient safety strategy for KRI, it would be important to establish local training centres and promote better knowledge and skills by clearly identifying the objectives of the proposed training courses and impose a duty on healthcare practitioners to successfully complete the course.[71] Additionally, within the KRI healthcare providers, training managers need to be employed to ensure the successful use of new knowledge by overseeing the functions of healthcare practitioners.[72]

Conclusion

This chapter has critically analysed the patient safety strategies under the current healthcare system of KRI. It started by providing an overview of the KRI healthcare system. The particular focus was on healthcare finance, dual healthcare practice and clinical governance. It considered the negative impact of political instabilities on the healthcare budget allocation which is currently underfunded.[73] As the result, the policy makers are attempting to prevent patient safety failures under short-term solutions only.[74] As a patient safety strategy, it is recommended that KRI resolve budget constraints and ensure better access to healthcare through the implementation of an 'Accountable National Health Service' (A-NHS).[75] Subsequently, this chapter determined that dual healthcare practice by physicians had a negative impact on patient safety. This is mainly because physicians spend most of their time in private clinics and are, thus, failing to treat patients in public hospitals within a reasonable time. Furthermore, clinical governance under the healthcare system fails to clarify sufficiently the expected standards of healthcare through the implementation of clinical guidelines and regulations.

The chapter also considered future patient safety strategies for KRI including the implementation of an Incident Reporting System. Additionally, the introduction of 'a culture of data for action' through the Health Information System was regarded as the second future strategy of patient safety. A further strategy concentrated on improving healthcare performance through education and training,

69 WHO, *Exploring patient participation in reducing healthcare related safety risks*, 2013, p. 4; A. Alkhenizan and C. Shaw, 'Impact of accreditation on the quality of healthcare services: a systematic review of the literature', *Annals of Saudi Medicine* 2011, 31(4):407.

70 Towfik-Shukur and Khoshnaw, 'The impact of health system governance and policy processes', p. 4.

71 WHO, Report on the regional consultation, pp. 8–9.

72 Allsop and Saks, *Regulating the health professionals*, p. 84; Towfik-Shukur and Khoshnaw, 'The impact of health system governance and policy processes', p. 5.

73 Towfik-Shukur and Khoshnaw, 'The impact of health system governance and policy processes', p. 1; Miller and Buker, *Legal Education in Iraqi Kurdistan.*

74 Di Stefano Pironti, *Ministry of Health.*

75 Anthony, et al., 'Health Sector Reform in the Kurdistan Region – Iraq'.

which will help to ensure understanding and subsequent use of new knowledge gained under the training courses.

Overall, it can be argued that, although KRI is currently experiencing political instabilities and budget constraints, the KRG has taken a number of patient safety initiatives to reduce patient safety failures.

References

Alkhenizan A. and Shaw, C., 'Impact of accreditation on the quality of healthcare services: a systematic review of the literature', *Annals of Saudi Medicine* 2011, 31(4):407.

Allsop, J. and Saks, M., *Regulating the Health Professions* (2002).

Anthony, C. R. et al., 'Health sector reform in the Kurdistan Region – Iraq: financing reform, primary care, and patient safety', *RAND Health*, 2014. www.rand.org/pubs/periodicals/health-quarterly/issues/v4/n3/02.html (accessed 9 Jan 2018).

Anthony, C. R. et al. 'Strengthening health care in the Kurdistan Region of Iraq' (2017) *RAND Research Briefs* 1, www.rand.org/pubs/research_briefs/RB9990.html.

Doctors of the World, *Access to healthcare in the UK*, 2015). www.doctorsoftheworld.org.uk/files/2015–09–18_DOTW_Access_to_healthcare_final.pdf (accessed 15 January 2017).

Donaldson, L. J. and Scally, G., 'Clinical management and the drive for quality improvement in the NHS in England', *British Medical Journal* 1998, 1727.

Goodwin, N. et al., *Improving the quality of care in general practice: report of an independent inquiry by the King's Fund*, London: The King's Fund 2011.

Hamanajm, J., 'Kurdistan Board of Medical Specialties', 2014. www.kbms.org/?page=aboutus (accessed 24 January 2018).

Handel, D. A., et al., 'Using information technology to improve the quality and safety of emergency care', *Academic Emergency Medicine*, 2011, 18(6):e45–51.

Hasan, F. M., 'A quantitative analysis about the prevalence of PTSD after the chemical attack I Halabja/Kurdistan, Iraq', *European Psychiatry* 2010, 25(1):344.

Inglesby, T., 'Incident reporting systems', *Patient Safety & Quality Healthcare* 2014. www.psqh.com/analysis/incident-reporting-systems-reporting-and-prevention/ (accessed 9 January 2018).

IRFAD, *Healthcare in Iraq: Iraq Healthcare System*, 2014). www.irfad.org/healthcare-in-iraq/ (accessed 9 December 2017).

Kathrin, M., et al., 'Global Research Priorities to Better Understand the Burden of Iatrogenic Harm in Primary Care: An International Delphi Exercise', *PLOS Medicine* 2013, 2.

Keogh, B., *Review into the quality of care and treatment provided by 14 hospital trusts in England: overview report*, London: ISO, 2013.

KRG Cabinet, 'Ministry of Health: More health services needed for IDPs', 29 September 2014, KRG. http://cabinet.gov.krd/a/d.aspx?s=040000&l=12&a=52300.

Kurdish News Network, 'Kurdistan parliament warns Kurdistan Doctors Syndicate', 2018. www.knnc.net/en/full-story-38310–28-False (accessed 28 January 2018).

Legemaate, J., *Exploring patient participation in reducing health-care-related safety risks*, World Health Organisation, 2013, p. 14.

Legido-Quigley, H., et al., *Assuring the quality of healthcare in the European Union*, Geneva: European Observatory on Health Systems and Policies, 2008.

Medical Protection Society, *Professionalism – what does it look like?* MPS, 2015.

Miller, E. and Buker, C., 'Legal education in Iraqi Kurdistan', *Stanford Lawyer* 2015, 93. https://law.stanford.edu/stanford-lawyer/articles/legal-education-in-iraqi-kurdistan/ (accessed 20 July 2017).

Moloney, S., 'Medical misadventure: compensation, accountability and regulating standards of practice', *Medico-Legal Journal of Ireland* 2000, p. 2.

Moore, M. et al., 'The future of health care in the Kurdistan Region – Iraq: toward an effective, high-quality system with an emphasis on primary care', *RAND Health* 2014, 4(2):17, 19.

Pironti, A. Di Stefano, *Ministry of Health: more health services needed for IDPs*, KRG, 2014.

Scally, L. J. and Donaldson, G., 'Clinical governance and the drive for quality improvement in the new NHS in England', *British Medical Journal* 1998, 61–65.

Shabila, N. P. et al., 'Iraqi Health System in Kurdistan Region: medical professionals' perspectives on challenges and priorities for improvements', *Conflict and Health* 2010, 4:19. www.conflictandhealth.com/content/4/1/19 (accessed 25 March 2014).

Shawis, R. S., 'Kurdistan Regional Government – Iraq Ministry of Health medical registration and licensing body is a pre-requisite for good medical practice', 2011, KRG. www.duhokhealth.org/files/Lecture%202-%20Rang%20shawis-GMC%20PresentationNew%20Microsoft%20PowerPo.pdf (accessed 29 January 2018).

Stokes, S. C., 'Clientelism', in Boix, C. and Stokes, S. C. (eds), *The Oxford Handbook of Comparative Politics*, Cambridge: Cambridge University Press, 2009.

The Kurdish Heritage Foundation of America, 'Kurds and Kurdistan: facts and figures', *The International Journal of Kurdish Studies* 1992, 5.

Towfik-Shukur, A., Khoshnaw, H., 'The impact of health system governance and policy processes on health services in Iraqi Kurdistan', *BMC International Health and Human Rights* 2010, June (8):1.

Waladbagi, S., 'Private hospitals are the new face of medical services', *Kurdish Globe* 2011.

WHO, *WHO draft guidelines for adverse event reporting and learning systems*, 2005.

WHO, *Health Information System: toolkit on monitoring health systems strengthening*, 2008. www.who.int/healthinfo/statistics/toolkit_hss/EN_PDF_Toolkit_HSS_Information Systems.pdf (accessed 30 January 2018).

WHO, *Exploring patient participation in reducing healthcare related safety risks*, 2013.

WHO, *10 facts on patient safety*, 2014. www.who.int/features/factfiles/patient_safety/en/ (accessed 20 March 2014).

WHO, *Guide for developing national patient safety policy and strategic plan*, 2014.

WHO, *Report on the regional consultation on improving quality of care and patient safety in the Eastern Mediterranean Region, Jeddah Saudi Arabia*, 2014.

WHO, *Iraq: Primary Healthcare*, 2017. www.emro.who.int/irq/programmes/primary-health-care.html (accessed 9 December 2017).

WHO, *Safer primary care*, 2014. www.who.int/patientsafety/safer_primary_care/en/ (accessed 20 March 2014).

Yu, Angela, et al., *Patient Safety 2030*, 2016, National Institute for Health Research.

16 Patient safety and the health transition

Understanding and addressing the high level of lifestyle-related non-communicable diseases in the Pacific region

Roy Smith

Introduction

The burden of non-communicable diseases (NCDs) is transitioning from high income to low and middle income countries at a rapid pace due to the twin processes of globalisation and development and is now considered the leading cause of death globally.[1] Patient safety meanwhile has, until recently, mainly focused on health care in clinical settings and not considered the importance of working upstream in health systems to prevent ill health or considered the need to tackle the broader, structural determinants of health. The World Health Organisation (WHO), however, has now taken the lead in arguing for the need to tackle health problems upstream through a health systems perspective with more of a focus on primary health care systems, communities and context.[2] This chapter uniquely progresses this approach through a case study of the Pacific region and contends that there is a need to understand and tackle the drivers of NCDs through an international development perspective.

The island states of the Pacific region have some of the world's highest rates of hypertension, cardiovascular disease, obesity and Type 1 and 2 diabetes.[3] Whilst this is an issue that has long been recognised by regional governments and overseas donor agencies, there has been relatively slow progress in tackling these health problems. In terms of patient safety regimes, this is partly because the context and drivers underpinning these trends are a complex mix of not only lifestyle choices but also lifestyle options. Shifting patterns of agriculture and diet are partly the result of changes to the physical environment, particularly among the low-lying atoll nations such as Kiribati and Tuvalu, which are facing challenging climatic conditions and related rise in sea level. This has resulted in a marked shift away from traditional practices of food production and consumption. Increased reliance on imported foodstuffs has tended to be dominated by processed foods with high levels of fat, sugar and salt. In addition, internal migration and urban drift from outer islands to capital islands has led to

1 *The Lancet*, 'Global Burden of Disease Study', *The Lancet*, 2017, vol. 390, 10100:1083–463.

2 WHO, *Patient safety: making health care safer*, World Health Organisation 2017.

3 J. Parry, 'Pacific Islanders pay heavy price for abandoning traditional diet', *Bulletin of the World Health Organization* July 2010, 88(7):481–560.

increased levels of population density, adding to pressure on cultivatable land. Other health-related factors include incidences of inadequate sanitation and more general inabilities of national governments to be able to provide suitable health and welfare infrastructure for their growing populations.

Improving patient safety in the Pacific region can be informed by initiatives from other parts of the world. For example, Jennifer Sancho has drawn on empirical data from the small island states of the Caribbean region to indicate how lessons learned there might be applied to Pacific islands facing similar patient safety challenges.[4] More broadly, the WHO has developed a Patient Safety Framework with a focus on Africa that can be referred to here in relation to the islands of the Pacific region.[5] This framework approach will be used here to assess the extent to which Kiribati and Tuvalu are facing the challenges of an increasing prevalence of NCDs and other aspects of developing an effective patient safety regime. Recognising that many developing countries face a shortage of medical technologies and appropriately trained clinicians, the WHO framework model places an emphasis on development partnerships. As with most partnerships this tends to be relatively asymmetrical and driven by the more dominant donor partners of the industrialised world. This raises some questions in relation to the dynamics of such relationships, and the broader context of international trade and other forms of power. This analysis will consider the implications of such a dynamic, especially when many of the patient safety issues and concerns under consideration here can be linked to underlying international patterns and structures that have actively disadvantaged these island communities.

WHO's Patient Safety Framework has three key target actions: 1) to strengthen health support systems and patient safety; 2) to build patient safety capacity and 3) to advocate and communicate for patient safety. To take these actions forward the framework consists of six steps. Beginning with the above partnership development, this is followed by a needs assessment, gap analysis, action planning, action and finally evaluation and review.

Mainstream media sources from outside of the Pacific region have largely focused on the environmental threats of sea-level rise and the potential consequences of complete inundation and the prospect of whole populations needing to migrate. Whilst this remains a real possibility for some of the more at risk communities in the region the immediate concern for Pacific islanders is to deal with their day-to-day experiences. The dominant narrative discourse on living on these islands has been variously described in terms of 'vulnerability', 'resilience' and now almost exclusively with regard to 'adaptation' to the apparent inevitability of climate change-induced challenges. From a patient safety perspective, health concerns need to be viewed as multi-faceted and with many inter-related factors coming into play. The political economy of health involves numerous stakeholders and influencing variables. These range from the environmental issues

4 J. Sancho, 'Health reform in Trinidad and Tobago: lessons for the Pacific islands?' *Pacific Health Dialog* 1997, 4(1):130–7.

5 World Health Organisation, *The African Partnerships for Patient Safety Framework*, Geneva: WHO, 2012.

mentioned above through to individual patterns of behaviour via local, national and international actors – both public and private. In this chapter, patient safety will be looked at in its broadest sense. Meaning the whole population of the territories under consideration will be addressed, with awareness that for NCDs there are preventative measures that can be promoted. Ideally, future generations will be protected from becoming patients in need of treatment for NCDs.

Current policies to address patient safety among Pacific island communities are largely focused on the health of individuals, with a key aspect of this being attempts to address the lifestyle issues that have been linked to very high levels of NCDs in the region. This is seen as a priority area for both Pacific island governments and also, crucially in terms of the funding of projects, international donor agencies. Individual patterns of behaviour are certainly one of the key elements of patient safety. However, lifestyle choices can only be fully understood and addressed if a more holistic assessment is made to put these choices in the context of the options available to individuals and communities.

Options and choices

In most industrialised nations, medical literature and media coverage of NCDs has tended to focus on the lifestyle choices and behaviour of individuals.[6] While this is undoubtedly a significant contributing factor in relation to the incidence of NCDs it is only one aspect of this issue. For some individuals and their wider communities the type of behaviour and the lifestyle choices open to them can be severely restricted. In the Pacific region, the communities inhabiting low-lying atolls have experienced a major transition from predominantly, and relatively isolated, subsistence economies to ones that are increasingly connected to, and dependent upon, external relations.

The island communities under consideration here have their own unique characteristics, but also share a very high incidence of NCDs. Both of these territories have experienced health and environmental transitions whereby, despite easier access to advanced medical information and practices, there are growing concerns around food and water insecurity and the impacts this has on opportunities to follow a healthy diet. Historically these island communities have always experienced periods of 'feast and famine' due to localised impacts such as droughts or crop damage caused by tropical storms. However, with greater connectivity and interaction with other territories the availability of some sort of food supply is now reasonably constant, apart from in the immediate aftermath of particularly devastating extreme weather events. What is now of more concern is the quality of imported foodstuffs. These, usually processed, foods feed into the obesity and diabetes crises experienced by these communities.[7] Some degree of personal responsibility has to

6 World Economic Forum, *Human-centric health: behaviour change and the prevention of non-communicable diseases*, Geneva: WEF, 2017.

7 A. M. Thow, 'Trade and nutrition transition: strengthening policy for health in the Pacific', *Ecology of Food and Nutrition* 2013, 50(1):18–42.

be allowed for in terms of what amount of such foods, and carbonated drinks with very high sugar content, are consumed. Yet it would be a distortion of this situation, and therefore how to respond, if the broader context of these actions was not taken into account.

Many factors lead to the creation of food and water insecurity in these communities. Importantly it should be noted that in some of the outer islands of these territories the situation is very different with many people on these islands living much more 'traditional' lifestyles closer to subsistence, albeit with occasional but regular contact with the main, capital islands. The popular perception of Pacific islands is often one of relatively sparsely populated communities living some sort of idyllic Paradise existence. There are a small number of examples where there remains a relatively close proximity to this stereotype. However, for Kiribati and Tuvalu this is not the norm. Urban drift has meant that in each of these territories at least half of the overall population now live on their main, capital islands. In terms of population, density areas such as South Tarawa in Kiribati has one of the highest numbers of people per square kilometre in the world.[8] These countries' main islands are the seats of government, which is the largest employer in each of these territories. They also tend to be where the head offices of any private sector companies are based, plus the offices of overseas donor agencies. These capital islands also benefit from the highest level of investment in infrastructure and related services, including health services. This level of population pressure means that there is a corresponding loss in cultivatable land on these islands. Some households do still maintain small plots of land to grow vegetables, and rear chickens and possibly pigs. Yet these methods of food production represent only a relatively small proportion of the regular household diet. Imported foodstuffs are bought in what are increasingly cash-based economies. This has implications for what type and quality of food individuals and families can afford to buy, with healthier options often being more expensive. Even where islanders are trying to maintain local food production this is not always possible due to rising sea levels, storm surges and the loss of freshwater resources.

The topography of these low-lying atolls means that they are subject to frequent flooding and seawater permeating through the base rock with saltwater intrusion and the salination of freshwater lenses.[9] This has implications for the traditional methods of root crop production, such as taro pits. Once saltwater enters and remains in these pits the crops begin to rot rather than reach maturity. Coastal erosion is also a problem when this undercuts the roots of coconut and pandanus trees, further depleting traditional sources of food. Under such circumstances, the shift to more 'Western' diets is understandable, given the significant decline in previous alternatives. This raises the question of where agency, and therefore responsibility, lies with regard to addressing and reversing current trends of increasing prevalence and related consequences of NCDs in these communities.

8 United Nations Population Fund, *Population and development profiles: Pacific island countries*, UNFPA, Pacific Sub-regional Office, Suva, 2014.

9 C. Woodroffe, 'Reef-island topography and the vulnerability of atolls to sea-level rise', *Global and Planetary Change* 2008, 62:77–96.

Agency and responsibility

As mentioned above, individuals do have some level of personal responsibility to minimise unhealthy patterns of behaviour and make the most of what health promotion initiatives are available to them. Yet with limited options on offer, this has to be taken into account when judging the choices individuals make. This leads to questioning where broader responsibility at the national, regional and even international level might lie. In the first instance, the Ministry of Health for each national jurisdiction has a degree of responsibility for the health and well-being of their territory's citizens. In the context of the Pacific region, the extent of the NCD crisis has been acknowledged for some time with numerous national initiatives and the raising of this issue at the regional level. In June 2011, Pacific Ministers of Health met in Honiara, Solomon Islands and issued a communique highlighting the need for NCDs to be addressed as a priority issue. This initiative was reinforced at the 42nd meeting of the leaders of the Pacific Island Forum, held in Auckland, New Zealand shortly thereafter. Tackling NCDs was also one of the key issues discussed at the UN Conference on Small Island Developing States held in Apia, Samoa in 2014.[10] In June 2016 Tonga hosted a Pacific NCD summit meeting.[11] This was a high-level event with a welcome by the King of Tonga and a keynote address from Helen Clark, Administrator of the UN Development Programme and former Prime Minister of New Zealand. Such events illustrate how NCDs are now firmly established as a standing agenda item for Pacific governments and related donor agencies, as are the negative impacts of climate change. However, few reports and communiques from these meetings are explicit in making the connections between human-induced climate change, food security and patient safety.

In 2011, the Asian Development Bank (ADB), one of the major financial investors in the region, produced a report on food security and climate change in the Pacific.[12] The tone of this report was, understandably given it was produced by the ADB, predominantly focused on the economic consequences of climate change, although social and environmental factors were noted. Changing patterns in Pacific diets were highlighted. Fresh fish being replaced by canned fish and corned beef; root crops, breadfruit and bananas replaced by white rice, bread and instant noodles; and water and coconut water replaced by sweetened soft drinks. In terms of preparation, where food has traditionally been eaten raw, grilled or baked in an earth oven it is now often fried. The nutritional consequences of these changes in diet have had implications for the health of individuals, but there are also negative impacts on national economies. NCDs are highlighted as accounting for three quarters of all deaths across the Pacific region and 40–60% of total healthcare expenditure. Whilst not explicitly discussing the issue of personal responsibility

10 www.sids2014.org.

11 Secretariat of the Pacific Community, Pacific NCD Summit: translating global and regional commitments into local action, SPC, Noumea, 2016.

12 Asian Development Bank, *Food security and climate change in the Pacific: rethinking the options*, Manila: ADB, 2011.

there is an interesting aspect to the ADB's report, and numerous similar considerations of the causes of and responses to NCDs in the Pacific region. For the ADB, and many other external institutions engaging with the region, their focus tends to be more on local events and, therefore, localised remedies. By highlighting the behaviour of individuals the implicit assumption is what is required is behavioural change to address the identified problem with this behaviour. There is an internal logic to this assessment and diagnosis. It does not deny the role of national governments and Ministries of Health in having some degree of responsibility towards promoting and maintaining certain levels of public health. However, in terms of agency, the emphasis on individual behaviour suggests that individuals are predominantly responsible for the health of themselves and their dependants.

The WHO has produced a Global Action Plan for the Prevention and Control of NCDs.[13] This provided a model for a Western Pacific Regional Action Plan.[14] In line with the ADB report, both of these plans focus on individual behaviour, and from a largely economic perspective. The first table in the Western Pacific plan is entitled 'Very cost-effective interventions for the prevention and control of NCDs'. In this plan, cost-effectiveness is defined as generating 'an extra year of healthy life for a cost that falls below the average annual income or gross domestic product per person'. As an economic indicator, this cost can be highly variable as national economies may perform much better in one financial year compared to another. For the small island developing states considered here, they have relatively low GDP per capita. World Bank data for 2016 show this as USD 3,083 for Tuvalu and only USD 1,449 for Kiribati. Interestingly, the desired result of a 'healthy life' is not explicitly linked to GDP per capita in terms of whether this person would still be making an economic contribution to the national economy. The emphasis appears to be more on avoiding the health-related costs associated with NCDs. This table is also notable when looking at the 'Risk factor / disease' categories. None of them considers the broader risks associated with climate change, unequal trade relations et cetera.

The risk factors in the above action plan include: tobacco use; harmful use of alcohol; unhealthy diet; physical inactivity; cancer; cardiovascular diseases and diabetes. Each factor is linked to a range of policy options and potential interventions. The majority are aimed at altering individual behaviour, again placing the emphasis on the choices people make rather than the options available to them. Tobacco use interventions focus on health education campaigns; banning tobacco advertising, promotion and sponsorship; increasing excise taxes on tobacco products to make them less financially attractive and legislating to introduce smoke-free environments in indoor workplaces, public places and on public transport. Arguably some of these do focus on the context within which the decision to use tobacco products is taken, but the emphasis remains on

13 World Health Organisation, *Global Action Plan for the Prevention and Control of Non-communicable Diseases (2013–2020)*, Geneva: WHO, 2013.

14 World Health Organization, Western Pacific Region, *Western Pacific Regional Action Plan for the Prevention and Control of Non-communicable Diseases (2014–2020)*, WHOWPR, 2014.

altering individual patterns of behaviour. Similarly, the recommendations for tacking the harmful use of alcohol emphasise pricing policies to make alcoholic beverage increasingly expensive to purchase. This approach, as with taxation on tobacco products, also has the added benefit of contributing to the national exchequer. Should they choose to, governments could ring-fence such revenue to be directed towards the provision of health services. If this were publicised it would have the combined benefits of raising both revenue and awareness of the negative consequences of excessive smoking and drinking.

Physical activity is simply addressed in terms of implementing public awareness campaigns. Whilst such initiatives are always to be welcomed they, again, often fail to address broader issues that have led to many islanders undertaking less strenuous activities than older generations. Subsistence lifestyles in Pacific island environments involve high levels of physical activity. Taro pits have to be dug, coconut trees are climbed, but canoes that were once paddled have often been replaced by boats with outboard motors. To recommend islanders visit their local gymnasium, should such a facility be available to them, overlooks the underlying causes of increased morbidity. There appears to be a missed opportunity here to both increase physical activity and return to more traditional methods of fishing and crop cultivation. Should such initiatives be undertaken this would clearly also have a positive impact on health, as it would encourage the return to a pre-Western-influenced diet. Changing land use because of colonial influence in the Pacific region has had far-reaching socio-economic and cultural impacts. McLennan and Ulijaszek highlight the ongoing significance that changes introduced by the British, French and other colonisers continue to have on contemporary Pacific island communities.[15] While GDP per capita increased during the colonial period as more economic value was extracted from these territories, via activities such as mining or the production of copra, most of this wealth went overseas with little residual benefit for the local inhabitants. On the contrary, as their environment was often degraded and patterns of land use moved away from locally focused subsistence activities, islanders began the process of reduced physical activity combined with increased reliance on the imported foodstuffs noted above. Health education activities will perhaps inevitably focus on encouraging individuals to undertake more physical activity. However, a more holistic, and therefore more inclusive and effective, approach should locate such activity within a much broader socio-economic and cultural context.

Individuals, communities and context

A deeper analysis of patient safety and health transition in these communities demonstrates that behavioural change, or the inability to do so, needs to be understood in relation to a myriad of complex factors and their interrelations. Whereas Western, industrialised societies tend to place a greater

15 A. McLennan and S. J. Ulijaszek, 'Obesity emergence in the Pacific islands: why understanding colonial history and social change is important', *Public Health Nutrition*, 2015, 18(8):1499–505.

emphasis on individualism, most Pacific island societies place greater emphasis on communal relationships and activities. Even with increased urbanisation and changes in traditional village life the cultural bonds, norms and values often continue to endure. For example, communal feasting and other attitudes towards food extend well beyond the nutritional value of what foodstuffs are on offer. There can be cultural significance in how much a community member contributes to a shared meal. The nutritional quality of what is provided is less of an issue than how far it can be shared among the group. Even if an individual knows that the food on offer will be low in nutrition but high in calories this has to be balanced against the social expectation of eating a reasonably large portion, or several portions, of what is being offered. Roger Haden has written about Pacific eating habits.[16] Although predominantly a recipe book that tries to highlight the more traditional ingredients of Pacific island meals, he also provides some cultural context explaining how these communal meals represent far more than the consumption of food. Traditional food preparation, including the catching of fish or the preparing of earth ovens, has been a communal activity. This also reinforced gendered roles and other forms of communal identity. Moving away from such communal activities has led to some elements of stress and strain within these communities. This is particularly evident in the urban areas where traditional patterns of land tenure and usage have been disrupted.

Any individuals and communities undergoing significant transitions will face challenges of adjustment and adaptation. Health transitions are influenced and informed by socio-economic and cultural considerations. In the case of the low-lying atolls of the Pacific region, these pressures are compounded by the potentially existential threat of mass relocation. Although not commonly considered in the context of mainstream approaches to NCDs the uncertainty and related stress associated with potential relocation is an under-researched field of study. Stress factors can lead to increased consumption of unhealthy foodstuffs, alcohol and tobacco. These are all key ingredients for the likelihood of contracting some form of NCD. In this respect, it is surprising that the Regional Action Plan for Prevention and Control of NCDs does not list stress and related behaviours as a major risk factor. Other studies have looked at the notable rise in mental disorders in the Pacific region. In a study published in 2015 Charlson, Diminic and Whiteford state that 'Major depressive disorder (MDD) is now responsible for the largest proportion of disability in the Pacific region'.[17] They also cite research from Australia and the UK which indicates that 'men with mental disorders die, on average, 15 years earlier than the general population; women with mental disorders die, on average, 12 years earlier, commonly as a result of suicide or co-morbid physical health conditions'. The health conditions referred to here will almost certainly be linked to some form of NCDs. Clearly not all Pacific islanders will necessarily suffer from

16 R. Haden, *Food culture in the Pacific islands*, Westport: Greenwood, 2009.

17 F. J. Charlson, S. Dininic, and H. A. Whiteford, 'The rising tide of mental disorders in the Pacific region: forecasts of disease burden and service requirements from 2010 to 2050', *Asia and Pacific Policy Studies* 2015, 2(2):280–92.

mental disorders because of changing socio-economic and cultural pressures. However, this is likely to be a contributing factor to some islanders adopting unhealthy lifestyles.

The importance of community affiliation and identity formation is particularly strong in Pacific island states. Arguably, similar dynamics of communalism exist around the world, but there are some particular aspects of life in Pacific island locations and societies that make such bonds all the more important. Historically, the low-lying atoll states of the Pacific region have been relatively isolated from the rest of the world. Even today, with generally reliable access to telecommunication networks, the physical distance from other states, the time taken and cost of travelling overseas and the generally homogenous nature of most of the societies under consideration here means that most residents continue to have a strong sense of their identity linked to their home territory. This identification with location is an issue not only in terms of national identity but also at the sub-national level. Most Pacific island states do not consist of a single island. More commonly, they are a collection of islands and atolls spread over large areas of the ocean. For example, someone from the island of Abaiang in Kiribati may still strongly identify themselves with their home island, even when they have been resident in the main island of Tarawa for many years. In some case people born on the main island may identify with their outer island heritage, especially if they have visited members of their extended family that still live in the outer islands. Familial heritage ties remain strong, and often associated with very specific land areas, despite increased internal relocation and overseas migration. Some individuals adjust and cope with relocation better than others do. This may partly be explained in terms of individual psychology and the extent to which relocation or migration was their preferred choice.

The movement of people is as old as the evolution of Homo sapiens. Pacific islanders have been referred to as the 'nomads' of the Pacific with a history of ocean-sailing vessels covering great distances between islands. The dominant narrative of these territories being seen as small island states can be challenged if they are thought of more as large oceanic states. That said, in the colonial and post-colonial era the focus has shifted more towards land-based issues. Sailing between islands for trading and cultural purposes has reduced dramatically as each of the island states, which are often colonial constructs in terms of their international boundaries, are now tied into a much more extensive web of international patterns of trade. Even fishing, which has been a central feature of island life for many generations, has now been appropriated by external forces. While fishing revenue still accounts for a significant proportion of export earnings for many Pacific island states, they have limited capacity for deep-water fishing and most of this fishing is undertaken under licence by fleets from other states. As such, the island economies only see a very small percentage of the true value of their fish stocks. Such patterns of investment/exploitation by external actors illustrate the dilemma that many so-called 'developing' economies face. To what extent are these communities better off for engaging with the outside world? The increased incidence of NCDs is, if not entirely, predominantly associated with the introduction of external products and patterns of behaviour.

The dependency dilemma

World system theory and other dependency approaches to international development, as pioneered by authors such as Wallerstein and Frank, consider the cost and benefits of less powerful states engaging with the more powerful core economies.[18] Given the contrast between the relatively contained, subsistence lifestyles of pre-colonial Pacific island communities and the contemporary external influences that now permeate, at least, the main urban centres of these islands, they are useful barometers for testing this hypothesis. Some benefits are readily identifiable, including in the healthcare sector. Immunisation programmes and various forms of technology transfer have undoubtedly saved and prolonged lives. Advances in telecommunications have enabled remote diagnosis and treatment and a range of e-health initiatives.[19] Yet, as already made clear when it comes to the prevalence and control of NCDs in these communities, the vast majority of products and associated behaviours that lead to NCDs have been introduced from outside of the region. This epitomises the dependency dilemma whereby individuals and communities wish to engage with the benefits of interconnectivity with the wider world, but also have to be aware and mindful of the potentially negative consequences of such contact.

Theoretically, Tuvalu and Kiribati are both fully independent political entities with sovereign control over clearly defined land and exclusive economic zones of maritime territory. They all have legal control of large-scale fisheries and potentially valuable seabed resources. Yet they are also among the most aid dependent nations. The World Bank reports that the Pacific islands receive significantly more overseas development assistance (ODA) than other regions of the world. Sub-Saharan Africa is often assumed to receive the bulk of such assistance, but in per capita terms, this region receives only USD 54, compared to USD 64 for the Caribbean and USD 469 for the Pacific islands region.[20] In part, this disparity can be explained by the practicalities and cost-effectiveness of aiding a relatively small population spread over a large area, albeit with some very dense concentrations of people on the capital islands. The nature of the aid also varies across regions with Sub-Saharan Africa's large land area requiring investment in large-scale road and rail infrastructure. Pacific islands do have some infrastructure needs in terms of maintenance of runways, port facilities and inter-island ferries, but not on the same scale as Africa. The focus in the Pacific is more on individual-orientated

18 I. Wallerstein, *The capitalist world-economy*, Cambridge: Cambridge University Press, 1979; A. G. Frank, *Dependent accumulation and underdevelopment*, London: Macmillan, 1978.

19 Y. Ishibashi, H. Juzoji, T. Kitano and I. Nakajima, 'ITU e-health training program for Pacific island community with the support of the Sasakawa Peace Foundation', *Journal of Medical Systems*, 2011, 35(3):345–51.

20 C. Wilson, 'Pacific nations need help away from aid', *Inter Press Service News Agency*, Sydney, 29 January, 2014.

aid, such as promoting health and education. This is commendable, but given the ongoing rise in NCDs, this does raise the question of how effective this approach is. As a health initiative, there are elements of both curative and preventative approaches. In extreme cases of advanced diabetes toe, foot or lower leg amputations may be required. As an operative procedure, this is not something that could be satisfactorily undertaken in the remote outer islands that lack the required surgical facilities. In terms of dependency, it is clearly more beneficial for the individuals involved that their home governments have good relations with neighbouring states that can provide such facilities, albeit at a cost. Yet it would be far better if such conditions did not develop in the first instance, or if the signs of them were detected and addressed at an earlier stage. Donor countries are now investing more heavily in health education campaigns in an attempt to focus on preventative measures. However, this still often fails to address the underlying issues which, regardless of how much information is available, remain at the root cause of many incidences of NCDs.

A study by Tin et al. published in 2013 investigated the experience of a sample of Pacific islanders who had diabetes-related amputations and attempted to discover what earlier interventions could have prevented these procedures.[21] This is included in the dependency section as the results highlight both important aspects of the nature of the NCDs crisis and the fact that, once again, it is external actors who are driving this research agenda. In this group of respondents, the average length of time between being diagnosed with diabetes and eventual amputation was 10.5 years. The main reason for the eventual need for surgery was a delay in seeking treatment. One of the questions asked was how much information these patients had about foot care with only 11% saying they had insufficient knowledge about foot care. Increasing such knowledge from close to 80% to even higher than this should be an aspiration, but this suggests that health education programmes may not be a priority issue. People are generally aware of the dangers of a poor diet and consuming soft drinks with high sugar content, as they also appreciate the ill-effects of smoking and excessive drinking. The findings on delay in treatment is difficult to interpret as it is not completely clear if this means the respondents would have sought treatment had it been available, or if they simply failed to take advantage of what treatment was available to them. Whatever the answer it is apparent that treatment centres do need to be accessible and individuals with early diagnosis of diabetes should be taking up the treatment services available to them.

Dependency theory is relevant to NCDs in the Pacific region not so much in terms of the level of healthcare available via ODA and technology transfer, but by the way in which other forms of dependency limit and restrict islanders' options to adopt healthy lifestyles. As 'peripheral' economies, they are engaged in unequal and disadvantaging trade relations. Arguably, some export revenue is

21 S. T. W. Tin, E. Gadabu, G. Iro, J. Tasserei, and G. Colagiuri, 'Diabetes-related amputations in Pacific island countries: a root cause analysis of precipitating events', *Diabetes Research and Clinical Practice* 2013, 13(2):230–4.

better than no export revenue, but it should be recognised that little of the true value of their resources, notably their fish stocks, finds its way into these nations' coffers. This, in turn, has implications for the ability of these governments to provide adequate health care and tackle the many factors noted above that influence Pacific islanders' behaviour in relation to adopting the healthiest lifestyles available to them. Having provided a broader theoretical and empirical context this analysis now focuses more closely on what is actually happening at the local level within each of these communities.

Patient safety in Kiribati

Responsibility for healthcare provision in Kiribati lies with the Ministry of Health and Medical Services.[22] The structure of this Ministry is divided between three key areas – Hospital (Curative) Services, Public Health Services and Nursing Services. Patient safety policies in Kiribati, as with many health services worldwide, tend to commit more resources to the curative rather than the preventative. This is not to say that preventative initiatives do not take place, such as campaigns based around No Tobacco Day or reducing intake of alcohol, but the highest rates of expenditure are geared towards the treatment of individuals once they are diagnosed with an illness or disease and are regarded as 'a patient'. Life expectancy in Kiribati is approximately 60 and it has the highest under-5 mortality rate in the Pacific region. The leading causes of death are acute respiratory infections, wounds and sores, diarrhoeal diseases, cardiovascular disease and liver disease.[23]

A key aspect of patient safety is the level of treatment that the government can provide. Recalling the WHO framework model, a needs assessment and gap analysis for Kiribati demonstrates an inadequate level of provision of trained clinicians. Nursing Services provide basic nurse training. This is a three-year programme with an intake of 25–30 students each year. Even assuming all of these students successfully complete their training this level of investment is not keeping pace with the growth in demand for qualified clinicians. Beyond this basic level of training further qualifications can be gained as either a hospital nurse or public health nurse. More specialist health training for I-Kiribati is available overseas and can be supported by international donors, usually Australia or New Zealand. As a proportion of a limited overseas aid budget, the numbers of such training scholarships are very small. It is more likely that trained medical staff from overseas will visit Kiribati for a temporary period. Whilst the majority of these are likely to originate from the main donor countries of Australia and New Zealand some have also come from other countries further afield, such as Cuba.

In terms of medical infrastructure Kiribati faces significant practical difficulties associated with its geography and the inability to provide adequate patient safety measures across the whole of a very spread out and diverse territory. Understandably, the key medical facilities are located in the main urban area of

22 See generally, www.health.gov.ki

23 http://savekiribati.com/health.php.

the main island of Tarawa. There are four hospitals, the largest of which, the Tungaru Central Hospital, has 120 bed spaces. This is where any visiting specialist medical practitioners would be based. The next largest hospital, the Southern Kiribati Hospital, has a capacity of only 40 beds. In the outer islands, there are a number of health centres with some qualified clinicians although, for anything more serious than minor illness or injuries, patients would need to be referred and transported to one of the main facilities. In this regard, patient safety is monitored and responded to in a centralised, top-down manner with the Ministry of Health coordinating national strategies and priorities. This demonstrates a certain level of bureaucratic and administrative competence but, at least in relation to NCDs, does not explain why their incidence continues to increase. To fully understand this situation a more holistic analysis is required looking at individual behaviours and the socio-economic and cultural contexts within which these take place.

Patient safety in Tuvalu

Tuvalu operates a similar patient safety regime to Kiribati, only on a much smaller scale. There is only one hospital, the Princess Margaret Hospital, based on the main island of Funafuti. In addition there are a further eight medical centres based on the outer islands. Nurses, rather than fully qualified doctors, staff these centres. Despite the relative shortage of trained clinicians, qualified health staff attend 98% of births and the same percentage of one-year olds are part of an immunisation programme. Although almost all of the population are using a treated water supply, only 83% have access to adequate sanitation facilities.[24] Tuvalu's Department of Pharmacy also trains nurses in the correct ordering and administration of required drugs and medicines. With a population of only approximately 10,000, compared with Kiribati's 100,000, there are fewer practical constraints to achieving close to universal patient safety and general healthcare provision. That said, the government of Tuvalu, and related donor agencies, are still facing an ongoing increase in the incidence of NCDs.

The current Strategic Health Plan for Tuvalu runs from 2009 to 2018.[25] This plan identifies a number of outcomes, strategies and performance indicators. A key focus of this plan is health administration in relation to patient safety. In particular, the plan questions the efficiency of the Tuvalu Medical Treatment Scheme, especially in relation to the high cost of referral rates for overseas treatment. Although much of this treatment is paid for as part of New Zealand's ODA to Tuvalu, the plan notes that such costs are a considerable drain on this budget and diverts funding from other potential development projects. The plan also notes that funding is, as with Kiribati, geared more towards curative treatments rather than more cost-effective preventative projects. As a patient safety issue, and in relation to how governments tend to operate, it is understandable that there will be a more immediate focus on those issues that present themselves

24 www.commonwealthhealth.org, 2017

25 Government of Tuvalu, *Strategic Health Plan, 2009–2018*, Ministry of Health, 2009.

in terms of medical referrals and requests for curative treatment. Longer-term planning clearly exists in relation to major infrastructure projects, such as the development of ports or transport networks. But when it comes to preventative healthcare, especially when associated with types of behaviour where individuals are seen as having at least some degree of control, such initiatives appear to be given less priority.

The focus of Tuvalu's Strategic Health Plan in relation to patient safety includes some aspects of institutional development with regard to attempting to ensure appropriate policies and monitoring procedures are in place, and adequately funded. However, in relation to NCDs the focus remains largely on attempting to change individual patterns of behaviour. As noted above though many of the lifestyle behaviours adopted are drawn from a relatively limited set of options. This is particularly the case when considering diets. This illustrates a key difficulty for both Kiribati and Tuvalu as they attempt to promote patient safety policies. Both governments have clearly defined health strategies designed to tackle NCDs and other healthcare issues. Yet the level of NCDs and related healthcare costs continues to rise. In part this is due to the, albeit understandable, focus on curative rather than preventative measures. Underlying this though are socio-economic, environmental and cultural issues that work against health promotion initiatives. It is only by taking a broader, more holistic view of the context within which individual behaviour is determined that greater progress in this area of healthcare is likely to take place.

Conclusion

The patient safety regimes in the Pacific islands considered here have been broadly understood to include preventative measures that aim to avoid islanders needing to become patients requiring NCD treatment. There has also been a recognition that the currently unhealthy behaviour patterns leading to an increase in NCDs needs to be placed within the context of seeing that some of the unhealthy choices being made are largely determined by the inaccessibility of healthier choices. In particular, this relates to the shift away from traditional forms of food production and the physical activities associated with such practices.

The regional and broader international community plays a significant role in how patient safety with regard to NCDs are experienced in the Pacific region. There are some significant positives in terms of the acknowledgement of NCDs as a crisis reaching epidemic proportions. The Regional Action Plan cited above does go some way towards addressing this problem. Donor agencies are also active in supporting initiatives to combat the rise and spread of NCDs. Yet, there are also more negative aspects of international relations that have had, and continue to have, negative impacts on these territories. Post-colonial attitudes and relations, notably with regard to patterns of trade, disadvantage these communities. The greenhouse gas emissions produced by the industrialised nations are contributing to the climate change and sea-level rise that is having a direct impact on the Pacific island nations maintaining food security. The narrative discourse of climate change negotiations highlights adaptation rather than mitigation. This suggests that the dominant international powers are placing less of a priority on cutting their emissions and more on expecting the communities suffering the greatest negative impacts from climate change to adapt to 'inevitable' sea-level rise and its consequences.

Preventing and controlling NCDs is a leading aspect of promoting patient safety in the Pacific region, and a growing issue worldwide. Most of the initiatives to date have tended to focus on challenging and altering individual patterns of behaviour. This analysis acknowledges that unhealthy behaviour does need to be addressed. However, it is also crucial that the choices individuals make are often made in the face of limited options that are available to them. Some of these options can be influenced at the local level, but very many are subject to broader, systemic factors in the global political economy. Without an awareness and acknowledgement of this point, any initiatives that only focus on individual choices, without considering the range of options from which these choices are made, are unlikely to tackle the ongoing spread of NCDs in the Pacific region and elsewhere.

References

Asian Development Bank, *Food Security and Climate Change in the Pacific: Rethinking the Options*, Manila: ADB, 2011.

Charlson, F. J., Dininic, S. and Whiteford, H. A., 'The rising tide of mental disorders in the Pacific region: forecasts of disease burden and service requirements from 2010 to 2050', *Asia and Pacific Policy Studies*, 2015, 2(2):280–92.

Frank, A. G., *Dependent accumulation and underdevelopment*, London: Macmillan, 1978.

Government of Tuvalu, *Strategic Health Plan, 2009–2018*, Ministry of Health, 2009.

Haden, R., *Food culture in the Pacific islands*, Westport: Greenwood, 2009.

Ishibashi, Y., Juzoji, H., Kitano, T. and Nakajima, I., 'ITU e-health training program for Pacific island community with the support of the Sasakawa Peace Foundation', *Journal of Medical Systems* 2011, 35(3):345–51.

Lancet, The, 'Global Burden of Disease Study', *The Lancet*, 2017, 390, 10100:1083–463.

McLennan, A. and Ulijaszek, S. J., 'Obesity emergence in the Pacific islands: why understanding colonial history and social change is important', *Public Health Nutrition* 2015, 18(8):1499–505.

Parry, J., 'Pacific islanders pay heavy price for abandoning traditional diet', *Bulletin of the World Health Organization* 2010, 88(7):481–560.

Sancho, J., 'Health reform in Trinidad and Tobago: lessons for the Pacific Islands?' *Pacific Health Dialog* 1997, 4(1):130–7.

Secretariat of the Pacific Community, *Pacific NCD Summit: translating global and regional commitments into local action*, SPC, Noumea, 2016.

Thow, A. M. et al., 'Trade and nutrition transition: strengthening policy for health in the Pacific', *Ecology of Food and Nutrition* 2013, 50(1):18–42, 2013.

Tin, S. T. W., Gadabu, E., Iro, G., Tasserei, J. and Colagiuri, G., 'Diabetes-related amputations in Pacific island countries: a root cause analysis of precipitating events', *Diabetes Research and Clinical Practice* 2013, 13(2):230–4.

United Nations Population Fund, *Population and development profiles: Pacific island countries*, UNFPA, Pacific Sub-regional Office, Suva, 2014.

Wallerstein, I., *The capitalist world-economy*, Cambridge: Cambridge University Press, 1979.

Wilson, C., 'Pacific nations need help away from aid', *Inter Press Service News Agency*, Sydney, 29 January 2014.

Woodroffe, C., 'Reef-island topography and the vulnerability of atolls to sea-level rise', *Global and Planetary Change* 2008, 62:77–96.

World Economic Forum, *Human-centric health: behaviour change and the prevention of non-communicable diseases*, Geneva: WEF, 2017.

World Health Organisation, *The African partnerships for patient safety framework*, Geneva: WHO, 2012.

World Health Organisation, *Global action plan for the prevention and control of non-communicable diseases (2013–2020)*, Geneva: WHO, 2013.

World Health Organisation, Western Pacific Region, *Western Pacific Regional Action Plan for the Prevention and Control of Non-communicable Diseases (2014–2020)*, WHOWPR, 2014

WHO, *Patient safety: making health care safer*, World Health Organisation, 2017.

www.commonwealthhealth.org/pacific/tuvalu/health_systems_in_tuva/.

www.health.gov.ki.

http://savekiribati.com/health.php.

www.sids2014.org.

17 The Japanese Obstetric Compensation System for Cerebral Palsy – a case study of a no-fault compensation system

Shin Ushiro[1]

Introduction

The study group of the Ministry of Health, Labour and Welfare (MHLW), charged with investigating the education of junior paediatricians and obstetricians, was set up during 2002–2004 to address concerns surrounding balancing resources in the context of the burdens that stem from providing advanced treatments, emergency medicine and high-risk treatment. It studied the introduction of a new system that may be effective in achieving an appropriate balance between these competing variables. A no-fault compensation system was evaluated and proposed.

Introduced in 2009, the Japanese Obstetric Compensation System for Cerebral Palsy (JOCS-CP) provides investigation and prevention, and also monetary compensation on a no-fault basis. This initially was introduced in response to the growing concerns about the deterioration of perinatal care and low birth rate in Japanese society. Under strong political leadership, this system was launched by the Japanese Council for Quality Health Care (JQ) with the help of relevant scientific societies, experts, organisations, individuals and the government. The JQ has initiated such strategies as review, compensation, investigation and prevention that serve as major pillars of the JOCS-CP since the system was established. In appreciating the work and impact of the JOCS-CP, this chapter will provide an introduction to the background and development of a no-fault system which has earned a unique place in Japanese society and which provides potential guidance to other health care systems for improving patient safety.

The Japan Obstetric Compensation System for Cerebral Palsy

History of the system – conflict over cerebral palsy and compensation for patients

In 2004, the number of new medicine-related lawsuits was analysed by the Ministerial Study Panel: the highest frequency of such cases was for Obstetrics

1 i) Executive board member, Japan Council for Quality Health Care (JQ); ii) Professor and Director, Division of Patient Safety, Kyushu University Hospital.

and Gynaecology (OG). It has been assumed that the cases filed against OG comprise a significant share of cerebral palsy cases. Traditionally, the reasons for occurrence of cerebral palsy has been poorly understood. However, its existence can evoke conflict between family members and physicians. Most cerebral palsy cases are caused by factors outside of the control of the attending obstetricians and midwives. However, it is also true that there are cases caused by poor procedures that do not accord with the latest guidelines and standards.[2] It is, however, not easy to distinguish the former from the latter. Obstetricians and relevant experts have studied and explored the possibility of drawing up a no-fault compensation system that covers the whole of Japan to overturn the current situation, which is characterised by high frequency of conflict. The enthusiasm of Japanese obstetricians for the no-fault-based compensation system was also observed in a novel entitled *No-Fault* by the then Professor of Obstetrics and Gynaecology of University Hospital.[3] This described the risks Japanese obstetricians faced in terms of being exposed to conflicts, including lawsuits.

Establishment of the no-fault compensation system in Japan

The Japan Medical Association (JMA) has studied the potential of introducing a no-fault compensation system for cerebral palsy since the early 1970s. A report issued by the JMA in 1972 touched on the following three items to support development of the system:[4]

a) When medical errors take place, prompt compensation should be made in cases in which a physician turns out to be liable for the error;
b) a new national compensation scheme should be devised covering a case that is not attributable to medical intervention i.e. an error that inevitably occurs in clinical practice;
c) the new system should work independently from the pre-existing court system for settling disputes.

A response to recommendation (a) was almost immediate, with the launch of the JMA Physician's Liability Compensation System in 1973. However, an independent no-fault scheme was not implemented for almost three decades. By 2000, there were growing concerns about patient safety in OG, the reducing number of obstetricians and the falling birth rate in Japan. In 2006, the Policy Research Committee of the Liberal Democratic Party (LDP), a committee of leading

2 Japan Society of Obstetricians and Gynecologists (JSOG) and the Japanese Association of Obstetricians and Gynecologists (JAOG), 'Guidelines for Obstetrical Practice in Japan 2017', available only in Japanese.

3 Takashi Okai, 'No-fault', Tokyo: Hayakawa Shobo, 2007, available only in Japanese.

4 Committee on Legal Affairs, Japan Medical Association (JMA), 'Legal Proceeding of Medical Accident and the Relevant Theory', *The Journal of Japan Medical Association* 1972, 68(2):183–203.

politicians, produced a report that came to be known the 'LDP framework'.[5] It spelled out the significance of a no-fault compensation system specifically for cerebral palsy, stating that 'it is usually difficult to identify malpractice in an adverse event during delivery and those cases are apt to be contended in a court. Frequent dispute is one of the reasons for the shortage of obstetricians.'[6] It proposed to secure a safe and trustworthy perinatal care system that could benefit not only the obstetrician but also the patient and family. It suggested that the new system should (i) compensate the patient who developed an impairment possibly caused by an obstetric adverse event; (ii) settle conflicts at the earliest stage; and (iii) establish a system that could improve the quality of obstetric care, by investigating cerebral palsy cases.

Given their experience in developing patient safety interventions, the JQ set up the 'Division of Introductory Work on the Japan Obstetric Compensation System for Cerebral Palsy' in 2007. The committee members intensively argued over the practical issues for the launch of the system and eventually issued a report detailing the design of the system in January 2008. The JOCS-CP was subsequently launched on January 1, 2009.[7]

What does 'no-fault' mean in JOCS-CP?

There are multiple definitions of no-fault compensation. For example, the compensation system for drug side effects that has been carried out by the Pharmaceuticals and Medical Devices Agency (PMDA) has been described as no-fault compensation system because it compensates individuals who suffer drug side effects regardless of identifying negligence in medicine.[8] The premise of such a system is that the drug was likely to cause the adverse effect even if prescribed and administered in an appropriate way, in accordance with the accompanying drug information sheet. Concerning the JOCS-CP, the LDP framework stated that the JOCS-CP should compensate patients with cerebral palsy which has been caused by the circumstances of delivery, regardless of negligence by obstetricians. Therefore, cerebral palsy obviously caused by congenital reasons, e.g. major cerebral anomaly, rather than via the obstetric procedure are excluded from the eligibility criteria that could be deemed as premises of the system. Therefore, although there is a wide variety of definitions ascribed to no-fault compensation, it seems that any definition primarily shares the idea that compensation is provided regardless of identifying negligence.

5 Policy Research Committee, The Liberal Democratic Party, 'The framework of the no-fault compensation system in obstetric care', 23 Jan 2006. Accessory material of the 12th meeting (www.sanka-hp.jcqhc.or.jp/documents/committee/pdf/obstetrics_3.pdf); available only in Japanese.

6 Ibid.

7 Japan Council for Quality Health Care (JQ), 'Japan Obstetric Compensation System for Cerebral Palsy (JOCS-CP)' (www.sanka-hp.jcqhc.or.jp/index.html), available only in Japanese. See also 'Guide to The Japan Obstetric Compensation System for Cerebral Palsy', 2014. www.sanka-hp.jcqhc.or.jp/documents/english/bira_english_color_201407.pdf.

8 Pharmaceuticals and Medical Devices Agency (PMDA), 'Relief Services for Adverse Health Effects'. www.pmda.go.jp/english/index.html.

Overview of JOCS-CP

Compensation framework

There are two major pillars to the JOCS-CP, namely compensation and investigation/prevention (Fig.17.1).

Of these, the compensation pillar works with a mechanism of indemnity insurance provided by an alliance of indemnity insurance firms on business contract with JQ, as indicated in the 'The Framework of the No-fault Compensation System in Obstetric Care' (Fig. 17.2).[9]

Initially, a childbirth facility registers with the JOCS-CP. It then agrees in principle to compensation and investigation with pregnant women in case a baby develops profound cerebral palsy.[10] A premium is paid to the indemnity insurance firm through the JQ and this then pays the related lump sum to the indemnity insurance firm. In cases where a baby develops profound cerebral palsy, the case is reviewed by the Review Committee to see if it meets the eligibility criteria for compensation. If the case is approved, monetary compensation is provided from the childbirth facility. However, the compensation money is paid from the indemnity insurance firm directly to the patient/family. Approved patients receive a lump sum of approximately 6 million JPY. They are subsequently paid further compensation in 20 annual instalments of 1.2 million JPY. The monetary compensation in JOCS-CP is partly derived from a lump sum childbirth payment which is paid by the public health care insurance system.[11] This linkage between compensation and public health insurance reportedly gives the JOCS-CP system a quasi-public nature.

In 2009, 419 people were eligible for compensation.

Despite being a voluntary system, 99.9% of all childbirth facilities have registered with the JOCS-CP. It appears that this take-up rate has been strongly influenced by the commitment of professional and research councils for perinatal care, as well as the MHLW.

Framework of the expert review process for profound cerebral palsy

Along with the standard compensation agreement, a childbirth facility files a petition to JQ.[12] The documents for petition include the certification form of profound cerebral palsy diagnosed by a qualified physician. As scientific knowledge and expertise are necessary for the diagnosis, those who work on the certification

9 See JQ, guides, note 7.

10 Website of relevant information for registered facility in the JOCS-CP. www.sanka-hp.jcqhc.or.jp/organization/office.htm , available only in Japanese.

11 Ibid. As indicated in the LDP framework, the lump sum childbirth allowance was raised by the Ministry of Health, Labour and Welfare (MHLW) by the amount of insurance premium in response to the probable increase of the childbirth fee determined by the childbirth facility (2015: 16,000 JPY (265 USD or 225 EUR), 2009–2014: 30,000 JPY (140 USD or 120 EUR).

12 JQ, 'Proceedings for petition in the Japan Obstetric Compensation System for Cerebral Palsy (JOCS-CP)'. www.sanka-hp.jcqhc.or.jp/application/flow.html, available only in Japanese.

need to be a certified expert of the Japanese Society of Child Neurology and/or a registered physician, defined by Article 15 of the Act on Welfare of Physically Disabled Persons. These practitioners are registered with JOCS-CP and are identified on its website for the convenience of guardians of affected children.[13]

The petition is put forward for review in the relevant committee of the JQ to determine eligibility. The review process is fundamentally carried out on a documentary basis, with close reference to the 'General criteria' (Fig.17.3) and the 'Exclusion criteria' (Fig. 17.4).

In the case of approval, the result is authorised at the JQ's board meeting. The approval is conveyed to the family, followed by prompt payment of monetary compensation. Those who are not eligible could be approved on a case-by-case basis according to additional criteria (Figs.17.5–17.8). There is a deduction rule that the JOCS-CP does not allow a patient/family to receive compensation through the scheme in addition to damages awarded in legal proceedings. Therefore, the amount of any damages payment is deducted from the payment of JOCS-CP. Given that JOCS-CP compensation payments will always be larger than any possible damages award, this discourages patients from seeking legal remedies in court. This may have contributed to the reduction in the quantity of lawsuit cases related to cerebral palsy.

Of the 2,980 petitions filed, 2,233 cases have been approved by the Review Committee, whereas 740 cases were found not to be eligible according to the criteria of JOCS-CP. The reasons for non-eligibility are studied by the Steering Committee of the JOCS-CP. The major reasons for exclusion were demonstrated in Table 17.2. The most common features among non-eligible cases are those that did not meet case-by-case review criteria such as pH of umbilical arterial blood exceeding 7.1 and/or fetal heart rate not meeting the patterns indicating hypoxia during labour and delivery

All the cases approved for compensation in the Review Committee go on to the production of an Investigation Report. The investigative work of the JCOS-CP will now be explored.

Investigation of cerebral palsy

Compilation of Investigative Report

Investigation is one of the major pillars of JOCS-CP that aims to not only prevent cerebral palsy but also to mitigate conflict and bring it to an early settlement. To achieve these goals, an Investigative Report is delivered to both the childbirth facility and to the patient/family. This report is compiled through intensive scientific investigation, with sufficient data collected from the relevant childbirth facility and including the voice of the patient's family. During the years of taking preparatory

13 JQ, List of registered physician engaged in the diagnostic certification in the JOCS-CP. www.sanka-hp.jcqhc.or.jp/doctor/list.html, available only in Japanese. As of 2016, 518 practitioners are currently registered.

steps and the early years of operation of JOCS-CP, there were obstetricians who were aggressively opposed to delivering the Investigative Report as they believed that the report caused conflict and even lawsuits that had never happened in times before JOCS-CP. On the other hand, there were obstetricians and patient representatives who claimed that the reports generated by experts would meet the high expectations of guardians of children born with cerebral palsy, leading to the mitigation of conflict.

JQ has established seven sub-committees for producing the Investigative Report (Fig. 17.9).[14]

Cases approved in the Review Committee are allotted to each sub-committee for drafting such reports. Each committee yields approximately 400 reports annually. The membership of the sub-committee comprises of five obstetricians, including the Chair and four drafting members, two neonatologists, one midwife and two lawyers, including one who works on the physician's side and another who works on the family's side. Physicians and midwives principally work in the sub-committee from a medical point of view. Lawyers play a role in crafting a report in a standardised fashion with clear points of contention and in a manner that makes it easy for the patient/family to understand. The revised process for disclosure has been valid since November 2015. 1,606 reports have been produced by the committee. Anonymised report summaries are published on the JOCS-CP website and original copies can be requested from the JQ, following review by an ethics committee.[15]

The aim and the policy of Investigative Reports are included in the Investigative Manual as described below:

a) The investigative report does not aim at accusing someone but at elucidating the probable cause of profound cerebral palsy and to recommend ameliorating measures for preventing similar event.
b) The report should be easy for patient/parents, the citizens of Japan and lawyers to understand.
c) The investigation should be carried out taking not only data during delivery but wider contextual data, including history of diseases and terms of pregnancy.
d) Delivery procedure and management of pregnancy should be reviewed in terms of what was an appropriate procedure or management at the moment in which the event in question took place. Retrospective assessments should be avoided due to the negative influences of hindsight bias.
e) Ameliorating measures conducive to better perinatal care should be explored from the retrospective viewpoint.[16] Prospective and retrospective viewpoints should not be confused to avoid hindsight bias.

14 JQ, Investigative work of the Japan Obstetric Compensation System for Cerebral Palsy (JOCS-CP). www.sanka-hp.jcqhc.or.jp/outline/function.html, available only in Japanese.

15 JQ, 'Disclosure proceedings of the Investigative Report of the Japan Obstetric Compensation System for Cerebral Palsy (JOCS-CP). www.sanka-hp.jcqhc.or.jp/outline/disclosure.html, available only in Japanese.

16 JQ, 'Guidance to deal with questions from the guardians in investigational work'. www.sanka-hp.jcqhc.or.jp/documents/analysis_other/bunseki_approach_201604.pdf, available only in Japanese.

Preventability of cerebral palsy

Whether or not to include an assessment of the preventability of cerebral palsy was one of the most controversial issues faced by the Investigation Committee at its inception. There was a worry among obstetricians, as represented by the Chair of the committee, that the report might bring about conflicts, including lawsuits, if it stated that cerebral palsy could have been prevented in a specific case. Obstetricians were afraid of the report possibly accusing them of negligence contrary to the policy and aim of the investigation, despite claiming that it did not aim to accuse anyone, but was rather aimed at elucidating the probable cause of profound cerebral palsy and to recommend ameliorating measures for preventing similar events. On the other hand, some members of the committee, including patient representatives, claimed that the report should explore the possibility of avoidance of cerebral palsy to create preventative measures which are effective in real terms. Ultimately, the committee proposed that the policy on this issue was to be dealt with by the Chair in consideration of the view that investigations require the frank and committed involvement of medical professionals.

A final agreement was reached in December 2009. Below are extracts from the committee's report outlining the advised position for investigations:[17]

a) The guidance to describe the 'The item to consider for better obstetric/perinatal care' in the Investigative Report.

   - Measures which are helpful, or possibly helpful, for prevention should be described in 'The item worthwhile to consider for better obstetric/perinatal care' of the Investigative Report by taking every possibility for prevention into account through intensive and retrospective investigation with known results on the procedure and/or management during pregnancy and delivery. Avoidance of cerebral palsy should not be mentioned in Investigative Report.
   - For example, in 'The item worthwhile to consider for better obstetric/perinatal care' of the investigational report, the item is described in a way as 'It is desirable to take education and training of neonatal resuscitation', 'It is strongly recommended that caesarean section or forceps delivery is conducted immediately after it turned out that vacuum delivery was not effective'.
   - If multiple measures for prevention are proposed, it should be clear to others how such measures are to be prioritized in practice.
   - If it transpires that cerebral palsy was caused by an obviously poor or dangerous management and/or procedure, the childbirth facility should be urged to improve the management and/or procedure as soon as possible. Therefore, the Investigational Report should clearly mention to the cause of cerebral palsy and the preventative measure.

17 JQ, Working Group for Investigations, 'Preliminary Investigative Report of a case for practice by preliminary working group for investigation (Vol. 2), Mar 2010'. www.sanka-hp.jcqhc.or.jp/documents/analysis_other/100420mogibukai_3.pdf. Available only in Japanese. The extract has been translated into English by the author.

b) Guidance to deal with questions from guardians in investigational work

- ○ The committee should answer the family's question from a medical viewpoint in the Investigational Report as far as it possibly can.
- ○ Even if the family raise the question 'How could the cerebral palsy in our case have been prevented?', the committee should describe the answer in as much detail as possible.
- ○ The answer to the question from the family is written in a document as 'Annex'.
- ○ The answer to the question from the family i.e. 'Annex' is to be delivered not only to the family but to the childbirth facility.
- ○ The 'Annex' should not be disclosed by JOCS-CP, while it is admitted that the disclosure by the family could not be restrained.

Survey on the effects of Investigative Reports

Investigative work was launched by the JOCS-CP, according to the LDP framework, on the premise that the Investigative Report would be accepted by both the childbirth facility and the guardian and could lead to effective improvements in quality and safety in perinatal care. A survey testing this premise was conducted in 2015.[18] It seemed that both childbirth facilities and guardians are in favour of the report, choosing 'Very good' and 'Fairly good' in 73% of respondents from childbirth facilities and similarly 65% from guardians (Figs. 17.10, 17.11).

Among respondents who are in favour of the report, the most common reason given by both childbirth facilities and guardians was 'Investigation was conducted by a third party' (Figs. 17.12, 17.13), suggesting that neutrality or fairness was an important factor. However, it is notable that guardians answered 'Not very good' in 14% of respondents, in contrast to only 3% from childbirth facility (Figs. 17.10, 17.11). The reason for the answer was mostly attributed to 'Cause of cerebral palsy was not eventually identified' (Fig. 17.3). Actually, 36.3% of the Investigative Reports concluded that the cause was unclear or unknown (Table 17.3). It seems that guardians expect the JOCS-CP to elucidate the cause of cerebral palsy, given that investigations conducted by experts in perinatal care never fail to disclose probable causes in all the cases.

Amelioration of perinatal care

The investigational reports are aggregated and systemically analysed by the Prevention Committee to generate knowledge for improving quality in obstetric/perinatal care, particularly through the prevention of cerebral palsy.

18 Steering Committee of the Japan Obstetric Compensation System for Cerebral Palsy (JOCS-CP) Material No.5, 34th. www.sanka-hp.jcqhc.or.jp/documents/committee/pdf/obstetric_meeting_34.pdf. Available only in Japanese.

The JOCS-CP publishes a Prevention Report annually, including data for some 1,192 cases.[19] Preventative measures have been disseminated by JOCS-CP as effectively as possible by introducing the knowledge gained from other projects of JQ, such as the Adverse Event Reporting and Learning System etc.[20]

Specifically, the Prevention Reports that have been published contain analysis including: i) quantitative and epidemiological analysis of maternal data, clinical course of pregnancy, delivery and neonatal period and institutional human resources and health care provision systems and ii) thematic analysis of the causes of cerebral palsy, as described in Investigative Report; records on fetal heart rate monitoring; administration of uterine-contracting agents; clinical procedures, such as forced delivery and neonatal resuscitation; the type of devices the facility has for delivery; and organisational structures, and other resources, for birth care.

Aggregative analysis provides the probable causes of cerebral palsy approved in JOCS-CP. Table 17.3 indicates that placental abruption and bleeding and umbilical factors are the most common causes of cerebral palsy in JOCS-CP, followed by intrauterine infection and uterine ruptures. However, it should be reiterated that investigational reports failed to identify the causes of cerebral palsy in 36.3 % of approved cases, suggesting that, despite advances in research, cerebral palsy is still not fully understood.

It appears that non-clinicians do not fully appreciate this fact. Therefore, it may be worthwhile disseminating this information as a means of informing and managing expectations in the investigation process.

The Prevention Reports published so far are available on the homepage of the JOCS-CP in a user-friendly manner. The 'Guideline for Obstetrical Practice in Japan 2017', edited and supervised by the Japan Society of Obstetricians and Gynaecologists (JSOG) and the Japanese Association of Obstetricians and Gynaecologists (JAOG), applied knowledge presented in the thematic analysis of the Prevention Report. Therefore, it has been increasingly recognised that the JOCS-CP gives updated knowledge on obstetric care to medical professionals in perinatal care.

The full content of the Prevention Report is distributed not only to medical professionals but extracted information is also given to pregnant women and families in a leaflet that is easy to understand.[21] The information which is presented to medical professionals and pregnant women can be usefully compared. Leaflets designed for medical practitioners demonstrate the significance of obtaining the consent of pregnant women in cases of inducing labour by a uterine-contracting agent. It includes the types of information which should be included in consent

19 JQ, 'Prevention Report and Recommendation of the Japan Obstetric Compensation System for Cerebral Palsy (JOCS-CP)'. www.sanka-hp.jcqhc.or.jp/documents/prevention/index.html. Available only in Japanese.

20 JQ, National Adverse Event Reporting and Learning System www.med-safe.jp/contents/english/index.html.

21 JQ, Recommendation booklets, leaflets and posters released by the Prevention Committee in the Japan Obstetric Compensation System for Cerebral Palsy (JOCS-CP). www.sanka-hp.jcqhc.or.jp/documents/prevention/proposition/. Available only in Japanese.

forms, such as the indication of the drug, possible associated treatments, alternative methods of administration of the drug, side effects of the drug and the measures to ensure patient safety during labour and delivery. Similarly, a leaflet for pregnant women and others offers an alert on early skin-to-skin contact of a mother with her baby in which several educational items such as informed consent, observation, safe positioning and maintaining the body temperature of a baby are highlighted. Patient representatives of the Prevention Committee have greatly contributed to the production of these materials intended for pregnant women, mothers with newborn babies and family members.

Scientific and educational activities for obstetricians

Childbirth facilities are entitled to submit petitions for access to data such as medical charts, labour and delivery records, fetal heart rate monitoring and other data generated by midwives. The data is highly meaningful not only for subsequent proceedings for compensation but for the creation and dissemination of educational materials. Traditionally, it has been difficult to obtain data on cerebral palsy on such a large scale, as cerebral palsy occurs so infrequently that even large-scale research hospitals cannot gather enough data for systematic analysis. However, the launch of the JOCS-CP in response to deteriorating perinatal care system in Japan provided an opportunity not only to improve perinatal care in Japan but to also collect data on profound cerebral palsy at a national level. Therefore, a working group was set up to craft educational guidance on the correct interpretation of the fetal heart rate monitoring record. Previously a number of different records were studied by academic obstetricians. The working group successfully compiled and issued a book entitled 'Proper Reading of Fetal Heart Rate Monitoring Record for Profound Cerebral Palsy'[22] in which 43 examples of fetal heartrate recordings are illustrated, with comments on the pitfalls in interpretations. A number of scientific meetings and courses of education and training in Japan adopted this guide as a textbook, so that the proper knowledge of cardiotocogram (CTG) interpretation would spread among obstetricians and midwives.

Furthermore, the MHLW has been cooperative in distributing these educational materials through local governments. As the data on profound cerebral palsy grows, JQ internally launched a database that comprises data gained from individual Investigative Reports and from documents provided on petition by claimers. Another working group was established in JOCS-CP to conduct research based on a case study with data from a large-scale database on perinatal care with or without cerebral palsy. A scientific paper that described obstetric factors specific to cerebral palsy was accepted for the first time by *PLOS ONE*, an open access journal, in 2016.[23] Subsequently, another scientific paper was published

22 JQ 'Proper Reading and Pitfalls of Reading Fetal Heartrate Monitoring Record of Profound Cerebral Palsy' (www.sanka-hp.jcqhc.or.jp/documents/english/index.html).

23 Junichi Hasegawa et al., 'Relevant obstetric factors for cerebral palsy: from the Nationwide Obstetric Compensation System in Japan'. *PLOS One* 2016 https://doi.org/10.1371/journal.pone.0148122.

in *Obstetrics & Gynaecology*, also an open access journal, in 2018.[24] The paper observed relevant obstetric factors significantly linked to irregular fetal heart rate patterns in pregnant women with hypertensive disorder of pregnancy (HDP). Placental abruption and light-for-gestational-age were supposed to be factors related to HDP. It claimed that pregnant women with HDP should be placed under intensive observation and management so that they would avoid developing fetal hypoxia during labour. The working group has been conducting similar case-control studies with the data of JOCS-CP to elucidate more detailed features to improve the prevention of cerebral palsy. Consequently, the research facet of JOCS-CP has continually attracted academic obstetricians, further entrenching the significance of the JOCS-CP.

Effect of the JOCS-CP on lawsuit trends

The JOCS-CP aims at preventing conflict and bringing it to early settlement, whilst achieving quality improvement in perinatal care. To evaluate whether the introduction of the JOCS-CP has had an impact in this regard, the annual figures of damages requests to childbirth facilities was examined. Notably, fears that there would be an increase in these requests was not observed. In this regard, the 'Medical Lawsuit Cases Settled in Court released from the Medical Lawsuit Committee of the Supreme Court of Japan[25] has demonstrated a rapid decline for OG in recent years (Fig. 17.14).

Focusing on 2009, when the JOCS-CP was launched, both the term 2007–2008, in which the system was planned and drawn up, and the next term (2009 and later), in which the system was launched and implemented, revealed a declining trend, again suggesting that there was no surge of conflicts in relation to the JOCS-CP. The Supreme Court of Japan issued 'A Report on Expediting Lawsuit Proceedings' which acknowledged the decrease and stated 'The JOCS-CP has dealt with a significant number of cases of cerebral palsy, possibly affecting the trend of the lawsuit case'.[26]

Conclusion

The JOCS-CP was launched in response to the deteriorating perinatal care system in Japan. The successful launch of the system owes a great deal to the cooperation of a range of individuals and organisations, including experts in obstetrics, scientists, lawyers engaged in law suits related to medicine, indemnity

24 Junichi Hasegawa et al., 'Relevant obstetric factors associated with fetal heart rate monitoring for cerebral palsy in pregnant women with hypertensive disorder of pregnancy'. *Obstetrics & Gynaecology* 2018. http://onlinelibrary.wiley.com/doi/10.1111/jog.13555/abstract

25 Supreme Court of Japan, 'Website of the Committee on Medicine of the Supreme Court of Japan'. www.courts.go.jp/saikosai/iinkai/izikankei/index.html, available only in Japanese.

26 Supreme Court of Japan, 'A report on expedition of lawsuits: ⊠: verification of social background factors; study by types of conflict'. www.courts.go.jp/vcms_lf/20524011.pdf, 2013, available only in Japanese.

insurance firms, lawmakers associated with the LDP and the MHLW. Analysis of this intervention has revealed that the system has been effective in improving the quality and safety of perinatal care through the use of the various materials produced in the JOCS-CP. This intervention represents a new departure for patient safety in Japan. Additional discussion is required in relation to the need to overhaul and review aspects of the programme. The possibility of expanding the specific scope of cerebral palsy and of introducing other medical specialties or conditions into the programme could also be considered. This system is somewhat unique in that it is operated within the private sector, but is supported by the government. This constitutes a valid system of public/private cooperation. In that regard, JOCS-CP could be viewed as a social experiment that could build a useful and efficient system that would prepare the nation to cope with changes in medicine, the law and society.

On behalf of the Japan Council for Quality Health Care (JQ), I truly thank Dr Takashi Okai (1947–2017) for his tireless work and dedication as a chair of the Investigation Committee in JOCS-CP, in coordinating the argument in the committee and producing over one thousand standardised Investigative Reports even during days in bed of his final hospital admission.

References

Committee on Legal Affairs, Japan Medical Association (JMA), 'Legal Proceeding of Medical Accident and the Relevant Theory', *The Journal of Japan Medical Association* 1972, 68(2):183–203.

Hasegawa, Junichi, et al., 'Relevant obstetric factors for cerebral palsy: from the Nationwide Obstetric Compensation System in Japan'. *PLOS One* 2016 https://doi.org/10.1371/journal.pone.0148122.

Hasegawa, Junichi, et al., 'Relevant obstetric factors associated with fetal heart rate monitoring for cerebral palsy in pregnant women with hypertensive disorder of pregnancy'. *Obstetrics & Gynaecology* 2018.

Japan Council for Quality Health Care (JQ), 'Japan Obstetric Compensation System for Cerebral Palsy (JOCS-CP)' (www.sanka-hp.jcqhc.or.jp/index.html), available only in Japanese. See also 'Guide to The Japan Obstetric Compensation System for Cerebral Palsy', 2014. www.sanka-hp.jcqhc.or.jp/documents/english/bira_english_color_201407.pdf.

Japan Society of Obstetricians and Gynecologists (JSOG) and the Japanese Association of Obstetricians and Gynecologists (JAOG), 'Guidelines for Obstetrical Practice in Japan 2017', available only in Japanese.

JQ, 'Disclosure proceedings of the Investigative Report of the Japan Obstetric Compensation System for Cerebral Palsy (JOCS-CP). www.sanka-hp.jcqhc.or.jp/outline/disclosure.html, available only in Japanese.

JQ, 'Guidance to deal with questions from the guardians in investigational work'. www.sanka-hp.jcqhc.or.jp/documents/analysis_other/bunseki_approach_201604.pdf, available only in Japanese. http://onlinelibrary.wiley.com/doi/10.1111/jog.13555/abstract

JQ, 'Investigative work of the Japan Obstetric Compensation System for Cerebral Palsy (JOCS-CP)'. www.sanka-hp.jcqhc.or.jp/outline/function.html, available only in Japanese.

JQ, 'List of registered physician engaged in the diagnostic certification in the JOCS-CP'. www.sanka-hp.jcqhc.or.jp/doctor/list.html, available only in Japanese.

JQ, 'National Adverse Event Reporting and Learning System'. www.med-safe.jp/contents/english/index.html.

JQ, 'Prevention Report and Recommendation of the Japan Obstetric Compensation System for Cerebral Palsy (JOCS-CP)'. www.sanka-hp.jcqhc.or.jp/documents/prevention/index.html. Available only in Japanese.

JQ, 'Proper Reading and Pitfalls of Reading Fetal Heartrate Monitoring Record of Profound Cerebral Palsy'. www.sanka-hp.jcqhc.or.jp/documents/english/index.html.

JQ, 'Recommendation booklets, leaflets and posters released by the Prevention Committee in the Japan Obstetric Compensation System for Cerebral Palsy (JOCS-CP)'. www.sanka-hp.jcqhc.or.jp/documents/prevention/proposition/. Available only in Japanese.

JQ, 'Preliminary Investigative Report of a case for practice by preliminary working group for investigation (Vol. 2), Mar 2010'. www.sanka-hp.jcqhc.or.jp/documents/analysis_other/100420mogibukai_3.pdf. Available only in Japanese.

JQ, 'Proceedings for petition in the Japan Obstetric Compensation System for Cerebral Palsy (JOCS-CP)'. www.sanka-hp.jcqhc.or.jp/application/flow.html, available only in Japanese.

Okai, Takashi, 'No-fault', Tokyo: Hayakawa Shobo, 2007, available only in Japanese.

Pharmaceuticals and Medical Devices Agency (PMDA), 'Relief Services for Adverse Health Effects'. www.pmda.go.jp/english/index.html.

Policy Research Committee, The Liberal Democratic Party, 'The framework of the no-fault compensation system in obstetric care', 23 Jan 2006. Accessory material of the 12th meeting (www.sanka-hp.jcqhc.or.jp/documents/committee/pdf/obstetrics_3.pdf). Available only in Japanese.

Steering Committee of the Japan Obstetric Compensation System for Cerebral Palsy (JOCS-CP) Material No.5, 34th. www.sanka-hp.jcqhc.or.jp/documents/committee/pdf/obstetric_meeting_34.pdf. Available only in Japanese.

Supreme Court of Japan, 'A report on expedition of lawsuits: VI: verification of social background factors; study by types of conflict'. www.courts.go.jp/vcms_lf/20524011.pdf, 2013, available only in Japanese.

Appendix

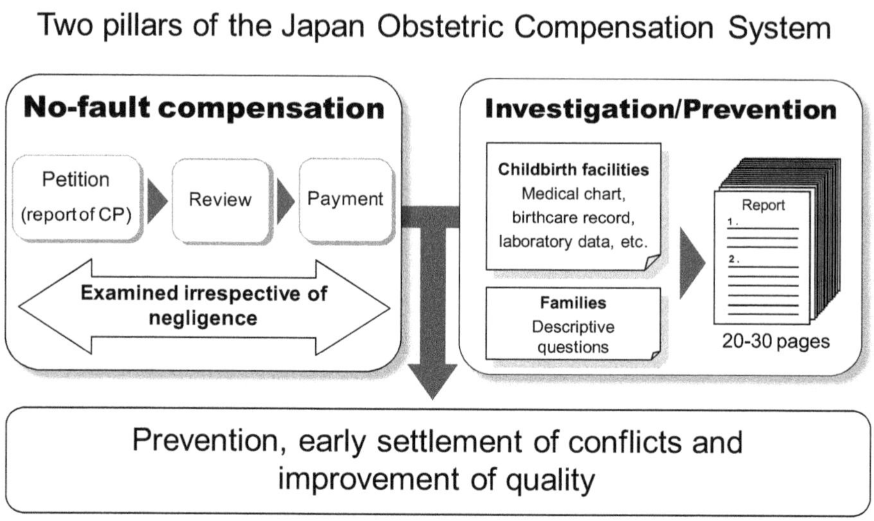

Figure 17.1 Two pillars of the Japan Obstetric Compensation System

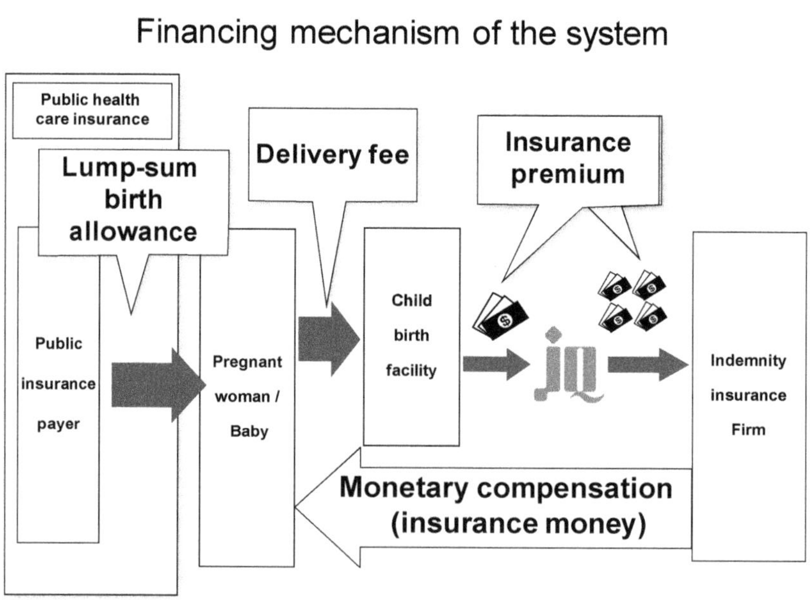

Figure 17.2 Financing mechanism of the system

Eligibility criteria (2009) for compensation

1. General criteria

A) Gestational week and birth weight
Born at **33rd gestational week or later** and birth weight at **2,000 grams or over**

B) Degree of Severity
Certified as **1st or 2nd class of severity** according to the Japanese Social Welfare System for the disabled

Figure 17.3 Eligibility Criteria (2009) for Compensation

Eligibility criteria (2009) for compensation

2. Exclusion criteria

Cerebral palsy "clearly caused" by factors defined by below exclusion criteria is not approved.

A) Congenital causes
Bilateral broad cerebral malformation, chromosomal disorders, genetic disorders, congenital metabolic disorders or other congenital abnormalities

B) Neonatal causes
Infections after birth etc.

Figure 17.4 Eligibility Criteria (2009) for Compensation

Eligibility criteria (2009) for compensation

3. Case-by-case criteria

A) Patient delivered **during 28 to 32 gestational week** may be approved based on a "**Case-by-Case Review**" by "**Individual criteria**" in careful reference to the evidence of hypoxic event during delivery.

B) Degree of severity (same as in 'general criteria') Certified as **1st or 2nd class of severity** according to the Japanese Social Welfare System for the disabled.

Figure 17.5 Eligibility Criteria (2009) for Compensation

Case-by-case criteria

A case consistent with A) and B) and/or C) is approved on case-by-case basis.

A) 28 weeks ≤
B) Umbilical arterial blood pH≥7.1
and/or
C) Specific deceleration patterns on Cardiotocography (CTG)

Figure 17.6 Case-by-case criteria

C) Specific deceleration patterns on CTG (2009)

Any patterns of 'a' AND 'any of b-d' is allowed eligible for the individual criteria.

a. Loss of variability of the baseline

AND

b. Late decelerations observed at 50% or over of uterine contractions
c. Variable decelerations observed at 50% or over of uterine contractions
d. Severe bradycardia with reduced variability of the baseline

Figure 17.7 C) Specific deceleration patterns on CTG (2009)

C) Specific deceleration patterns on CTG (2015)
Any patterns of 'a-h' is allowed eligible for the individual criteria.

* Items underlined are included in criteria of 2009

a. Abrupt and continuous bradycardia
b. Late decelerations observed at 50% or over of uterine contractions*
c. Variable decelerations observed at 50% or over of uterine contractions*
d. Loss of variability of the baseline*
e. Severe bradycardia with reduced variability of the baseline*
f. Sinusoidal pattern
g. APGAR score (1min) at '3' or below
h. Arterial/venous blood gas pH below 7.0 within one hour after birth

Figure 17.8 C) Specific deceleration patterns on CTG (2015)

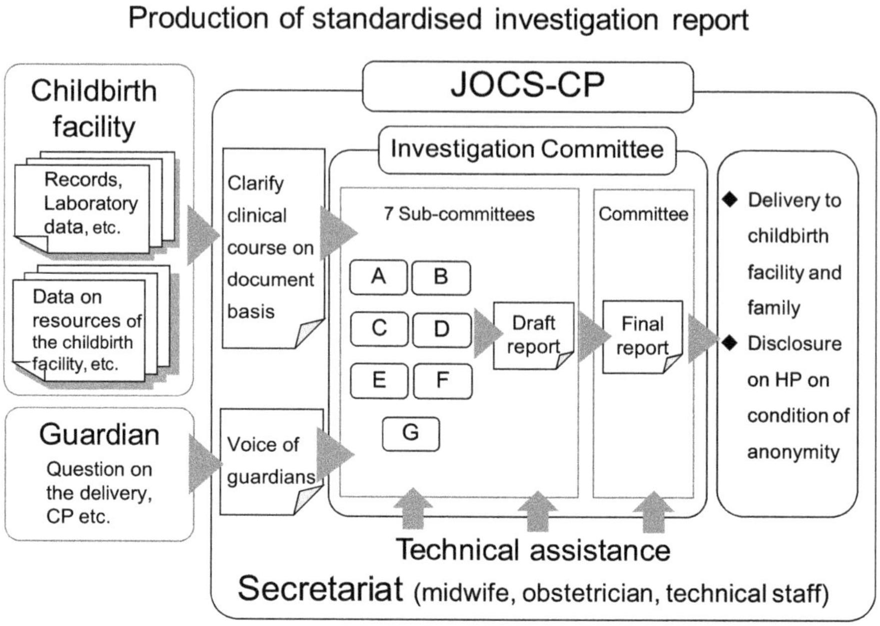

Figure 17.9 Production of standardized investigation report

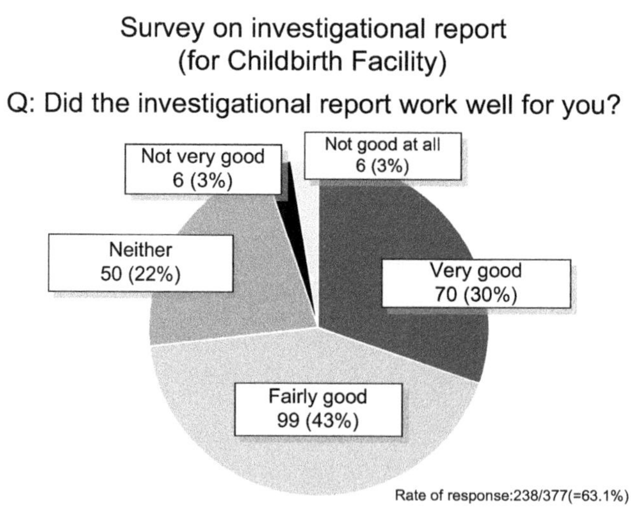

Figure 17.10 Survey on investigational report (for Childbirth Facility)

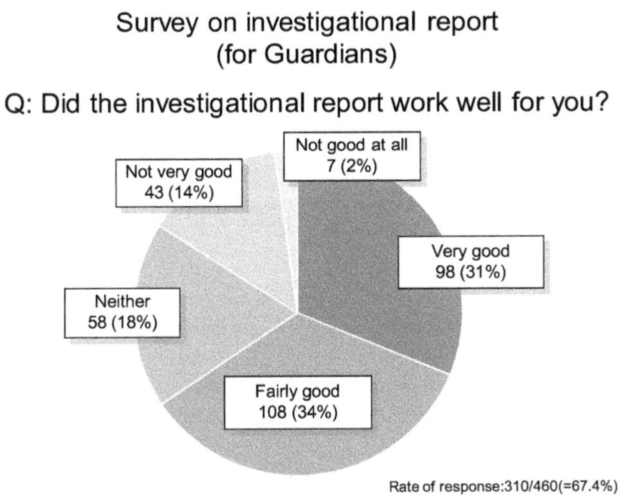

Figure 17.11 Survey on investigational report (for Guardians)

Survey on investigational report (for Childbirth Facility)

Q: Did the investigational report work well for you?

	Reasons for 'Very good' and 'Fairly good' groups		%
1	Analysis was done by a third body	148	88
2	Supposedly, lead to improvement of obstetric care	78	46
3	Cause was identified	61	36
4	Sense of distrust was mitigated against childbirth facilitiy and physicians	30	18
5	Others	8	5

	Reasons for 'Not so good' and 'Not good at all' groups		%
1	Skeptical about fairness and/or neutrality in investigation	9	75
2	Supposedly, never lead to improvement of obstetric care	7	58
3	Cause was not eventually identified	7	58
4	Sense of distrust grew against childbirth facility and physicians	6	50
5	Others	2	17

Rate of response:238/377 (=63.1%)

Figure 17.12 Survey on investigational report (for Childbirth Facility)

Survey on investigational report (for Guardians)

Q: Did the investigational report work well for you?

	Reasons for 'Very good' and 'Fairly good' groups		%
1	Analysis was done by a third body	177	86
2	Supposedly, lead to improvement of obstetric care	102	50
3	Cause was identified	94	46
4	Sense of distrust was mitigated against childbirth facilitiy and physicians	20	10
5	Others	14	7

	Reasons for 'Not so good' and 'Poor' groups		
1	Cause was not eventually identified	16	84
2	Sense of distrust grew against childbirth facility and physicians	10	62
3	Supposedly, never lead to improvement of obstetric care	8	56
4	Skeptical about fairness and/or neutrality in investigation	7	48
5	Others	5	10

Rate of response:310/460(=67.4%)

Figure 17.13 Survey on investigational report (for Guardians)

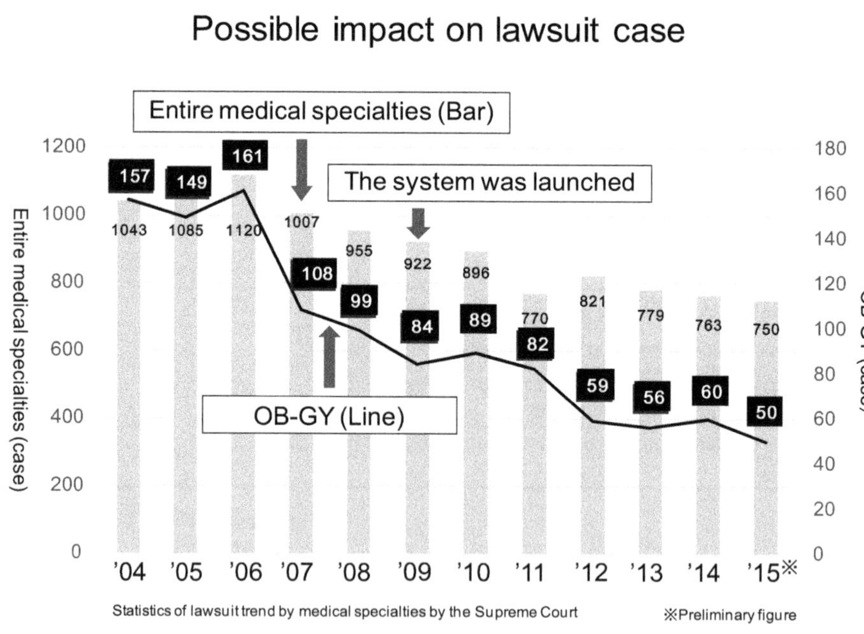

Figure 17.14 Possible impact on lawsuit case

Table 17.1 Statistics of eligible case by birth year

As of Dec 31, 2017

Birth year	*No. case reviewed*	*No. case processed*			*In process*
		Eligible	*Not Eligible*	*Not Eligible (Re Submission Allowed)*	
2009	561	419	142		0
2010	523	382	141		0
2011	502	355	147		0
2012	507	356	148		3
2013	343	264	54	24	1
2014	274	214	41	18	1
2015	199	176	8	15	0
2016	71	67	2	0	2
Total	2,980	2,233	683	57	7

Table 17.2 Reasons of cases excluded

As of Dec 2017

Not-eligible	Do not meet the criteria for case-by-case review	338	pH of umbilical arterial blood at birth is over 7.1, Do not meet criteria of Fetal Heart Rate Pattern
	Obviously caused by congenital factors and/ or factors that broke out during neonatal term or later	160	Bilateral brain anomaly, chromosomal abnormality, genetic abnormality and other congenital abnormalities
	Do not meet the definition of cerebral palsy	85	Physical impairment due to progressive brain factors
	Do not meet the criteria on the degree of physical impairment	81	Able to walk in practical manner
	Others	19	Childbirth earlier than 28 gestational weeks
Not-eligible (Re-submission allowed)	Cases which are uncertain of eligibility due to the preliminary diagnosis by a physician but are possibly approved by future submission	57	**Uncertain of eligibility on submission due to be unable to forsee degree of impairment**
Total		740	

Table 17.3 Causes of CP approved in the JOCS-CP*

Identified single cause in individual case	*596*	*50.0*
Placental abruption or placental bleeding	**205**	**17.2**
Placental abruption	201	16.9
Abruption of placenta previa or low lying placenta	4	0.3
Factors related to umbilical cord	173	14.5
without umbilical cord prolapse	142	11.9
(with morphological abnormality of the cord)	(46)	(3.9)
without umbilical cord prolapse	31	2.6
Intrauterine infection	29	3.4
GBS infection	20	1.7
Herpes encephalitis	9	0.8
Other infections	12	1.0
Uterine rupture	30	2.5
Fetomaternal transfusion	27	2.3
Discordance of blood perfusion in twin(e.g. Twin to Twin Transfusion Syndrome; TTTS)	24	2.0
Placental dysfunction or hypofunction	21	1.8
(with pregnancy-induced Hypertension)	8	(0.7)
Maternal respiratyopry/circulatory dysfunction	15	1.3
without amniotic embolism	9	0.8
with amniotic embolism	6	0.5
Cerebral hemorrhage of the fetus	15	1.3
Others	45	3.8
Identified multiple causes in individual case	**163**	**13.7**
Umbilical factors other than those related to umbilical cord	95	8.0
Placental dysfunction or hypofunction	50	4.2
Infection	36	3.0
Placental abruption	20	1.7
Causes uncertain and/or unspecified	**432**	**36.3**
Total	**1191**	**100.0**

*Cited from 2017 Report on prevention of CP

Table 17.4 List of themes included in the Prevention Report

1 Vacuum delivery
2 Uterine contracting agent
3 Kristeller maneuver-Pressing maneuver on uterine fundus
4 Fetal heart rate monitoring during delivery
5 Umbilical factor except for umbilical prolapse
6 Umbilical prolapse
7 Intrauterine infection
8 Uterine rupture
9 Placental abruption
10 Maternal education for early detection of placental abruption
11 Premature birth

12	Multiple pregnancy
13	Pregnancy Induced Hypertension
14	Detonated all transfusion syndrome
15	Neonatal care
16	Neonatal resuscitation
17	Case in no need of neonatal resuscitation by the time five min after birth
18	Follow up statistics of the past themes
19	Medical chart recording
20	Maternal transport system

Table 17.5 Structure of thematic analysis

Section	*Description*
i Preface	Summary of the theme including aims, status quo etc is briefly stated.
ii Overview of the theme	Quantitative analysis is shown in tables and figurse on healthcare data of period of pregnancy and classified data of perinatal care
iii Collective analysis of aggregated reports	Collective analysis is applied to cause of CPs, procedural review and suggestions/recommendations.
iv Referential data in relation to the theme	Status quo of the theme is described quoting relevant references such as scientific papers, guidelines, ongoing programs of scientific societies, etc.
v Suggestion/ Recommendation	Suggestions/recommendations from prevention committee is consolidated. A) To those who are engaged in perinatal care B) To scientific societies and professional societies C) To the central and local governments

Table 17.6 Title of educational leaflets

1	For maternal use For better understanding of neonate For better understanding of informed consent on delivery For better understanding of placental abruption
2	For the use of obstetricians, midwifes and other medical professionals engaged in perinatal care Neonatal care Flowchart of artificial rupture of membrane Flowchart of metreurysis Informed consent on administering uterine contraction agent
3	Form of informed consent on administering uterine contracting agent

18 Conclusion

Global patient safety – power of the dream

Clayton Ó Néill, Morgan Shimwell and John Tingle

Introduction: Raisa and her story

> *My grandfather had oesophageal cancer, initially diagnosed as being inoperable. However, a second opinion recommended the removal of the tumour, by way of removal of the oesophagus. This operation had to be aborted when the tumour, which was lying on the aorta, was 'tugged' by the surgeon, causing the aorta to burst, and my grandfather to die. There were many questions posed by the family in the days following his death. Should this procedure have been recommended? Were my grandfather and the immediate family made aware of the dangers and possible adverse effects of the operation? Was there a lack of care during the operation? Would he have died anyhow? We wrote to the hospital querying the manner of his death and received a lovely personal letter from the surgeon explaining how the death of my grandfather in this manner, no matter how awful, might have been better than the alternative – peg feeding. There was no suggestion in the letter of any error and we happily came to an acceptance that my grandfather had 'fallen in love with easeful death'. This big picture diagnosis of 'better to have died like X, than to have lived like Y' had, of course, some validity. But hindsight and perusal of my grandfather's medical charts convinced me that the small errors that day also had an impact on the eventual outcome. There was difficulty accessing a consultant that weekend, and all decisions were made by a junior house officer. There was a difficulty getting the amount of blood required when my grandfather's aorta burst and insufficient staff on hand to properly deliver the blood transfusions. When he died, we were dazed and no one explained what had happened, and what steps had been taken or not taken. We were unsure then and remain unsure now whether there was cause to complain or sue, or is it just better to let sleeping dogs lie?*

The picture painted above by Raisa about possible or perceived errors (or non-errors) could be replicated in many hospitals, jurisdictions and countries. Various iterations of the Hippocratic Oath have all called for '*First do no harm*'. The chapters of this book attest to a painful irony about healthcare the world over: those who aim to relieve suffering and improve the quality of life may cause great harm.

The question asked in each chapter has been: how do we minimise the iatrogenic harms of the medical encounter? It is hoped that, by sharing experiences from other jurisdictions, we can begin to move forward in answering this question.

The editors of this collection see the chapters of this book as threads of a plait – they exist within themselves, but when they interconnect they form a unified, stronger whole. Patient safety is much the same: made up of a number of fragile, contingent policies, procedures and practices, the only way to ultimately strengthen the systems for protecting patients from the harms caused by the healthcare environment is to carefully weave these together; to enmesh the principles with the practice. And this should not have to be an isolated effort, led by trailblazers from within one hospital, one country or one region. Rather, patient safety must be a collective effort. Perhaps this has been the greatest flaw of national patient safety strategies to date: they have been overly introverted, when they should have looked outwards as well.

This book is global in nature, but it unashamedly never tried to escape the local. The two perspectives are inextricably bound: the local becomes global and the global becomes local. Small, localised errors can beget, nurture and nourish systemic errors, with bigger consequences. The chapters in this book have highlighted a number of ways in which different countries have produced and developed patient safety systems and measures, to greater and lesser success. Throughout, there is a recognition by almost all contributors that there is a need for good policy, a specific and well-calibrated patient safety agenda, subject to requisite checks and balances. But the formulation and embedding of policy is, itself, not enough – it must meet good practice.

There is a familiar narrative to the formation of patient safety policies. When errors occur in healthcare, this is usually followed by root-cause analysis to determine who or what was responsible. This may lead to the proposal of a new procedure, to be adhered to by all. The new procedure is usually reviewed and monitored, sometimes with a double-check system of some kind, gaining new insights through a fresh pair of eyes. In theory, fine – in practice, problematic. The top-down imposition of safety improvement processes rarely integrates with the real practices of those working within this imagined framework; rather it is overlaid, ill-fitting and likely discarded or shunned. For example, if a review of an error indicates that the hours that doctors work on a particular day need to be reduced but budgetary restrictions and/or doctors' desire to work overtime do not allow for these changed work practices, then a disparity can exist between what new policy requires and what practice dictates. There is, perhaps, a failure to dig down into the minutiae of how recommendations to ease patient safety issues might work out in practice.

At this stage, it should be apparent that patient safety is incredibly complex and a 'one approach fits all' attitude cannot be taken when looking at the differing interpretations from country to country. Each country is, indeed, unique and that uniqueness must be respected and understood by anyone attempting to institute global safety norms. Cultural differences exist throughout the jurisdictions discussed in this book, as manifest in differing representations of the relationship between the doctor and the patient, the existence or non-existence of prevailing compensation cultures and the availability of health resources. The law and regulations that underpin patient safety practices differ in the detail. There is no expectation, or want, for a globalised set of policies that seek to iron out differences in local practices. However, there is a fundamental commonality shared by all countries in the world: healthcare systems are made up of *people* – whether patients or practitioners – all deserving of respect and protection, at all times. It is easy to forget this basic idea, and to immerse oneself in concepts, policies and intervention design. It was the stark message of the Francis Report into the horrendous failings in Mid Staffordshire NHS Foundation Trust in the UK which documented the ways in which the worst affected patients had been stripped of their humanity, and the failure of 'systems' to prevent it from happening.[1]

This should be the starting point for any patient safety standard, local or global: how do we preserve, protect and promote the humanity of those who are participating (voluntarily or involuntarily, in health or sickness) in our healthcare systems? This is not idealised and unachievable; it is not disrespectful of context, of cultures or pressures. It is a guiding principle that radiates from the heart of healthcare, transcending geographical, legal, social and political boundaries.

Global patient safety: themes

Critical junctures

Despite the variety of experiences offered in the chapters of this book, a recurrent theme throughout is the presence of 'defining moments' in the development narrative of patient safety movements. Almost each country has its own critical juncture in which healthcare institutions – whether national healthcare systems, or localised quality and safety practices – attempt to change the trajectory of their safety policies. As Tingle notes in Chapter 1, a frequently cited example of pivotal turns in the West is the publication, in 2000, of *Organisation with a memory* in the UK and *To err is human* in the US. Both of these seminal reports document a programme for reform in reflection on the ever-present systemic risks facing patients in two of the most developed healthcare systems in the world. Yet, 18 years later, there has been no real paradigmatic change. In 2018, the Royal College of Physicians in the UK reported that 64% of doctors feel that patient safety has deteriorated over the past year.[2]

Other countries have their own critical junctures, to perhaps greater success than the UK and the US. Oman is perhaps the most overtly promising: following

1 Robert Francis QC, *Report of the Mid Staffordshire NHS Foundation Trust Public Inquiry*, 6 February 2013. www.gov.uk/government/publications/report-of-the-mid-staffordshire-nhs-foundation-trust-public-inquiry (accessed 27 March 2018). See, also, the submission to the Public Inquiry from the Patients Association, *Patients not numbers, people not statistics*, Patients Association, 2009.

2 Royal College of Physicians, *NHS reality check: update 2018*, London: Royal College of Physicians, 2018). Available at www.rcplondon.ac.uk/projects/outputs/nhs-reality-check-update-2018 (accessed 13 March 2018).

systemic, deep healthcare reform in the 1970s by Sultan Qaboos bin Said al Said, Oman has undergone an almost complete transformation in its healthcare safety profile, becoming one of the most successfully performing systems in the world. To a slightly lesser extent, the establishment of the independent Health Accreditation Institute in 2009 in Thailand also marked a dramatic shift in the direction of the country's safety and quality commitments. Since then, there have been notable improvements in the development of holistic patient safety initiatives, being implemented initially in hospitals but more recently across the health sector as a whole. Similarly, the development of the Japanese Obstetrics Compensation Scheme for Cerebral Palsy, from around 2005, has also triggered a series of medical, legal and social shifts in relation to investigating, remedying and seeking to prevent medical errors giving rise to life-changing consequences.

Unfortunately, the closest that the UK has come to its own real 'cultural moment' in patient safety is the Francis Report on the Mid Staffordshire scandal. Both within the UK, and across a range of countries featuring in this book, the traumas visited upon patients have had a ripple effect across healthcare systems, triggering periods of public reflection on our expectations of the caring environment. But, as Herring explained in Chapter 2, although the NHS is making some progress following the Report, at the time of the scandal a plethora of safety regulations already existed. This prompts us to question whether more of the same top-down interventions is really the most appropriate and promising solution available to developed countries like the UK. McHale also discussed the Francis Report and how initiatives, such as the duty of candour and the concept of a safe space, could impact upon potential future incidents involving patient safety. Endorsing the introduction of a duty of candour incumbent upon health professionals involved in adverse events, McHale was somewhat more sceptical about the proposed 'safe investigative space': 'the construction of the safe space itself may cause some major problems for justice and accountability where adverse clinical harms have been caused'.[3]

The issue of governance and leadership was also present throughout this book. For example, Mannion et al. ('Board governance for better, safer healthcare')[4] stressed the requirement of effective leadership to quality improvement processes. This was echoed in Limpanyalert's chapter, 'Thailand'. However, from the Thai experience, the author stressed that, whilst it was vital to 'develop a core group of leaders to lead and facilitate the [patient safety] movements at various levels', this was but one ingredient in a successful patient safety culture.[5] Rather, committed leaders had to be complemented by motivated healthcare professionals, who are given their own sense of place and involvement within the framework of patient safety.

Cultures of fear

It is self-evident that the likes of the disgraceful events at Mid Staffordshire NHS Trust cannot take place again. It is hoped that the Francis Report has made

3 Chapter 6.
4 Chapter 4.
5 See the Conclusion of Chapter 12.

healthcare practitioners more aware of the need to provide patients with dignified and safe treatment/care.[6] However, there is a fine line between enhancing a greater sense of accountability for patient safety, and instilling a culture of fear amongst those whose primary purpose is to help relieve pain and suffering. In many countries, there is a stark relationship between medical error and the tort of negligence. The fear of litigation was explained by Foster in his discussion of how issues such as too much openness or autonomy could potentially be damaging to patient safety, and by Herring in relation to the duty of candour. In jurisdictions such as the UK and the US, attempts have been made to minimise the number of claims and the ensuing potential for compensation (e.g. the safe space, duty of candour, no-fault system).[7] However, these attempts have not made any major impact to date. In the UK, the NHS is at a crossroads: the impact of compensation claims, and the related damages, has been insurmountable.

However, this is by no means a Western problem. Similar concerns have been raised by a number of contributors from a range of countries. For example, Palceja and Bankava argued that the fear of litigation amongst health professionals has a heightened dimension in Latvia, given the lack of clarity in law over the determination of liability.[8] They note a number of discrepancies between the domestic regulatory framework, which is itself composed of a number of (at times) inconsistent legal provisions, and the EU Patient Safety Directive. The overall effect has, in the authors' opinion, fostered an overly cautious healthcare system which constantly presupposes and allocates blame for error. This is in spite of the development of a supposed 'no-fault' compensation system.

A similar problem has been raised in other countries. Despite its success in improving healthcare quality, Oman has begun to experience difficulties with healthcare providers fearing reprisals when reporting adverse health incidents. Al Maqbali and Al-Mandhari frame this as a problem caused by the cultural perception of error-as-blame amongst patients, and the public more generally.[9] They note that media reportage of healthcare failures has a particular role to play in managing public expectations about the ability of healthcare professionals to prevent such errors from arising; in particular, the media have a particular opportunity and ability to frame these outcomes in a strongly negative light. There is a tension between informing the public about potential systemic failings and the need for transparent investigations which may (indeed should) not always call for individual accountability.

However, there is a paradoxical nature to clinical litigation which this book seeks to raise. Although a number of chapters characterise rising litigation rates as a flaw in patient safety systems, Onyemelukwe argues that in Nigeria, there is a need for increased litigation by patients against deficient healthcare

6 Francis, Report of the Mid Staffordshire NHS Foundation Trust Public Inquiry.
7 See, in particular, Chapters 2, 3, 6 and 9.
8 Chapter 11.
9 Chapter 8.

providers.[10] She calls for 'more medical negligence suits, quicker court and disciplinary processes, and [an increase in] patients' rights awareness' as a means of ensuring accountability. This is not a recommendation taken in ignorance of the detrimental effects of over-litigation in other jurisdictions. Rather, the author is rightly concerned that the lack of litigation in transitioning countries is reflective of a sense of enforced passivity amongst patients. By actively encouraging patients to become more demanding of their health rights, patient safety 'champions' (NGOs, health lawyers, patient groups) can create pressure on health providers to comply with the new raft of quality and safety litigation introduced in Nigeria. However, this must be complemented by a concurrent increase in the health-literacy of the public. The editors would hope that progressive changes at the grass roots of the patient safety culture would, over time, reduce the need for reactive litigation, becoming a measure of last resort.

Of course, litigation as a tool of regulation is all about balance. Arguably, in the US and the UK, the seemingly limitless litigation costs are a sign of Western 'excess' – the balance between preventative and remedial action has not yet been adequately struck. In these countries, litigation is bearing the burden of the patient safety framework when it should be providing a backstop against any backward slide from the ideals of active learning following transparent investigation and reporting.

Responsibility and accountability – whose job is it anyway?

Patient safety is not just about the actual policies and hospital practices. It is, at its core, about the patient. However, can patient safety, at times, be compromised by the patients themselves? A number of chapters argue that we have to give some level of responsibility to the patient. Ó Néill's chapter differed from others in the sense that it does not focus particularly on costs issues or adverse events or scandals. Instead, he considers the role of religious or cultural beliefs in relation to how they can actually have an (adverse?) impact on the safety of patients.[11] This chapter was English law focused, but the refusal of treatment by Jehovah's Witnesses or ritual male circumcision are global issues. His call for a widening of the definition of patient safety to include the actions of patients themselves could be relevant to all jurisdictions. Similarly, Seden and Kamoga's analysis of patient safety in Uganda recognises the connection between it and the vindication of patients' rights.[12] Their discussion of the lack of accountability of healthcare workers, as well as the lack of patient empowerment, resonates with other jurisdictions covered in this book.

The experience of Thailand is remarkably refreshing on this issue. The patient safety framework in that country is characterised by collaborative efforts to develop practices and policies which can be meaningfully adopted in healthcare institutions. Blending the top-down oversight functions of regulatory bodies, such as

10 Chapter 14.
11 Chapter 7.
12 Chapter 13.

the Health Accreditation Institute, with the bottom-up experiential expertise of health practitioners, Thailand appears to strive towards the creation of a collective sense of responsibility for patient safety that is not as evident from any of the other countries on offer in this collection. The 'Communities of Practice', serving as learning–sharing platforms for groups of practitioners with aligned expertise, allow for the formation and review of safety policies which reflect the abilities, interests and needs of local health communities, whilst contributing to the national patient safety dialogue. By forming deep connections with the World Health Organisation (WHO), these contributions are further enmeshed into the regional and global framework of quality and safety standards and ideals. This system of reciprocal knowledge exchanges between regulator and regulated appears to have much to offer for those countries with long histories of (ineffectual) top-down initiatives.

Health resources as safety obstacles

This book includes countries across the development spectrum. Yet, regardless of differences in relative economic strength and stability, a further recurrent global theme has been the inhibitive effects of fluctuating health resources. The lack of material resources (whether economic, technological or human) has been regarded as a key challenge in effecting patient safety improvements. The developing and transitioning countries featured in this collection all raise this as a significant problem. For example, Omer, in Chapter 15, explored the deleterious effects on healthcare of the persistent political and civil instability of the Kurdistan Region of Iraq over the last three decades. She notes that for every 10,000 patients there are, on average, only 11 physicians available. Whilst public funds are allocated to medical services, there is little logic to the way that services are funded; consequently, 60% of the region's health needs are not adequately funded.

In contrast, Oman has, in some ways, become a victim of its own success. The sustained investment in healthcare since the 1970s has meant that the sector has bloomed, being able to offer a more comprehensive (not to mention safer) range of services for the vast majority of its population. However, Al Maqbali and Al-Mandhari note that, whilst this has led to an increase in public demands and expectations for quality services, there has not be a concurrent increase in the number of health practitioners available to meet these needs. Rather, there is now a deficit in tertiary, specialist health professionals which has negatively impacted upon the quality and safety of these services. This naturally raises concerns about the sustainability of the rapid growth in the Omani heath sector and careful attention will need to be paid to the levels of patient care and satisfaction to ensure that the nation does not speed towards a dramatic 'cliff edge' in the near future.

In a particularly novel approach, Smith argued in Chapter 16 that the patient safety profile of a nation can only be truly understood, appreciated and responded to if it is deeply contextualised with reference to the determinants of (ill) health. The author argued that there is a systemic need for patient safety initiatives to 'work upstream' in the healthcare process. In doing so, he concurrently calls for 'a recognition that the currently unhealthy behaviour patterns leading to an increase in [non-communicable diseases] needs to be placed within context in seeing that some of the unhealthy choices being made [by patients] are largely determined by the inaccessibility of healthier choices'. Thus, Smith most closely ties together the macro and micro in this globalised safety dynamic. Without tending overly towards nihilism, there is something to be said for improving patient safety by keeping patients out of the healthcare system for as long as possible.

Patient safety into the future

The development of patient safety over time, its current role and the future of it played a key role in much of the book's discussions. The future is an unknown country. We can only guess. However, initiatives, such as *Patient Safety 2030* are welcomed as they give a forward reaching perspective on enhancing global patient safety policies, practices, laws and attitudes. As it stands, no system or jurisdiction is perfect. An important message is that most countries are identifying patient safety as being a key priority. It is likely that it will become an even greater priority as new medical advances take shape. Recently, fractured societies and political landscapes have taken root. For example, Brexit will have implications for (EU) cross-country patient safety. What about patients who share facilities in the Republic of Ireland and Northern Ireland? Brexit might curtail travel to other countries in the EU for medical treatment. Let us not forget, in the UK, how many politicians (not to name names!!) put slogans on red buses claiming, 'We send the EU £350 million a week, lets fund our NHS instead'. There will be shifts as a result of Brexit. The fact that the UK will not be answerable to the Court of Justice of the European Union (CJEU) and EU legislation will bring about changes: *we know what we are, but not what we may be*![13] The current efforts to nullify the advances in healthcare in America under Obamacare will potentially radically change and, perhaps, set back advances in healthcare provision.

What can the Government/policy makers and healthcare providers do to change the systemic cultures that exist and negate effective patient safety? Perhaps, as in the UK and the US, as well as other jurisdictions, everything is too hierarchical. Currently, a top-down approach exists. Instead of that linear trajectory, a circular approach that can go backwards as well as forwards (patient–surgeon–hospital–policy) might be more suitable. This would put the patient at the epicentre of all of this, rather than bottom of the pyramid, as arguably it stands at the moment. Maybe, the model needs a cross-pollination from patient to policy. Patient representatives could be more involved in constructing or commenting on policy documents. However, this change needs to happen at a cultural level, in schools, in the workplace, in the home. In many ways, encountering safety initiatives in the hospital is far too late.

13 William Shakespeare, *Hamlet* (first published between 1599 and 1602, reproduced by Wordsworth Editors, 1992), Act 4, scene 5.

As we consider patient safety policy into the future, let us examine the recent publication from the WHO, entitled *Patient safety: making healthcare safer.*[14] It also recognises the global nature of patient safety and that 'although health systems differ from country to country, many threats to patient safety have similar causes and often similar solutions'.[15] The report recognises the unsustainable nature of the current global issue, resulting in the compromising of health results, endangering of patients and the overall distrust of health services.[16]

In a report, entitled *Patient safety 2030*, the Patient Safety Translational Research Centre at Imperial College London argue that in the many years following the publication of *To err is human*:

> . . .safety has become embedded in the lexicon of policymakers, healthcare professionals and the media in most developed countries. We've untangled some of the root causes of error and have implemented specific interventions which have shown immense promise in reducing patient harm. On the other hand, research and intervention continue to be concentrated in particular settings of care and as serious policy priorities, safety and quality have received far less attention in developing nations than is deserved. With this report we have reached a watershed. If we are to save more lives and significantly reduce patient harm we need to adopt a holistic, systematic approach that extends across professional, cultural, technological and procedural boundaries.[17]

They argue that it is time to reflect upon the lessons of the past 15 years in order for systems to improve by 2030. Their report calls for an improved system of accountability in order to ensure that patients throughout the world can access safe and effective healthcare.[18] They recognise that patient safety is a global issue, but crucially argue that 'there is significant untapped potential in this global movement'.[19] The report states that three elements are required:

1 The movement needs to be actually *global* and needs to include countries that, to date, have been more or less ignored.[20]
2 It needs to be *focused*: 'while safety is a common goal across countries, some issues are more dependent on the local context and require tailored solutions. International collaboration should focus on identifying high-level

14 World Health Organisation, *Patient safety: making health care safer*, WHO, 2017. www.who.int/patientsafety/publications/patient-safety-making-health-care-safer/en/ (accessed 27 March 2018).
15 Ibid., p. 1.
16 Ibid., p. 3.
17 Patient Safety Translational Research Centre at Imperial College London and Imperial College Healthcare NHS Trust, *Safety 2030*, www.imperial.ac.uk/media/imperial-college/institute-of-global-health-innovation/centre-for-health-policy/Patient-Safety-2030-Report-VFinal.pdf, p. 4.
18 Ibid.
19 Ibid., p. 5
20 Ibid.

trends and raising awareness of common issues, including measurement of a core set of high-level indicators'.[21]

3 The movement must also be *coordinated* in order to make best use of the impact of the respective countries. It is also important that efforts are not repeated.[22]

These three visionary pillars of global consideration, specific-focus and explicit coordination, if implemented with rigour and cohesion, could make a significant contribution to universal patient safety. Our view is that in order to improve the current state of patient safety, countries do not need to reinvent the wheel. Whilst the country infrastructures are different, the great generic feature is that we are dealing with human beings. The concept of reverse innovation is useful: developed countries can learn from less developed countries in how they use patient safety tools. Also, developing countries may provide better insights than developed countries, as they may use the tools more efficiently.

General conclusions

Overall, it is submitted that countries can learn from what happens in other countries and good practice can be emulated. This global perspective has the potential to improve the worldwide patient safety culture – a culture that respects the rights of patients and recognises the positive impact of patient safety on spiralling litigation costs, potential errors and patient satisfaction, *inter alia*. However, it is a bit worrying that practice differs so radically from country to country, at times. Obviously, for all countries, there is a rocky road ahead, but the growing understanding of patient safety is endorsed. We argue that there is a need for joined-up thinking in this regard, at a global level, so that patients are broadly experiencing the same sort of practices from country to country.

1 Patient safety *matters*.
2 It is a *global* concern.
3 The procedures that are put in place to promote patient safety differ from jurisdiction to jurisdiction. They differ in their degree of effectiveness. They differ in terms of the political or geographical landscape in with they are operationalised. They differ in the forms of leadership applied and in terms of the financial resources available to them. No one country has a perfect system. There are lacunae in all. There is, however, a sense that all this varying practice is propelled by a united commitment to bringing about a situation where patients are safe from medical error and the harm created by same. There is also a tentative acknowledgement that patients themselves have a role to play in their own safety.
4 There are number of layers of learning. The first layer is a recognition that some things work better than others and we can learn from this and apply it

21 Ibid.
22 Ibid.

> to our own jurisdiction. Secondly, the book challenges the notion that developed countries know it all and have the 'best' practices in place. The reverse innovation suggested by the book brings into play the idea that much is to be learnt from developing nations. There are gaps in the book, gaps that relate to the absence of other countries and other practices, but also, perhaps, gaps in terms of our conceptual understanding of how and why patient safety practices grow and develop within these jurisdictions. We have learnt quite a lot about what is in place. We have, perhaps, not learnt sufficiently about why these mechanisms were in place.

Patient safety is not given high enough priority. Efforts to reduce error need to be prioritised even more. Commentators in this book have indicated how atrocities occur even with detailed systems in place.[23] Global trends exist in the context of patient safety, and these trends are quite positive. It is somewhere on the agenda and there are parallels in practice from country to country. An issue has emerged in this collection as to how money for the healthcare system is managed. The reality is that financial resources play a part in making people safe, but it is not the only factor. We need a concrete relationship between policy and practice. In digging down into the chronology of error, we have to learn from the aviation model: it is not just the major steps that have to be taken – we have to dig down into the minutiae. Patient safety has to become the mantra of all!

And so, this book has laid bare some of what must be said about the topic of patient safety, a topic that resonates in the local cottage hospital, in a busy city A & E unit, in the hospice of the dying and the gravely ill, in the corridors and bedrooms of old people's nursing homes, in this country, in far countries, in this continent and in farther continents, for wherever people live, there will be sickness, there will be healers, there will be cures, and there will always be mistakes. What this book has highlighted is the importance of trying to ensure that these mistakes are minimised and that patients are safe in their healthcare environments. Efforts to promote patient safety are many, varied and laudable. The fight to lessen error and adverse effects of healthcare provision goes on, enriched by the global commitment to the promotion of good practice, but constrained, perhaps, by harsh financial realities that beset healthcare providers and by the regulatory, legislative and hierarchical structures that underpin healthcare across a range of jurisdictions. The aim is worthwhile, the cause is great, the pursuit lives on.

References

Francis, Robert, *Report of the Mid Staffordshire NHS Foundation Trust Public Inquiry*, 6 February 2013. www.gov.uk/government/publications/report-of-the-mid-staffordshire-nhs-foundation-trust-public-inquiry (accessed 27 March 2018).

Patient Safety Translational Research Centre at Imperial College London and Imperial College Healthcare NHS Trust, *Safety 2030*. www.imperial.ac.uk/media/imperial-college/institute-of-global-health-innovation/centre-for-health-policy/Patient-Safety-2030-Report-VFinal.pdf (accessed 27 March 2018).

23 For example, Herring in Chapter 2.

Public Inquiry from the Patients Association, *Patients not numbers, people not statistics*, Patients Association, 2009.

Royal College of Physicians, *NHS reality check: update 2018*, London: Royal College of Physicians, 2018. Available at www.rcplondon.ac.uk/projects/outputs/nhs-reality-check-update-2018 (accessed 13 March 2018).

Shakespeare, William, *Hamlet*, (first published between 1599 and 1602, reproduced by Wordsworth Editors, 1992), Act 4, scene 5.

World Health Organisation, *Patient safety: making health care safer*, WHO, 2017. http://apps.who.int/iris/bitstream/10665/255507/1/WHO-HIS-SDS-2017.11-eng.pdf?ua=1 (accessed 27 March 2018).

Index

Page numbers in *italics* refer to figures. Page numbers in **bold** refer to tables.

For Product Safety Concerns and Information please contact our EU representative GPSR@taylorandfrancis.com
Taylor & Francis Verlag GmbH, Kaufingerstraße 24, 80331 München, Germany

www.ingramcontent.com/pod-product-compliance
Ingram Content Group UK Ltd.
Pitfield, Milton Keynes, MK11 3LW, UK
UKHW022013180926
475701UK00003B/337
* 9 7 8 0 3 6 7 5 8 7 1 8 5 *